CORPORATE ISSUERS

CFA® Program Curriculum
2025 • LEVEL I • VOLUME 3

WILEY

CONTENTS

How to Use the CFA Program Curriculum

The CFA® Program exams measure your mastery of the core knowledge, skills, and abilities required to succeed as an investment professional. These core competencies are the basis for the Candidate Body of Knowledge (CBOK™). The CBOK consists of four components:

A broad outline that lists the major CFA Program topic areas (www .cfainstitute.org/programs/cfa/curriculum/cbok/cbok)

Topic area weights that indicate the relative exam weightings of the top-level topic areas (www.cfainstitute.org/en/programs/cfa/curriculum)

Learning outcome statements (LOS) that advise candidates about the specific knowledge, skills, and abilities they should acquire from curriculum content covering a topic area: LOS are provided at the beginning of each block of related content and the specific lesson that covers them. We encourage you to review the information about the LOS on our website (www.cfainstitute.org/programs/cfa/curriculum/study-sessions), including the descriptions of LOS "command words" on the candidate resources page at www.cfainstitute.org/-/media/documents/support/programs/cfa-and -cipm-los-command-words.ashx.

The CFA Program curriculum that candidates receive access to upon exam registration

Therefore, the key to your success on the CFA exams is studying and understanding the CBOK. You can learn more about the CBOK on our website: www.cfainstitute .org/programs/cfa/curriculum/cbok.

The curriculum, including the practice questions, is the basis for all exam questions. The curriculum is selected or developed specifically to provide candidates with the knowledge, skills, and abilities reflected in the CBOK.

CFA INSTITUTE LEARNING ECOSYSTEM (LES)

Your exam registration fee includes access to the CFA Institute Learning Ecosystem (LES). This digital learning platform provides access, even offline, to all the curriculum content and practice questions. The LES is organized as a series of learning modules consisting of short online lessons and associated practice questions. This tool is your source for all study materials, including practice questions and mock exams. The LES is the primary method by which CFA Institute delivers your curriculum experience. Here, candidates will find additional practice questions to test their knowledge. Some questions in the LES provide a unique interactive experience.

DESIGNING YOUR PERSONAL STUDY PROGRAM

An orderly, systematic approach to exam preparation is critical. You should dedicate a consistent block of time every week to reading and studying. Review the LOS both before and after you study curriculum content to ensure you can demonstrate the knowledge, skills, and abilities described by the LOS and the assigned reading. Use the LOS as a self-check to track your progress and highlight areas of weakness for later review.

Successful candidates report an average of more than 300 hours preparing for each exam. Your preparation time will vary based on your prior education and experience, and you will likely spend more time on some topics than on others.

ERRATA

The curriculum development process is rigorous and involves multiple rounds of reviews by content experts. Despite our efforts to produce a curriculum that is free of errors, in some instances, we must make corrections. Curriculum errata are periodically updated and posted by exam level and test date on the Curriculum Errata webpage (www.cfainstitute.org/en/programs/submit-errata). If you believe you have found an error in the curriculum, you can submit your concerns through our curriculum errata reporting process found at the bottom of the Curriculum Errata webpage.

OTHER FEEDBACK

Please send any comments or suggestions to info@cfainstitute.org, and we will review your feedback thoughtfully.

Corporate Issuers

Organizational Forms, Corporate Issuer Features, and Ownership

INTRODUCTION

1

This learning module introduces the Corporate Issuers topic area, which covers the fundamentals of how corporations are organized and governed and how they make operating, investing, and financing decisions. Financial analysts must have a strong understanding of corporate issuers because they are the largest type of issuer in financial markets globally; many analysts are focused entirely on analyzing and investing in their debt or equity instruments. In the first lesson of this module, we describe and compare the legal organizational forms of businesses, emphasizing their similarities and differences and important implications for investors. The second lesson focuses on the corporate organizational form and its key features, such as the separation of ownership and management, limited shareholder liability, access to financing, and tax issues. In the final lesson, we compare privately held and public corporate issuers, including the mechanisms of how corporate issuers go public and are taken private.

LEARNING MODULE OVERVIEW

- Businesses are legally organized as sole proprietorships, partnerships, or limited companies, which differ by several attributes, including legal identity, owner–manager relations, owner liability, taxation, and access to financing. In practice, organizational forms are jurisdiction specific; our focus is on common characteristics.

- The limited company form, often known as the corporation, offers advantages over the other two forms by improving the ability to raise capital, through limited shareholder liability, the separation of ownership and management, and fewer restrictions on the number of owners and transferring ownership. In most jurisdictions, there are two types of limited companies: private limited companies and public limited companies.

- Private limited companies tend to have some restrictions on ownership but pass-through taxation like partnerships. Public limited companies have no ownership restrictions, but their income can be taxed at both the company and shareholder level. While public limited companies do not have to go public by selling their shares on an exchange, it is this form that is most suitable for becoming a publicly traded company.

- Corporate shareholders elect a board of directors that appoints executive management to operate the company. Shareholders effect change primarily through their ability to replace directors.

- Corporations that seek external financing in financial markets, known as corporate issuers, can utilize either public or private markets, and these choices have implications for the liquidity and price transparency of the company's securities, as well as its ability to raise future financing and the degree to which it must disclose information.

- Corporate issuers can change their status from privately held to publicly traded (or "listed") through a variety of mechanisms, including an initial public offering. Publicly traded issuers can be taken private through several mechanisms, including a leveraged buyout.

- Shareholders of corporate issuers include not only individuals and institutional investors, such as pension funds and mutual funds, but also governments, non-profits, and other corporations.

LEARNING MODULE SELF-ASSESSMENT

These initial questions are intended to help you gauge your current level of understanding of this topic.

1. Fill in the two blanks below using the two of the following four possible terms:

    Sole proprietorship

    General partnership

    Limited partnership

    Public limited company (corporation)

    A _____ likely has the greatest access to financing, while a _____ likely has the least access to financing.

Solution:

A <u>public limited company (corporation)</u> likely has the greatest access to financing, while a <u>sole proprietorship</u> likely has the least access to financing. A primary difference across organizational forms is access to financing to fund investments. The sole proprietorship is limited to its individual owner's ability to invest her own money and borrowing capacity as an individual. At the other end of the spectrum, a public limited company can access a broad array of outside investors by issuing debt and/or equity securities.

2. Which of the following organizational forms provides for the *least* owner liability of business debts?

   A. General partnership

   B. Private limited company

   C. Sole proprietorship

   Solution:

   B is correct. In both the sole proprietorship and general partnership forms of organization, the owners are personally liable for all debts assumed by the company. In a private limited company, owner (shareholder) liability is limited to the value of their ownership stake.

3. Voting rights of a corporate issuer's shareholders generally refer to which of the following?

   A. The ability of the corporation to vote in political elections

   B. The direct ability to elect a chief executive officer of the company

   C. The ability to elect members of the company's board of directors

   Solution:

   C is correct. The voting rights of shareholders generally allow them to elect board members as well as vote on other matters outlined in the company's charter. The board of directors has the responsibility to hire (or retain) the company's chief executive officer (CEO); thus, voting rights do not give shareholders the *direct* ability to hire the CEO. Despite the status of a corporation as a distinct legal entity, this status does not provide voting rights in political elections.

4. Explain how the following situation reflects double taxation on the corporate organizational form: The corporation pays a 21% tax rate on pre-tax income of USD100 million. The corporation distributes USD10 million to its shareholders. Individuals pay a 20% tax on dividend income.

   Solution:

   The corporation pays USD21 million in income taxes at the corporate level and, collectively, the shareholders pay USD2 million in individual income taxes on dividends received. In total, USD23 million in income taxes were paid on the pre-tax income of USD100 million. Effectively, the USD10 million paid as dividends was taxed twice, first as business income and again as personal income.

5. True or false: The term "public" for a public corporate issuer means that the company is wholly or partially owned by a government.

   A. True

   B. False

   Solution:

   B is correct. The statement is false because while a public corporate issuer could be owned partly by a government, this condition is not necessary. The term "public" refers only to the fact that a company's equity securities are traded on an exchange and thus are available for investment by the public.

6. Fill in the blanks:

A public company's shares can be exchanged on a _____,
while a private company's shares suffer from a lack of price

_____.

Solution:

A public company's shares can be exchanged on a <u>stock exchange</u>, while a
private company's shares suffer from a lack of price <u>transparency</u>.

2   ORGANIZATIONAL FORMS OF BUSINESSES

☐ | compare the organizational forms of businesses

In most market economies, there are three general types of organization, each with
distinct purposes, stakeholders, and governing legal frameworks: for-profit organizations, known as **businesses** or **companies**; not-for-profit non-governmental
organizations, or simply non-profits; and governments.

The focus of this and subsequent modules are businesses, because financial analysts are important participants in the markets for their financial resources. However,
non-profits and governments often are investors in businesses, which will be covered
in later lessons. Governments as issuers of debt and other securities are covered in
modules on fixed income.

Organizational Forms of Businesses

Business owners choose a legal **organizational form** that defines how returns, risks,
and ownership and operational responsibilities are distributed. There are three general
forms common to most jurisdictions.

Exhibit 1: Organizational Forms of Businesses

The organizational forms of businesses differ by several attributes:

- *Legal identity:* Whether the business is legally considered a separate entity
  or person apart from its owners
- *Owner–manager relationship:* The relationship between the owner(s) of the
  business and those who manage the business

- *Owner liability:* The extent to which owners are personally legally liable for actions or debts undertaken by the business
- *Taxation:* The treatment of business profits or losses for tax purposes
- *Access to financing:* The ability to raise capital to fund expansion and distribute risks

Every jurisdiction has its own specific versions and variants of organizational forms, including different names for them. We are not attempting to provide an exhaustive treatment of jurisdictional specifics; rather, we provide the general and common attributes that analysts must know to ask the right questions in their own research on specific investment candidates and business cases.

Sole Trader or Proprietorship

The simplest organizational form is the sole trader or proprietorship, shown in Exhibit 2. In a sole proprietorship, the owner provides the capital needed to start and operate the business and retains full control over management, while participating fully in the firm's financial returns and risks. In some jurisdictions, this form is the default form, requiring no formal legal registration, and is dissolved when the owner ceases business activity or dies.

Exhibit 2: Sole Trader or Proprietorship

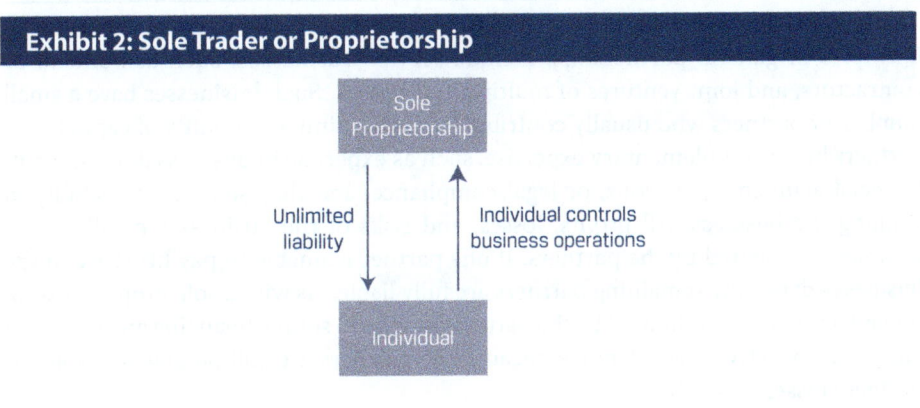

An example of a sole proprietorship is a family-owned business. The individual owner usually uses savings or a personal loan to start the business and to run daily operations and retains full management control. The owner retains all return (profits), which is taxed as personal income, and is personally responsible for losses and obligations of the business, such as debts.

While sole proprietorships comprise the largest *number* of businesses in most market economies and are preferred by small business owners for their simplicity and flexibility, their growth is constrained by an owner's ability to access financing, assume risk, and serve as the sole owner.

Partnerships

Partnerships allow multiple owners to pool their resources and share business risk and return. There are three common types in most jurisdictions: general partnerships, limited partnerships, and limited liability partnerships.

A **general partnership**, shown in Exhibit 3, has two or more owners called partners or **general partners (GPs)**. General partnerships are like sole proprietorships, with the important distinction that they allow for additional resources to be brought into the business by the additional owners, along with the sharing of business risk and return. Partnerships are often formed and governed by a written partnership agreement that outlines specific partner roles and responsibilities and the sharing of profits, losses, and obligations. However, a written agreement is not required; partnerships can be formed verbally or incidentally through actions.

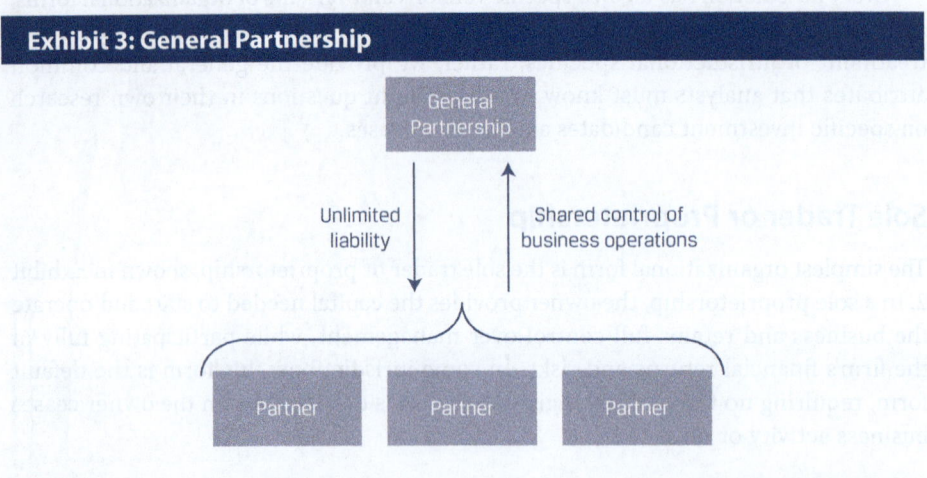

Exhibit 3: General Partnership

Examples of general partnerships include service businesses, such as builders or contractors, and joint ventures of multiple businesses. Such businesses have a small number of partners who usually contribute equal or similar amounts of capital. The partners bring complementary expertise, such as expertise in business development, financial acumen, operations, or legal/compliance, and they share responsibility in running the business. All profits, losses, and risks of the business are collectively assumed and shared by the partners. If one partner is unable to pay his share of the business's debts, the remaining partners are fully liable. As with a sole proprietorship, potential for growth is limited by the partners' ability to source financing and expertise and their collective risk tolerance because the partners are still personally liable for business losses and debt.

Exhibit 4 shows a type of partnership called a **limited partnership**, which addresses some of the shortcomings of general partnerships. In a limited partnership, there must be at least one general partner (GP) with unlimited liability that often manages the business. Remaining partners, however, called **limited partners (LPs)**, have limited liability, meaning their losses are limited to the size of their investment in the limited partnership, and may not have any management responsibilities. With limited liability, personal assets are considered separate and thus protected from the obligations of the business. All partners are entitled to a share of the profits and losses as specified in the partnership agreement, with GPs typically receiving a larger portion in exchange for their greater risk and personal liability. Partnership agreements are customized and negotiated by the partners and can be highly complex, with multiple partnership tiers that have varying profit and loss sharing arrangements.

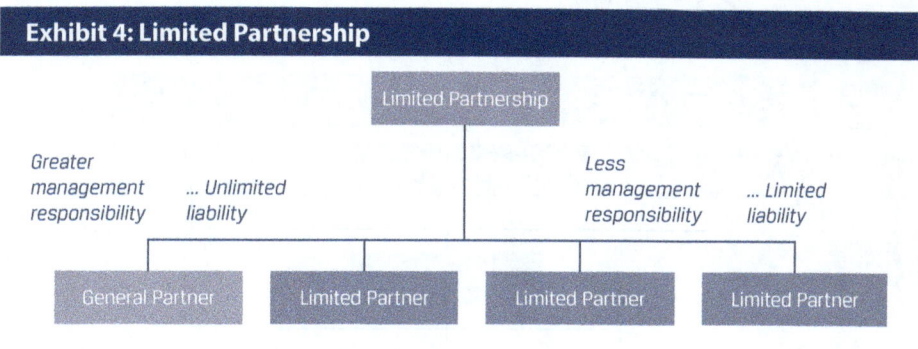

Exhibit 4: Limited Partnership

In a limited partnership, while financial risk and reward are shared, such resources as capital and expertise are typically limited to what the partners can contribute, and limited partners usually grant managerial responsibilities to the GP, which entails risk. Partnership agreements are customized and often limit the transferability of ownership interest or expansion beyond a small group of partners. Like sole proprietorships, partnerships are typically **pass-through businesses** for tax purposes. Pass-through businesses are not taxed at the entity level, passing on all their profits or losses to the partners who are taxed personally. Business income from these entities is passed through and taxed regardless of whether income was actually distributed or retained in the partnership and reinvested.

In some jurisdictions, there is a special form of limited partnership known as a **limited liability partnership (LLP)**, which does not require a general partner and is instead composed entirely of limited partners, thus resolving the risk of unlimited liability for the GP. Instead, all partners have limited liability, and the partners share in management responsibilities, typically appointing one or more partners as managing partners. In some jurisdictions, such as the United States, LLPs are permitted only for professional services firms, such as law, accounting, engineering, and architecture, and have limits on the number of partners and legal restrictions on equity investment.

Limited Companies

Finally, a **limited company** has many similarities to limited partnerships but includes several more features that allow greater access to financing and expertise for growth. In many jurisdictions, there are two types of limited companies: private limited companies and public limited companies.

The **private limited company** is similar to a limited partnership. But the form includes limited liability for *all* owners, improved transferability of ownership interests by dividing ownership into units called **shares** that are more easily tradeable, and a distinction between owners and managers. Owners, known as **shareholders** or members, elect a **board of directors** to manage the company and authorize any distributions of profits to owners. Boards of directors typically appoint professional managers. Private limited companies are known by many names in different jurisdictions, including limited liability company (LLC) and S corporation in the United States, G.K. in Japan, SARL in France, GmbH in Germany, and company with limited liability in China.

Exhibit 5: Organization of Limited Company

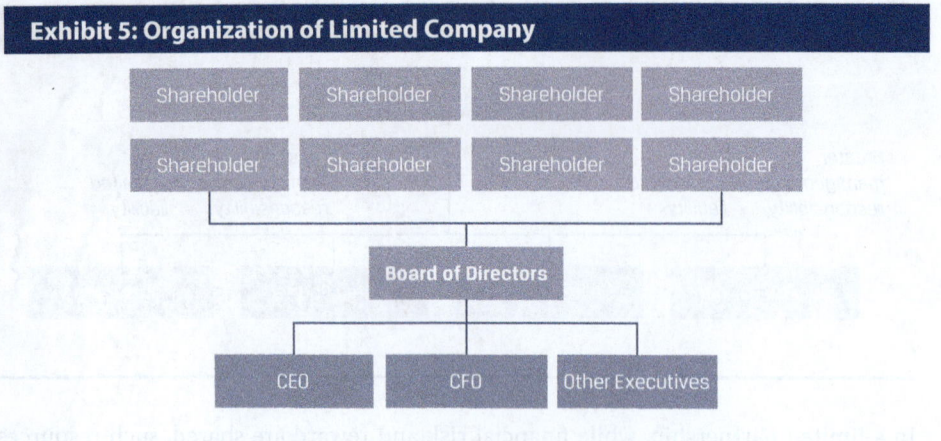

In many jurisdictions, including the United States, private limited companies have legal limits on the number of owners and require votes for transferring ownership interest but are pass-through businesses (like LPs), meaning that taxes on business income are paid only at the shareholder, not company, level.

Finally, **public limited companies**, often called **corporations**, are similar to private limited companies but in most jurisdictions face no legal restrictions on the number of owners or ownership transferability, while still featuring limited liability and separation of ownership and management. For these reasons, public limited companies are the most suitable form for companies that seek to go public and are the dominant organizational form globally by revenues and asset values. However, public limited companies are disadvantaged in most jurisdictions compared to the other organizational forms in one respect: taxation. While other forms are taxed only on business income and loss at the owner (personal) level, public limited companies are taxed at the business level and *again* at the personal level if profits are distributed to shareholders. But if profits are retained and reinvested in the company, the shareholder level of tax does not apply, which makes this organizational form more suitable for companies intending to retain profits to fund investment.

Public limited companies are known by different names in different jurisdictions, including C-corporation in the United States, corporation in China, Société anonyme in France, AG in Germany, and K.K. or stock company in Japan. Examples are numerous, including most if not all well-known multinational companies.

EXAMPLE 1

Simon Property Group

Simon Property Group ("Simon") is one of the largest owners of retail real estate in the world, with over $33 billion in assets. Its assets primarily include shopping centers in the United States and some retail properties in Europe and Asia. Simon is organized in two layers, each with a distinct organizational form.

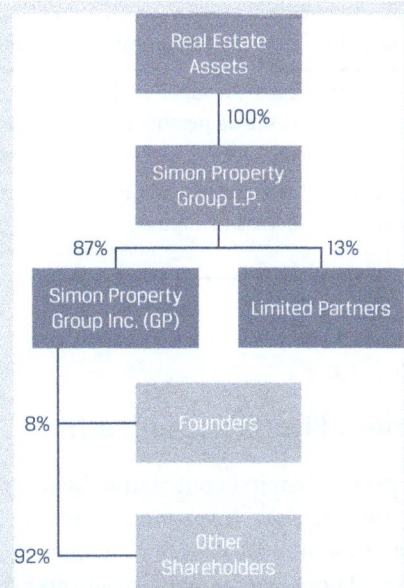

The retail real estate assets are wholly owned by Simon Property Group L.P., a limited partnership. Its partners include Simon Property Group Inc., the general partner, and approximately 200 limited partners. The general partner has full managerial responsibilities and unlimited liability and has an ownership interest of 87% in the partnership.

Importantly, the general partner, Simon Property Group Inc., is itself a corporation. It is broadly owned by thousands of shareholders, including the founding family, which owns 8% of shares. Simon Property Group Inc. has a single asset: its partnership interest in Simon Property L.P.

Simon's structure allows co-investing with limited partners, full management control, and receiving most of the income from the assets, while benefiting from broad access to financing, because while the GP has unlimited liability, its *shareholders* have limited liability. Partnerships composed of entities with limited liability, such as corporations, are common because they shield the ultimate owners (in this case, shareholders of Simon Property Group Inc.) from business risk but allow for the sharing of profit and loss in the underlying business.

The key distinctions between sole proprietorships, partnerships, and public limited companies or corporations are outlined in Exhibit 6.

Exhibit 6: Features of Sole Proprietorships, Partnerships, and Corporations

Feature	Sole Proprietor	General Partnership	Limited Partnership	Corporation
Legal Identity	No separate legal identity; extension of owner	No separate legal identity; extension of partner(s)	No separate legal identity; extension of partner(s)	Separate legal entity
Owner–Operator Relationship	Owner operated	Partners operated	GP operated	Board and management operated
Owner Liability	Sole unlimited liability	Shared unlimited liability	GP has unlimited liability; LPs have limited liability	Limited liability

Feature	Sole Proprietor	General Partnership	Limited Partnership	Corporation
Taxation	Pass-through: Profits taxed as personal income	Pass-through: Profits taxed as personal income	Pass-through: Profits taxed as personal income	Corporation income taxed; distributions (dividends) taxed as personal income
Access to Financing	Limited by owner access to capital	Limited by partner access to capital	Limited by GP/LP access to capital	Unbounded access to capital, unlimited business potential

EXAMPLE 2

How Are Investment Funds Organized?

Investment funds are pools of capital contributed by one or more investors for earning returns and managing risks. Investment funds are like other companies in a market economy: They hire professional management to invest capital, sometimes with additional borrowed money, in various assets to achieve return objectives subject to risk constraints. Major differences between funds and other companies include employing few people directly, primarily investing in financial instruments rather than operating assets, diversification of assets, and having specific rather than general objectives (e.g., exceed a benchmark rate of return).

Two common organizational forms for investment funds are corporations and limited partnerships, as illustrated in the following two diagrams. When organized as a corporation, fund investors hold shares that represent their proportionate interests in the pool of underlying assets. When organized as a limited partnership, fund investors hold partnership units that either represent their proportionate interests in the pool of underlying assets or varying interests of specific assets.

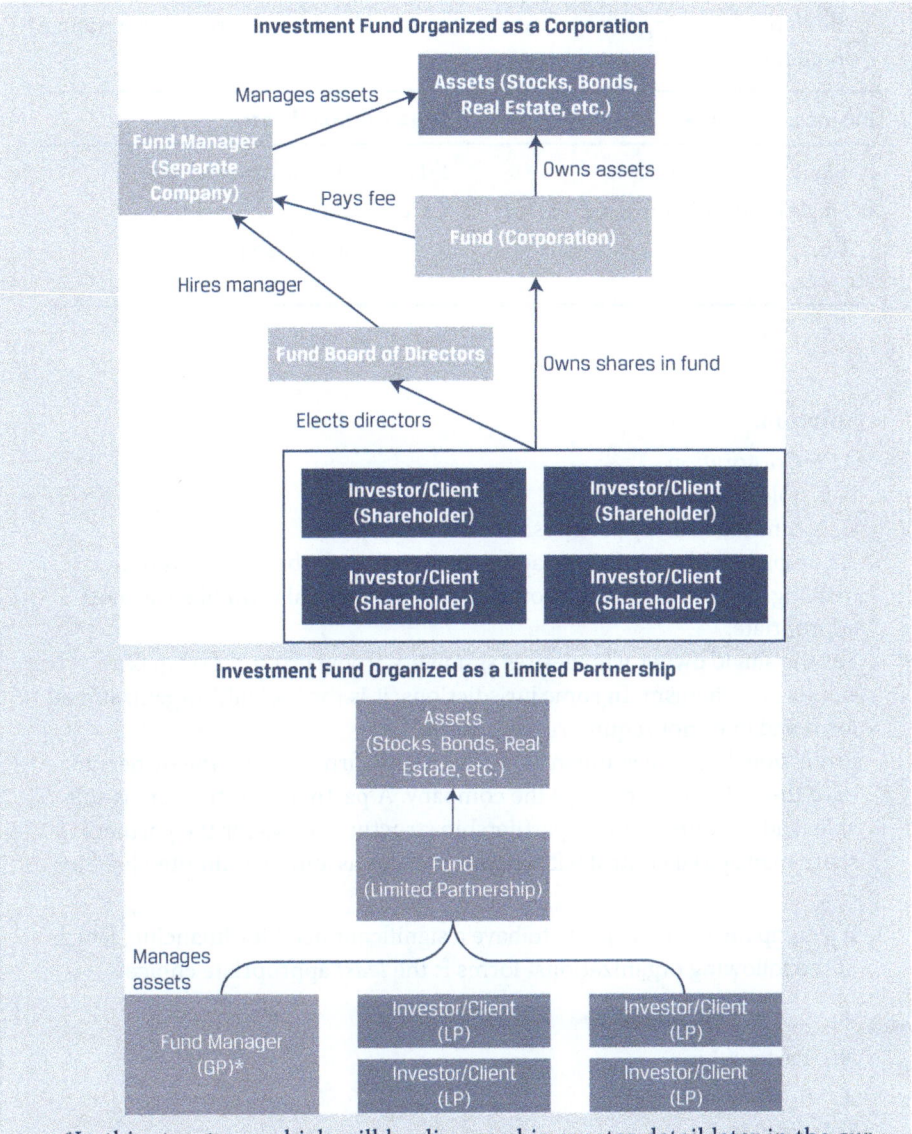

Investment Fund Organized as a Corporation

Investment Fund Organized as a Limited Partnership

*In this structure, which will be discussed in greater detail later in the curriculum in lessons on alternative investment, fund managers typically create a wholly owned private limited company entity that serves as the GP to protect the fund manager from unlimited liability.

QUESTION SET

1. Identify two features that distinguish a general partnership from a limited partnership.

   Solution:

   Owner–manager relationship: The management of a general partnership is typically shared by the general partners, while in a limited partnership, the general partner often exercises most managerial responsibilities.

   Owner liability of business debts and obligations: In a general partnership, the partners are personally legally liable for business debt and actions undertaken by the company. In a limited partnership, only the general partner faces personal liability; limited partners' liability is limited to their investment in the partnership.

2. Match the following business attributes with the most appropriate organizational form.

Business Attribute	Organizational Form
A. Significant capital needs	1. Limited liability partnership
B. Single owner, desires simplicity	2. Corporation
C. Company provides professional services	3. Sole proprietorship

Solution:

A. 2. Corporation
B. 3. Sole proprietorship
C. 1. Limited liability partnership
A company with significant capital needs will want broad access to financing. In such a case, the corporate organizational form likely is most appropriate.
For the single owner who desires simplicity, a sole proprietorship is a suitable mechanism. In some jurisdictions, it is the "default" organizational form and does not require registration.
Professional service companies, such as a law firm, require the owners to have the skill sets to manage the company. A partnership structure is suitable, and a limited liability partnership structure allows for the partners to share managerial control without any partner assuming unlimited liability.

3. If a company owner expects to have a significant need for financing, which of the following organizational forms is the *least* appropriate choice?

A. Corporate

B. Partnership

C. Sole proprietorship

Solution:

C is correct. A sole proprietorship is limited in financing to the owner's funds and by the amount the owner can borrow personally. A partnership expands access to financing by adding owners, spreading risk, and adding borrowing capacity. The corporate form provides for the broadest access to financing because there are no limits to the number of shareholders and, with limited liability, shareholders are relatively more comfortable with the company borrowing.

4. Fill in the blanks in the following sentence:

_____ liability is a benefit to the corporate organizational form, but the form does face a possible disadvantage because of _____ taxation of distributed business income.

Solution:

<u>Limited</u> liability is a benefit to the corporate organizational form, but the form does face a possible disadvantage because of <u>double</u> taxation of distributed business income.

5. True or False: Partnerships are typically taxed at the entity level rather than at the individual partner level.

   A. True

   B. False

   Solution:

   B is correct. Partnerships are typically pass-through entities, meaning that business income earned by the partnership is passed through to the partners according to the terms of partnership agreement, and each partner is taxed at the personal level.

KEY FEATURES OF CORPORATE ISSUERS   **3**

☐ │ describe key features of corporate issuers

The prior lesson addressed several advantages of the corporate organizational form over others, such as limited owner liability, owner–manager separation, and improved access to external financing. In this lesson, we explore the features of corporations in greater depth. Corporations that raise capital in the financial markets, known as **corporate issuers**, are essential for financial analysts to understand, because they raise more capital from investors than even governments worldwide.

Legal Identity

A corporation is a legal entity separate and distinct from its owners formed through the filing of articles of incorporation with a regulatory authority. Corporations share many of the rights and responsibilities of an individual and may engage in similar activities. For example, a corporation can enter into contracts, hire employees, sue and be sued, borrow and lend money, make investments, and pay taxes.

Large corporations frequently have business operations in many different geographic regions and are subject to each regulatory jurisdiction where

- the company is incorporated,
- the business is conducted, and
- the company finances itself

and for such activities as

- registration,
- financial and non-financial reporting and disclosure, and
- capital market activities (issuance, trading, investment).

Owner–Manager Separation

A key feature of most corporations is the separation between those who own the business (the shareholders) and those who operate it, as represented by the board of directors and management. In a corporation, shareholders are largely removed from the day-to-day operations of the business. Instead, shareholders elect a board of directors that, in turn, appoints executive-level management, such as the chief executive officer, who is accountable for investing, financing, and operating decisions. Directors and managers have a primary responsibility to act in the best interest of shareholders and, indirectly, all stakeholders. The separation of ownership and management enables the corporation to obtain financing from a larger universe of potential investors who do not need (or want) to be involved in management.

If a board or management does not act in shareholders' best interests, shareholders can enact change through exercising **voting rights** attached to their shares—for example, by voting to replace the board of directors—though this can take time. Influencing operations or changing management outright using engagement and voting rights is a strategy pursued by some investors and will be discussed in detail in later lessons.

Owner/Shareholder Liability

Risk is shared among all shareholders, who face limited liability. That is, the maximum amount shareholders can lose is what they have invested in the company (i.e., the value of their shares can fall to zero but no further), and they are not responsible for the debts of the corporation unless they separately, specifically guarantee them.

Shareholders share in the risk and return of the company in proportion to their share ownership unless the corporate charter specifies differently. Unlike partnerships, ownership units are divided into shares of smaller unit size, allowing investors to more easily purchase or sell ownership interests as represented by their shares. For example, some issuers have more than 1 billion shares outstanding, meaning that ownership interests are divided into extremely small increments. Additionally, some corporations issue multiple types or classes of shares with different risk and return characteristics, which will be discussed in a later lesson. Exhibit 7 shows the relationship between owners and the corporation.

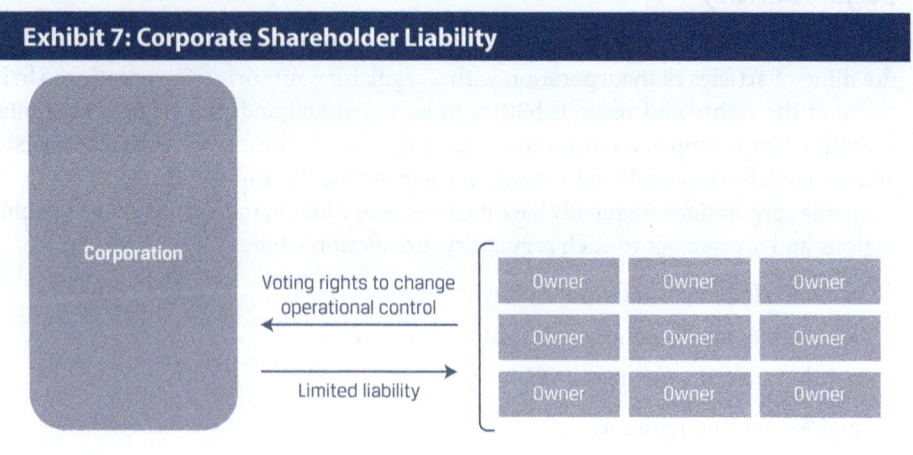

Exhibit 7: Corporate Shareholder Liability

External Financing

The separation between ownership and management allows corporations to access external financing more easily than other business structures because purchasing a share is the only requirement to become an owner. While more expensive to form and operate than other forms, the corporate form is typically preferred when capital needs exceed what could be raised by an individual or small group of partners. Financing may be provided by individuals or by institutions, such as mutual funds, pension funds, banks, governments, non-profits, and other corporations.

Corporations are financed in two ways: with **equity**, by selling shares to investors or reinvesting profits, and with borrowings, or **debt**, in the form of loans, bonds, and leases. Equity investors (shareholders) have a right to receive any distributions of profits, known as **dividends**, while debt must be repaid on a pre-specified date in the future with interest. Equity or debt financing can be raised based on a private contractual agreement between an issuer and investors or in the form of a **security**, a standardized instrument that might be tradeable among investors on a public exchange, which will be covered in the next lesson.

Exhibit 8 shows the relationship between debt and equity on a corporation's balance sheet and how these are related to its assets.

Exhibit 8: Financial and "Economic" Balance Sheet

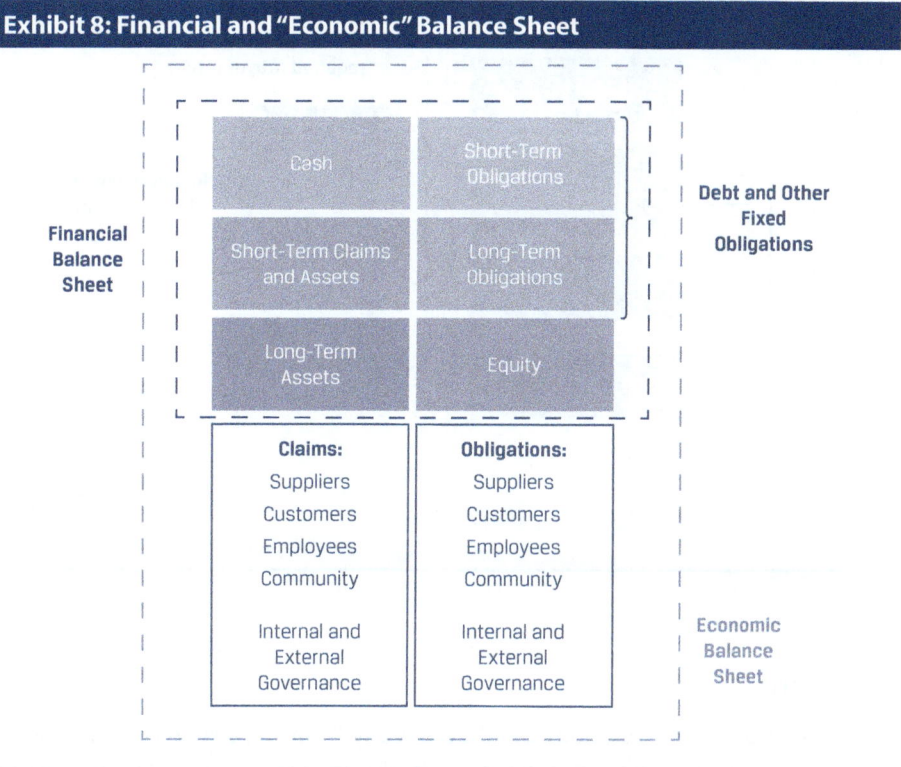

While the "financial" balance sheet at the top of Exhibit 8 shows an issuer's assets (left-hand side) and its sources of financing (right-hand side) from short term to long term measured in financial terms, other intangible or hard-to-quantify assets or liabilities of a firm, such as the human capital associated with its employees and supplier and customer relationships, are included on what may be referred to as an issuer's broader "economic" balance sheet.

Similarly, Exhibit 9 shows an issuer's income statement and distinguishes between its financial income or net income once fixed obligations have been met and its "economic" profit, or return to a firm's owners in excess of what they could have earned elsewhere on different investments, known as their required rate of return on equity.

Exhibit 9: Financial and "Economic" Income Statement

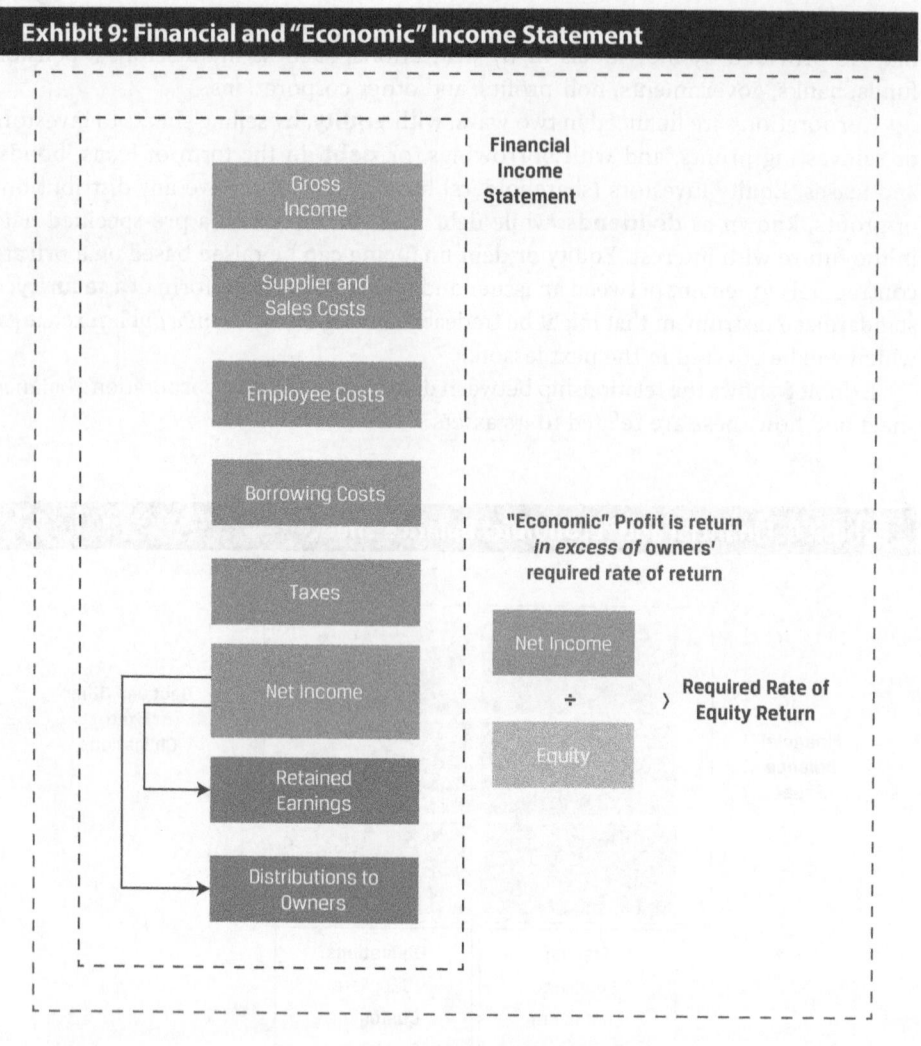

Taxation

While taxation for corporations can differ greatly from country to country, the corporation is ultimately subject to the tax authority and tax code governing the issuer's tax reporting, payment, and status. In most countries, corporations are taxed on their profits. Taxable profits are usually *not* the same as profits reported on financial statements, because tax codes and accounting standards differ.

In many countries, shareholders pay an additional tax on distributions (dividends) that are passed on to them. This is referred to as the **double taxation** of corporate profits. In some countries, shareholders do not pay a personal tax on dividends if the corporation has paid tax previously on the earnings distributed to shareholders or shareholders receive a personal tax credit for their proportional share of taxes paid by the corporation. In other countries, corporations pay no tax at all or may face different tax regimes within one country.

EXAMPLE 3

Double Taxation of Corporate Profits

1. The French retail giant Auchan Holding generated pre-tax income of €838 million last year and paid corporate taxes of €264 million. Investors in France also pay a 30% tax on dividends received. If Auchan had fully distributed its after-tax income to investors as a dividend and all its investors are in France, what is the total tax rate as a percentage of Auchan's pre-tax income?

   Solution:

Pre-Tax Income	€838
Corporate Taxes (31.5%)	€264
After-Tax Income	€838 − €264
	= €574
Distributed Dividend	€574
Investor Dividend Tax (30%)	€574 × 0.30
	= €172.2
Total Tax Rate	(€264 + €172.2)/€838
	= 52.1%

   If the after-tax income of €574 million were paid to investors as a dividend, investors would pay €172.2 million in personal taxes on the dividends received. Total taxes paid would be €436.2 million (€264 million at the corporate level plus €172.2 million at the personal level), resulting in a total tax rate of 52.1%.

Despite the tax disadvantage illustrated in the prior example, the corporate form remains attractive for several reasons. While corporate shareholders are taxed on distributions, sole proprietors and partners are often taxed on all profits regardless of whether they are distributed as dividends (exceptions exist with allowances for profit reserves). This difference makes the corporate structure attractive to businesses that expect to reinvest undistributed profits in, for example, additional capacity for growth. Also, in jurisdictions where corporate tax rates are lower than personal income tax rates, it can be advantageous to "store" profits in the business.

QUESTION SET

1. Explain why the separation of ownership from management allows for corporate issuers to have greater access to capital.

   Solution:

   By separating ownership from management responsibilities, corporations can attract a broad range of owners, especially individuals and institutions, who do not want to be involved in management but would like to participate as investors.

2. Fill in the blanks in the following sentence:

Limited liability of shareholders refers to the fact that the _____ amount shareholders may lose on their investment is the _____ paid to buy the shares.

Solution:

Limited liability of shareholders refers to the fact that the <u>maximum</u> amount shareholders may lose on their investment is the <u>price</u> paid to buy the shares.

3. In which of the following situations does the double taxation of the corporate organizational form matter the *least*?

   A. The company expects to pay all its after-tax income as a dividend to shareholders each year.
   B. The company's shareholders reside in a tax jurisdiction with a high tax rate on dividend income.
   C. The company is expecting to reinvest all its after-tax profits each year into growth of the business.

   Solution:

   C is correct. Reinvestment of all profits implies that the company pays no dividend to shareholders, and thus, no double taxation occurs.
   A is incorrect. Double taxation occurs because dividend income is taxed at both the corporate level and the shareholders' personal levels. If all after-tax profits are distributed, shareholders are taxed twice on the business's income.
   B is incorrect because a high tax rate on shareholders' dividend income received would be a strong impetus to retain profits, find alternative means of distributing profits, or change the organizational form.

4. Referring to the Auchan Holding example in this lesson, calculate the amount of the tax disadvantage (in euros) Auchan has in its corporate form compared to if it were organized as a limited partnership. Recall that Auchan's pre-tax profit was €838 million, the corporate tax rate was 31.5%, the personal income tax rate was 30%, and all after-tax profits were distributed.

   Solution:

   If Auchan were organized as a limited partnership, its pre-tax profit would be passed through to the owner(s) and taxes would only be paid at the personal level. Thus, total taxes paid would be €251.4 million (= €838 million × 0.30), or €184.8 million lower than total taxes paid under the corporate organizational form, and this tax of €251.4 million would be paid regardless of whether the partnership distributed the profit to partners.

5. Corporate issuers are characterized by all of the following *except*:

   A. Corporate income is taxed at both the corporate and personal levels.
   B. Owners do not need to be involved in management of the company.
   C. The owners of the corporation are not legally distinct from the corporation.

   Solution:

   C is correct. A corporation is a legally separate entity from its owners.

A is incorrect because corporate income is taxed at both the corporate and personal levels unless the company pays zero dividends.

B is incorrect because shareholders are not required to exercise management control over the company. While in some cases, a large shareholder may serve as senior management or be on the board of directors, most shareholders do not take on management responsibilities.

PUBLICLY VS. PRIVATELY OWNED CORPORATE ISSUERS

4

☐ | compare publicly and privately owned corporate issuers

For corporations, "public" and "private" (or "listed" and "unlisted") are often defined by whether the company's shares are listed and tradeable on an **exchange**. Somewhat confusingly, this is different from the discussion of private and public limited companies in an earlier lesson; most public or listed companies are public limited companies, but public limited companies are not obliged to list their shares on an exchange.

Exhibit 10: Publicly vs. Privately Owned Limited Companies

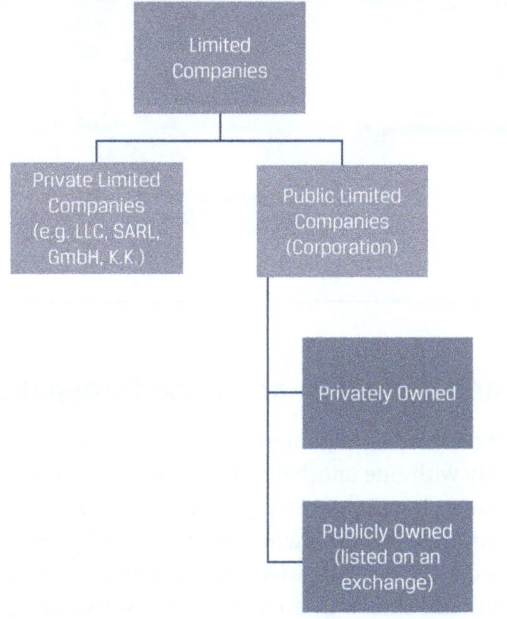

An exchange, which for equities is referred to as a **stock exchange**, is a rules-based, open access market venue where financial instruments are traded, with price and volume transparency accessible by issuers, investors, and their intermediaries. In addition to an exchange listing, primary features distinguishing public and private companies include

- the ability to transfer ownership between investors,

- the process of issuing new shares, and
- registration and disclosure requirements.

A **public (listed) company** has some or all of its shares listed and traded on an exchange. These shares may be widely held or involve a majority or controlling owner. Shareholders may include individuals, employees, institutions on behalf of individuals (e.g., pension funds), other corporations, governments, and non-profits. The shares that are traded actively—and thus are not held by insiders, strategic investors, or sponsors but are more freely available on exchanges—are known as an issuer's **free float**. Free float is often expressed as a percentage of total shares outstanding.

EXAMPLE 4

L'Oréal S.A., the world's largest beauty company, is a French société anonyme, or public limited company. It has been public since listing its shares on the Paris Stock Market (now Euronext) in 1963. As of 31 December 2021, L'Oréal had approximately 535 million shares outstanding.

L'Oréal's shares are mostly owned by Francoise Bettencourt Meyers, her family, and Nestlé (a large, listed Swiss consumer goods company), and the remainder—the free float, approximately 44% of shares—is owned by institutional investors, individual investors, and L'Oréal employees.

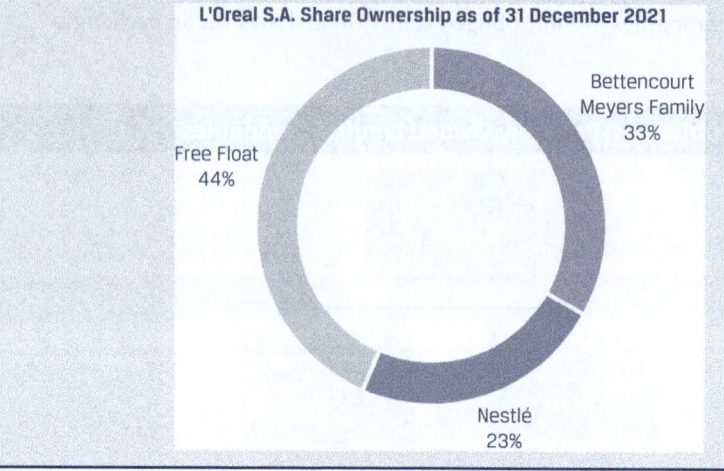

L'Oreal S.A. Share Ownership as of 31 December 2021

Exchange Listing, Liquidity, and Price Transparency

An exchange listing allows ownership to be more easily transferred because investors transact directly with one another in the secondary market on the exchange. An investor can become a shareholder in a public company by executing a buy order in a brokerage account or reduce an ownership position by executing a sell order. This can be done immediately for a relatively small number of shares in a liquid stock or take longer for many shares in a company whose shares trade infrequently. An exchange listing provides share price transparency, allowing investors to track how a company's value changes.

Exhibit 11: Public Companies—Share Ownership Transfer

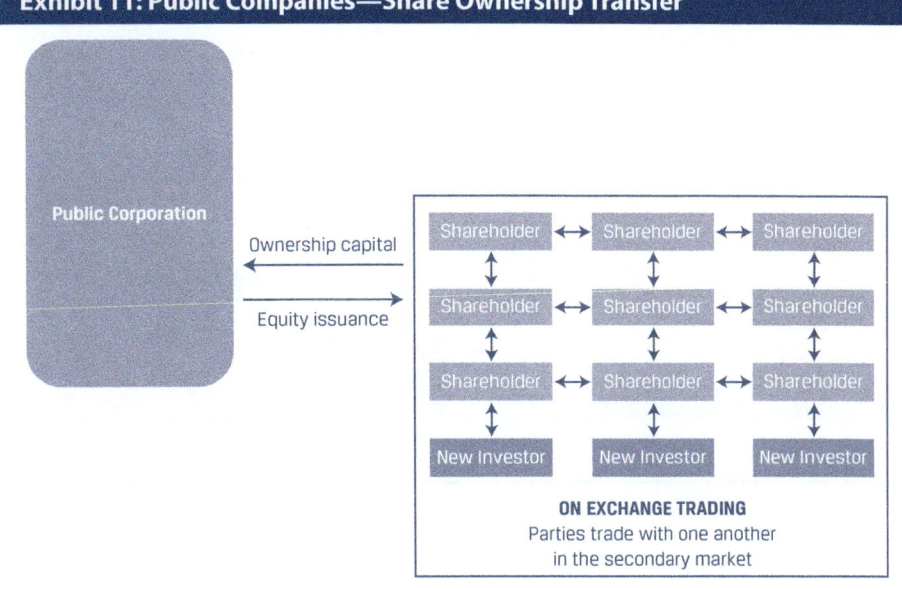

In contrast, the shares of a **private company** are not listed (do not trade on an exchange), so no visible company valuation or share price transparency exists. This makes ownership transfer between investors far more difficult than for a public company. A private company shareholder seeking to sell shares must find a willing buyer, and the two parties must negotiate a price. Even then, the company may refuse the transfer of ownership. Private company shareholders must exercise patience. Their investment is usually locked up until the company is acquired for cash or shares by another company or it goes public.

Private companies do, however, provide benefits that may outweigh the downside of limited transferability of shares. Private companies typically have fewer shareholders, meaning that controlling owners and management are accountable to fewer stakeholders. Second, many early-stage companies are private. If successful, an investor in their equity could earn high returns. Finally, private companies have few disclosure requirements, which are costly to comply with, and there are few regulations and costs associated with raising financing in private transactions. While some claim that private status results in improved performance from greater focus on the long term, as opposed to focusing on quarterly earnings and other short-term measures associated with listed companies, the empirical evidence for short-termism among listed companies is thin at best.[1]

Share Issuance

Corporate issuers may issue additional equity shares in the capital markets from time to time. For a public issuer, these shares can be traded in the secondary market once they're issued. In contrast, private companies finance smaller amounts in the primary market (private debt or equity) from fewer investors who typically have longer holding periods. Exhibit 12 and Exhibit 13 illustrate differences in public and private company share issuance and relative size of financing.

---

1 Mark J. Roe, "Stock Market Short-Termism's Impact," European Corporate Governance Institute (ECGI) Law Working Paper No. 426/2018, Harvard Public Law Working Paper No. 18-28 (22 October 2018).

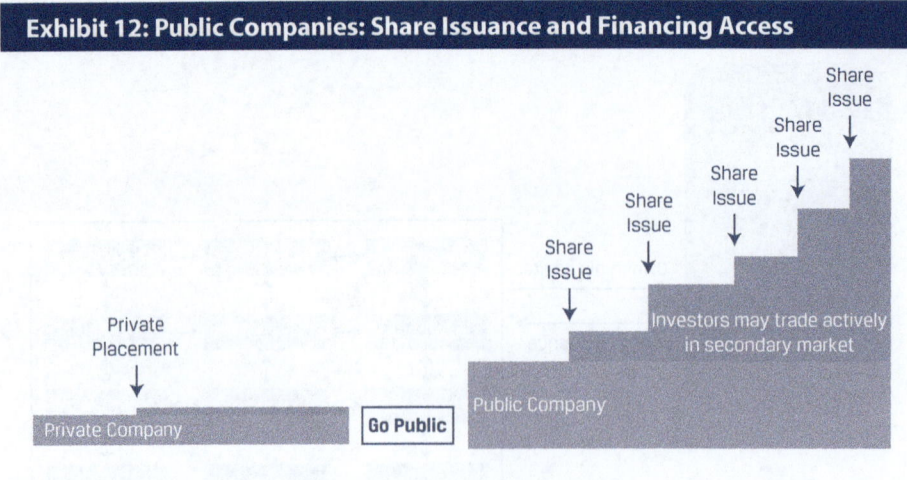

Exhibit 12: Public Companies: Share Issuance and Financing Access

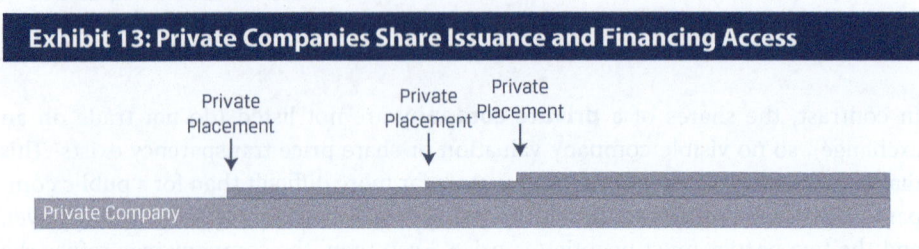

Exhibit 13: Private Companies Share Issuance and Financing Access

Private company investors are typically invited to purchase shares in the company through a **private placement** whose terms are outlined in a legal document (public companies can also conduct private placements, subject to regulatory constraints). Private company investors may be limited to qualified or so-called **accredited investors** or **sophisticated investors**, or those deemed to be able and willing by regulatory authorities to assume the greater risk of a non-public offering.

Registration and Disclosure Requirements

Perhaps the defining attribute of public companies is transparency and disclosure. Public companies must register with a regulatory authority and are subject to compliance and reporting requirements. For example, companies with securities listed on US exchanges (e.g., NYSE and NASDAQ) must file audited financial statements and other information on a quarterly basis with the Securities and Exchange Commission (SEC), which are then accessible to the public on the SEC's EDGAR (Electronic Data Gathering, Analysis, and Retrieval) system or on the company's website. In the European Union, financial statements must be reported in the EU's standardized ESEF (European Single Electronic Format) in the registry of domicile, at least semiannually. Public companies' annual reports regularly exceed 100 pages.

Besides qualitative information and financial reports, public companies must also disclose major changes in the holding of voting rights and other information that may affect security prices, such as management and director stock transactions. Significant share purchases and sales by management may contain information for investors, such as management's confidence in exceeding expectations or leading to questions about a company's business strategy.

Private companies are generally not subject to the same level of regulatory disclosures, although many rules pertain to both private and public companies (such as prohibitions against fraud and the obligation to file corporate tax returns). While not required, some private firms disclose pertinent information directly to owners as well as lenders, especially if they hope to be able to raise additional financing in the future. Exhibit 14 and Exhibit 15 compare typical entity relationships for public and private companies.

Exhibit 14: Public Companies: Typical Entity Relationships

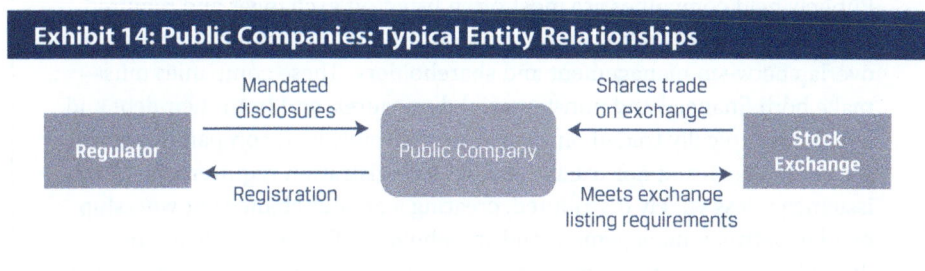

Exhibit 15: Private Companies: Typical Entity Relationships

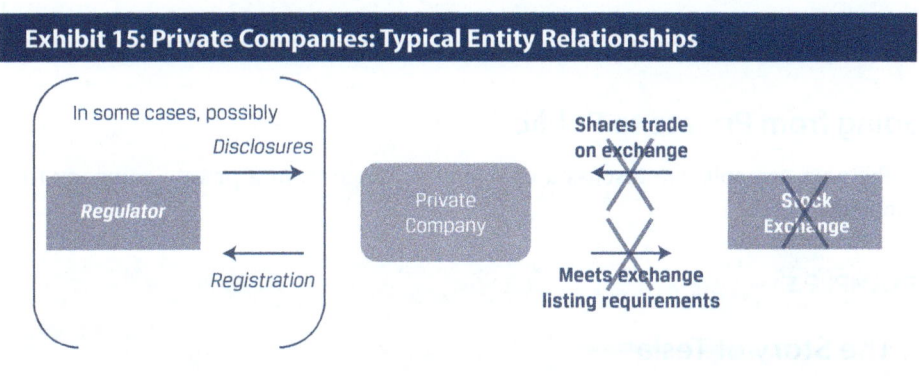

KNOWLEDGE CHECK

1. Match the applicable company characteristic in the left column with the category that best describes it (publicly held, privately held, both) on the right.

Exchange listed	Publicly held/Privately held/Both
Owner/manager overlaps	Publicly held/Privately held/Both
Registered	Publicly held/Privately held/Both
Share liquidity	Publicly held/Privately held/Both
Non-financial disclosure required	Publicly held/Privately held/Both
Negotiated debt and equity sales	Publicly held/Privately held/Both

Solutions:

Exchange listed	Publicly held
Owner/manager overlaps	Privately held
Registered	Publicly held
Share liquidity	Publicly held
Non-financial disclosure required	Both
Negotiated debt and equity sales	Privately held

Publicly held companies are most often listed on exchanges and required to register shares. Their shares are typically liquid with minor ownership overlap between management and shareholders. These companies must make both financial and non-financial disclosures, and both their debt and equity are typically traded on exchanges. Privately held companies are neither exchange listed nor usually subject to registration requirements. Share issuance is less widely distributed, creating a greater chance of ownership overlap between management and shareholders. Private company shares are illiquid. Generally, these companies are required to make only non-financial disclosures. The sale of their equity and debt is privately negotiated between company insiders and capital providers.

Going from Private to Public

In the next example, we discuss a company's change from a private company to a public one.

EXAMPLE 5

The Story of Tesla

In 1997, engineer Martin Eberhard and computer scientist Marc Tarpenning started a company called NuvoMedia to make an electronic book reader called the Rocket eBook, a precursor to Amazon's Kindle. Three years after it was founded, NuvoMedia was sold for $187 million.

Soon after, the two entrepreneurs formed a new company focused on making electric sports cars. They named the company Tesla Motors in honor of the inventor Nikola Tesla, forming a corporation in 2003. As a high-risk, capital-intensive endeavor, they used some of their new-found wealth and sought other cofounders with expertise in electric vehicles and fundraising capabilities. Elon Musk, an entrepreneur with a shared vision in the commercialization of electric sports cars, joined the team, as did Ian Wright and J. B. Straubel, the company's chief technical officer.

In addition to investing $6.3 million in Tesla in 2004, making him the largest shareholder, Musk helped raise money from venture capitalists. Musk became CEO in 2008, the year Tesla released its first vehicle, the Roadster. In 2010, Musk led Tesla's initial public offering, which raised $226 million. Over the next several years, Tesla shifted from sports cars to passenger vehicles, greatly expanding its vehicle production and product line, and in 2016, it also entered the photovoltaics market. In 2017, it changed its name from Tesla Motors to Tesla, Inc., to reflect its diversification into energy storage. The company continued global expansion of automobile production, issuing several billion dollars in three secondary equity offerings in 2020. Tesla moved its headquarters from California to Texas and reached a $1 trillion market capitalization in 2021.

The evolution of Tesla, Inc., over less than 20 years of existence from a startup to a firm among those with the largest market capitalization globally was assisted by the flexibility of its organizational form as a corporation. Tesla was able to obtain significant financing from both debt and equity investors and retain key employees, including Musk, with equity-based compensation.

Private companies may become public companies ("go public") in three ways: IPO, direct listing, or acquisition.

Exhibit 16: Three Ways Private Companies Go Public

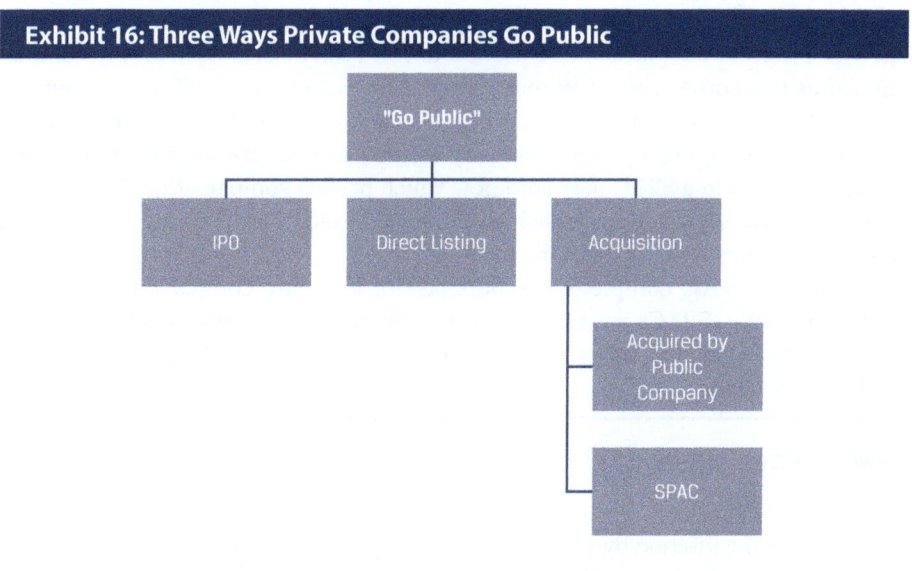

Tesla Motors became a public company using an **initial public offering (IPO)**. To complete an IPO, companies must meet specific exchange listing requirements and usually engage financial intermediaries known as investment banks to underwrite the sale of new shares. Proceeds from the sale of new shares go to the issuing corporation, and its shares begin trading on an exchange.

Private companies can also go public through a far less common method known as a **direct listing**, which differs from an IPO in two important ways. A direct listing does not involve an underwriter and no new shares are issued, so no capital is raised. Instead, the company simply lists existing shares on an exchange at a price determined by the market, and shares become available to the public as they are sold by existing shareholders. Although direct listings, compared with IPOs, may take place more quickly and at a lower cost, they are usually undertaken only by larger, more established companies with a recognized brand, as in the following example.

EXAMPLE 6

In early 2018, Sweden-based music streaming company Spotify Technology SA became the first foreign issuer to go public via direct listing on the New York Stock Exchange (NYSE). Founded in 2006, Spotify secured multiple rounds of venture capital equity financing and also raised debt prior to going public. Unlike other private companies seeking to go public, Spotify was a well-known brand and an established company, having entered the US market in 2011, with over

70 million global subscribers and over $5 billion in revenue during the prior year. When announcing its direct listing, Spotify said it chose this financing route because it could list without diluting existing shareholders, offer liquidity to existing shareholders, and provide equal access to buyers and sellers.

Alternatively, a private company may become public via an acquisition. This may occur indirectly if the company is acquired by another that is already public. In such cases, the acquiring company is usually larger, so an investor in the combined entity has minimal exposure to the private company that was acquired.

Another means of going public via acquisition is through a **special purpose acquisition company (SPAC)**, which is a transaction like the reverse merger that was popular in the 1990s and early 2000s. A SPAC is a shell company, often called a "blank check" company, that exists solely for the purpose of acquiring an unspecified private company sometime in the future. SPACs raise capital and go public through an IPO. Proceeds are placed in a trust account and can be disbursed only to complete an acquisition; otherwise, they must be returned to investors. SPACs are publicly listed, often specialize in a particular industry, and have a finite time period, such as 18 months, to acquire a private company before proceeds are returned to investors. While investors in a SPAC may not know which private company the SPAC will buy, they may have expectations based on the SPAC executives involved or comments these individuals have made in the media.

Once the SPAC completes the purchase of a private company, that company becomes public. SPACs are replacing the formerly used reverse merger process of going public, which typically used a dormant listed company with a previous business and trading history.

KNOWLEDGE CHECK

1. Match the method by which a private company can go public with the most closely related term.

   Going Public Method:

IPO	"blank check," existing shareholder, underwriter
Direct listing	"blank check," existing shareholder, underwriter
SPAC	"blank check," existing shareholder, underwriter

   Solution:

IPO	underwriter
Direct listing	existing shareholder
SPAC	"blank check"

   An IPO is facilitated by investment banks that underwrite, or guarantee, the offering. A direct listing does not involve an underwriter, and no new capital is raised. Instead, the company is simply listed on an exchange, and shares are sold by existing shareholders. A SPAC is a shell company often called a "blank check" company because it exists solely for the purpose of acquiring an unspecified private company sometime in the future.

2. True or false: Accredited investors are the capital providers qualified by regulators to invest in public companies. Justify your answer.

   Solution:

   The statement is false. Accredited investors are judged by regulators to have the sophistication for understanding and assuming the risks that come with investing in *private*, not public, companies.

Going from Public to Private

Public companies may also decide to go private. A "take-private" or "go-private" process involves investors acquiring all of the company's publicly traded shares and delisting the company from the exchange. The investors must typically pay a premium above the current share price and often use debt to finance the acquisition. Go-private transactions are initiated by investors who believe that actions could be taken that would result in a higher valuation than that reflected in the current share price. Going private puts these investors in control and takes the company out of public view, which may be beneficial. These actions undertaken with greater private control might include management changes, selling assets, restructuring, or realizing cost savings that are expected to exceed the premium paid and financing costs. Once these actions are complete, investors may take the company public again several years later if they are able to achieve the desired valuation at that time.

Public versus private company trends can provide insight into market developments. For example, many emerging economies have a growing number of public companies, while the opposite is occurring in developed economies. Emerging economies are usually characterized by higher rates of growth, a transition to more open market structures, and foreign capital inflows. This is consistent with a growing number of listed companies on an emerging economy's domestic stock exchange.

A declining number of listed public companies in developed markets is a result of several factors. One cause is a higher number of mergers and acquisitions, which reduces the number of independent listed companies. Another is the growing number of private capital sources available, such as venture capital and private equity, allowing companies to access needed capital while avoiding the additional cost, regulatory burden, public scrutiny, and compliance costs associated with a public listing. Another factor is that many private companies simply choose to remain private because it preserves control by incumbent owners and management.

The Varieties of Corporate Owners

Corporations offer a great deal of flexibility in ownership and objectives. As discussed earlier, shareholders include not only individual and institutional investors but also other corporations, governments, and non-profits, which may be controlling owners.

Governments sometimes create legally separate corporations while maintaining 100% or varying levels of ownership. For example, a sovereign government may establish a wholly owned corporation but create a board of directors and management structure, along with compliance and reporting requirements, such as the issuance of audited financial statements. This structure provides increased transparency to taxpayers and external investors (limited to debt investors in this case) as to whether the corporation achieves its objectives and generates a profit or a loss, which must be financed from the government's budget. This structure is used by the United States

Postal Service (USPS), while postal services in some countries, such as the Netherlands (KPN), the United Kingdom (Royal Mail), and Germany (Deutsche Post), are partly or fully investor owned.

Government-owned corporations exist in both developed and emerging economies, in some cases to supply public goods, such as infrastructure, which creates positive externalities, and in others to earn profits in a major domestic industry. For example, government-owned corporations are common in developed economies among postal systems, railways, and other infrastructure, such as airports. In emerging economies, state-owned or state-controlled enterprises often operate in a dominant domestic industry, such as basic commodities or energy. Financial intermediaries, such as banks, are also often first established as government institutions in these markets. As the economy seeks foreign and domestic capital from the private sector to expand and diversify, government companies are often gradually transferred to private sector ownership via an IPO, as in the following example.

EXAMPLE 7

Saudi Aramco IPO

Nearly 50 years after oil was first discovered in Saudi Arabia, the government issued a decree creating the Saudi Arabian Oil Company (Saudi Aramco) to take control of and carry out petroleum and natural gas production in the country. To partially finance a plan to diversify the Saudi economy and reduce reliance on oil, the Saudi government announced its intention in 2016 to raise up to $100 billion on global exchanges by selling a 5% stake in the company, valuing Saudi Aramco at $2 trillion. Given IPO delays and a lower, $1.7 trillion valuation, in 2019, the Saudi government opted to scale down its plans, selling a 1.5% stake on the domestic Saudi stock exchange for $25.6 billion instead. Despite the smaller size, this transaction was the largest IPO to date and created the world's most valuable publicly traded corporation at the time.

In other instances, industry deregulation and/or technological change is the catalyst for a shift from government to private sector ownership. For example, the telecommunications industry shifted from government-owned monopolies across developed and less developed economies in the 1980s to many private sector corporations and varying degrees of government ownership today. This expanded access to capital has greatly enhanced the industry's ability to invest in rapidly evolving cellular technology. In the area of power generation, a similar shift from government to private sector has occurred, leading to greater diversification of energy production, as well as recently leading to investment in sustainable and renewable sources of energy, as in the case of Public Power Corporation S.A.

EXAMPLE 8

Public Power Corporation S.A.

The largest electric power company in Greece, Public Power Corporation (PPC), was established as a state-owned and -managed corporation by the Greek government in 1950. Following Greece's entry into the EU, PPC lost its domestic power generation monopoly. In response to the European Electricity Directive separating power generation, transmission, and distribution, the company issued an IPO in 2001 for 34% of its shares and reduced government ownership further, to 51%, through subsequent share raises over the next few years. The company is phasing out coal-fired power plants and shifting to renewable energy sources, and in 2021, it announced a further share capital increase of EUR750 million combined with a reduction in government ownership, from 51% to 34%.

Corporate shareholders also commonly include non-profits, such as foundations and endowments, some of which have grown to significant size. In addition to financial objectives, non-profits typically have societal and other non-financial responsibilities to their beneficiaries, as in the following example.

EXAMPLE 9

Novo Nordisk Foundation and Novo Nordisk A/S

The Denmark-based Novo Nordisk Foundation is the largest private foundation in the world. It has a dual objective: to provide a stable basis for the commercial and research activities conducted by investee companies within and to support scientific and humanitarian purposes. Through its holding company, Novo Holdings A/S, the foundation is the largest and controlling shareholder of the for-profit, listed Danish biopharmaceutical company Novo Nordisk A/S.

QUESTION SET

1. A corporate issuer has the following attributes: It has no need for new equity financing, its debt needs are well satisfied through its existing credit facility with a bank, and it has a majority owner that exercises management control of the company. Is this corporate issuer more likely public or private?

   A. Public

   B. Private

   Solution:

   B is correct. The lack of need for new equity capital implies less reason to have exchange-listed stock, as does the ability to operate the business with the current debt capacity available under its existing credit facility. The majority owner exercising management control could possibly imply either public or private status, although combined with the first two attributes, it is doubtful that such a company would be public.

2. Which of the following does *not* reflect a primary difference between an initial public offering (IPO) and a direct listing?

   A. Whether or not employees own shares in the private company

   B. Whether or not new capital is raised

   C. Whether or not an underwriter is used

   Solution:

   A is correct. A company with employee shareholders can go public with either an IPO or a direct listing; employee shareownership does not differ by the choice of transaction.

   C is incorrect. An IPO uses an underwriter to manage the process and underwrite the purchase of new shares, while a direct listing does not.

B is incorrect. An IPO raises new capital for the listing company by issuing new shares to the public, while a direct listing does not; it lists only existing shares.

3. Describe two benefits of being a public company and two reasons that an issuer may instead prefer to be private company.

Solution:

Benefits of public status:

- Public listing allows the company to access capital from a broader range of investors, thus making larger capital raises more feasible.
- Public listing allows for price transparency for investors and ease of trading because of stock exchange listing. This may be especially beneficial if employees own significant stock, because listing creates a market for these shares.

Benefits of private status:

- Fewer disclosure requirements, thus reducing compliance costs and perhaps conferring competitive advantages because information can be kept private.
- Fewer stakeholders, thus allowing for improved access to communication channels.

4. Identify a major reason why a national government would be a 100% shareholder in a corporate issuer, and discuss two factors that may cause a national government to reduce its ownership in a state-owned company.

Solution:

A national government may choose to be the 100% owner of a company that provides public goods to the national economy, such as infrastructure and public safety, that would either not be provided by private means or be delivered inequitably or inefficiently. In some cases, a country may have natural resources, such as crude oil, and the national government may use a wholly owned corporation for production and to invest profits in ways that benefit its country.

Two possible reasons that a country may reduce its ownership in a state-owned company include (1) opportunities to bring in foreign capital and diversify the country's economy, such as the case highlighted by the Saudi Aramco example, and (2) a push for privatization and deregulation to potentially lower costs through competition and motivate innovation, as highlighted by the postal services examples.

5. A public company acquires a private company. Is the acquired company public or private after the acquisition? Explain the rationale for your choice.

   A. Public

   B. Private

Solution:

A is correct. Even though the acquired company will not have its own shares, the shareholders of the acquirer own the formerly private company, though the percentage of assets of the combined company attributable to the acquired company may be small. The acquirer's board of directors and management now operate the newly acquired company.

PRACTICE PROBLEMS

The following information relates to questions 1-5

Dee's Arbor Group Inc. (DAG Inc.) is a large international investor in timber and forest assets located on the North and South American continents. DAG Inc. is the general partner of DAG LP, a limited partnership that is the 100% owner of the timber and forest assets. DAG LP is controlled by DAG Inc. and its limited partners; the limited partners own a 20% stake in the partnership, while DAG Inc. holds the remaining majority stake.

DAG Inc.'s shares are listed on stock exchanges in the United States and Canada. DAG Inc. is organized as a special corporate form available in its jurisdiction in which it does not pay corporate income taxes so long as it distributes all of its net income as dividends to its shareholders and complies with other conditions. In the current and past fiscal years, DAG Inc. has complied with all of these conditions.

DAG Inc.'s shares are owned by various members of the Dee family, who hold several key senior management positions at DAG Inc. and DAG LP, and collectively they own 30% of the shares of DAG Inc. The remainder of DAG Inc.'s shares are owned by a variety of individual and institutional investors, none of whom own more than 5%. The following diagram shows the organizational structure of DAG Inc. and DAG LP.

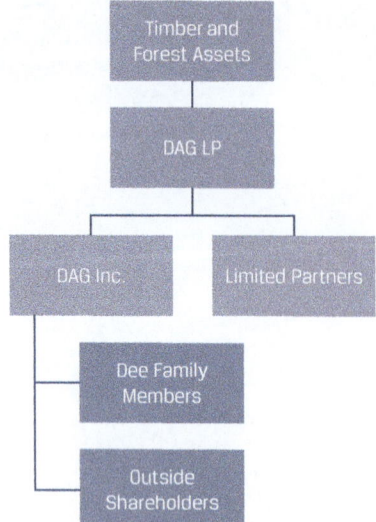

1. What percentage of the timber and forest assets are effectively owned by the Dee family members in this scenario?

   A. 24%

   B. 30%

   C. 80%

2. Which of the following best describes the taxation of DAG Inc. and DAG LP?

   A. DAG LP pays tax based on its pre-tax income.

    B. Shareholders of DAG Inc. pay tax based on dividend income.

    C. DAG Inc. pays tax based on its pre-tax income.

3. Which of the following best describes DAG LP and DAG Inc.?

    A. Neither DAG LP nor DAG Inc. is managed by a majority owner.

    B. DAG Inc. has limits to its ability to raise new capital because of the dividend requirement on its corporate form.

    C. DAG Inc. faces unlimited liability as the general partner, while DAG Inc.'s status as a corporation implies that its shareholders face limited liability.

4. What is a significant difference between the limited partners of DAG LP and the outside shareholders of DAG Inc.?

    A. Managerial responsibilities

    B. Taxation of income from the partnership

    C. The ability to vote and replace members of the DAG Inc. board of directors

5. Which of the following rationales would be most consistent with the Dee family's choice to create this complex organizational structure instead of simply organizing as a limited partnership?

    A. It provides management control without the need for majority ownership by the family, while maintaining limited liability.

    B. The complex structure eliminates the potential for double taxation.

    C. The complex structure avoids potential problems associated with outside investors exercising voting rights.

SOLUTIONS

1. A is correct. The Dee family effectively owns 24% of the timber and forest assets. They own 30% of the shares of DAG (the publicly traded corporation), and they own 80% of the limited partnership (which owns the assets): 24% = 30% × 80%.

2. B is correct. DAG Inc. is organized as a special corporate form available in its jurisdiction in which it does not pay corporate income taxes. DAG LP, as a limited partnership, is a pass-through entity. DAG Inc. shareholders pay tax on dividend income.

    A is incorrect. DAG LP is a limited partnership. Partnership income is passed through to each partner, and the partners pay tax at the personal level.

    C is incorrect. DAG Inc. is organized as a special corporate form available in its jurisdiction in which it does not pay corporate income taxes.

3. C is correct. DAG Inc. is the general partner of DAG LP and thus has unlimited liability in the partnership. However, as a corporation, DAG Inc.'s shareholders have limited liability for its losses and obligations.

    A is incorrect. DAG LP is 80% owned by DAG Inc., the general partner that manages the partnership. DAG Inc. is 30% owned by the Dee family, who holds several key managerial positions.

    B is incorrect. As a public company, DAG Inc. can raise new equity by issuing shares on an exchange. The dividend requirement is not a binding limit on its ability to raise capital but, rather, might be an attractive feature to prospective investors.

4. C is correct. The limited partners of DAG LP are not shareholders of DAG Inc., so they do not have voting rights in the corporation. Additionally, because the limited partners own only 20% of the partnership, they also have little ability to remove DAG Inc. as the general partner. In contrast, outside shareholders own 70% of DAG Inc. and have voting rights. They could use their collective ownership to effect change in the management of DAG Inc.

    A is incorrect. Neither the DAG LP limited partners nor the outside shareholders of DAG Inc. have managerial responsibilities. The general partner has managerial responsibilities of the partnership, and the board of DAG Inc. has managerial responsibilities of the corporation.

    B is incorrect. Owing to the special corporate form of DAG Inc., both the corporation *and* the limited partnership are pass-through entities. Therefore, neither the partnership nor the corporation pays entity-level income taxes, but both the limited partners and shareholders are responsible for personal income taxes.

5. A is correct. The Dee family can effectively control management of the timber and forest assets with only a 24% effective ownership stake in the partnership. If the family had opted for a limited partnership as the organizational form, they likely would need a much higher ownership stake to assert management control and would have unlimited personal liability.

    B is incorrect. The double taxation problem is not an issue in the more complex structure, nor is it a problem in the partnership structure, because both are pass-throughs.

    C is incorrect. The complex structure potentially creates problems because of the existence of outside shareholders constituting a majority of votes.

Investors and Other Stakeholders

INTRODUCTION

1

Corporate issuers are financed with debt and equity. Debt and equity securities have different risk and return profiles for both issuers and investors. This learning module discusses these differences and their implications, while also considering the perspectives of a broader group of stakeholders beyond debtholders and shareholders. We introduce these groups and discuss potential conflicts of interest among them. Balancing stakeholder interests is important, as both issuers and investors have increasingly incorporated environmental, social, and governance factors into their decision-making processes. Analysts assess ESG factors to better evaluate issuers' expected future performance and risk profile.

LEARNING MODULE OVERVIEW

- Corporate issuers are financed with debt and equity. Debt is a financing source with a finite length, and interest and principal payments are promised on pre-specified future dates. Debtholders have a priority claim over shareholders to an issuer's cash flows and assets.

- Equity is a source of permanent financing, and no promises of repayments or distributions to shareholders are made. Equity is a residual claim on an issuer's cash flows and assets.

- From the perspective of an issuer, debt is riskier than equity. From the perspective of an investor, equity is riskier than debt. The proportion of debt in a firm's capital structure affects both the potential return and the risk of cash flows.

- Conflicts of interest may exist between debtholders and shareholders. Debtholders' payoff is limited to promised interest and principal payments, while shareholders' payoff is theoretically unlimited as increases in firm value over the value of debt accrue to shareholders.

- Besides debt and equity investors, corporate stakeholders include the board of directors, managers, employees, customers, suppliers, governments, society in general, and the environment. The stakeholder theory of corporate governance broadens the focus of corporate decision-making beyond that of the shareholder theory.

- Environmental, social, and governance (ESG) considerations are becoming more important to both investors and analysts. ESG factors affect firms' values and can present both risks and opportunities.

LEARNING MODULE SELF-ASSESSMENT

These initial questions are intended to help you gauge your current level of understanding of this learning module.

Complete each statement by selecting the most appropriate term in parentheses.

1. _____ make permanent capital available to issuers. (debtholders, shareholders)

   Solution:

   Shareholders make permanent capital available to issuers.
   Debtholders is incorrect. Debt has a finite maturity, though it can be far in the future.

2. _____ have a residual claim against a firm's cash flows. (debtholders, shareholders)

   Solution:

   Shareholders have a residual claim against a firm's cash flows.
   Debtholders is incorrect. Debtholders have a *priority* claim over shareholders to a firm's cash flows and assets.

3. The shareholder theory of corporate governance is _____ than the stakeholder theory. (narrower, broader)

   Solution:

   The shareholder theory of corporate governance is narrower than the stakeholder theory.
   Stakeholders are groups and individuals with a vested interest in a firm's success and include, but are not limited to, shareholders.

4. ESG considerations are an explicit objective in the _____ theory of corporate governance. (shareholder, stakeholder)

   Solution:

   ESG considerations are an explicit objective in the stakeholder theory of corporate governance.
   The stakeholder theory seeks to balance the interests of shareholders with the interests of a broader group that relate to ESG considerations.

5. The estimated impact of ESG factors on corporate issuers' financial and share price performance has _____ over time. (decreased, remained the same, increased)

Solution:

The estimated impact of ESG factors on corporate issuers' financial and share price performance has <u>increased</u> over time. This impact is the result of changing consumer and investor preferences, increased regulations and taxes related to ESG factors, and the rising threat of climate change.

6. ESG factors are increasingly recognized as _____ by analysts. (quantifiable, qualitative)

Solution:

ESG factors are increasingly recognized as <u>quantifiable</u> by analysts. Historically, ESG factors were considered negative externalities with no direct effect on firms' financial statements. Increasingly, analysts are quantifying the effects of ESG factors and including them in firm valuation and investment decision-making.

FINANCIAL CLAIMS OF LENDERS AND SHAREHOLDERS

2

☐ | compare the financial claims and motivations of lenders and shareholders

Debt Versus Equity

The prior module established that corporations finance their assets with debt and equity. We now turn our attention to the nature of these claims, their relative risk versus return for both issuers and investors, and potential conflicts of interest that may arise between lenders and shareholders.

Debt and Equity Claims

Exhibit 1 shows the relationship between a corporation's assets and the claims of its debt and equity investors that finance them. Exhibit 2 shows that assets are used to generate income to pay interest to debtholders, while remaining profits are either reinvested or distributed to shareholders.

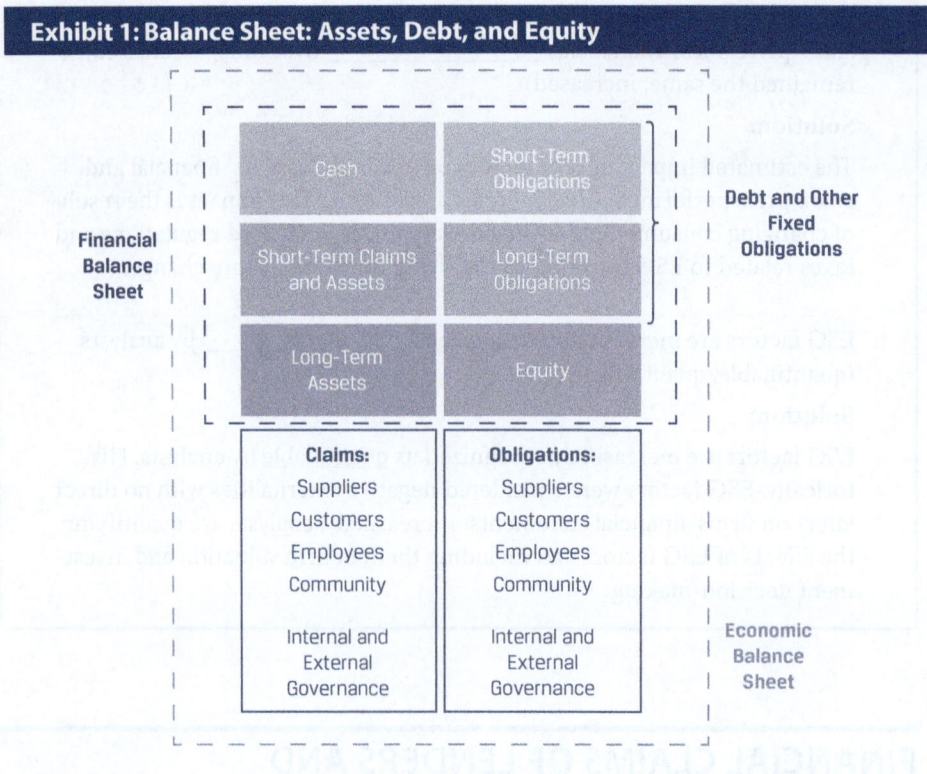

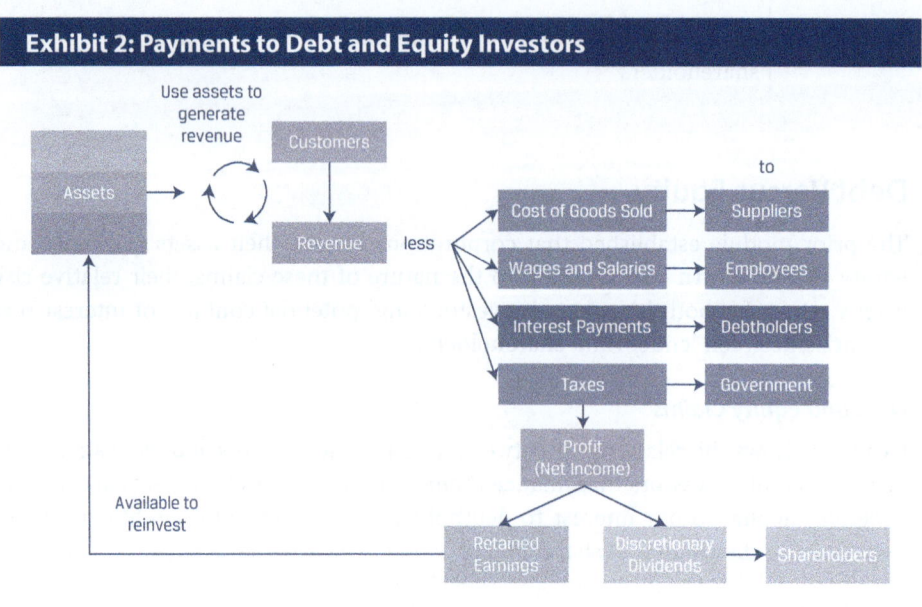

Debtholders, or lenders, provide capital with a *finite* maturity. Issuers agree to make promised interest payments and to repay principal on pre-specified dates. Lenders have no decision-making power within the corporation, but debt contracts can be structured to protect lenders by imposing financial requirements and/or legal claims on certain assets of the corporation if the debt is not repaid as agreed. As shown in Exhibit 2, interest payments are paid before any distributions to equity investors and are a priority claim against a company's assets and cash flows.

Equity investors make *permanent* capital available to issuers; issuers generally do not commit to future dividends or repayments to shareholders. Rather, equity is a *residual* claim against company cash flows—whatever is left after expenses, investments, and debt payments. Cash distributions to equity investors are at the discretion of the board of directors. In contrast to lenders, equity investors have voting rights on important company matters such as choosing the board of directors, which appoints and oversees management.

In addition to interest payments to debtholders, other claims that must be satisfied before any shareholder distributions are made include payments to suppliers, employees, and governments (in the form of taxes). If a firm is dissolved and its assets are liquidated, these priority claims must be met before equity investors receive anything.

Because debt is a priority, fixed, and finite claim on assets and cash flows, it is a less costly form of financing for issuers: it is lower risk for investors than equity (though, as will be discussed, increasing debt increases risk for a company's equity investors). Another difference between debt and equity is that debtholder interest payments are usually treated as a tax-deductible expense, reducing taxable income, while dividends paid to shareholders are not.

KNOWLEDGE CHECK

1. Identify whether the attribute on the left is a feature of debt or equity.

Legal repayment obligation	Debt, Equity
Residual asset claim	Debt, Equity
Discretionary payments	Debt, Equity
Tax-deductible expense	Debt, Equity
Finite term	Debt, Equity
Voting rights	Debt, Equity

Solution:

Legal repayment obligation	Debt
Residual asset claim	Equity
Discretionary payments	Equity
Tax-deductible expense	Debt
Finite term	Debt
Voting rights	Equity

Whether offered in the form of a loan or a bond, debt involves a contractual obligation with priority interest and principal claims. Equity investors receive discretionary distributions and have a residual claim to assets. Equity dividend payments are not tax deductible. Debt requires contractual interest and principal payments, with interest expense being tax deductible for the issuer. Debt has a finite term and confers no decision-making power, while equity has an unlimited term and includes voting rights.

Debt Versus Equity: Risk and Return

As established earlier, debtholder claims are fixed and finite, while equity owners have ongoing claims to a firm's current and future profits. While firms usually start with equity financing, those with more predictable cash flows may choose to borrow rather than sell additional ownership stakes to finance assets. The trade-offs between debt and equity financing for both issuers and investors are best shown by the following example.

EXAMPLE 1

Equity- versus Debt-Based Balance Sheet Financing

Consider a firm with assets 100% fully financed by equity and an identical firm financed with 75% debt and 25% equity.

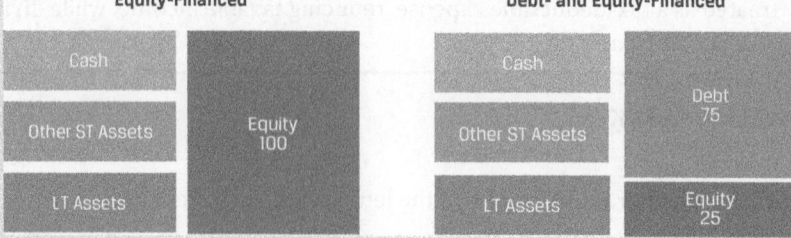

Assume that both firms have revenue, over a period, of 100 and operating expenses of 70. Ignore income taxes.

---

1. If we assume interest expense of 15 for the period, calculate net income for each firm and compare their returns on equity (ROE) for the period. Explain why ROE is higher when debt financing is used.

   Solution:

   Solve for net income by subtracting expenses from revenue, and divide net income by total equity to solve for the one-period return on equity:

Equity-Financed		Debt- and Equity-Financed	
Revenue	100	Revenue	100
Less: Operating Expenses	−70	Less: Operating Expenses	−70
		Less: Interest Expense	−15
Net Income	30	Net Income	15
Total Equity	100	Total Equity	25
Return on Equity	**30%**	**Return on Equity**	**60%**

   Return on equity is higher when debt is used, because the interest cost of debt is lower than the firm's return on assets. Interest rate on debt = 15/75 = 20% versus return on assets = 30/100 = 30%.

---

2. Calculate returns on equity for the period if the firms experience a 20% increase and a 20% decrease in revenue (from Question 1), assuming expenses remain unchanged.

   Solution:

   Solve for net income and return on equity given the increase and decrease in revenue as follows:

20% *Increase* in Revenue			
Equity-Financed		**Debt- and Equity-Financed**	
Revenue	120	Revenue	120
Less: Operating Expenses	–70	Less: Operating Expenses	–70
		Less: Interest Expense	–15
Net Income	50	Net Income	35
Total Equity	100	Total Equity	25
Return on Equity	**50%**	**Return on Equity**	**140%**

20% *Decrease* in Revenue			
Equity-Financed		**Debt- and Equity-Financed**	
Revenue	80	Revenue	80
Less: Operating Expenses	–70	Less: Operating Expenses	–70
		Less: Interest Expense	–15
Net Income	10	Net Income	**(5)**
Total Equity	100	Total Equity	25
Return on Equity	**10%**	**Return on Equity**	**(20%)**

This example demonstrates the greater potential shareholder return when debt financing is used—but also the greater risk. In particular, the net loss in the downside case for the issuer financed with debt and equity raises the possibility that it may be unable to meet future debt payments. The variation in ROE for the company financed with debt and equity is significantly higher than the ROE variation for the all-equity-financed company.

From an issuer's perspective, debt financing is less costly but involves greater risks than equity financing, because it commits the issuer not only to interest and principal payments but also to any restrictions that lenders impose in the debt contract. The greater use of debt for a given amount of equity financing, known as **financial leverage**, increases the likelihood that the firm may be unable to meet its promised obligations to lenders, resulting in bankruptcy and potential liquidation. The firm faces no such risk in the case of equity financing, as shareholders are not promised any distributions or repayments.

From an investor's perspective, stocks are riskier than bonds because shareholders hold residual rather than fixed claims against the firm. As shown in Example 1, the profits available for distribution to shareholders can vary greatly, depending on the performance of the firm as well as financial leverage. If a corporation is successful, there is theoretically no limit to how much equity owners could earn on their investment. But if the firm performs poorly, owners can lose their entire investment if the firm is liquidated and debtholders take control of the assets. Due to their limited liability, however, shareholders cannot lose more than their initial investment.

While debt financing adds risk, equity holders often prefer it to an issuer raising additional equity to fund growth, because additional share issuance reduces the fractional firm ownership of existing shareholders, known as **dilution**. The downside of dilution may be offset by an expectation that the firm will generate enough incremental profit to compensate.

EXAMPLE 2

Financing an Investment with Debt, Equity, or Cash on Hand

Consider the same equity-financed firm as in Example 1 and its choices for financing a new investment in long-term assets of 20. The pertinent details in the firm's initial balance sheet are shown below. Revenue before the investment is 100, expenses are 70 and are expected to remain unchanged, interest on new debt financing is 20%, and the return on the new investment is 30%. Ignore income taxes.

Initial Balance Sheet			
Cash	30		
Other assets	20		
LT assets	50	Equity	100

1. Compare the firm's returns on equity if it finances the investment with debt, shares, or cash on hand. Discuss the results of the comparison.

   Solution:

Issue Shares		Borrow		Cash on Hand	
Cash 30		Cash 30		Cash 10	
Other 20		Other 20	Debt 20	Other 20	
LT assets 70	Equity 120	LT assets 70	Equity 100	LT assets 70	Equity 100

	Issue Shares	Borrow	Cash on Hand
Revenue	106	106	106
Less: Operating Expenses	70	70	70
Less: Interest		4	
Net Income	36	32	36
Equity	120	100	100
ROE	30%	32%	36%

Financing the investment by issuing shares produces the lowest ROE due to the dilution from additional equity. Because the investment produces a return equal to the beginning ROE, there is no change in ROE. Financing with debt produces a higher ROE, because the interest rate on debt is lower than the return on the new investment and no new shares are issued, so equity does not increase. The highest ROE is produced by using cash on hand, which avoids both the increase in equity and the interest cost of new debt.

Exhibit 3 shows this shareholder payoff asymmetry over time as a function of firm value.

Exhibit 3: Firm Value and Shareholder Payoff

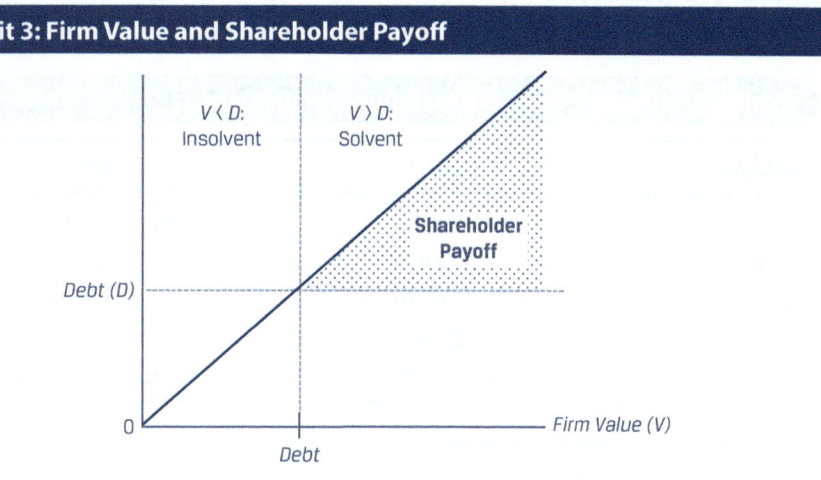

If the firm is solvent—that is, its value (V) exceeds the value of its debt (D)—then the value to shareholders is the positive difference between the firm's value and the value of its debt. Potential upside gains to shareholders are limited only by the future value of the firm. If a firm becomes insolvent, with a debt value greater than that of its assets ($V < D$), shareholders lose their entire investment and debtholders take control of the firm.

Exhibit 4 shows this asymmetry from the perspective of debtholders.

Exhibit 4: Firm Value and Debtholder Payoff

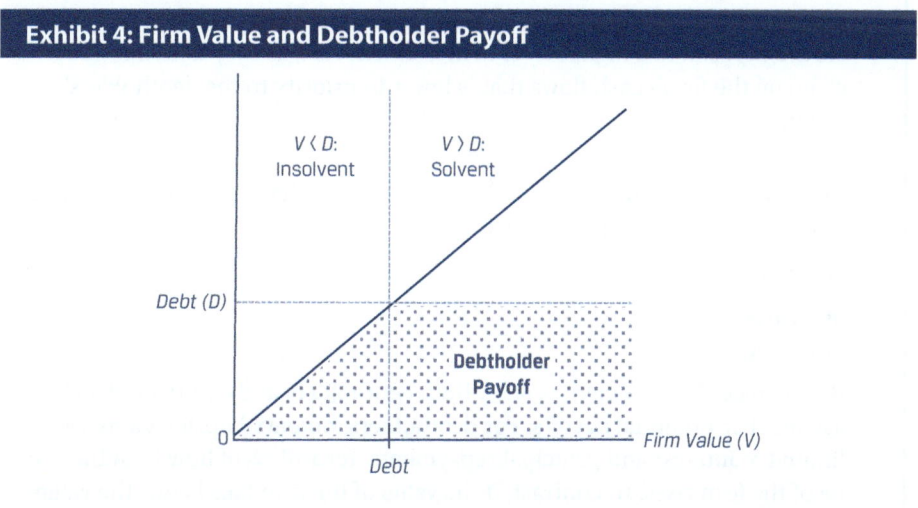

Lender returns are limited to promised interest and principal payments so long as the firm is solvent, regardless of firm performance and financial leverage. In contrast, if firm value falls below that of debt, the firm is declared insolvent and debtholders seek to recover their capital from remaining firm assets. Note that if we add the shaded areas for the shareholder payoff and the debtholder payoff, we get the diagonal line showing the total value of the firm as debtholders are owed promised payments and equity holders get the residual.

While equity owners seek to maximize firm value (to increase their payoff), bondholders seek to ensure the timely repayment of principal and interest, with the company maximizing its ability to meet its debt obligations. These perspectives are summarized in Exhibit 5.

Exhibit 5: Investor Perspectives: Equity versus Debt

Attribute	Equity	Debt
Tenor	Indefinite	Term (e.g., 3 months, 10 years)
Return potential	Unlimited	Capped
Maximum loss	Initial investment	Initial investment
Investment risk	Higher	Lower
Desired outcome	Maximize firm value	Timely repayment

KNOWLEDGE CHECK

1. Corporate equity and debt holders share the same investor perspective with respect to:

   A. maximum loss.

   B. investment risk.

   C. return potential.

   Solution:

   A is correct. For both equity and debt holders, their initial investment represents their maximum possible loss. The return potential is theoretically unlimited for equity holders, while it is capped for debtholders. Equity holders are exposed to a higher level of investment risk, as they hold a residual claim on the firm's cash flows that is lower in priority to the debtholders' claim.

2. **True or False:** Debtholders, unlike equity holders, have symmetric potential downside losses and upside gains.

   A. True.

   B. False.

   Solution:

   B is correct; the statement is false. Both debtholders and equity holders have asymmetric potential payoffs. For debtholders, potential upside gains are limited to interest and principal repayments, regardless of how high the value of the firm rises. In contrast, if the value of the firm falls below the value of its debt, debtholders can lose up to their initial investment.

   For equity holders, equity value is determined as the value of the firm less the value of its debt. Potential upside gains to shareholders are limited only by the future value of the firm, while shareholder losses, like those of debtholders, are limited to their initial investment.

Conflicts of Interest among Lenders and Shareholders

While both lenders and owners are compensated from the same firm cash flows, the differing risk and return profiles of debtholders and shareholders create potential conflicts of interest.

Shareholders seek to maximize residual cash flows, or firm profits, once other obligations are met. Since these investors lose their entire investment in the case of insolvency but have unlimited upside return potential, they prefer that management pursue projects with greater calculated risks and higher potential returns while maximizing the use of debt financing. Additionally, shareholders can demand higher cash dividends, which can increase leverage, thereby increasing risk for debt investors. Example 1 illustrated the greater potential equity return associated with the use of leverage.

Bondholders seek to maximize the likelihood that they will receive timely interest and principal payments; they derive no benefit from greater leverage used to pursue projects with higher risks given limited upside. As a result, bondholders generally prefer that management invest in less risky projects that increase cash flow certainty. Since they have no voting rights over management decisions, bondholders seek to impose contractual restrictions such as requiring cash flow coverage for debt payments and/or limiting a firm's financial leverage. These restrictions prevent a firm from taking actions that may benefit shareholders but reduce the firm's likelihood of debt repayment in the future.

QUESTION SET

1. Which of the following groups has a residual claim on an issuer's cash flows?

    A. Employees

    B. Debtholders

    C. Shareholders

    Solution:

    C is correct. Shareholders are residual claimants to a firm's cash flows and receive discretionary distributions after priority claims (e.g., employee compensation, supplier payments, interest expenses, and taxes) are met.

2. Which is more sensitive to changes in firm value: debt or equity? Explain your answer.

    Solution:

    Equity is more sensitive to changes in firm value, because debtholders have fixed, priority claims while equity holders have residual claims whose value is contingent on future firm profits. On the one hand, if firm value increases, residual value accrues to shareholders while debtholder payments do not change. On the other hand, reductions in firm value fall first on equity holders. If firm value falls below debt value and the firm is declared insolvent, equity holders typically receive nothing and debtholders take control of the firm and often seek to liquidate its assets.

3. Interest payments to debtholders are:

    A. residual payments.

    B. at the discretion of the board.

C.   deductible for corporate income tax purposes.

Solution:

C is correct. Interest payments on debt are tax deductible for the firm.

A is incorrect. Debtholders have priority claims on the cash flows of the firm over shareholders.

B is incorrect. Interest payments are contractual, not discretionary like shareholder dividends.

---

4.   All of the following are characteristics of debt *except*:

   A.   limited liability.

   B.   unlimited return.

   C.   priority in payment.

Solution:

B is correct. Shareholders, not debtholders, have the potential for unlimited return.

A is incorrect. Debtholders and shareholders both have limited liability.

C is incorrect. Debtholders have a priority claim over shareholders to a firm's cash flows.

---

5.   All else being equal, a jurisdiction increasing its corporate income tax rate would most likely lead to _____ (lower/higher/the same) use of debt financing by issuers.

Solution:

Higher. An increase in the corporate income tax rate would likely result in a higher mix of debt. Interest payments on debt are tax deductible, so an increase in the tax rate would reduce the after-tax cost of debt financing, all else being equal, thus making debt financing relatively more attractive than equity financing.

3

CORPORATE STAKEHOLDERS AND GOVERNANCE

☐ | describe a company's stakeholder groups and compare their interests

The prior lesson addressed the claims, relative risks and returns, and potential conflicts among debtholders and shareholders. Corporations operate in a complex ecosystem where the interested parties are a much broader group than shareholders alone. These parties depend on the company—and the company depends on them—for economic success, though their short- and long-term goals may be in conflict. A corporation's ability to maximize shareholder return and meet debt and other obligations may be either compromised or enhanced by the actions of these parties, known as **stakeholders**. A stakeholder is any individual or group with a vested interest in a company. Financial analysts must understand and incorporate these groups and their actions into their assessment of a firm's expected performance and risk profile.

Primary stakeholder groups and their roles in a corporation include:

- debt and equity investors;

- a board of directors that supervises the corporation's activities;

- managers who execute the board's strategy and run operations;

- employees who provide human capital for the firm's operations;

- customers who demand the company's products and services;

- suppliers who provide the raw materials and goods and services not generated internally, including functions that are outsourced;

- governments that establish rules and regulations, collect taxes, and provide a variety of public goods and services; and

- other individuals and the non-human environment affected by the company's products and processes.

Exhibit 6 illustrates the primary stakeholder groups and describes their involvement with the corporation.

Exhibit 6: Key Stakeholder Groups

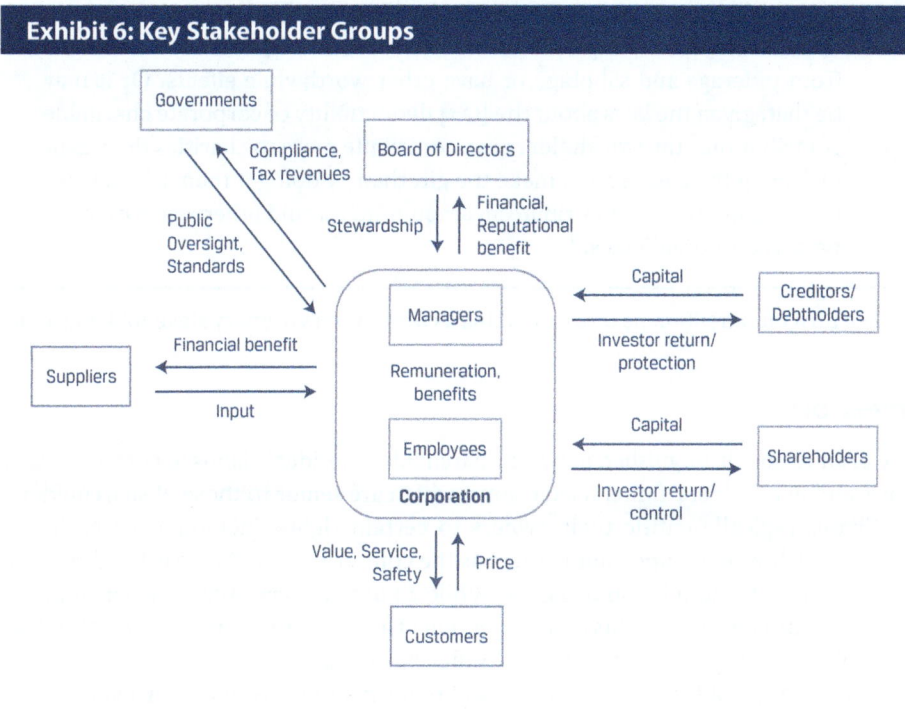

Shareholders versus Stakeholders

In a typical corporation, shareholders elect the board of directors, which hires managers to serve the interests of shareholders. The interests of other parties—such as creditors, employees, customers, and even society—are considered only to the extent that they affect shareholder value. This concept is referred to as the **shareholder theory of corporate governance**.

In contrast, the **stakeholder theory of corporate governance** suggests that corporate governance should consider *all* stakeholder interests, not just those of shareholders. For example, it is often suggested that environmental, social, and governance (ESG) considerations be an explicit objective of the board of directors and management. This approach gives rise to several challenges, including:

- complexity of balancing multiple objectives;

- defining, measuring, and balancing non-shareholder objectives;

- competing globally if competitors do not face similar constraints; and
- direct costs of adhering to higher ESG standards.

SHAREHOLDER VERSUS STAKEHOLDER THEORIES OF CORPORATE GOVERNANCE

The shareholder and stakeholder theories of corporate governance are not necessarily at odds with each other. In a famous 1970 essay espousing the shareholder theory, "The Social Responsibility of Business Is to Increase Its Profits," economist Milton Friedman noted as much, particularly if management is taking a long-term perspective:

> "It may well be in the long-run interest of a corporation that is a major employer in a small community to devote resources to providing amenities to that community or to improving its government. That may make it easier to attract desirable employees, it may reduce the wage bill or lessen losses from pilferage and sabotage or have other worthwhile effects. Or it may be that, given the laws about the [tax] deductibility of corporate charitable contributions, the stockholders can contribute more to charities they favor by having the corporation make the gift than by doing it themselves, since they can in that way contribute an amount that would otherwise have been paid as corporate taxes."[1]

We turn our attention next to describing a corporation's primary stakeholder groups.

Investors

The prior lesson distinguished between shareholders' residual claims to corporate cash flows and debtholders' finite, fixed claims, which are senior to those of shareholders.

Shares typically entitle their owners to certain rights, including the exclusive right to vote on such important matters as the composition of the board of directors, mergers, and the liquidation of assets. While all debtholders usually establish issuer requirements and lender rights at the inception of a debt contract, **private debtholders** and public debtholders (**bondholders**) differ in several ways.

Private debtholders, such as banks and other institutions that offer loans, credit facilities, and leases, often hold a debt investment to maturity. They typically have direct access to company management and non-public information, which lowers information asymmetry. Since an individual bank or private lender can be a critical source of financing, particularly for a small or mid-sized company, they may have great influence over the company. The relaxation of debt restrictions and extension of further credit—or refusal to do so—by a single private lender can be far more impactful for companies with limited access to capital markets than for those with broad debt market access.

Private lenders may also have a wider variation in their risk appetite, approach, behavior, and relationships with borrowers. For example, a commercial real estate lessor may primarily care about receiving lease payments, the upkeep of the real estate, and whether it can renew or re-lease the asset at attractive rates. In other cases, a lender

---

1 Friedman, Milton. "A Friedman Doctrine—The Social Responsibility of Business Is to Increase Its Profits," *The New York Times*, 13 September 1970, https://www.nytimes.com/1970/09/13/archives/a-friedman -doctrine-the-social-responsibility-of-business-is-to.html?smid=url-share.

may hold *both* debt and equity in a company or take a more equity-like approach to evaluating the business. Finally, some private lenders specialize in lending to businesses as they either approach, or are in, bankruptcy.

Bondholders, which are often institutional investors and asset managers, rely on public information such as financial statements to make investment decisions. These investors usually have little to no influence over an issuer's operations, relying instead on the terms of the debt contract negotiated at inception. While it is relatively more difficult to gain the consent of bondholders versus private lenders to change the terms of an existing agreement, bondholders can sometimes exercise significant influence if a firm in financial distress must restructure outstanding public debt.

Board of Directors

A company's board of directors is elected by shareholders to advance shareholders' interests. The board is responsible for hiring the CEO and monitoring company and management performance. Boards often include both **inside directors** (including founders and current and former managers) and **independent directors** (no material relationship with the company, including employment, family ties, and so on), who may better represent the interests of minority shareholders. Major stock exchanges maintain corporate governance standards with which listed companies must comply, and these standards often include director independence requirements. For example, the London Stock Exchange requires at least half of the directors of listed companies to be independent, and the Singapore Exchange listing rules state that "there should be a strong and independent element on the board" with a majority of non-executive directors. Besides independence, corporate governance standards also typically require boards to include a diversity of backgrounds, expertise, and competencies. Director duties are mandated by laws that vary by jurisdiction, but directors are usually required to display a high standard of prudence, care, and loyalty to the company.

While the single-tier board structure is prevalent in the USA and the UK, a two-tier corporate governance structure is common in Continental Europe and is legally mandated in some countries (e.g., Germany). Under the two-tier model, a separate **supervisory board** is elected to oversee the activities of the board of directors. The supervisory board consists solely of independent directors from among corporate stakeholders, including shareholders, employees, labor unions, the public at large, and, in some cases, government representatives for firms with state ownership. While the board of directors remains responsible for strategy and management oversight in the two-tier system, the supervisory board may appoint or dismiss board members and must approve selected board decisions, among other duties.

Although most boards hold simultaneous elections for specific terms (e.g., all board members elected annually or bi-annually), some companies have **staggered boards**, with directors divided into groups elected separately in consecutive years. It takes several years to replace a full staggered board, which limits the ability of shareholders to effect a major change of control at the company. However, staggered board elections allow for continuity without constant reassessment of strategy and oversight by new board members, which may introduce short-termism into company strategy. Staggered boards are common in Australia and several European countries.

Managers

Led by the chief executive officer (CEO), managers are responsible for determining and implementing the strategy of the corporation, under the oversight of the board of directors, as well as day-to-day operations. Senior executives and other high-level managers are usually compensated via a base salary in cash and an annual bonus that often involves cash and stock, as well as a multi-year, stock-based incentive plan and other benefits. In addition to preventing manager attrition, compensation structures are designed to align manager interests with those of shareholders and other stakeholders.

Employees

A corporation relies on the labor and skills, or **human capital**, of its employees to provide its goods and services. In return, employees typically seek competitive compensation and benefits, development opportunities, job security, and a safe and healthy work environment. In some industries and/or countries, workers join labor unions to collectively negotiate compensation, benefits, working conditions, and other matters with management. Employees may have an equity investment in their employer through equity-based participation plans (such as profit sharing, share purchases, or stock options) beyond their financial interests as employees. For most employees, equity ownership is a minor component of total compensation but can be significant in some cases.

Customers

Customers expect a company's products or services to satisfy their needs at a reasonable price while meeting applicable quality and safety standards. Depending on the product or service and their relationship with the company, customers may seek ongoing support, product guarantees, and after-sale service. While major corporate customers may exercise significant influence over a company, the loyalty and satisfaction of retail customers are also often correlated with revenue and profit growth. The environmental or social impact of products is of growing importance to customers. For example, brand boycotts and shareholder actions in response to negative environmental and social effects, as well as product-related controversies, may adversely affect sales and profits.

Suppliers

A company's suppliers include suppliers of raw materials and intermediate goods as well as software and outsourced services like call centers and payroll. Suppliers are often also short-term creditors with a primary interest in being paid in a timely manner for products or services delivered.

When a company is in financial distress, the financial position of its suppliers may be affected as well as their willingness to extend additional credit to the company. However, suppliers also have long-term interests in companies, as they seek to build and maintain mutually beneficial relationships. Supplier interest in a company's long-term stability is important when products are specialized and one or both parties have invested in the relationship through product design, training, or customization.

Governments

Governments seek to advance the interests of their constituencies and ensure the well-being of the economies over which they preside. Because corporations have a significant effect on economic output, capital flows, employment, social welfare, and the environment, among other factors, regulators have an interest in ensuring that corporations comply with applicable laws. Moreover, corporations and their employees are a major source of tax revenue.

EVOLUTION OF STAKEHOLDERS AND CORPORATE GOVERNANCE AT VOLKSWAGEN AG

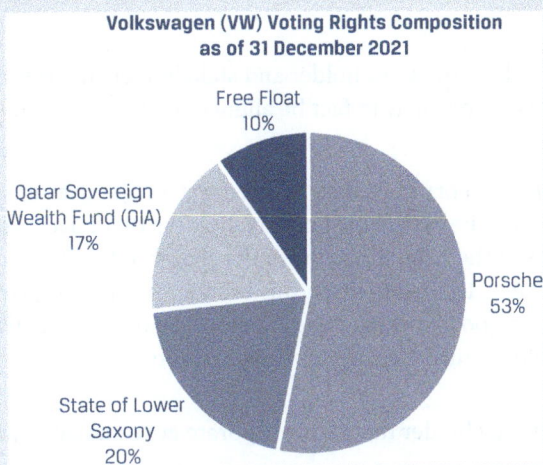

Volkswagen (VW) Voting Rights Composition as of 31 December 2021

- Free Float 10%
- Qatar Sovereign Wealth Fund (QIA) 17%
- Porsche 53%
- State of Lower Saxony 20%

Source: Volkswagen AG 2021 Annual Report

Volkswagen AG (VW) was fully government owned from 1937 until it issued public shares in 1960. The German state of Lower Saxony, where VW is the largest private employer, retained a 20% share of voting rights. A German law (the "Volkswagen law") was enacted when VW went public, requiring *over* 80% of votes for major matters to pass, effectively giving the state veto power.

German auto rival Porsche AG (wholly owned by the Porsche family) sought to take over Volkswagen in 2007. Instead, the two companies merged in an equity deal that left the Porsche family as VW's largest shareholder.

While the Porsche family's majority voting rights give it power over the board of directors, the supervisory board is equally divided between labor and shareholder representatives. Given its 20% voting stake and the Volkswagen law, the government of Lower Saxony partners with labor representatives to promote the retention of local employees by vetoing domestic plant closures, cost reductions, and other measures that adversely affect union employees.

KNOWLEDGE CHECK

1. Which stakeholders would *most likely* realize the greatest benefit from a significant increase in the market value of the company?

   A. Creditors

   B. Customers

   C. Shareholders

   Solution:

   C is correct. Shareholders have residual claims on the company, and their wealth is directly related to the market value of the company. A is incorrect because creditors are usually not entitled to any additional cash flows (beyond interest and debt repayment) if the company's value increases. B is incorrect because, though customers may have an interest in the company's stability and long-term viability, they do not benefit directly from a higher company value.

QUESTION SET

1. Briefly discuss how the shareholder and stakeholder theories of corporate governance may in fact be aligned with each other.

   Solution:

   The stakeholder theory considers balancing the objectives of shareholders, debtholders, and the broader set of stakeholders that have a vested interest in the success of the firm. It may be in the shareholders' best interests in the long run to make decisions within this broader framework. For example, high wages and good working conditions can lead to productive employees and low employee turnover, which boosts profits.

2. Applying the stakeholder theory of corporate governance requires:

   A. balancing multiple objectives only.

   B. measuring non-shareholder objectives only.

   C. both balancing multiple objectives and measuring non-shareholder objectives.

   Solution:

   C is correct. To implement the stakeholder theory of corporate governance, it is necessary to both measure non-shareholder objectives and balance the objectives of shareholders and non-shareholders.

3. Identify and explain a method of aligning the interests of shareholders, managers, and employees.

   Solution:

   Aligning manager and employee interests with those of shareholders can be accomplished with performance- and/or share-based compensation. Shareholders seek an increase in profits and firm value, and performance-based compensation—such as bonuses based on profit or shareholder return measures, or profit sharing with employees—would align manager and employee interests with shareholder interests. Awarding shares or stock options to employees and managers increases alignment, as employees and managers become shareholders themselves.

4. Compared with public debtholders (e.g., bondholders), private debtholders (e.g., banks, lessors):

   A. have less influence over company management.

   B. have access to non-public information about the company.

   C. are less likely to consent to changes in the debt contract.

   Solution:

   B is correct. Private debtholders, including banks and other direct lenders, typically have direct access to management and non-public information, which lowers information asymmetry.

   A is incorrect. Private debtholders typically have more influence over company management than bondholders do.

   C is incorrect. Private debtholders have closer and more bespoke relationships with borrowers than bondholders do and thus are more likely to allow changes in the debt contract, such as changing covenants.

5. Which of the following board structures would most limit shareholders' ability to effect a major change in the management of a firm?

   A. Majority inside, staggered

   B. Majority independent, staggered

   C. Majority independent, non-staggered

   Solution:

   A is correct. A board with a majority of inside directors could more easily resist outside change than one with a majority of directors who were independent of management. Also, a staggered board would allow only a portion of the directors to be voted out each year, so it would take several years to replace a majority of directors.

CORPORATE ESG CONSIDERATIONS

4

☐ | describe environmental, social, and governance factors of corporate issuers considered by investors

Debt and equity investors are increasingly taking a *stakeholder* rather than a purely *shareholder* perspective by prioritizing environmental, social, and governance (ESG) factors in making investment decisions. Corporate issuers include these factors when setting strategic objectives as well as in their operating, investing, and financing decisions.

Exhibit 7 summarizes key ESG factors of importance to investors.

Exhibit 7: Environmental, Social, and Governance (ESG) Factors

Environmental	Social	Governance
Conservation of the natural world	**Consideration of people and relationships**	**Standards for running a company**
▪ Climate change	▪ Customer satisfaction	▪ Board composition
▪ Air and water pollution	▪ Data protection and privacy	▪ Audit committee structure
▪ Biodiversity	▪ Gender and diversity	▪ Bribery and corruption
▪ Deforestation	▪ Employee engagement	▪ Executive compensation
▪ Energy efficiency	▪ Community relations	▪ Lobbying
▪ Waste management	▪ Human rights	▪ Political contributions
▪ Water scarcity	▪ Labor standards	▪ Whistleblower schemes

Source: CFA Institute

Governance factors such as shareholder voting rights, board composition, and compensation practices are widely available and quantifiable, making it relatively straightforward for a financial analyst to evaluate the soundness of a firm's governance. Consequences of poor corporate governance have long been understood by analysts and shareholders. In contrast, incorporating *environmental* and *social* factors into investment decision-making has evolved more slowly. While many environmental and social issues exist, identifying which of these factors are most likely to affect company performance, and how and when they will do so, is often less clear.

ESG considerations are of increasing importance for three reasons:

1. The material financial impact of ESG factors on corporate issuers has risen. Both shareholders and debtholders have suffered substantial losses due to environmental disasters, social controversies, and governance deficiencies.

2. Interest in the environmental and social impacts of investments has grown, particularly among younger clients, who increasingly demand that newly acquired or inherited wealth, as well as pension contributions, be managed with ESG considerations in mind.

3. As government stakeholders continue to prioritize climate change and social policies, revised regulations are forcing corporate issuers to adapt their business practices to meet more stringent ESG criteria.

Environmental and social issues, such as climate change, air pollution, and societal impacts of company products and services, have historically been treated as **negative externalities**, or costs not borne by the company and its investors. But increased stakeholder awareness and stronger regulations are forcing companies to internalize environmental and societal costs in their income statements, either explicitly or implicitly, for responsible investors.

While ESG factors were once regarded as intangible or qualitative information, improved identification and analysis, as well as enhanced corporate disclosures, have resulted in increasingly quantifiable information.

KNOWLEDGE CHECK

1. ESG considerations are increasingly relevant for which of the following reasons (select up to three options)?

   A. Many in the new generation of investors are demanding that investment strategies incorporate ESG factors.

   B. ESG issues are having more material impacts on companies' valuations.

   C. Environmental and social issues are being treated as negative externalities.

   Solution: A and B are correct.

   A is correct. A growing number among the new generation of investors increasingly demand that their inherited wealth or pension contributions be managed using investment strategies that systematically consider material ESG risks, as well as negative environmental and societal impacts, of their portfolio investments.

   B is correct. ESG issues are having more material impacts on companies' valuations. Many investors have suffered substantial losses due to corporate mismanagement of ESG issues, resulting in environmental disasters, social controversies, and governance deficiencies.

   C is incorrect. Environmental and social issues are less frequently treated as negative externalities than in the past. Increased stakeholder awareness and stronger regulations are forcing companies to internalize environmental and societal costs in their income statements, either explicitly or implicitly, for responsible investors.

Environmental Factors

The materiality of environmental factors can vary significantly across industries. An ESG factor is **material** when that factor is believed to have a significant impact on a company's results or business model. For firms in natural-resource-intensive industries, environmental factors often have a *direct* material effect on operations, while in other cases the impact may be material but *indirect* in nature. Environmental factors generally considered material by investors include climate change, pollution and waste, resource and land use, ecological footprint, and biodiversity.

Climate change considerations are often framed as either **physical risks** or **transition risks**. Physical risks include damage to or destruction of assets by severe weather, which is expected to significantly increase in frequency as the climate changes. Physical risks can often be insured against or diversified. Transition risks are losses related to the transition to a lower-carbon economy, which may result from regulations or shifting consumer demand. For example, a coal producer's revenues may decline materially if its electric utility customers switch to lower-emission fuel sources and renewables. A specific instance of transition risk for energy companies and their investors is **stranded assets**, or emission-intensive reserve assets at risk of becoming unviable, thereby reducing their value (e.g., even if an oil well were to produce oil from 2029 to 2059, production might have to cease early due to regulations or uneconomical prices). Analysts may find it difficult to assess this risk for energy companies, given uncertainties of regulations and break-even prices.

Adverse material environmental effects can arise from decisions based on inadequate governance or errors in judgment. For example, oil spills, industrial waste contamination, and local resource depletion can result from poor environmental standards, breaches of safety standards, or unsustainable business models. Such events can be costly in terms of regulatory fines, litigation, clean-up expenses, and reputational risk.

EMISSIONS AND WASTE AS AN ENVIRONMENTAL RISK

Environmental issues such as emissions and waste have historically been treated as externalities and have thus not been fully addressed in companies' financial reporting. However, with growing awareness among stakeholders, including regulators, companies may face financial liabilities for pollution, contamination, and the emission of toxic or carcinogenic substances and therefore must manage these risks. Gross mismanagement of these risks may result in a company not only incurring severe financial penalties but also losing permanently its license to operate.

In 2019, the collapse of Dam I of the Córrego do Feijão Mine in Brumadinho, Brazil, resulted in the spillage of millions of tons of mud; 270 lives were lost, and the nearby Paraopeba River was contaminated. The mine was owned and operated by Vale, a multi-national Brazilian mining corporation. Vale has since been accused of hiding information about the dam's instability for years to avoid damaging its reputation. Several company employees, including its ex-CEO, and its auditor, TÜV SÜD, were charged with murder and environmental crimes. Vale was fined millions of dollars by the Brazilian government and reached an agreement in 2021 to repair all environmental damage and pay USD7 billion to the families of victims killed in the disaster.

Social Factors

Social factors typically pertain to a firm's practices concerning, and their impacts on, its employees and human capital, customers, and communities in which it operates. Compensation, turnover, worker health, training and safety, employee morale, employee diversity, customer data privacy, and community relations can all affect a company's ability to sustain its performance over the long run. Minimizing social risk can lower a company's costs through higher employee productivity, lower employee turnover, reduced litigation potential, and reduced reputational risk.

DATA PRIVACY AND SECURITY AS A SOCIAL RISK

Data privacy and security addresses how companies gather, use, and secure personally identifiable information and other meta-data collected from individuals. In some industries, such as internet software and services, this issue includes managing the risks associated with government requests that may result in violations of consumers' civil and political rights.

As more services are offered online, consumers often unknowingly leave a large digital footprint using such services. Some information may be personally identifiable in nature, leaving users vulnerable to theft or misuse of data. As reported in the *2019 Cost of a Data Breach Report* released by IBM and Ponemon Institute, the average cost of a data breach is USD3.9 million.

Mismanagement of data and privacy and security breaches can have materially significant consequences for both a company's business model and its financial performance. For example, lax cybersecurity measures at Equifax, a US-based consumer credit reporting agency, led to a data breach and the theft of identity and financial data of over 140 million US citizens in 2017. Equifax has incurred hundreds of millions of dollars in expenses arising from the breach and has faced numerous lawsuits and investigations.

In a separate case, Facebook, a leading US-based social media platform, shared the personal data of over 80 million users with a third-party consultancy without users' consent. The consultancy gathered psychological profiles of users and accessed their contacts to influence voters in US elections, leading to one of the largest US government fines (USD5 billion) imposed in the technology sector to date—and to a significant decline in user trust. Facebook's subsequent renaming as Meta Platforms in late 2021 was considered by some analysts a means of distancing itself from the corporation's privacy and other social issues.

Governance Factors

As outlined in an earlier lesson, corporate governance and stakeholder management address issues that include:

- company ownership and voting structure;
- relevance of board skills and experience to current and future company needs;
- alignment of management compensation with company results;
- strength of company shareholder rights versus peers; and
- company effectiveness in managing long-term risks and sustainability.

Analyses of these areas and questions—typically found in issuers' proxy statements, annual reports, and sustainability reports—can provide important insights about the quality of management and sources of risk. Corporate governance will be discussed in greater depth in the next learning module.

SIEMENS AG BRIBERY SCANDAL AND CORPORATE GOVERNANCE CHANGES

In 2006, German police raided the headquarters of Siemens AG, the largest industrial manufacturing firm in Europe, as officials uncovered one of the largest corporate corruption cases in history. German and US investigators subsequently discovered that the payment of bribes to foreign government officials by Siemens employees to secure sales and contracts was standard operating procedure for decades, with total bribery payments exceeding EUR1 billion (dating back to 2001). While hundreds of Siemens employees were dismissed and the firm faced over EUR3 billion in fines, the disgorgement of profits, and other costs, the failure of leadership led to substantial upheaval at the board and senior management level as well as the establishment of new governance policies.

Both the supervisory board and the managing board chairmen resigned, and for the first time in its 160-year history, Siemens hired a CEO from outside the company and most senior managers were dismissed. As the prior boards were found to lack sufficient understanding of, or engagement with, the business, both the new supervisory board and the new managing board included members with insight into operational activities and active decision-making. The new managing board was composed of the CEO, CFO, head of HR, and representatives from key operational units as well as the areas of supply chain management and sustainability, legal, and compliance. The firm increased its scrutiny and oversight of many regional businesses, whose prior autonomy had resulted in significant violations. Finally, to rebuild trust with internal and external stakeholders, Siemens instituted a firmwide anti-corruption policy designed to prevent, detect, and respond to compliance breaches.

Evaluating ESG-Related Risks and Opportunities

Recall from an earlier lesson that debt and equity investors have different claims to the same cash flows of a corporation. The process of identifying and evaluating ESG-related factors that affect these cash flows is therefore similar for both equity and corporate credit analyses.

The question of *how* and *when* ESG factors affect corporate cash flows rests on differences in their effect on the value of debt and equity claims.

- Once identified, the material effects of ESG factors must first be quantified in financial terms—that is, how are the firm's discounted future cash flows positively or negatively affected by these factors?

- In the case of significant long-term adverse ESG-related events, equity claims are usually immediately and disproportionately affected, as they represent residual claims to future company cash flows. For example, in the Vale dam disaster, the Equifax data breach, and the Siemens bribery scandal cited earlier, all three firms experienced a sharp share price decline in the wake of the event.

- While adverse ESG-related events also affect the value of debtholder claims, these finite, fixed obligations are usually less affected than equities by such events unless the firm's ability to make interest and principal payments is adversely affected. In the Vale, Equifax, and Siemens examples, all three saw their respective issuer-specific cost of debt rise, and each experienced a credit rating downgrade shortly after the adverse event. Vale saw its debt rating briefly reduced to speculative grade following the dam collapse. In more extreme cases, debtholders may force a company into bankruptcy and experience significant losses in liquidation.

- In general, the effects of adverse ESG-related events often differ depending on maturity. For example, an analyst may believe a coal company has long-term risk from potential asset write-downs—that is, stranded assets due to regulatory changes or shifts in demand—which would likely have a greater negative effect on debt maturing in ten years versus short-term debt maturing in twelve months.

Analysts evaluate potential positive and/or negative effects of material ESG-related factors, whose financial impact is reflected in a company's projected financial statements and ratios—with future expected cash flows discounted at an appropriate rate and sensitivity and/or a scenario analysis used to weigh different outcomes for debt and equity holders.

For example, an analyst might increase her forecast of a hotel company's operating costs because of the impact of excessive employee turnover—lost productivity, reduced customer satisfaction, and increased expenses for employee searches, temporary workers, and training programs. As another example, an analyst might choose to lower the discount rate for a food company that is expected to gain a competitive advantage by transitioning to a sustainable source of a key ingredient in its products.

QUESTION SET

---

1. Historically, analysts have best been able to evaluate a company's:

   A. social practices.

   B. governance practices.

   C. environmental practices.

   Solution:

   B is correct. Corporate governance factors are well understood and quantifiable by analysts, including the consequences of poor corporate governance. In contrast, the inclusion of environmental and social factors in investment decision-making has evolved more slowly. The results of evaluating the effects of environmental and social factors on firm performance are often less clear.

---

2. Historically, environmental and social issues have been treated as _____. However, they are increasingly being recognized as _____. (negative externalities, internalized costs).

   Solution:

   Historically, environmental and social issues have been treated as <u>negative externalities</u>. However, they are increasingly being recognized as <u>internalized costs</u>.

   It was previously assumed that the negative consequences of poor firm decisions did not fall on the firm's capital suppliers but, rather, on society. Now, analysts consider these increasingly internalized company costs by estimating their effects on firm financial performance, by incorporating them into discount rates and risk assessments, and by screening or adjusting position sizes of companies that have poor ESG practices.

3. Stranded assets best represent _____. (physical risk, transition risk)

   Solution:

   Stranded assets best represent <u>transition risk</u>.

   Transition risks are losses related to the transition to a lower-carbon economy. An oil well may become a stranded asset due to government regulations or changes in consumer preferences that affect the price of oil or otherwise impair an issuer's ability to fully realize the asset value. Physical risks include damage to property stemming from extreme weather, which is expected to increase in both frequency and severity due to climate change.

4. Explain the importance of materiality of ESG factors for a financial analyst.

   Solution:

   An ESG factor is considered material when it has a significant impact on a company's results or business model. An analyst attempts to evaluate potential positive or negative effects of material ESG-related factors—for example, by incorporating them into a company's projected cash flows and/or discount rates or through an investment candidate screening process. While an issuer may have many ESG factors to consider, analysts prioritize those that are material given the opportunity cost of analysts' time.

5. A company's effectiveness in managing long-term risks and sustainability is best classified as a:

   A. social factor.

   B. governance factor.

   C. environmental factor.

   Solution:

   B is correct. Corporate governance and stakeholder management address issues that include a company's effectiveness in managing long-term risks and sustainability. Management effectiveness can be assessed through an evaluation of the company's financial and non-financial performance over the long run, along with a comparison against industry peers to isolate controllable variables.

PRACTICE PROBLEMS

The following information relates to questions 1-3

Consider a firm with assets of 200 fully financed by equity and an identical firm financed with 80% debt and 20% equity. Assume both firms have revenue over a period of 200 and non-debt operating expenses of 140.

1. If we assume an interest rate of 20% for the period, calculate net income for each firm and compare their returns on equity for the period, ignoring income taxes.

2. Calculate the return on equity for the period if the firms experience a 20% increase and decrease in revenue (from Question 1), assuming operating expenses remain unchanged.

3. Consider the same all-equity-financed firm as in Question 1 and its choices for financing a new investment in LT assets of 40. The pertinent details in the firm's initial balance sheet are shown below. Revenue before the investment is 200, operating expenses are 140 and are expected to remain unchanged, interest on new debt financing is 20%, and the return on the new investment is 30%.

   Calculate the ROE for the firm if it finances the investment with debt, the issuance of new shares, or cash on hand and compare the results. Discuss the results of the comparison.

Initial Balance Sheet

Cash	60		
Other assets	40		
LT assets	100	Equity	200

Share Issuance		Debt Issuance		Cash on Hand	
Cash 60		Cash 60		Cash 20	
Other 40		Other 40	Debt 40	Other 40	
LT assets 140	Equity 240	LT assets 140	Equity 200	LT assets 140	Equity 200
Revenue	212	212		212	
Less: Operating Expenses	140	140		140	
Less: Interest		8			
Net Income	72	64		72	
Total Equity	240	200		200	
ROE	30%	32%		36%	

4. A company has developed a long-term relationship with its major supplier. The supplier has developed complex systems that integrate with those of the compa-

ny and has an agreement to receive payment within 30 days for goods delivered. Discuss the supplier's stakeholder relationship with the firm. Why would high financial leverage be inconsistent with the supplier's interests?

5. Explain why a company's management might not act in the best interests of shareholders.

SOLUTIONS

1. Solve for net income by subtracting expenses from revenue, and divide net income by total equity to solve for the one-period return on equity:

Equity-Financed		Debt- and Equity-Financed	
Revenue	200	Revenue	200
Less: Operating Expenses	−140	Less: Operating Expenses	−140
		Less: Interest Expense*	−32
Net Income	60	Net Income	28
Total Equity	200	Total Equity	40
Return on Equity	**30%**	**Return on Equity**	**70%**

*Interest expense with 80% debt financing = 160 × 0.20 = 32.

2.

20% _Increase_ in Revenue			
Equity-Financed		**Debt- and Equity-Financed**	
Revenue	240	Revenue	240
Less: Operating Expenses	−140	Less: Operating Expenses	−140
		Less: Interest Expense	−32
Net Income	100	Net Income	68
Total Equity	200	Total Equity	40
Return on Equity	**50%**	**Return on Equity**	**170%**

20% _Decrease_ in Revenue			
Equity-Financed		**Debt- and Equity-Financed**	
Revenue	160	Revenue	160
Less: Operating Expenses	−140	Less: Operating Expenses	−140
		Less: Interest Expense	−32
Net Income	20	Net Income	(12)
Total Equity	200	Total Equity	40
Return on Equity	**10%**	**Return on Equity**	**(30%)**

Like the example in the lesson, the use of debt increases the variance in return on equity.

3. Financing the investment with new shares produces the lowest ROE among the three financing options. However, since the investment produced a return equal

to the beginning ROE, there was no change in ROE from the initial case. Financing with debt produced a higher ROE, because the interest rate on debt was lower than the return on the new investment and no new shares were issued, avoiding dilution. The highest ROE was produced by using excess cash on hand, which avoids both dilution and the interest cost of debt.

4. The supplier has a clear vested interest in the success and survival of the company, so it is considered a stakeholder. The supplier extends short-term credit to the company and has a long-term interest in the success of the company because it has invested in integrated complex systems. High financial leverage would not be in the best interest of the supplier, because it presents both short-term risk that the company may be unable to make payments for goods delivered and long-term risk for the investment made to integrate the supplier's complex systems with those of the company.

5. Managers are in a principal-agent relationship with a company's shareholders. Managers, overseen by the board of directors, serve as agents who should act in the best interests of the company's shareholders. However, in some cases, managers may put their own interests ahead of shareholders' interests. Examples include insufficient effort, excessive perquisite consumption (e.g., corporate jets, elaborate offices), and failure to take appropriate risks or make investments in an effort to safeguard their jobs. Oversight by a majority independent board and compensation to align managers' interests with shareholders', such as performance-based and equity-based compensation schemes, are mechanisms to mitigate these conflicts of interest.

Corporate Governance: Conflicts, Mechanisms, Risks, and Benefits

LEARNING OUTCOMES

Mastery	The candidate should be able to:
☐	describe the principal-agent relationship and conflicts that may arise between stakeholder groups
☐	describe corporate governance and mechanisms to manage stakeholder relationships and mitigate associated risks
☐	describe potential risks of poor corporate governance and stakeholder management and benefits of effective corporate governance and stakeholder management

INTRODUCTION

1

Corporations are complex structures with stakeholders beyond owners, lenders, and managers. Corporate governance involves the creation and maintenance of a system of checks, balances, and incentives that addresses conflicting interests among these stakeholders. In this Learning Module, we first identify key aspects of the relationships between these parties and the potential conflicts that may arise. In the second lesson, we turn to the various mechanisms established to manage these conflicts, settle disputes, and mitigate risk. Finally, we highlight the benefits of strong corporate governance and stakeholder management policies as well as the risks of weak policies and their potential impact on corporate performance.

> **LEARNING MODULE OVERVIEW**
>
> - A principal-agent relationship is created when one party (a principal) hires another party (an agent) to perform a task or service. The relationship can exist with or without a contract. The agent is expected to act in the principal's best interest.
>
> - In many cases, the agent possesses more information than the principal, and conflicts arise where the interests of the principal and the agent diverge. In a corporation, shareholders are a <u>principal and elect directors (an agent)</u>, who appoint managers (another agent), who are charged with maximizing shareholder value.

- Given the complex ecosystem of stakeholders in a corporation, the rights, responsibilities, and powers of each stakeholder must be considered when establishing an appropriate governance structure by striking a balance among the interests of these groups while meeting corporate objectives.

- A sound governance structure consists of mechanisms to ensure adherence to rules and regulations imposed by external authorities as well as to meet the unique requirements of internal stakeholders. These mechanisms include financial reporting, general and extraordinary meetings, compensation, debt covenants, and more.

- Weak corporate governance, unmanaged conflicts of interest, or inadequate stakeholder management can place firms at a competitive disadvantage. Strong governance practices and a proper balance among stakeholders' interests are often reflected in increased competitiveness and operational efficiency, better control processes, and improved performance.

LEARNING MODULE SELF-ASSESSMENT

These initial questions are intended to help you gauge your current level of understanding of this learning module.

1. The following statements relate to the ecosystem of stakeholders in a corporation. Complete each statement by selecting one of the following: agent, principal, contractual, principal-agent, employer-employee

   In a corporation, the board of directors is elected to act as a(n) _____.

   In a corporation, shareholders are a(n) _____.

   Customers have a(n) _____ relationship with a corporate issuer.

   Solution:

   In a corporation, the board of directors is elected to act as an <u>agent</u>.
   In a corporation, shareholders are a <u>principal</u>.
   Customers have a <u>contractual</u> relationship with a corporate issuer.

2. Conflicts arise where the interests of a principal and an agent diverge, resulting in agency costs. Identify and explain an example of an agency cost for a corporate issuer.<QuestionType>essay</QuestionType>

   Solution:

   An example of an agency cost for public companies is the cost of hiring an external independent auditor for the financial statements and internal controls. Audit fees are paid by the issuer, a cost borne by the shareholders, to mitigate the risk that financial reports are materially misstated or deviate from generally accepted accounting principles.

3. Match the mechanism to manage relationships or settle disputes with the applicable stakeholder

1. Shareholders	A. Ad hoc committee
2. Creditors	B. Proxy contest
3. Management	C. – Stock-based compensation

Solution:

1. B is correct. Proxy contests are one mechanism for shareholders to pursue changes in corporate control.
2. A is correct. When a company is struggling to meet its debt obligations, an ad hoc committee may be formed by a group of bondholders to approach the company with potential options to restructure their bonds.
3. C is correct. Stock-based compensation seeks to align the interests of management and shareholders.

4. A(n) _____ may be called when requested by a specific minimum number of calling shareholders, as detailed in the company's bylaws or charter.

Solution:

An extraordinary general meeting (EGM) may be called when requested by a specific minimum number of calling shareholders, as detailed in the company's bylaws or charter.

5. Studies have shown that improvements in corporate governance practices _____ (increase/decrease) the likelihood of a credit rating _____ (upgrade/downgrade), which tends to _____ (increase/decrease) the cost of debt.

Solution:

Studies have shown that improvements in corporate governance practices increase the likelihood of a credit rating upgrade, which tends to decrease the cost of debt.

6. What types of questions should analysts consider about a company's corporate governance and stakeholder management?<QuestionType>essay</QuestionType>

Solution:

Key questions analysts should consider about a company's corporate governance and stakeholder management include the following:

- What is the company's ownership and voting structure?
- How well do board members' skills and experience match the current and future needs of the company?
- How closely does the management team's compensation and incentive structure align with factors expected to drive overall company results?
- Who are the significant investors in the company?
- How strong are company shareholder rights versus its peers?
- How effective has management been in taking a long-term perspective on risks and sustainability?

2   STAKEHOLDER CONFLICTS AND MANAGEMENT

☐ describe the principal-agent relationship and conflicts that may arise between stakeholder groups

A corporation is a legal entity with a complex ecosystem of stakeholders. Corporate stakeholder relationships include contractual, principal-agent, and other relationships as illustrated in Exhibit 1.

Exhibit 1: Principal-Agent and Other Relationships

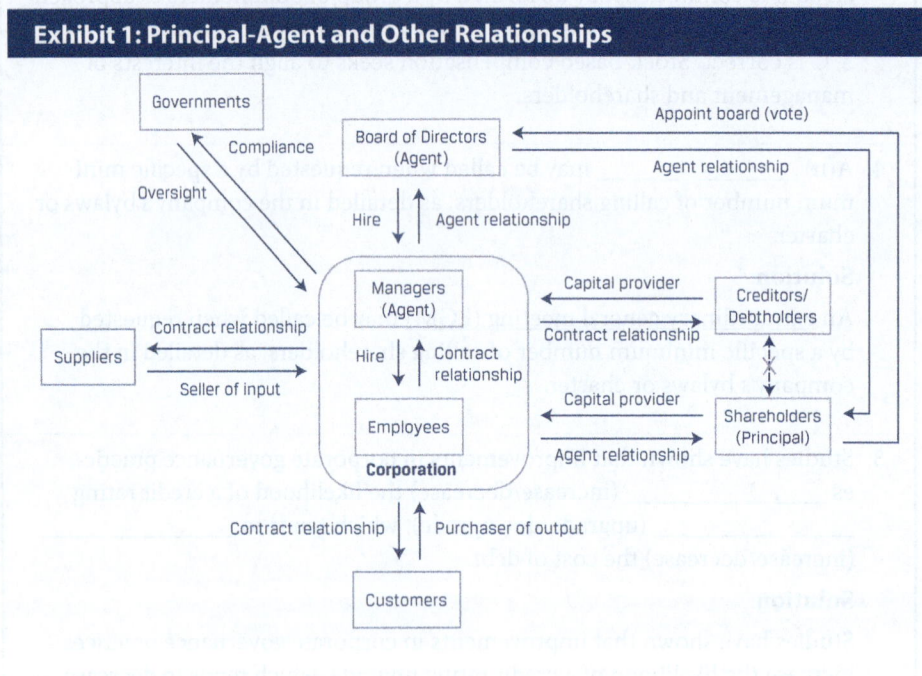

A **principal-agent relationship** (or agency relationship) is created when one party (a principal) hires another party (an agent) to perform a task or service and can be present with or without a contract governing the relationship. An agent is expected to act in the principal's best interest, and the relationship involves trust and expectations of loyalty and diligence. In many cases, the agent possesses more information than the principal, which means that the principal is often unable to directly verify that the agent is acting in the principal's best interest. Conflicts arise where the interests of the principal and agent diverge, resulting in **agency costs**, which can be direct, such as the costs of hiring monitoring agents (e.g., a board of directors hiring an auditor), or indirect, like the forgone profits and economic benefits of lost opportunities.

In a corporation, shareholders are a principal and elect directors (an agent), who are expected to pursue shareholders' interests by hiring managers (another agent) to maximize shareholder value. Shareholders and lenders demand higher returns and risk premiums when faced with greater information asymmetry due to the greater potential for conflicts of interest. Principal-agent relationships and potential conflicts arise in several areas within corporations.

Shareholder, Board Director, and Manager Relationships

Directors and managers have more information about a company's performance, risks, and investment opportunities than outsiders such as shareholders and lenders. This information asymmetry lowers shareholders' ability to assess the performance of directors and managers, weakening their capacity to identify and dismiss poor performers. While all companies have some degree of asymmetric information, it is more pronounced for companies competing in many markets and geographies, those that sell complex products, and companies with lower levels of institutional ownership and free float.

In practice, compensation is the principal tool used to align the interests of management and shareholders. While management compensation seeks to motivate managers to maximize shareholder value, manager and shareholder interests may diverge in the following common ways:

- Insufficient effort. Managers may be unable or unwilling to make investments, manage costs appropriately, or make hard decisions like shutting down unprofitable business lines. They may conduct too little monitoring of employees or assert too little control, leading to unintentional risks and litigation. Finally, managers may allocate too little time to their role because they are committed to political or charitable activities, personal investments, or serving as directors or managers of other companies.

- Inappropriate risk appetite. Compensation dominated by stock grants and options can motivate excessive management risk-taking, as option holders participate only in upside share price moves. Similarly, little or no use of stock grants and options in compensation plans can lead to unduly risk-averse corporate decision-making and the inability to attract talent. This misalignment may be at odds with the company's value creation objective or shareholders' desire for higher-risk, higher-reward endeavors. Since investors can hold diversified portfolios, they may have a higher risk tolerance than managers, whose reputation and time are concentrated in a single company.

- Empire building. Management compensation and status are typically tied to business size (e.g., total revenues, number of employees), which can incentivize managers to seek "growth for growth's sake," such as acquisitions that do not increase shareholder value.

- Entrenchment. Directors and managers want to retain their jobs. Tactics to do so include copying competitors and peers, avoiding risks, and pursuing complicated transactions and restructurings that they are uniquely suited to manage. Directors may avoid speaking out against management, even if speaking out is in the interest of shareholders or other stakeholders.

- Self-dealing. Managers may exploit firm resources to maximize personal benefits, such as excessive perquisites (private airplanes, club memberships, personal security), or defraud investors by misappropriating assets. The smaller a manager's stake in the company, the less they bear these costs themselves, reducing their desire to maximize firm value.

KNOWLEDGE CHECK: SHAREHOLDER AND MANAGER/DIRECTOR RELATIONSHIPS

1. A construction firm has the opportunity to invest in a high-risk, high-reward capital infrastructure project. Which of the following could be a reason why the company decides not to pursue the project?

   A. The compensation of managers is closely tied to the size of the company's business.

   B. Management receives excessive all-cash compensation.

   C. Management has recently received a generous options reward in the company's shares.

   Solution:

   B is correct. When compensation—particularly if it is excessive—is entirely in cash, the risk tolerance of managers may be too low, as they are inclined to protect their cash compensation. Additionally, there may be little upside for them if the project performs well.

   A is incorrect, as it describes the "empire building" phenomenon that would likely result in the decision to grow the company at any cost in an attempt to secure higher compensation.

   C is incorrect, as it would likely lead to an alignment of managers' interests with those of shareholders.

Controlling and Minority Shareholder Relationships

Corporate ownership is generally classified as dispersed or concentrated. Dispersed ownership involves many shareholders, none of whom can exercise control over the corporation. In contrast, concentrated ownership reflects an individual shareholder or a group (known as **controlling shareholders**), who can exercise control over the corporation. The group may involve a family, another company (or companies), or government.

While we have been discussing shareholders as a homogeneous group with shared interests, in fact shareholders are often a heterogeneous group with different interests, such as a founding family with a large percentage of their wealth held in company stock who thus desire management to diversify the company to achieve stability. This desire would be at odds with that of **minority shareholders** who hold diversified portfolios and would prefer that management focus on maximizing shareholder value, as they can diversify cheaply on their own. Conversely, a controlling shareholder may also be a long-term shareholder with a multi-year or multi-decade perspective, while some minority shareholders may seek quick gains from cost cutting, selling assets, or share repurchases. Shareholders can communicate with one another and form voting blocs to advocate for their interests more effectively.

Share ownership percentages alone may not necessarily reflect whether company control is dispersed or concentrated. Differences in shareholder voting schemes, as well as a **share class** with different voting rights, give rise to varying degrees of control among shareholders. In contrast to a simple structure of one vote per shareholder, a **dual-class structure** involves one share class (e.g., Class A) that carries one vote per share and is publicly held and traded and another share class (e.g., Class B) that carries several votes per share and is held exclusively by company insiders or founders. A dual-class structure allows certain stakeholders to effectively control the company even if they do not hold most of the shares outstanding. These stakeholders—who can avoid voting-power dilution if new shares are issued—control board elections, strategic decisions, and all other significant matters. CFA Institute has long advocated against dual-class structures, because they permit one group of shareholders to have disproportionate power and potentially override the will of the majority for their own personal interest. In cases where dual-class structures are legal, CFA Institute advises issuers to clearly disclose such arrangements and their implications for investors. For more on CFA Institute's advocacy on this and other corporate governance topics, visit www.cfainstitute.org/advocacy.

Magna International Inc., a Canadian auto parts company, started off with two classes of shares. Class A shares had one vote per share, and Class B shares had 500 votes per share. The founder, Frank Stronach, and his family were able to control 75% of the voting rights while owning only 3% of the total shares by holding Class B shares. Investors were frustrated that the founder and members of his family secured millions in consulting fees, salaries, bonuses, and stock options despite weakness in the stock price. Shareholders voted for a single-class share structure in an extraordinary general meeting, creating an agreement that Stronach would leave the company after paying out CAD870 million over five years.

KNOWLEDGE CHECK: DUAL-CLASS SHARE STRUCTURE

1. Which of the following *best* describes dual-class share structures?

    A. Dual-class share structures can be easily changed over time.

    B. Company founders can maintain significant power over the organization.

    C. Conflicts of interest between management and stakeholder groups are less likely than with single-class share structures.

    Solution:

    B is correct. Under dual-class share systems, company founders may control board elections, strategic decisions, and other significant matters. A is incorrect, because dual-class share systems are difficult to dismantle once adopted as the voting control within dual-class systems is held exclusively by company insiders or founders. C is incorrect, because conflicts of interest between management and stakeholders are *more* likely than with single-class share structures owing to the potential control element in dual-class systems.

Shareholder versus Creditor Interests

Despite their financial claims to the same cash flows of a corporation, the difference in debt versus equity claims gives rise to potential conflicts of interest, as outlined in the previous module. For example, debtholders with a fixed claim tend to be risk averse and prefer that the corporation take actions to ensure sufficient cash flow to meet its debt obligations. For this reason, debtholders tend to prefer that a company raise more equity and limit shareholder distributions. Shareholders, however, tend to prefer greater leverage and shareholder distributions rather than dilutive equity issuance.

This potential conflict is greater for long-term debt, as the passage of time exposes debtholders to changes in business conditions, strategy, and management behavior. As a result, long-term creditors are more likely to impose contractual limits on leverage and shareholder distributions.

KNOWLEDGE CHECK: STAKEHOLDER RELATIONSHIPS

1. A controlling shareholder of Stillcreek Corporation owns 55% of Stillcreek's shares, and the remaining shares are spread among a large group of shareholders. In this situation, conflicts of interest are *most likely* to arise between:

   A. shareholders and bondholders.

   B. the controlling shareholder and managers.

   C. the controlling shareholder and minority shareholders.

   Solution:

   C is correct. In this ownership structure, the controlling shareholder's power is likely more influential than that of minority shareholders. Thus, the controlling shareholder may be able to exploit its position to the detriment of the interests of the remaining shareholders. A and B are incorrect, because the ownership structure in and of itself is unlikely to create material conflicts between shareholders and bondholders or shareholders and managers.

EXAMPLE 1

Leverage and Other Stakeholders: KLD Marine Ltd.

KLD Marine Ltd. (KLD) is a small, debt-free manufacturer of welded metal boats with domestic and international sales in a highly competitive and cyclical market. KLD is the primary employer in a small, remote town. Sales are through a network of dealers, who typically sell three or four different boat brands. Of the company's 50 employees, about half are specialized aluminum welders, with most others in sales and management. The primary purchased input for KLD's boat production is sheet aluminum. KLD's sole aluminum supplier is a large, multi-national company with many clients. KLD has never paid dividends but has substantial retained earnings that finance the company's assets. KLD has recently decided to borrow heavily so it can pay a large, one-time dividend to shareholders.

1. Which of the following stakeholder groups will be most negatively affected by the increase in leverage?

   A. The welders employed by the company

   B. The company's dealers

   C. The supplier of aluminum to the business

   Solution:

   A is correct. As employees, the welders could face loss of employment if the company were to become financially distressed with the increase in leverage. And since their skills are very specialized, they would probably have difficulty finding another job locally. In a small and remote town, employment opportunities are likely to be limited for specialized workers.

   B is incorrect. The dealers might suffer lost sales if KLD were to fail, but they could likely replace KLD with a competing brand.

   C is incorrect. The aluminum supplier would probably suffer the least impact, since it is large and KLD is likely not a sizable proportion of its sales.

2. Is it likely that any of these groups would be affected positively?

Solution:

In all cases, impacts are negative. Note that for modest borrowing, these effects would be minor.

QUESTION SET

1. Which of the following stakeholders are *most likely* to demand higher returns and risk premiums when faced with greater information asymmetry due to the greater potential conflicts of interest?

   A. Directors and managers

   B. Suppliers and customers

   C. Shareholders and lenders

   Solution:

   C is correct. Greater information asymmetry increases risk for shareholders and lenders, who will seek to be compensated for taking that risk with a lower share price or multiple and a higher yield on debt investments.

   A is incorrect, because directors and managers have more information about a company's performance, risks, and investment opportunities than outsiders, such as shareholders and lenders.

   B is incorrect, because while suppliers and customers are outsiders with information asymmetry, their relationship is contractual and not based on investment return.

2. An analyst is examining the governance of several companies in her coverage area and learns that one of the CEOs is highly involved in political and charitable activities. These activities may result in which one of the following misalignments of interests between management and shareholders?

   A. Self-dealing

   B. Entrenchment

   C. Insufficient effort

   Solution:

   C is correct. The CEO's outside activities could result in insufficient effort. Managers may allocate too little time to their role because they are committed to political or charitable activities, personal investments, or serving as directors or managers of other companies.

   A and B are incorrect, because while they are both examples of misalignments between management and shareholders, they are not the primary concern about management involvement in charitable and political activities, which tend to distract management rather than cause a direct conflict of interest or transaction that is not in shareholders' interests.

3. A _____ corporate ownership structure involves many shareholders, none of whom can exercise control over the corporation.

   Solution:

   A <u>dispersed</u> corporate ownership structure involves many shareholders, none of whom can exercise control over the corporation.

4. A company's management team, whose compensation includes significant stock grants and options, is pursuing a large debt-financed acquisition. The management team discusses how this acquisition may not align with the interests of all stakeholders, and it is proposed that they increase equity financing for the acquisition. Increasing equity financing for the transaction would increase support by which stakeholder?

   A. Debtholders

   B. Management

   C. Shareholders

   Solution:

   A is correct. Debtholders with a fixed claim tend to be risk averse and prefer that the corporation take actions to ensure sufficient cash flow to meet its debt obligations. For this reason, debtholders tend to prefer that a company raise more equity as opposed to increasing debt to a level that may increase default risk.

   B and C are incorrect, because management is aligned with shareholders through stock grants and options, and shareholders tend to prefer greater leverage rather than dilutive equity issuance.

5. Discuss the potential conflicts between controlling shareholders and minority shareholders in a dual-class structure.

   Solution:

   A dual-class structure allows stakeholders to effectively control the company by virtue of their ownership of a share class with superior voting rights. While it is possible for minority shareholders to change voting rights in their favor, it can be difficult and expensive to do so, as illustrated by the Magna International example.

3   CORPORATE GOVERNANCE MECHANISMS

☐ | describe corporate governance and mechanisms to manage stakeholder relationships and mitigate associated risks

Given the complex ecosystem of stakeholders in a corporation, the rights, responsibilities, and powers of each must be taken into consideration when establishing an appropriate governance structure by striking a balance among the interests of these groups while meeting corporate objectives. A sound governance structure seeks to ensure that a corporation has mechanisms in place that not only facilitate adherence to rules and regulations imposed by external authorities but also meet the unique requirements of internal stakeholders.

Corporate Reporting and Transparency

Corporate reporting and transparency are foundational to governance. Without them, external stakeholders would be unaware of the company's performance and position, and thus their ability to advocate for their interests would be severely weakened. Given its importance, reporting is mandated and regulated through legal, regulatory, and quasi-regulatory means (e.g., exchange listing requirements).

Investors have access to a public company's financial and non-financial information through annual reports, proxy statements, company disclosures, investor relations resources, and other sources. This reporting includes information on a company's operations, strategic objectives, audited financial statements, governance structure, ownership structure, remuneration policies, related-party transactions, and risk factors. Most jurisdictions and stock exchanges require that listed companies' annual financial statements be audited—and interim financial statements reviewed—by third-party independent auditors.

Private companies disclose information to the public only to the extent required by regulations or voluntarily. However, they will disclose information confidentially to their investors, but the content and form of that information are subject to negotiation between stakeholders rather than standardized like the reporting by public companies. Most jurisdictions do *not* require that private companies' disclosures be audited, though private companies are free to obtain an audit, which may improve their terms with investors.

Investors rely on corporate reports and information to:

- assess company performance and that of its directors and managers;
- make valuation and investment decisions;
- vote on key corporate matters or changes; and
- ensure compliance with legal commitments in debt contracts. As it is impractical for individual bondholders to track these bond requirements, a financial intermediary known as a trustee is hired to report on and manage payment administration for bondholders.

Shareholder Mechanisms

As residual owners of the company, shareholders seek to protect their ownership claims through a variety of control mechanisms over the company. While no standard set of shareholder rights exists, global investors usually rely on common rights and mechanisms outlined in the following sections. These mechanisms are often enshrined in securities laws and enforced by regulators.

Shareholder Meetings

General meetings—or an **annual general meeting (AGM)**, typically held once a year—enable shareholders to participate in discussions and vote on matters and transactions that are not delegated to the board of directors. Common matters presented for a shareholder vote at AGMs include the following:

- Board member elections
- Appointment of independent auditor
- Approval of annual financial statements, dividends, and director and auditor compensation
- Approval of equity-based compensation plans
- "Say on pay" non-binding votes on compensation plans

Extraordinary general meetings (EGMs) may be called when other resolutions requiring shareholder approval are proposed, or when requested by a specified minimum number of calling shareholders (or proportion of stock outstanding). Matters presented for a shareholder vote at EGMs are idiosyncratic but commonly include the following:

- Special elections of board members, usually proposed by shareholders
- Amendments to bylaws or articles of association
- Mergers and acquisitions, takeovers, and asset sales
- Capital increases
- Voluntary firm liquidation

Shareholders unable to attend a meeting in person usually authorize another party to vote on their behalf in a **proxy voting** process, typically by submitting a ballot electronically or by mail. Proxy voting is the most common form of investor participation in general meetings.

KNOWLEDGE CHECK

1. Which of the following statements about extraordinary general meetings (EGMs) of shareholders is true?

    A. The appointment of external auditors occurs during an EGM.

    B. A corporation provides an overview of corporate performance at an EGM.

    C. An amendment to a corporation's bylaws typically occurs during an EGM.

    Solution:

    C is correct. An amendment to corporate bylaws would normally take place during an EGM, which concerns significant changes to a company, such as bylaw amendments. A and B are incorrect, because the appointment of external auditors and a corporate performance overview would typically take place during the AGM.

Shareholder Activism

Shareholder activism involves investor strategies to compel a company to act in a desired manner. The primary motivation of shareholder activists is to increase shareholder value relatively quickly, although some activism involves social, political, or environmental considerations. Shareholder activists often pressure management to act using tactics such as initiating proxy fights, proposing shareholder resolutions, and publicizing issues of contention.

Hedge funds are among the predominant shareholder activists. Unlike most institutional investors, hedge funds base the majority of their fees on returns, granting them a significant stake in the financial success of an activist campaign. Also, hedge funds face fewer investment restrictions and are therefore able to take on large share positions using borrowed funds. Regulated investment entities such as mutual funds, however, are subject to investment restrictions (e.g., limitations on maximum position size, leverage, and ownership of distressed or illiquid securities) that limit these activities, although some large funds use their influence to encourage positive corporate action.

KNOWLEDGE CHECK

1. Which of the following *best* describes shareholder activists? Shareholder activists:

   A. help stabilize a company's strategic direction.

   B. have little effect on the company's long-term investors.

   C. are unlikely to alter the composition of a company's shareholder base.

   Solution:

   A is correct. Shareholder activists often narrow a company's strategic direction to focus on the few things that the company has historically done well, often shedding assets and closing divisions in the process.

   B is incorrect, because long-term investors in a company need to consider how shareholder activists affect the company, especially if the company is restructured and management is replaced.

   C is incorrect, because an activist *is* likely to change the investment thesis for a company toward restructuring, which may prompt a change in the shareholder base.

Shareholder Litigation

Shareholder activists may pursue additional tactics, such as litigation or lawsuits. One prominent type is **shareholder derivative lawsuits** (unrelated to financial derivative contracts), which are legal proceedings initiated against the board of directors, management, and/or controlling shareholders by a shareholder deemed to be acting on behalf of the company in place of its directors and officers, who have failed to adequately act for the benefit of the company. In many countries, laws restrict shareholders from pursuing legal action by either imposing minimum shareholder interest thresholds for such lawsuits or prohibiting them altogether.

Corporate Takeovers

Changes in corporate control via a takeover by shareholders or an acquirer may be pursued in several ways. One mechanism is the **proxy contest** (or proxy fight). In a proxy contest, a group seeking a controlling position on a company's board of directors attempts to persuade shareholders to vote for the group. Managerial teams can also be displaced through **tender offers** and **hostile takeovers**, which seek to take over a company through control of the board and thus management. A tender offer involves an invitation to shareholders to sell their interests directly to a group seeking to gain control. A contest for corporate control may attract arbitrageurs and takeover specialists, who facilitate transfers of control by purchasing shares from existing shareholders in the target company and later selling shares to the highest bidder. A hostile takeover is an attempt to acquire a company without the consent of the company's management.

Preservation of employment serves as an incentive for board members and managers to focus on shareholder wealth maximization. The threat of removal, however, can also have negative implications for a company's corporate governance practices if the company adopts anti-takeover measures, such as staggered board elections or a shareholder rights plan (commonly known as a **poison pill**), to reduce the likelihood of an unwanted takeover. Staggered board elections can dilute shareholder voting rights by preventing shareholders from replacing the entire board at any given election. A shareholder rights plan enables shareholders to buy additional shares at a discount if another shareholder purchases a certain percentage of the company's shares. Such plans increase takeover costs to any potential bidder.

Creditor Mechanisms

Creditors, including private lenders like banks as well as public bondholders, have several mechanisms available to protect their interests. The rights of creditors are established by laws and according to contracts executed with the company. Laws vary by jurisdiction but commonly contain provisions to protect creditors' interests and provide legal recourse.

Bond Indenture

The rights of bondholders are established through contracts executed with the company. A **bond indenture** is a legal contract that describes the structure of a bond, the obligations of the company, and the rights of the bondholders. The terms and conditions of lending agreements either require the company to perform certain actions (or meet certain requirements) or prohibit certain actions. Bondholders may also require that certain assets be pledged by an issuer to secure its promise to repay its obligations.

Creditor Committees

In some countries, official creditor committees, particularly for unsecured bondholders, are established once a company files for bankruptcy. Such committees are expected to represent bondholders during bankruptcy proceedings and to protect bondholder interests in restructuring or liquidation.

When a company is struggling to meet its obligations under an indenture, an **ad hoc committee** may be formed by a group of bondholders to approach the company with potential options to restructure their bonds. While members of an ad hoc committee do not officially represent all bondholders, their interests are often aligned with those of the broader bondholder group.

Board and Management Mechanisms

While the board of directors is central to a company's governance structure, boards routinely delegate specific functions to committees composed of a subset of their members. Board committees thoroughly consider, review, monitor, and follow up on matters that fall within their mandates, which may require specific expertise or independence.

Exhibit 2 outlines the three most common board committees (sometimes referred to as "core committees"), recommended by most corporate governance codes and required by some stock exchanges.

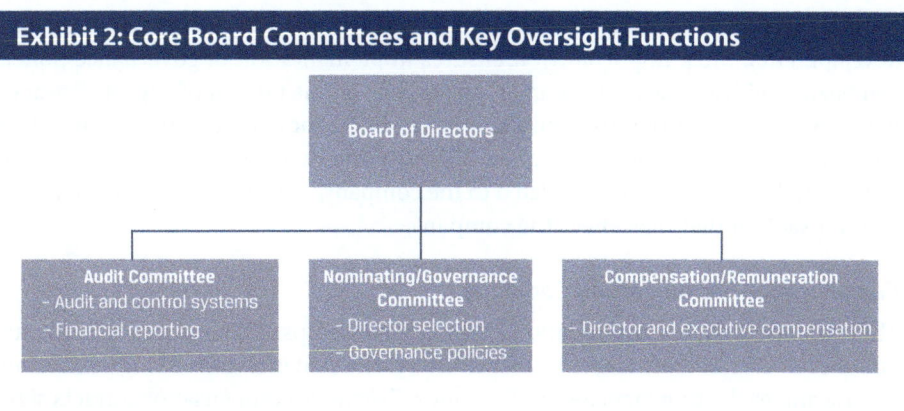

Exhibit 2: Core Board Committees and Key Oversight Functions

Board of Directors

Audit Committee	Nominating/Governance Committee	Compensation/Remuneration Committee
– Audit and control systems	– Director selection	– Director and executive compensation
– Financial reporting	– Governance policies	

These committees provide recommendations and reports to the board on a regular basis. When establishing committees, boards do not delegate their ultimate responsibility nor are they discharged of their duties. The board is required to review, challenge, and assure the content of any reports raised to it by the committees and to make the proper decisions.

Audit Committee

The audit committee is the most widely required and established board committee, which, according to best practices, should be composed solely of independent board members and include at least one director with accounting or financial management expertise. The audit committee monitors the issuer's financial reporting process, including the proper selection and implementation of accounting policies according to accounting standards and regulations in order to ensure the integrity of the financial statements. It supervises the internal audit function and ensures its independence and competence. The audit committee is also responsible for recommending the appointment of an independent external auditor and proposing its remuneration. It interacts and holds meetings with the external auditor. It receives reports from the internal and external auditors, proposes remedial actions for highlighted issues or matters, and follows up on them. In some cases, the audit committee may also oversee information technology security.

Nominating/Governance Committee

The nominating, or governance, committee is also typically composed of independent members, in accordance with best practices. This committee appraises director and manager candidates and oversees the board election process. It sets nomination procedures and policies, including board directorship criteria, the search for and identification of qualified candidates for board directorships, and the election process by shareholders. In designing its policies and in nominating candidates to the board, the committee ensures that the structure of the board is balanced and in alignment with governance principles and applicable codes.

The committee also oversees the establishment and enforcement of corporate policies, including:

- a corporate governance code;
- the charter of the board and its committees;
- a code of ethics; and
- a policy on conflicts of interest, among others.

It reviews these policies periodically to incorporate any necessary changes or developments. Most importantly, it ensures implementation of governance policies, compliance with applicable laws and regulations, and the pursuit of appropriate action if any issues or violations are identified. For example, policies on conflicts of interest and related-party transactions require directors and managers to disclose any actual or potential conflict of interest related to the company, as well as any material interests in a transaction that may affect the company.

Compensation/Remuneration Committee

The compensation, or remuneration, committee develops and proposes remuneration policies for the directors and key executives, which often includes setting performance criteria and evaluating manager performance. Executive compensation attracts significant investor attention, with a focus on aligning manager and shareholder interests. The laws in most jurisdictions, as well as best practices, require all compensation committee members to be independent directors because management should not assess its own performance.

Compensation plans often include a variable component—typically profit sharing, stock, or stock options—contingent on corporate or stock price performance. However, stock-based remuneration does not serve its purpose if managers can improve their personal gains at the expense of the company while limiting their exposure to weak stock performance. As a result, companies are increasingly designing incentive plans that discourage "short-termism" or excessive risk-taking by managers. Some incentive plans include granting shares, rather than options, to managers and restricting their vesting or sale for several years or until retirement. A long-term incentive plan delays compensation, either in part or in total, until a company's strategic objectives (typically performance targets) are met.

As a result of laws such as the Dodd-Frank Act in the USA or by choice, issuers are increasingly seeking shareholder views on executive compensation by conducting non-binding "say on pay" votes at the AGM. By allowing shareholders to express their views on remuneration-related matters, companies can limit the discretion of directors in granting excessive or inadequate remuneration.

Additional Committees

Companies can have multiple other board committees, which are often industry specific. Risk committees—common (in some jurisdictions, required) in the financial services industry—determine the risk profile and appetite of the company and ensure that the company has an enterprise risk management system in place whereby risks are identified, assessed, mitigated, and managed appropriately. Accordingly, risk committees oversee the setting of the risk policy and risk management annual plans and monitor their implementation. Insurance companies often have investment committees that ensure the company has adopted and adheres to rational and prudent investment and capital management policies.

Employee Mechanisms

By managing employee relationships, companies seek to respect employees' rights and avoid legal or reputational risks associated with employment matters. Employee relationship management (sometimes called human capital management) helps firms attract and retain talent and ensure that employees fulfill their responsibilities and are motivated to act in the company's best interest.

Employee rights are primarily protected through jurisdiction-specific labor laws, which define the standards for employees' rights and responsibilities and cover such matters as work hours, post-employment, health care and other benefit coverage, and paid leave. In most countries, employees have the right to form unions. Unions advocate on behalf of members to influence certain matters affecting employees, such as compensation and working conditions. Although not a common practice in many parts of the world, in some countries employees are represented on the board of directors—or supervisory board—of companies meeting certain size or ownership criteria (e.g., in Germany, Austria, and Luxembourg).

At the individual level, employment contracts specify the various rights and responsibilities of the employer and employee. Some companies have an **employee stock ownership plan (ESOP)** to help retain employees and further align their interests with those of the company. As part of an ESOP, a company establishes a fund consisting of shares and/or cash, which are granted to employees based on service or performance criteria and often include vesting periods.

Customer and Supplier Mechanisms

Both customers and suppliers enter into contractual agreements with a company that specify the products and services underlying the relationship, the prices or fees and the payment terms, the rights and responsibilities of each party, the after-sale relationship, and any guarantees. Contracts also specify actions to be taken and recourse available if either party breaches the terms of the contract.

Customers, owners, and other stakeholders increasingly use social media to voice or protect their interests or to enhance their influence on corporate matters. For example, negative media attention can adversely affect the reputation or public perception of a company or its managers and directors. Through social media, these stakeholders can instantly broadcast information with little cost or effort and are thus better able to compete with company management in influencing public sentiment.

Government Mechanisms

Laws and Regulations

Governments and regulatory authorities develop laws that companies must follow and monitor companies' compliance with those laws. Such laws protect and enforce property and contract rights, in addition to protecting the rights of a specific group such as consumers or the environment. Industries whose services, products, or operations are more likely to affect the public or stakeholder interests are typically subject to greater regulation. Examples include financial services, health care, and agriculture and food, as well as industries deemed to be in the national interest (e.g., defense).

Corporate Governance Codes

Many regulatory authorities have adopted corporate governance codes that consist of guiding principles for publicly traded companies. These codes require companies to disclose their adoption of recommended corporate governance practices or explain why they have not done so, known as a "comply or explain" approach. In Japan, for example, companies with no outside directors must justify why appointing outside directors is not appropriate. Some jurisdictions do not have national corporate governance codes but do make use of national corporate laws or regulations (e.g., Chile) or stock exchange listing requirements (e.g., India) to achieve similar objectives.

The USA does not have a national corporate governance code or law but does have national securities laws (e.g., the Securities Act and the Sarbanes-Oxley Act) that are enforced by a national regulator (the Securities and Exchange Commission). US stock exchanges have listing requirements that include numerous governance provisions, such as the requirement for majority independent boards. Additionally, most US companies are incorporated in a single state, Delaware, which does have state corporate laws that, in effect, serve the same purpose as a national corporate governance code.

QUESTION SET

1. Which of the following is typically used to represent creditors' interests?

   A. Ad hoc committee

   B. Poison pill

   C. Tender offer

   Solution:

   A is correct. An ad hoc committee is a group of creditors who approach an issuer in financial distress with options for debt restructuring.

   B is incorrect. A poison pill is used to protect shareholders, management, and the board from takeovers that could potentially undervalue the company or are otherwise unwanted.

   C is incorrect. A tender offer involves an invitation to shareholders to sell their interests directly to a group seeking to gain control.

2. A primary responsibility of a board's audit committee does not include:

   A. oversight of accounting policies.

   B. adoption of proper corporate governance.

   C. recommending remuneration for the external auditor.

   Solution:

   B is correct. The adoption of proper corporate governance is the responsibility of a corporation's governance committee.

   A and C are incorrect, because oversight of accounting policies and recommending remuneration for the external auditor are responsibilities of the audit committee.

3. Which of the following is true of shareholder activism?

   A. Shareholder activists rarely include hedge funds.

   B. Regulators play a prominent role in shareholder activism.

   C. A primary goal of shareholder activism is to increase shareholder value.

   Solution:

   C is correct. Although shareholder activism may involve social and political issues, shareholder activists' primary motivation is to increase shareholder value.

   A is incorrect, because hedge funds commonly serve as shareholder activists.

   B is incorrect, because regulators play a prominent role in standard setting, not shareholder activism.

4. True or False: Investors receive information similar in content and form, including audited disclosures, from both private and public companies.

   A. True

B. False

Solution:

False. Private companies disclose information confidentially to their investors, but the content and form of that information are subject to negotiation rather than standardized and regulated like the reporting by public companies. Most jurisdictions do not require that private companies' disclosures be audited, though they are free to obtain an audit.

5. Explain why staggered board elections weaken corporate governance.

Solution:

Staggered board elections can dilute shareholder voting rights by preventing shareholders from replacing the entire board at any given election. For example, if only 25% of the board is elected per year, it can take an activist three years to replace a majority of the board.

6. A company's compensation committee seeking to discourage excessive risk-taking by managers is *most likely* to design an incentive compensation plan that:

   A. allows directors and managers to have greater discretion over their remuneration.

   B. includes a variable component comprising stock options contingent on near-term stock performance.

   C. grants shares, rather than options, that vest over several years and are subject to minimum holding requirements.

Solution:

C is correct. Granting shares, rather than options, that vest over several years and must be held discourages "short-termism" or excessive risk-taking by managers.

A is incorrect. By allowing *shareholders* to express their views on remuneration matters, companies can limit the discretion of directors and managers in granting themselves excessive (or inadequate) remuneration, thus not allowing managers to have greater discretion over their own pay.

B is incorrect, because a variable component comprising stock options contingent on near-term stock performance may encourage excessive risk-taking by managers. Stock-based remuneration does not serve its purpose if managers can improve their personal gains at the expense of the company while limiting their exposure to weak stock performance.

CORPORATE GOVERNANCE RISKS AND BENEFITS   4

☐ describe potential risks of poor corporate governance and stakeholder management and benefits of effective corporate governance and stakeholder management

Corporate governance and stakeholder management play a critical role in the success or failure of corporations. Weak corporate governance, unmanaged conflicts of interest, and/or inadequate stakeholder management mechanisms can place firms at a competitive disadvantage to industry peers. In contrast, strong governance practices and a proper balance among stakeholders' interests are often reflected in increased competitiveness and operational efficiency, better control processes, and improved performance. The role of corporate governance and related mechanisms in mitigating risk extends beyond operations to include legal, regulatory, reputational, and financial risks.

Operational Risks and Benefits

Corporations with weak control systems, ineffective decision-making, or inefficient monitoring often face adverse results with respect to their operations, performance, and value. In the absence of adequate controls, one stakeholder group may benefit at the expense of others. For example, when the information available to managers is superior to that received by the board or shareholders, audit procedures are poor, or oversight is lacking, managers can make decisions solely for their own benefit. The following example demonstrates the level of fraud and mismanagement that can occur when corporate governance is inadequate.

THE RISE AND FALL OF THERANOS INC.

Founded in 2003, Theranos raised over USD700 million from venture capital and private investors and was valued at USD10 billion in 2014. The company and its founder and CEO, Elizabeth Holmes, sought to revolutionize health care with breakthrough technology to inexpensively and rapidly identify numerous medical conditions using a test based on a single drop of blood. Its board featured a variety of famous and influential directors over its history, including former US Secretaries of State and directors of the US Centers for Disease Control and Prevention.

In 2015, questions began to surface publicly around the company's blood-testing technology. Whistleblowers came forward to voice concerns about questionable practices, and it became clear that the technology was flawed and that blood test results had been falsified. In 2018, the company, CEO Holmes, and COO Ramesh Balwani were charged with "massive fraud" by the US SEC and the company ceased operations, resulting in a total loss to its shareholders as well as losses to other stakeholders. Holmes was found guilty of four counts of fraud in 2022.

Subsequent investigations uncovered many corporate governance failures at Theranos related to inadequate board composition and oversight, including the following:

- While the board was composed of highly accomplished and well-known individuals, most had little to no knowledge of medical technology.

- Given its lack of medical technology expertise, the board should have hired an independent expert to validate Theranos's innovative technology, which it failed to do. An expert would also have informed the board of the lack of peer-reviewed publications by Theranos, which is highly irregular in the industry.

- The board failed to raise concerns about not only the conflict of interest regarding Holmes's romantic relationship with Balwani but also his leadership role despite a lack of relevant industry experience.

- The board dismissed fraud allegations raised by whistleblowers and remained silent even after the whistleblowers were fired soon after making their allegations.
- Finally, Theranos operated without filling key management roles such as CFO and global compliance officer, among others.

Strong governance practices involve proper scrutiny and control at all corporate levels. These mechanisms allow for the mitigation of risk factors such as fraud, or at least their identification and control at early stages. Controls are enhanced when overseen by an effective independent audit committee. By having procedures for monitoring compliance with internal and external policies and regulations and for reporting any violations, a firm can mitigate the risks of being exposed to regulator questioning or legal proceedings and their associated costs.

In addition, formal procedures for dealing with conflicts of interest and related-party transactions ensure fair dealing and avoid hidden costs associated with preferential or unfair treatment in favor of a related party.

Effective governance also clarifies the delegation of authority and the reporting lines across a company, ensuring that employees have a clear understanding of their respective responsibilities. In addition, the governance, risk, and compliance (GRC) functions in the organization work in partnership to align interests. These arrangements improve decision-making processes and provide managers with flexibility to respond to opportunities and challenges in a constantly changing environment.

Internal auditors and other internal control mechanisms like compliance and legal departments are an equally important pillar of organizational and governance structures, as they aim to ensure that decisions and activities are properly monitored and controlled to prevent risks and misconduct. These mechanisms improve the operational efficiency of the company. Similarly, when the board defines the risk profile of the firm, sets its strategic direction, and supervises its implementation, managerial decisions and firm operations are better aligned with shareholder interests, paving the way for better operational results.

Legal, Regulatory, and Reputational Risks and Benefits

Compliance weaknesses in the implementation of regulatory requirements or the lack of proper reporting practices may expose a company to legal, regulatory, or reputational risks. In such cases, the company may be investigated by government or regulatory authorities for violation of applicable laws. A company may also be vulnerable to lawsuits filed by shareholders, employees, creditors, or other parties for breach of contractual agreements or company bylaws or for violation of stakeholders' legal rights. Improperly managed conflicts of interest or governance failures can cause reputational harm to a company, and its associated costs can be significant. Such risks are particularly acute for publicly listed companies subject to scrutiny by investors, analysts, and other market participants, as in the following example.

VOLKSWAGEN AG AND DIESELGATE

In 2014, an independent study revealed that certain Volkswagen (VW) diesel automobiles had abnormally high emissions in excess of legal limits. VW insisted for a year that the excess emissions were due to technical conditions before admitting to the US Environmental Protection Agency (EPA) in 2015 that it had deliberately manipulated emission test results using illegal software. The emissions software was installed in as many as 11 million Volkswagen and Audi vehicles worldwide, 500,000 of which were sold in the USA. Legal action was taken by governments in the USA, the EU, and elsewhere.

Whether company executives were aware of the illegal software remains unanswered. However, Volkswagen's reputation was severely damaged amid concerns about board independence, proper governance and oversight of the employees who installed the software, and the blatant violation of air quality standards in the communities where the cars were sold. While legal action continues against the company, its management, and certain employees, the impact of the scandal includes the following:

- VW's share price immediately fell by over a third in the days following the announcement of the scandal.
- VW CEO Martin Winterkorn resigned in 2015 and was criminally indicted in the USA and Germany on fraud and conspiracy charges.
- Volkswagen AG has incurred over EUR32 billion (USD37.7 billion) in vehicle recalls, fines, and legal costs.
- Ongoing shareholder lawsuits seek settlements against management and board directors totaling several billion euros in additional damages.

This example illustrates the importance of a company's reputation being based on strong governance and the ability to protect the interests of stakeholders, including customers, government authorities, and ultimately, in Volkswagen's case, shareholders. Employees, creditors, customers, and suppliers often seek to build and maintain long-term relationships with companies that have a reputation for respecting constituent and stakeholder rights. Such a reputation can enhance a company's ability to attract talent, secure capital, improve sales, and reach better terms with suppliers. In addition, ethics education and training for key stakeholders help support strong governance practices. Effective governance enables a company to mitigate risks, underlying conflicts of interest, and agency problems and to maintain stable operations.

Financial Risks and Benefits

Poor corporate governance, including weak management of creditors' interests, can affect a company's financial position and hinder its ability to honor its debt obligations. A rise in the possibility of corporate default has consequences well beyond creditors and shareholders, extending to managers, employees, and suppliers, and even society and the environment.

Governance arrangements that seek to manage creditor conflicts of interest restrict those corporate actions that would hinder the company's ability to repay its debt and thus reduce its default risk. Default risks are also mitigated by the proper functioning of audit systems, the transparency and better reporting of earnings, and the control of information asymmetries between the company and its capital providers. Lower default risks are associated with a lower cost of debt, as creditors typically require a lower return when their funds are better secured and their rights are protected.

Governance practices at shareholder meetings, as well as internal corporate mechanisms such as the board of directors and its committees, give investors greater assurance that their capital is well managed. These mechanisms help assure investors that their rights to participate in discussions, vote on important matters, and enjoy fair and equal treatment are protected. Investor confidence and the company's credibility in the marketplace are also enhanced by the appropriate and timely disclosure of material information concerning operating, financial, and governance activities. The improved transparency, the integrity of financial reporting processes, and an independent audit promote the trust of shareholders and market participants in both the quality of the firm's reported earnings and the fair representation of its financial position. These controls reduce investors' risk perception of well-governed firms and, therefore, the return required on capital invested in such firms. Consequently, good governance enhances the attractiveness of firms to investors, improves their valuations and stock performance, and reduces their cost of equity.[1] Studies have shown the following:

- Improved corporate governance practices increase the likelihood of a credit rating upgrade from speculative to investment grade, reducing the cost of debt.[2]

- Listed companies with experienced audit committees possessing financial expertise tend to have stronger market performance during a crisis.[3]

- Board diversity and independence appear to be key factors in firm valuation.[4]

Key questions analysts should consider about a company's corporate governance and stakeholder management include the following:

- What is the company's ownership and voting structure?

- Do board members' skills and experience match the current and future needs of the company?

- How closely does the management team's compensation and incentive structure align with factors expected to drive overall company results?

- Who are the significant investors in the company?

- How strong are company shareholder rights versus its peers?

- How effective is the company in managing long-term risks and sustainability?

An analysis of these areas and questions—for which a company's proxy statements, annual reports, and sustainability reports are a good starting point—can provide important insights about the quality of management and sources of potential risk.

QUESTION SET

---

1. Which of the following is *not* a benefit of an effective corporate governance structure?

    A. Operating performance can be improved.

    B. A corporation's cost of debt can be reduced.

    C. Corporate decisions and activities require less control.

    Solution:

    C is correct. A benefit of an effective corporate governance structure is to enable adequate scrutiny and control over operations.

---

1 Paul A. Gompers, Joy L. Ishii, and Andrew Metrick, "Corporate Governance and Equity Prices," *Quarterly Journal of Economics* 118, no. 1 (February 2003): 107–55; available at SSRN: https://ssrn.com/abstract=278920 or http://dx.doi.org/10.2139/ssrn.278920.

2 Sanjeev Bhojraj and Partha Sengupta, "Effect of Corporate Governance on Bond Ratings and Yields: The Role of Institutional Investors and Outside Directors," *Journal of Business* 76, no. 3 (2003): 455–75; available at JSTOR: https://doi.org/10.1086/344114 (accessed 28 May 2022).

3 H. Aldamen, K. Duncan, S. Kelly, R. McNamara, and S. Nagel, "Audit Committee Characteristics and Firm Performance during the Global Financial Crisis," *Accounting & Finance* 52, no. 4 (December 2012): 971–1000.

4 D. A. Carter, B. J. Simkins, and W. G. Simpson, "Corporate Governance, Board Diversity, and Firm Value," *Financial Review* 38, no. 1 (February 2003): 33–53; available at https://doi.org/10.1111/1540-6288.00034.

A is incorrect, because improved operating efficiency may indeed be a benefit of an effective corporate governance structure.

B is incorrect, because an effective governance structure can reduce investors' perceived credit risk of a corporation, thus potentially lowering the corporation's cost of debt.

2. An investment analyst would likely be *most* concerned about an executive compensation plan that:

   A. varies each year.

   B. is consistent with the compensation plans of a company's competitors.

   C. is cash-based only, without an equity component.

   Solution:

   C is correct. If an executive remuneration plan offers cash only, the interests of management and investors (and other stakeholders) may be misaligned. An equity-based compensation plan is commonly used to align management interests with those of shareholders.

   A is incorrect, because a plan that varies over time would typically be of less concern to an analyst compared with one that did not change.

   B is incorrect, because an analyst would likely be concerned if a company's executives were under- or overcompensated relative to competitors.

3. Benefits of effective corporate governance include all of the following *except*:

   A. avoidance of fraud.

   B. higher investor confidence.

   C. reduced cost of equity.

   Solution:

   A is correct. Effective corporate governance allows for the mitigation, not the avoidance, of risk factors such as fraud, or at least their identification and control at early stages.

   B and C are incorrect, as these are both benefits of effective corporate governance.

4. Your colleague suggests that governance and controls are bureaucratic and slow down decision-making and value creation at companies. Discuss.

   Solution:

   Strong governance practices and a proper balance among stakeholders' interests are often reflected in increased competitiveness and operational efficiency, better control processes, and improved performance. Studies have shown that listed companies with experienced audit committees possessing financial expertise tend to have stronger market performance during a crisis, and board independence and diversity appear to be key factors in firm valuation—particularly for initial public offerings—and play an important role in value creation and value protection for firms.

   However, governance and controls can be ineffective and slow down decision-making when the board is too big, there are too many managerial layers, managers lack relevant experience for their role, or the controls consist of a check-the-box approach that fails to produce relevant and actionable information.

5. True or False: So long as employees are not represented by labor unions or collective bargaining agreements, management and the board can ignore employee relations.

   A. True

   B. False

   Solution:

   False. For many companies, employees (human capital) are a crucial input to success and the largest category of cost. Employee relations are important whether or not employees are represented by labor unions or collective bargaining agreements, as the quality of their work directly affects customer experience and product or service quality. Employee attrition, productivity losses, the need for repeat training, and poor practices discussed in the press or social media are costly and could result in regulatory action. Companies that build and maintain positive, long-term relationships with employees can develop a competitive advantage.

PRACTICE PROBLEMS

The following information relates to questions 1–5

Kobe Steel Ltd. is a major Japanese steel manufacturer formed in 1905 that supplies global manufacturers of cars, planes, and trains. The company issued a report in March 2018 apologizing for falsifying data on the strength and durability of its aluminum, copper, steel products, and iron ore powder. Following the scandal, its stock sank to a five-year low and its cost of debt jumped to record levels.

An Independent Investigation Committee (IIC) investigated the misconduct and authored the report, which concluded that the misconduct resulted from (1) a management style that overemphasized profitability amid inadequate corporate governance, (2) the imbalanced operation of plants that resulted in reduced awareness of quality compliance among employees, and (3) insufficient quality control procedures that allowed the misconduct to take place. The report also emphasized that the company had "a culture that prioritized winning purchase orders and meeting delivery deadlines over ensuring quality."

The company committed to implementing various measures to prevent a recurrence of the misconduct. Regarding governance, measures included the following:

- Appointing an independent chairman of the board of directors
- Having at least one-third of the board of directors be independent
- Creating a nominating and compensation committee, consisting of a majority of independent directors, to serve as a voluntary advisory body to the board of directors
- Creating an independent quality supervision committee consisting of external experts
- Creating an audit and supervisory committee consisting of five members: two internal directors and three independent directors with backgrounds in legal, financial, and industrial fields

1. Identify three key stakeholder relationships for Kobe Steel and discuss their role in the misconduct or how they were affected.

2. Discuss the stakeholder incentives and the conflicts that arose between Kobe's management and the company's customers.

3. Which of the following is considered a best practice that would strengthen the measures discussed to prevent a recurrence of the misconduct?

   A. A shareholder rights plan

   B. A stock-based compensation plan

   C. An audit committee composed solely of independent board members

4. Discuss the financial risk implications of the post-scandal stock and bond prices

with regard to investor confidence.

5. Kobe Steel's governance failures *most likely* resulted in reduced:

   A. cost of debt.

   B. agency costs.

   C. growth opportunities.

SOLUTIONS

1.

Stakeholder 1	Stakeholder 2	Relationship Type	Role or Impact
Kobe Corporation	Customers (manufacturers of cars, planes, and trains)	Contractual	The company delivered an inferior-quality product that could have resulted in harm to the public.
Board of Directors	Kobe Corporation	Agent	The board failed to monitor the activities of the corporation, resulting in reputational damage, civil complaints, and legal action.
Managers	Employees	Contractual	The culture prioritized winning purchase orders and meeting delivery deadlines over ensuring quality.

2. The company supplied potentially faulty steel and other material inputs to manufacturers of cars, planes, and trains. The customers were incentivized by the advertised quality of the products, while management was incentivized by winning purchase orders and meeting delivery deadlines. A certain quality standard should have aligned interests, but instead the potential for profits created a conflict between the directors and customers.

3. C is correct. The company formed an audit and supervisory committee that included a majority of independent directors, but best practices would recommend an audit committee composed solely of independent members, with at least one director with accounting or related financial management experience.

   A is incorrect. A shareholder rights plan, also known as a poison pill, is used to defend against unwanted takeovers that could potentially undervalue the company, but it does not defend the company or shareholders against management or employee misconduct.

   B is incorrect. A stock-based compensation plan is used to align the interests of management with those of shareholders, though it might further incentivize risk-taking and misconduct, which is the issue in this case.

4. The stock price fell and the cost of debt increased, indicating that investor and creditor confidence in the company declined. Investors will have to assess how much the company's financial results benefited from the past misconduct and estimate the impact from (1) the company no longer falsifying data and (2) the loss of customer confidence even if the company fixes the issues. Strengthening governance to include best practices is a first step toward restoring investor confidence, but the impact on future sales and profitability is key to the stock price and cost of debt going forward.

5. C is correct. The misconduct likely caused reputational damage to Kobe among current and prospective customers, which reduces growth opportunities.

    A is incorrect, because bond yields jumped to record levels soon after the scandal was announced, suggesting a higher perceived default risk. Higher default risks are associated with a higher cost of debt, as creditors typically require a higher return when their funds are less secured and their rights less protected.

    B is incorrect, because Kobe is incurring higher agency costs in the wake of the governance failure by hiring an independent investigative committee, independent directors, and external quality assurance experts.

Working Capital and Liquidity

INTRODUCTION

1

Earlier lessons introduced the balance sheet of corporate issuers, composed of assets financed by liabilities (including debt) and equity. This learning module covers the analysis of *short-term* assets and liabilities, those that result in cash inflows or outflows within a year. The behavior of these assets and liabilities is primarily determined by an issuer's payment and delivery terms with its customers and suppliers. Subsequent modules cover issuers' *long-term* assets, liabilities, and equity financing. Short-term assets and liabilities are a key determinant of an issuer's ability to generate cash flows for investors, and mismatches between the timing and liquidity of assets and liabilities can have catastrophic effects on a firm. For these reasons and others, analysts closely scrutinize issuers' cash conversion and liquidity.

LEARNING MODULE OVERVIEW

- Issuers invest cash to generate revenues and profits. The cash conversion cycle is the length of time from paying suppliers to collecting cash from customers.

- The cash conversion cycle is measured as the sum of days of inventory on hand and days sales outstanding, less days payable outstanding. A short cash conversion cycle means that an issuer converts an investment in inventory into cash quickly, while a long cash conversion cycle means that an issuer converts its inventory investments into cash slowly.

- Collecting cash from customers sooner, delaying payments to suppliers, and reducing inventory levels relative to sales improve an issuer's cash conversion cycle.

- Working capital is defined as an issuer's short-term assets minus its short-term liabilities. Net working capital adjusts for non-operating accounts such as cash, marketable securities, and short-term debt. The ratio of net working capital to sales is closely related to an issuer's cash conversion cycle a long cash conversion cycle is associated with higher net working capital to sales, while a short cash conversion cycle is associated with lower net working capital to sales.

- An issuer's liquidity is primarily determined by the relative amounts and liquidity of its short-term assets and liabilities, which are determined by the issuer's business model. The long-run primary source of liquidity for most issuers is cash flow from operations. Secondary sources of liquidity are typically used in crises and impose significant costs, such as issuing equity, renegotiating contracts, selling assets, and filing for bankruptcy protection.

- Drags and pulls on liquidity affect an issuer's liquidity situation. Drags on liquidity reduce cash inflows and include such issues as uncollectible receivables and obsolete inventory. Pulls on liquidity are accelerations in cash outflows or interruptions in credit.

- Issuers may adopt a conservative, moderate, or aggressive approach to working capital management, and these approaches differ in the amount of working capital held on the balance sheet as well as in their reliance on external financing and the composition of short- and long-term financing.

LEARNING MODULE SELF-ASSESSMENT

These initial questions are intended to help you gauge your current level of understanding of this learning module.

1. Which of the following actions or events will most likely decrease an issuer's cash conversion cycle?

   A. Buying short-term marketable securities using cash on hand

   B. Offering customers a discount for payment received within 10 days

   C. Slowing of sales of certain goods due to changing preferences in styles

   Solution:

   B is correct. A prompt-payment discount would likely reduce days sales outstanding and, in turn, decrease the issuer's cash conversion cycle.
   A is incorrect, because increasing marketable securities by reducing cash does not affect the issuer's cash conversion cycle.
   C is incorrect, because the slowing of sales of certain goods would likely increase days of inventory on hand and, in turn, increase the issuer's cash conversion cycle.

2. Which of the following actions will most likely increase an issuer's liquidity?

   A. Forgoing a supplier's discount for prompt payments

   B. Relaxing terms for customers by lengthening the payment period

C. Purchasing short-term marketable securities with cash on hand
Solution:

A is correct. Forgoing the discount is using the supplier's financing and will result in the issuer stretching out payments on accounts payable, putting less drain on liquidity in the short run. This action increases the issuer's cash conversion cycle.

B is incorrect, because by relaxing credit terms, customers will take longer to pay, so this action increases the cash conversion cycle.

C is incorrect, because marketable securities are generally *less* liquid than cash, so this action would reduce liquidity. Even if the marketable securities are as liquid as cash (e.g., short-term Treasuries), this action would not materially affect liquidity.

3. The Plough Corporation reports the following items on its two most recent balance sheets (in millions)

	Fiscal Year-End	
	31 December 20X2	31 December 20X1
Cash	10	15
Short-term marketable securities	20	15
Accounts receivable	100	80
Inventory	200	150
Prepaid expenses	5	5
Accounts payable	100	120
Accrued expenses	50	60

Based on the cash ratio, the company has:

A. become less liquid.

B. become more liquid.

C. not changed regarding liquidity.
Solution:

B is correct. The cash ratios for the two fiscal year-ends are:

$$\text{Cash ratio, } 20X1 = \frac{15 + 15}{120 + 60} = \frac{30}{180} = 0.1667$$

$$\text{Cash ratio, } 20X2 = \frac{10 + 20}{100 + 50} = \frac{30}{150} = 0.20$$

The cash ratio has increased from 0.1667 to 0.20, indicating an increase in liquidity.

4. Which of the following events or activities is most likely to be a drag on liquidity?

A. Inventory that becomes obsolete

B. Making payments to suppliers earlier

C. Offering a discount to customers who pay within 10 days
Solution:

A is correct. As inventory becomes obsolete, it becomes more challenging to sell and inventory levels increase. This event is a drag on liquidity, because it slows cash flows.
B is incorrect, because making payments to suppliers earlier is a pull on liquidity.
C is incorrect, because offering a prompt-payment discount is likely to result in cash receipts sooner, which would improve liquidity.

5. Which of the following actions provides a secondary source of liquidity?

   A. Issuance of equity securities

   B. Collecting accounts receivable

   C. Taking advantage of a supplier's financing and paying on the net day, day 40

Solution:

A is correct. Primary sources of liquidity include cash on hand, borrowings, and cash flow from operations. Secondary sources of liquidity generate cash at a greater cost when primary sources are insufficient, such as issuing equity.
B is incorrect, because collection of accounts receivable is a primary source of liquidity.
C is incorrect, because supplier financing is a primary source of liquidity.

6. Classify each of the following actions as either a conservative or an aggressive approach to working capital management:

	Conservative	Aggressive
Minimize inventory levels		
Greater reliance on long-term debt and equity financing		
Lower level of short-term assets		
Greater reliance on short-term debt		

Solution:

	Conservative	Aggressive
Minimize inventory levels		✓
Greater reliance on long-term debt and equity financing	✓	
Lower level of short-term assets		✓
Greater reliance on short-term debt		✓

CASH CONVERSION CYCLE

2

☐ explain the cash conversion cycle and compare issuers' cash conversion cycles

A company's business operations are usually composed of several sequential steps. For a company that makes and sells physical goods, its operations include acquiring materials, producing inventory, selling products to customers, and collecting cash. These activities are known as the issuer's **operating cycle** and occur once or many times over a year, as illustrated in Exhibit 1.

Exhibit 1: Operating Cycle

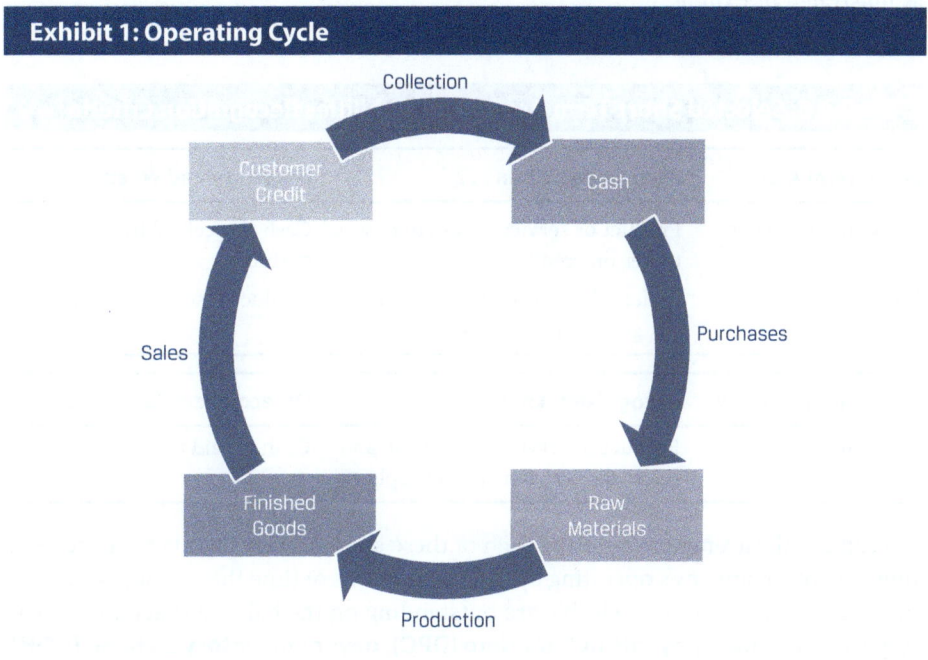

These activities result in cash outflows and inflows that usually do *not* occur at the same time as the activity. For example, materials are purchased and received by a firm but may not be paid for in cash until weeks or months later. Goods are sold to customers, but cash may not be received until weeks or months later. Finally, inventory may take time to produce or be ready for sale, such as in the spirits industry, where an aged product like whiskey can take years before it is ready to be sold to customers.

Future cash inflows within the operating cycle are recorded as short-term assets on issuers' balance sheets, while future cash outflows within the operating cycle are recorded as short-term liabilities. Issuers' financial statements often use the terms and associated definitions in Exhibit 2 for different types of future cash inflows and outflows.

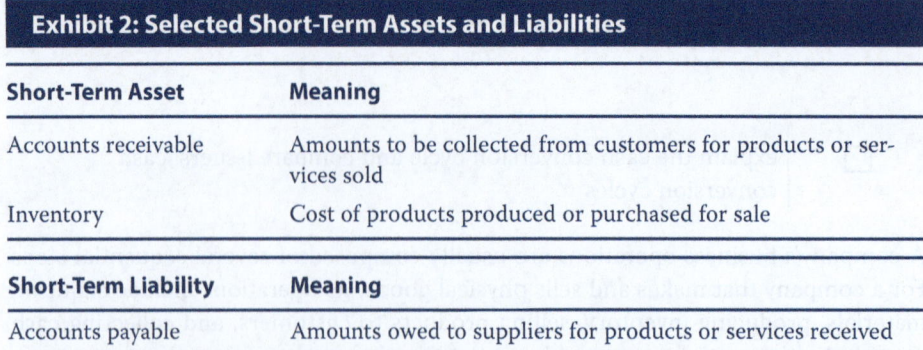

These short-term assets and liabilities are recognized based on the performance or occurrence of an activity and are derecognized when the cash inflow or outflow occurs, as illustrated in Exhibit 3.

Exhibit 3: Selected Short-Term Assets and Liabilities Recognition Criteria

Short-Term Asset	Recognized When . . .	Derecognized When . . .
Accounts receivable	Product or service is sold to customer on credit	Cash is received from customer
Inventory	Issuer takes ownership of materials, goods, supplies, etc.	Product is sold to customer

Short-Term Liability	Recognized When . . .	Derecognized When . . .
Accounts payable	Product or service is received, and issuer defers payment to supplier	Cash is paid to supplier

We can use the average duration of each of these short-term accounts to construct a timeline for a company's operating cycle. The amounts of time that accounts payable, inventory, and accounts receivable are outstanding on the balance sheet are known, respectively, as **days payable outstanding (DPO)**, **days of inventory on hand (DOH)**, and **days sales outstanding (DSO)**. The calculations of these amounts, known as **activity ratios**, will be discussed in detail later in the curriculum. An important quantity from this timeline for analysts is the **cash conversion cycle**: the amount of time between an issuer's paying its suppliers and receiving cash from customers (i.e., the time between derecognition of accounts payable and derecognition of accounts receivable). Formally, the cash conversion cycle, in days, is expressed in Equation 1 as:

Cash conversion cycle

= Days of inventory on hand + Days sales outstanding − Days payable outstanding

(1)

Exhibit 4 depicts the cash conversion cycle on a timeline within the broader operating cycle.

Exhibit 4: The Cash Conversion Cycle

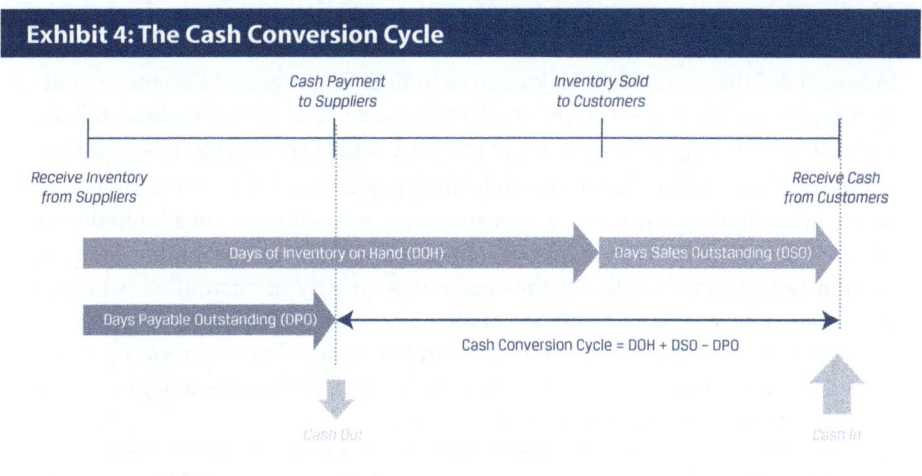

The cash conversion cycle is the number of days it takes a company to convert an inventory investment into cash receipts from customers. Therefore, the longer the cash conversion cycle, the longer a company needs financing to pay its bills, such as payroll, because it has not yet received cash from customers. In 2020, the average US-listed company had a cash conversion cycle of 78 days, though there was considerable variance by industry, as shown in Exhibit 5. Pharmaceutical manufacturers tend to have relatively long cash conversion cycles because they keep a considerable inventory of pharmaceuticals on hand. Airlines—a service business with minimal inventories of goods and mostly prepaid sales to customers in cash or credit cards—tend to have short cash conversion cycles.

Exhibit 5: 2020 S&P 1500 Industry Average Cash Conversion Cycles

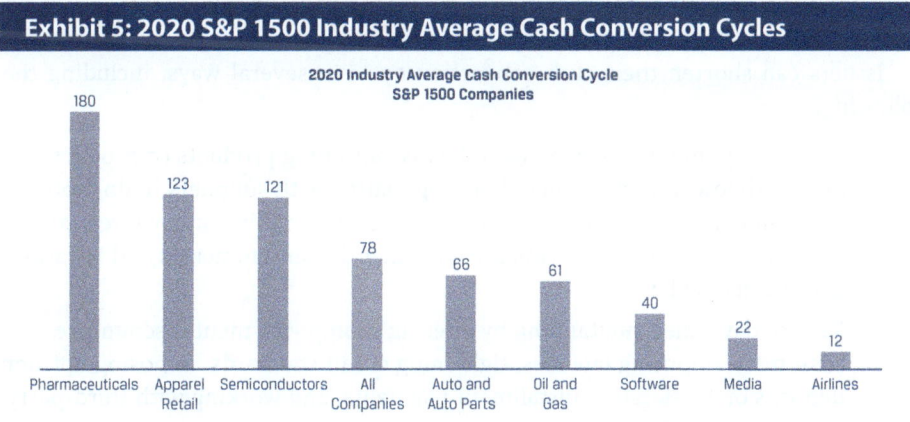

Source: JPMorgan Working Capital Index 2021. Authors' analysis.

The ideal scenario is a short or even negative cash conversion cycle, which means that cash invested in inventory is quickly returned for subsequent investment. A negative cash conversion cycle can result from receiving cash from customers before—in some cases, *well* before—suppliers are paid. This scenario results in cash that can be used elsewhere, reducing the need for alternative financing to fund operations.

INDITEX'S NEGATIVE CASH CONVERSION CYCLE

Industria de Diseño Textil, S.A., known as Inditex, is an apparel designer, manufacturer, and retailer listed on the stock exchanges of Madrid, Barcelona, Bilbao, and Valencia. Its largest brand concept is ZARA, which specializes in fast fashion.

Inditex has a unique business model in apparel, in which it leverages its vertically integrated supply chain to design, make, and sell numerous limited runs of inventories, enabling it to keep up with and influence customers' changing fashion tastes. Inditex sells off-the-rack items directly to customers (who pay with cash or credit cards), eschews stocking inventory to mitigate fashion risk, and sources raw materials from a vast number of suppliers over whom it has considerable leverage on payment terms. As a result, Inditex has a negative cash conversion cycle, as shown in the table below.

(in millions of EUR)	2021	2020
Accounts receivable	842	715
Inventories	3,042	2,321
Accounts payable	6,199	4,659
Sales	27,716	20,402
Cost of goods sold	11,902	9,013
Days sales outstanding	11	13
Days of inventory on hand	93	94
Days payable outstanding	190	189
Cash conversion cycle	−86	−82

Issuers can shorten their cash conversion cycle in several ways, including the following:

- Reduce days of inventory on hand by discontinuing products or product lines with low or niche demand, by negotiating with suppliers to do more frequent deliveries in order to establish "just in time" inventory levels, and by using data analytics to improve customer demand forecasts and to rationalize stocking levels.

- Reduce days sales outstanding by offering prompt-payment discounts to customers, imposing late fees, tightening credit standards, imposing upfront deposits or accelerating installment payments, and working with third-party collection agencies.

- Increase days payable outstanding by negotiating supplier contracts for longer terms. This approach may be feasible by establishing preferred suppliers—purchasing more in volume in exchange for better terms. However, it may result in suppliers charging higher prices or asking for deposits. The ability to lengthen days payable outstanding is highly dependent on the power dynamics between the company and its suppliers. If a company can purchase a critical component from only one supplier who sells to many others, it may not have the ability to negotiate better terms.

While extending days payable outstanding can improve the cash conversion cycle, suppliers typically offer discounts for prompt payment, such as requiring payment in 30 days but offering a 2% discount if payment is received within 10 days. If a company forgoes this discount in favor of paying in 30 days, it is implicitly borrowing from the supplier for 30 − 10 = 20 days at the cost of the forgone discount. One strategy is to borrow from a third party (e.g., a bank) at a relatively low interest rate, pay the supplier early to receive the prompt-payment discount, and later repay the bank. Such a strategy avoids the high cost of supplier financing but preserves cash, as shown in the following example.

EXAMPLE 1

Keown Corporation—Internal versus External Financing

Keown Corporation is an established manufacturer of custom paddleboards operating in the North American market. Keown operates its own manufacturing plant in Canada and sells its paddleboards exclusively through its website to avoid the cost of retail locations.

Most of Keown's sales take place during the North American summer season from May to August. Keown's customers expect orders to be filled immediately, so it must maintain substantial inventory to start the summer season or risk losing sales to competitors. Given the seasonality of the business, Keown is particularly focused on meeting customers' needs.

Since Keown lacks the necessary cash to pay its suppliers within 10 days, the CFO must decide whether to borrow from its bank at an effective annual rate (EAR) of 7.7% to take the prompt-payment discount offered by its supplier of materials or pay in 30 days. The terms from the supplier are 2/10, net 30.

1. Should Keown use the bank loan and pay the supplier within 10 days to receive the 2% discount, or simply forgo the discount and pay the supplier in 30 days?

Solution:

To compare the relative cost of the bank loan with that of the trade credit, we can calculate the effective annual rate on the trade credit. Essentially, we are calculating the interest rate on a loan for which the interest cost is the forgone discount and the term is the additional time Keown gets to pay; in this case, 30 − 10 = 20 days.

$$\text{EAR of Supplier Financing} = \left(\left(1 + \frac{\text{Discount \%}}{100\% - \text{Discount \%}}\right)^{\frac{\text{Days in Year}}{\text{Payment Period} - \text{Discount Period}}} \right) - 1$$

$$\text{Effective Annual Rate of Supplier Financing} = \left(\left(1 + \frac{2\%}{100\% - 2\%}\right)^{\frac{365}{30-10}} \right) - 1$$

$$\text{Effective Annual Rate of Supplier Financing} = 0.446 \text{ or } 44.6\%$$

Since the effective annual rate of 44.6% on the supplier financing is significantly higher than the 7.7% interest rate on the bank loan, Keown should borrow from its bank. That way, it will still be able to preserve cash but will pay a far lower interest rate on the financing.

A long cash conversion cycle may reflect industry or business model characteristics, but a longer cycle relative to competitors and a lengthening over time are of particular concern for analysts. A longer cycle may signal worsening customer demand, deteriorating customer financial health or credit quality, or the loss of bargaining power with suppliers.

EXAMPLE 2

Cash Conversion for US Discount Retailers

Consider the following activity ratios for large US discount retailers Walmart Inc., Target Corporation, Costco Wholesale Corporation, The TJX Companies, and Ross Stores for the 2021 calendar year, as shown below.

	Walmart	Target	Costco	TJX	Ross
Days sales outstanding	5	2	3	7	2
Days of inventory on hand	48	68	29	63	61
Days payable outstanding	47	75	34	47	63

1. Which company has the shortest cash conversion cycle? The longest?

   Solution:

   Cash conversion cycle = DSO + DOH − DPO

   Cash conversion cycle for Walmart = 5 days + 48 days − 47 days = 6 days

   Cash conversion cycle for Target = 2 days + 68 days −75 days = −5 days

   Cash conversion cycle for Costco = 3 days + 29 days − 34 days = −2 days

   Cash conversion cycle for TJX = 7 days + 63 days − 47 days = 23 days

   Cash conversion cycle for Ross = 2 days + 61 days − 63 days = 0 days

   Target has the shortest cash conversion cycle of the five companies.

2. These companies accept payment from customers at the point of sale in either cash or a debit or credit card. Does this fact align with the activity ratios presented?

   Solution:

   Yes, because days sales outstanding is small. Debit and credit card payments typically settle in a couple of days, and cash sales are settled immediately.

3. In examining annual reports, you find that approximately 54% of Costco's sales are food or food-related items, a larger percentage than that of the other companies, which sell a greater percentage of apparel and non-food items. Does this fact align with the activity ratios presented?

   Solution:

   Yes. Companies like Costco that sell perishable goods tend to have a lower number of days of inventory on hand, because inventory must be sold soon after receiving it from suppliers or else it spoils.

In addition to the cash conversion cycle, another measure analysts use to assess the efficiency of business operations is the amount of **working capital** used by the firm, particularly its quantity relative to sales so that it can be compared across time and firms. There are several definitions of working capital in practice. We distinguish between **total working capital**, formally defined in Equation 2 as a broad measure, and **net working capital**, defined in Equation 3 as a measure that excludes items that are less related to the cash conversion cycle or business operations, such as cash, marketable securities, and short-term debt.

Current assets
Minus: Current liabilities
Total Working Capital

(2)

Current assets, excluding cash and marketable securities
Minus: Current liabilities, excluding short-term and current debt
Net Working Capital

(3)

To control for size and for comparability across firms, total or net working capital is often expressed as a percentage of annual sales.

Consider the information on Licht Vernieuwend N.V. for the fiscal year ending 31 December 20X2, as shown in Exhibit 6. The total working capital is the difference between the current assets of EUR335 million and the current liabilities of EUR220 million, or EUR115 million. The net working capital excludes cash, marketable securities, and short-term bank loans from the calculation, giving a net working capital of EUR225 million – EUR160 million = EUR65 million.

Exhibit 6: Total and Net Working Capital Extracted from the Licht Vernieuwend N.V. Balance Sheet for the Year Ending 31 December 20X2		
	(in millions of EUR)	
Cash	40	
Marketable securities	70	
Accounts receivable	85	85
Inventory	130	130
Prepaid accounts	10	10
Total	335	225
Accounts payable	130	130
Accrued expenses	30	30
Short-term bank loan	60	
Total	220	160
Total working capital	115	
Net working capital		65

The cash conversion cycle and the ratio of working capital to sales are interrelated. Since receivables and inventories are often large components of short-term assets and payables are a large component of short-term liabilities, a short cash conversion cycle is associated with a low ratio of working capital to sales and vice versa.

INDITEX'S NEGATIVE CASH CONVERSION CYCLE AND WORKING CAPITAL

Continuing the earlier example, owing to Inditex's business model—which includes prompt payment from customers for off-the-rack apparel, limited runs of inventories with fast turnover, and a vast number of suppliers over which it has leverage—Inditex has not only a negative cash conversion cycle but also negative net working capital and negative ratios of net working capital to sales, as shown in the table below.

(in millions of EUR)	2021	2020
Accounts receivable	842	715
Inventories	3,042	2,321
Accounts payable	6,199	4,659
Net working capital	−2,315	−1,623
As a % of sales	−8.4%	−8.0%
Sales	27,716	20,402
Cost of goods sold	11,902	9,013
Days sales outstanding	11	13
Days of inventory on hand	93	94
Days payable outstanding	190	189
Cash conversion cycle	−86	−82

A high ratio of working capital to sales may be a result of industry characteristics, such as in the spirits industry, where inventory must age for several years before being sold to customers, or in the pharmaceutical industry, where companies hold a large amount of inventory, sometimes to comply with regulations. Besides cases of necessity, as illustrated in Example 1, or cases of compliance with regulations, issuers are generally better off holding less working capital and either using capital elsewhere on higher-return projects or returning capital to investors.

QUESTION SET

1. Classify each of the following actions by an issuer based on the likely effect on its cash conversion cycle:

	Effect on the Cash Conversion Cycle	
Action	Shorten	Lengthen
Offering larger discounts to its customers for payments received before the due date		
Paying suppliers sooner		
Lowering reliance on just-in-time inventory methods while increasing safety stocks of inventory		
Negotiating longer payment periods with its suppliers		
Tightening credit standards for its customers		

Solution:

	Effect on the Cash Conversion Cycle	
Action	Shorten	Lengthen
Offering larger discounts to its customers for payments received before the due date	✓	
Paying suppliers sooner		✓

	Effect on the Cash Conversion Cycle	
Action	**Shorten**	**Lengthen**
Lowering reliance on just-in-time inventory methods while increasing safety stocks of inventory		✓
Negotiating longer payment periods with its suppliers	✓	
Tightening credit standards for its customers	✓	

2. Identify the issuer with the longest cash conversion cycle and explain the effects of that length on that issuer relative to the other issuers.

	Issuer A	Issuer B	Issuer C
Days of inventory on hand	20	35	15
Days payable outstanding	15	10	5
Days sales outstanding	30	25	30

Solution:

Using:

$$\text{Cash conversion cycle} = \text{Days of inventory on hand} + \text{Days sales outstanding} - \text{Days payable outstanding}$$

	Issuer A	Issuer B	Issuer C
Days of inventory on hand	20	35	15
Plus: Days sales outstanding	30	25	30
Minus: Days payable outstanding	15	10	5
Cash conversion cycle	35	50	40

Issuer B has the longest cash conversion cycle, 50 days. By having the longest cycle, Issuer B is more reliant on alternative financing to support its operations relative to the other issuers.

3. Assuming no change in days sales outstanding and days of inventory on hand, an issuer in need of cash flow that forgoes the discount offered by its vendor for payments within 10 days and chooses to pay on the due date in 30 days is:

    A. shortening its cash conversion cycle.

    B. lengthening its cash conversion cycle.

    C. not affecting its cash conversion cycle.

    Solution:

    B is correct. The issuer that uses the vendor financing by delaying payments is increasing its days payable outstanding and thus lengthening its cash conversion cycle. The issuer is reducing its need for liquidity by taking advantage of the vendor financing at the cost of the forgone discount.

4. An issuer with limited cash flow is deciding which of its suppliers' credit terms are least costly. Which of the following credit terms offered to the issuer by its suppliers have the *lowest* effective interest rate?

  A. 1/10, net 50

  B. 2/15, net 40

  C. 3/15, net 60

Solution:

A is correct. The implicit financing cost that the issuer faces when forgoing a discount that the supplier or vendor offers is based on the amount of the forgone discount and length of the payment period beyond the discount period; 1/10, net 50 would permit the issuer to borrow for 50 − 10 = 40 days at a cost of only 1% of the purchase price (the forgone discount). The calculations for the cost of financing for each set of credit terms, expressed as an effective annual rate, are as follows:

$$\text{EAR of Supplier Financing} = \left(\left(1 + \frac{\text{Discount }\%}{100\% - \text{Discount }\%}\right)^{\frac{\text{Days in Year}}{\text{Payment Period}-\text{Discount Period}}} \right) - 1$$

$$\text{EAR of 1/10, net 50} = \left(\left(1 + \frac{1\%}{100\% - 1\%}\right)^{\frac{365}{50-10}} \right) - 1$$

$$\text{EAR of 1/10, net 50} = 0.096 \text{ or } 9.6\%$$

$$\text{EAR of 2/15, net 40} = \left(\left(1 + \frac{2\%}{100\% - 2\%}\right)^{\frac{365}{40-15}} \right) - 1$$

$$\text{EAR of 2/15, net 40} = 0.343 \text{ or } 34.3\%$$

$$\text{EAR of 3/15, net 60} = \left(\left(1 + \frac{3\%}{100\% - 3\%}\right)^{\frac{365}{60-15}} \right) - 1$$

$$\text{EAR of 3/15, net 60} = 0.280 \text{ or } 28.0\%$$

5. An issuer is comparing a bank loan at a rate of 15% with taking advantage of a supplier's terms of 1/14, net 30, paying on day 14. The best decision in terms of the lower cost of financing is to:

  A. forgo the discount and use the supplier's financing to pay on day 30.

  B. borrow from the bank to take advantage of the trade credit terms.

  C. use either option because the cost of the bank loan and the cost of the trade credit are identical.

Solution:

B is correct.

The cost of the supplier's trade credit, expressed as an effective annual rate, is 25.769%, which is higher than the 15% interest rate on the bank loan.

$$\text{EAR of Supplier Financing} = \left(\left(1 + \frac{\text{Discount }\%}{100\% - \text{Discount }\%}\right)^{\frac{\text{Days in Year}}{\text{Payment Period} - \text{Discount Period}}} \right) - 1$$

$$\text{EAR of 1/14, net 30} = \left(\left(1 + \frac{1\%}{100\% - 1\%}\right)^{\frac{365}{30-14}} \right) - 1$$

EAR of 1/14, net 30 = 0.25769 or 25.769%

A and C are incorrect, because the bank loan rate of 15% is lower than the effective annual rate, 25.769%, on the supplier's trade credit.

6. Consider the following balance sheet for an issuer:

Cash	100
Marketable securities	20
Accounts receivable	600
Inventory	800
Prepaid expenses	30
Property, plant, and equipment	10,000
Intangibles	500
Total assets	12,050
Accounts payable	980
Accrued expenses	70
Short-term debt	1,000
Long-term debt	2,000
Shareholders' equity	8,000
Total liabilities and equity	12,050

7. The issuer's net working capital is *closest* to:

A. −500.

B. 380.

C. 500.

Solution:

B is correct. Net working capital is defined as:

Current assets, excluding cash and marketable securities
Minus: Current liabilities, excluding short-term and current debt
Net Working Capital

Current assets, excluding cash and marketable securities:

Accounts receivable	600
Inventory	800
Prepaid expenses	30
Sum	1,430

Current liabilities, excluding short-term and current debt:

Accounts payable	980
Accrued expenses	70
Sum	1,050
Net working capital	380

A is incorrect, because cash, marketable securities, and short-term debt are mistakenly included in the calculation, resulting in the calculation of total working capital instead of net working capital.

C is incorrect, because cash and marketable securities are mistakenly included in the calculation.

3   LIQUIDITY

☐ | explain liquidity and compare issuers' liquidity levels

Liquidity for an individual asset or liability is its nearness to cash or settlement. Cash is already cash, so it is the most liquid asset, while inventories can take issuers significant time to sell and ultimately collect cash from customers and are thus less liquid than cash. Similarly, accounts payable due to a supplier in five days are more liquid than a lease payment due next month. Issuers report assets and liabilities on their balance sheet in descending order of liquidity. Assets and liabilities that are not expected to convert into cash or settle within 12 months are presented as long-term assets and liabilities. Exhibit 7 depicts the relative liquidity of short-term assets and liabilities.

Exhibit 7: Relative Liquidity of Short-Term Assets and Liabilities

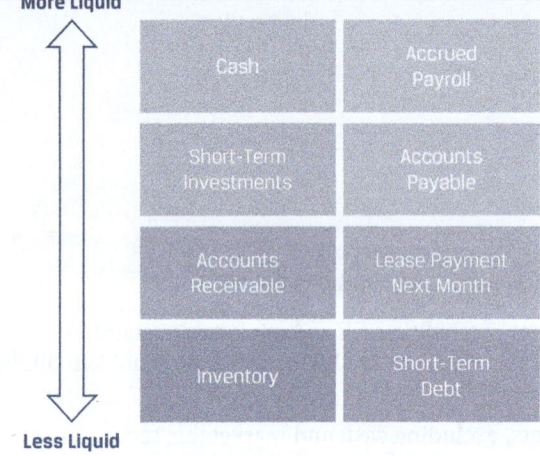

Liquidity for an *issuer* refers to its ability to meet its short-term liabilities. It is determined by the amounts and liquidity of its short-term assets and liabilities, which in turn are determined by an issuer's business model and cash conversion cycle. For example, if an issuer has 20 in total short-term liabilities and 100 in cash, it is highly liquid and will face no problem paying its short-term liabilities. If the reverse is true and the company has 20 in cash and 100 in short-term liabilities, the company will have to seek other sources of liquidity to meet its short-term liabilities.

Primary Liquidity Sources

Primary sources of liquidity represent the most readily accessible cash available to the company and include the following:

- *Cash and marketable securities on hand*, which is cash available in bank accounts or held as currency or securities that could be sold quickly without significant loss of value.

- *Borrowings*, from banks, bondholders, or suppliers' trade credit. While this source can yield cash to settle near-term obligations, it creates another obligation that will need to be repaid in the future.

- *Cash flow from the business*, though it takes time to generate, is a substantial source of liquidity for profitable firms. For example, if a firm has a liability of 40 due in six months but expects to generate 100 in cash from its operations over the next six months, it will not have to use cash on hand or borrowings to settle this liability. However, firms in an earlier stage of growth or earning net losses may not generate sufficient cash flows to meet liabilities.

While cash and securities on hand and borrowings are an important source of liquidity in the short run, an issuer's cash flow from its business is the primary long-term source of liquidity. For that reason, financial analysts closely track this information using a financial statement reported by issuers known as the **statement of cash flows**, the basic elements of which are shown in Exhibit 8.

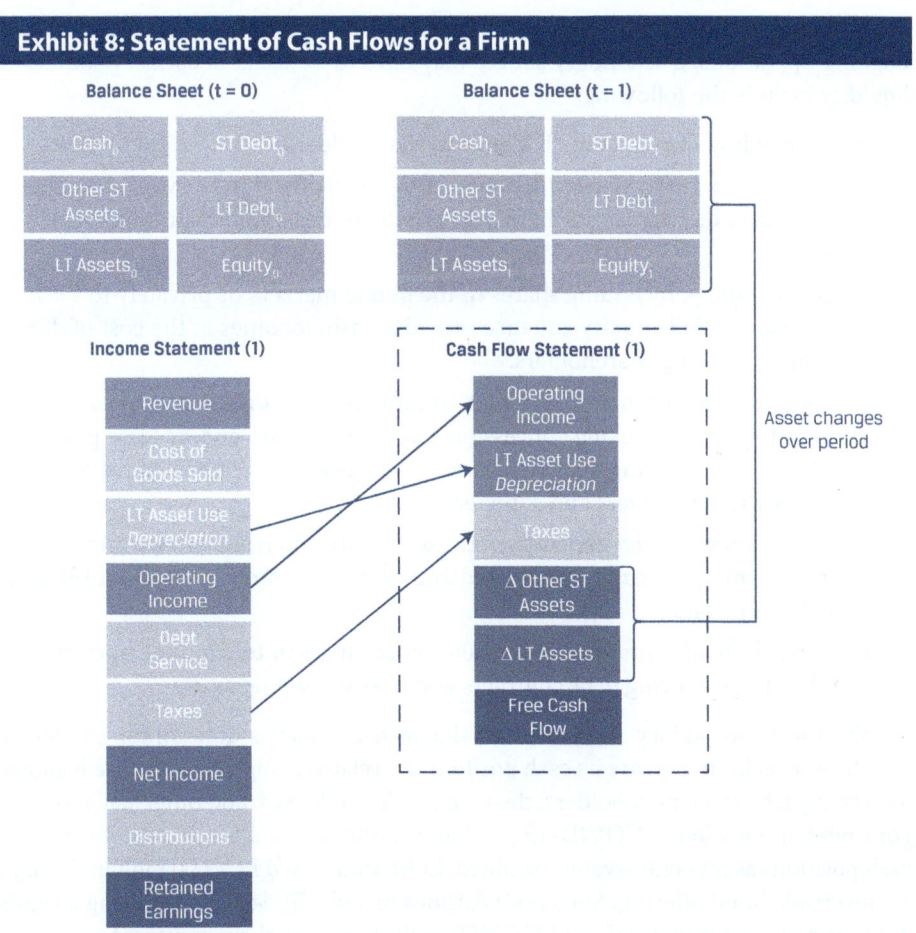

Exhibit 8: Statement of Cash Flows for a Firm

There are several measures of cash flows that analysts use or calculate from the statement of cash flows. **Cash flow from operations** is a cash profit measure over a period for an issuer's primary business activities, calculated as:

Cash received from customers
Plus: Interest and dividends received on financial investments
Minus: Cash paid to employees and suppliers
Minus: Taxes paid to governments
Minus: Interest paid to lenders
Cash flows from operations

(4)

However, this measure does not account for capital investments (covered in a subsequent learning module) that issuers make to improve operations or expand. Therefore, analysts calculate an additional measure known as **free cash flow** that accounts for this factor:

Cash flows from operations
Minus: Investments in long-term assets
Free cash flow

(5)

An alternative measure of free cash flow adds back interest paid to lenders in order to compute cash flows that are available for both debt and equity investors. This important topic will be addressed in greater detail later in the curriculum.

Secondary Liquidity Sources

While primary liquidity sources are preferable and are unlikely to affect a firm's ongoing operations, a secondary source may have to be used. Secondary sources of liquidity include the following:

- Suspending or reducing dividends to shareholders.

- *Delaying or reducing capital expenditures*, which will preserve cash in the near term but may result in missed opportunities and impair long-term value.

- *Issuing equity*, by issuing shares in the public markets or privately to select investors. While equity issuance provides cash, it comes at the cost of dilution for existing shareholders.

- *Renegotiating contract terms*, such as refinancing short-term debt to long-term debt; seeking concessions on interest, rent, and/or lease payments; restructuring debt covenants; and renegotiating payment or delivery terms with customers and suppliers.

- *Selling assets*, which depends on the degree to which short-term and/or long-term assets can be liquidated and converted into cash without substantial loss in value.

- *Filing for bankruptcy* protection and reorganization to continue operations while restructuring debt contracts and possibly selling assets.

The use of secondary sources often signals a company's deteriorating financial health, as it seeks to increase its cash position at a relatively high price or disadvantage to existing debt and equity holders, the company's employees, and other stakeholders. For example, early in the COVID-19 pandemic, airlines raised funds to shore up their cash positions as revenue severely declined: Lufthansa raised EUR600 million through a convertible bond offering, Singapore Airlines raised SGD$8.8 billion using a rights issue, and Delta Airlines deferred USD500 million in capital expenditures.

Example 3 shows the net proceeds from the primary and secondary sources of liquidity for an issuer in a liquidity crisis. It also shows the liquidation costs incurred by the company when those sources are used to raise funds. These costs can include the fees and commissions involved with the asset sale as well as any discount in asset value due to liquidity issues.

EXAMPLE 3

Estimating Keown Corporation's Cost of Liquidity

1. Keown Corporation is facing a liquidity crisis. As an analyst, you have identified four potential actions that Keown could take to raise funds. Your estimates of fair value for Keown's assets and liquidation costs are shown below.

Source of Funds	Fair Value (millions of CAD)	Liquidation Costs (%)
Sell short-term marketable securities	10	0
Sell select inventories and receivables	20	10
Sell excess real estate property	50	15
Sell a subsidiary of the firm	30	20

The liquidation costs include the fees and commissions for selling an asset as well as any reduction in value due to its illiquidity. In this case, liquidation costs for marketable securities are zero.

Net of liquidation costs, how much liquidity can Keown raise if all four sources of funds are used, and what are Keown's total liquidation costs?

A. 110 million, 9.5 million

B. 94.5 million, 15.5 million

C. 125.5 million, 15.5 million

Solution:

The gross and net amounts of liquidity raised are summarized in this table:

Source of Funds	Fair Value (millions of CAD)	Liquidation Costs %	Liquidation Costs (millions of CAD)	Net Proceeds (millions of CAD)
Marketable securities	10	0	0	10
Inventories and receivables	20	10	2	18
Real estate property	50	15	7.5	42.5
Subsidiary of the firm	30	20	6	24
Total			15.5	94.5

B is correct. Total net proceeds from the sales are CAD94.5 million, and the total liquidation costs incurred are CAD15.5 million.

Factors Affecting Liquidity: Drags and Pulls

A company's cash conversion cycle has significant effects on its liquidity position. Two classifications for negative forces on a firm's liquidity are drags and pulls on liquidity. A **drag on liquidity** occurs when cash inflows lag, creating a shortfall due to a decline in available funds. Alternatively, a **pull on liquidity** involves an acceleration of cash outflows or a situation where trade credit availability is limited, requiring companies to expend funds before they receive proceeds from sales that could offset the liability.

Major drags on receipts involve pressures from credit management and deterioration in other assets and include the following:

- *Uncollected receivables.* The longer customer receipts are outstanding, the greater the chance they will not be collected. As we will see in the following lesson, this drag is often measured by the average number of days that receivables are outstanding as well as the level of customer payment delinquencies as a percentage of receivables.

- *Obsolete inventory.* If inventory of finished goods is held for long periods, it might be an indication that it is no longer in demand by customers or can be sold only at a discounted price.

- *Borrowing constraints.* If credit conditions tighten due to adverse economic conditions, short-term debt becomes more expensive or unavailable.

In many cases, drags can be reduced by stricter enforcement of credit and collection practices, but this approach may also drive sales lower if customers are unwilling or unable to make a purchase if cash payment is required.

Managing cash outflows is of equal importance. If suppliers and other vendors who offer credit terms have greater market power over a firm or believe its financial position is weak, they might demand payment terms that strain the company's liquidity. Major pulls on liquidity include the following:

- *Making payments early.* By paying vendors, employees, or others before the due dates with no financial benefit, companies forgo the use of funds. Effective payment management means *not* making early payments.

- *Reduced credit limits.* If a company has a history of late payments, suppliers may cut the firm's credit outstanding at any time.

- *Limits on short-term lines of credit.* If a company's bank limits lending to it, the company may face liquidity constraints. Credit line restrictions can be government mandated, market related, or simply company specific.

- *Low liquidity positions.* Many companies face chronic liquidity shortages, often due to industry conditions or a weak financial position. This pull may be exacerbated by an aggressive approach to working capital management.

The following example addresses changes affecting Keown Corporation's liquidity position.

EXAMPLE 4

Drags and Pulls on Keown Corporation's Liquidity

1. Keown Corporation is experiencing liquidity challenges. As an analyst, you note three recent trends related to Keown's working capital:

   1. An increase in average days sales outstanding is a drag on liquidity.
   2. An increase in days of inventory on hand is a drag on liquidity.

3. An increase in credit limits by lenders is a pull on liquidity.

Which trend does *not* contribute to the firm's liquidity challenges?

A. The change in average days sales outstanding

B. The change in days of inventory on hand

C. The change in credit limits

Solution:

C is correct. The increase in credit limits is not a pull on liquidity but is in fact the opposite: it provides liquidity.

A is incorrect, because an increase in days sales outstanding is a drag on liquidity as it results in slower or delayed cash inflows.

B is incorrect, because higher days of inventory on hand is a drag on liquidity as it extends the cash conversion cycle.

Measuring and Evaluating Liquidity

The less liquid the company, the greater the risk it will experience financial distress if business conditions change unfavorably. Financial analysts are keenly interested in common measures to quantify and track changes in firm liquidity over time as well as to compare issuers' liquidity levels. To compare firms of different sizes with varying sources and uses of liquidity, financial *ratios* are frequently used. Liquidity assessment using financial ratios usually involves both **liquidity ratios** and the activity ratios introduced earlier in Example 2. Exhibit 9 summarizes the three most used liquidity ratios.

Exhibit 9: Key Liquidity Ratios

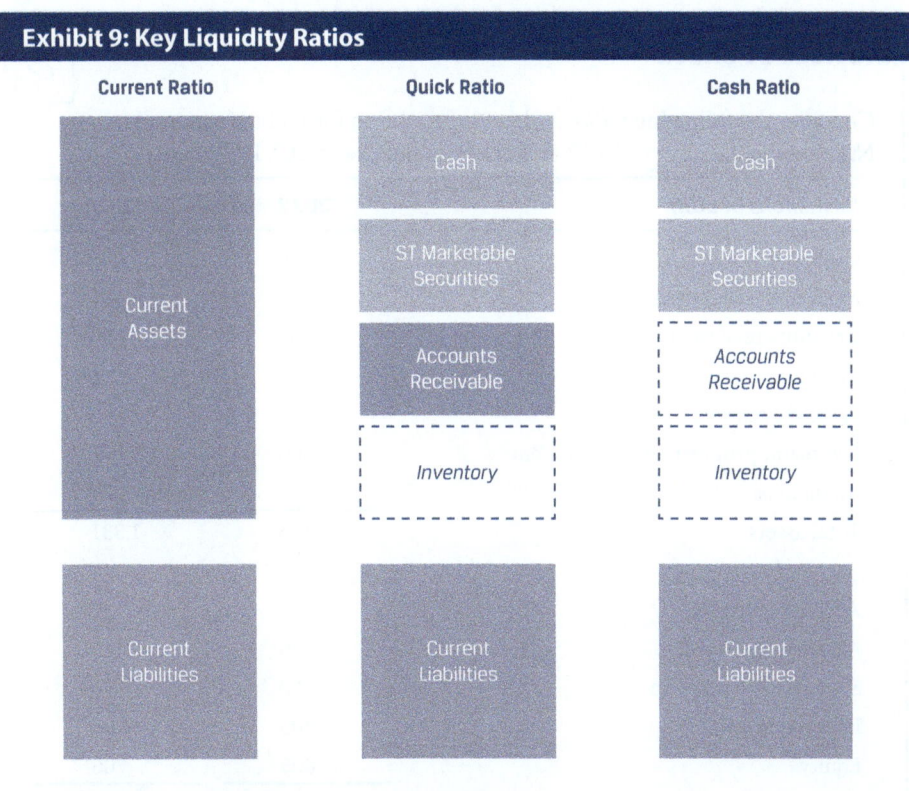

Liquidity ratios gauge a firm's ability to meet its short-term obligations from existing current assets. The broadest measure of liquidity is the **current ratio**, or ratio of current assets to current liabilities:

$$\text{Current ratio} = \frac{\text{Current assets}}{\text{Current liabilities}} \tag{6}$$

Recall from an earlier lesson that we defined total working capital as the *difference* between current assets and current liabilities. A firm with positive total working capital would therefore have a current ratio greater than one, with a higher current ratio representing greater liquidity under this aggregate measure, which includes all short-term assets.

This broad ratio is usually considered together with two narrower liquidity measures that exclude less liquid short-term assets. Recall that, unlike cash or short-term marketable securities, inventory and receivables are less readily convertible into cash. The **quick ratio** is a ratio of short-term assets to short-term liabilities that excludes inventory:

$$\text{Quick ratio} = \frac{\text{Cash} + \text{Short-term marketable instruments} + \text{Receivables}}{\text{Current liabilities}} \tag{7}$$

A firm able to meet its short-term obligations *without* liquidating inventory would therefore have a quick ratio greater than one. However, this scenario would require the firm to collect all receivables without delays or customer delinquencies. The **cash ratio** compares cash and short-term marketable securities with current liabilities and is the most conservative of these measures:

$$\text{Cash ratio} = \frac{\text{Cash} + \text{Short-term marketable instruments}}{\text{Current liabilities}} \tag{8}$$

A cash ratio equal to or greater than one indicates that a firm could satisfy all its short-term obligations without having to wait to sell inventory or collect receivables.

KNOWLEDGE CHECK

Consider the following balance sheet information for Licht Vernieuwend N.V. for the fiscal year 20X2 and the previous year, 20X1:

(in millions of EUR)	20X2	20X1
Cash	40	45
Marketable securities	70	90
Accounts receivable	85	90
Inventory	130	66
Prepaid accounts	10	15
Net plant, property, and equipment	1,000	950
Intangibles	90	75
Total assets	1,425	1,331
Accounts payable	130	140
Accrued expenses	30	15
Short-term bank loan	60	70
Long-term debt	400	400
Equity	805	706
Total liabilities and equity	1,425	1,331

1. Has net working capital changed from 20X1 to 20X2? If so, what was the primary driver of the change?

Solution:

Net working capital is defined as:

Current assets, excluding cash and marketable securities
Minus: Current liabilities, excluding short-term and current debt
Net Working Capital

Licht Vernieuwend N.V.'s net working capital each year is equal to:

(in millions of EUR)	20X2	20X1
Accounts receivable	85	90
Plus: Inventory	130	66
Plus: Prepaid accounts	10	15
Minus: Accounts payable	(130)	(140)
Minus: Accrued expenses	(30)	(15)
Net working capital	65	16

Licht Vernieuwend N.V.'s net working capital has increased from EUR16 million in 20X1 to EUR65 million in 20X2, largely owing to the increased investment in inventory from EUR66 million to EUR130 million.

2. Has the liquidity changed from 20X1 to 20X2 based on the:

i. cash ratio?

ii. quick ratio?

iii. current ratio?

Solution:

i. The cash ratio is defined as:

$$\text{Cash ratio} = \frac{\text{Cash + Short-term marketable instruments}}{\text{Current liabilities}}$$

$$\text{Licht's cash ratio, 20X1} = \frac{45 + 90}{140 + 15 + 70} = 0.60$$

$$\text{Licht's cash ratio, 20X2} = \frac{40 + 70}{130 + 30 + 60} = 0.50$$

Based on the cash ratio, Licht Vernieuwend N.V.'s liquidity has declined from 20X1 to 20X2.

ii. The quick ratio is defined as:

$$\text{Quick ratio} = \frac{\text{Cash + Short-term marketable instruments + Receivables}}{\text{Current liabilities}}$$

$$\text{Licht's quick ratio, 20X1} = \frac{45 + 90 + 90}{140 + 15 + 70} = 1.00$$

$$\text{Licht's quick ratio, 20X2} = \frac{40 + 70 + 85}{130 + 30 + 60} = 0.89$$

Based on the quick ratio, Licht Vernieuwend N.V.'s liquidity has declined from 20X1 to 20X2.

    iii. The current ratio is defined as:

$$\text{Current ratio} = \frac{\text{Current assets}}{\text{Current liabilities}}$$

Licht's current ratio, 20X1 $= \dfrac{45 + 90 + 90 + 66 + 15}{140 + 15 + 70} = 1.36$

Licht's current ratio, 20X2 $= \dfrac{40 + 70 + 85 + 130 + 10}{130 + 30 + 60} = 1.52$

    Based on the current ratio, Licht Vernieuwend N.V.'s liquidity has increased from 20X1 to 20X2.

3. Given the changes in liquidity ratios in Question 2, did the issuer become more or less liquid based on the most conservative liquidity ratio?

Solution:

The most conservative liquidity ratio is the cash ratio, as it measures the ability of an issuer to settle near-term obligations using only the most liquid assets: cash and short-term marketable instruments. Based on the cash ratio, Licht Vernieuwend N.V.'s liquidity has declined from 20X1 to 20X2.

QUESTION SET

1. Classify each of the following as either a drag on liquidity or a pull on liquidity:

	Effect on Liquidity	
Action	Drag	Pull
Customers delaying payments		
Inventory becoming obsolete		
Paying suppliers before due dates without a discount incentive		
Lender reducing a line of credit		
Vendors reducing trade credits		

    Solution:

	Effect on Liquidity	
Action	Drag	Pull
Customers delaying payments	✓	
Inventory becoming obsolete	✓	
Paying suppliers before due dates without a discount incentive		✓
Lender reducing a line of credit		✓
Vendors reducing trade credits		✓

2. Consider the following information from the Statement of Cash Flows for the Lucor Corporation:

Net income	1,000
Cash flow from operations	1,400
Cash flow from investing	(700)
Investment in long-term assets	(800)
Cash flow from financing	500
Funds from debt issue	600
Total net cash flow for the period	1,200

Lucor's free cash flow for this period is *closest* to:

A. 200.

B. 600.

C. 700.

Solution:

B is correct. Free cash flow is the difference between cash flow from operations and the investment in long-term assets, or

Free cash flow = 1, 400 − 800 = 600

3. An issuer is facing a liquidity crisis. Based on these estimations, complete the following table:

	Fair Value (millions of USD)	Liquidation Cost (% of fair value)	Liquidation Cost (millions of USD)	Net Proceeds (millions of USD)
Selling a production plant	1,000	20		
Selling short-term marketable securities	100	0		
Selling receivables	900	10		
Selling inventory	600	12		
Total				

Solution:

	(1) Fair Value (millions of USD)	(2) Liquidation Cost (% of fair value)	(3) Liquidation Cost (millions of USD)	(4) Net Proceeds (millions of USD)
Selling a production plant	1,000	20	200	800
Selling short-term marketable securities	100	0	0	100
Selling receivables	900	10	90	810
Selling inventory	600	12	72	528
Total				2,238

The liquidation cost in column (3) is the result of multiplying the column (1) and (2) entries. The net proceeds in column (4) are the result of subtracting the liquidation cost from the fair value, column (1). The total net proceeds is the sum of the net proceeds from each source in column (4).

4. Rank the following ratios from smallest (rank 1) to largest (rank 3) for a company that has inventory, accounts receivable, and payables:

Ratio	Rank
Cash ratio	
Current ratio	
Quick ratio	

Solution:

The denominator is the same for each of these ratios (current liabilities), so the differences among these ratios are attributable to the numerator. In the case of the cash ratio, the numerator is simply cash and short-term marketable securities. In the case of the quick ratio, receivables are added to cash and short-term marketable securities in the numerator. Finally, the current ratio has all current assets in the numerator.

Ratio	Rank
Cash ratio	1
Current ratio	3
Quick ratio	2

5. An issuer has the following current assets and current liabilities on its balance sheet:

Cash	200
Marketable securities	40
Accounts receivable	600
Inventory	800
Prepaid expenses	60

Accounts payable	500
Accrued expenses	50
Short-term debt	600

The issuer's cash and quick ratios, respectively, are closest to:

A. 0.2087; 0.7304.

B. 0.4363; 1.5273.

C. 0.5455; 1.6364.

Solution to 5:

A is correct.

The cash ratio is:

$$\text{Cash ratio} = \frac{200 + 40}{1,150} = 0.2087$$

The quick ratio is:

$$\text{Quic ratio} = \frac{200 + 40 + 600}{1,150} = 0.7304$$

MANAGING WORKING CAPITAL AND LIQUIDITY

4

☐ | describe issuers' objectives and compare methods for managing working capital and liquidity

The primary goal of working capital and liquidity management is to maximize firm value while maintaining ready access to funds necessary for day-to-day operations and obligations to creditors. Often, reaching this goal involves shortening the cash conversion cycle, estimating required liquidity, and minimizing any excess so that cash can be invested elsewhere in higher-return projects or returned to shareholders.

The realistic bounds of working capital and liquidity management depend on a firm's business model. For example, some types of manufacturing may involve more complex and lengthy conversion of inputs into finished goods, which may require that inventory be held for weeks or months. A distributor of less complex goods, however, may have just a few days of inventory on hand. Some businesses in the same industry require more investment in inventory and receivables than others. For example, retail businesses with multiple sales locations where finished goods are available for purchase, as well as those that offer customers sales on credit versus immediate payment, will need more working capital (in inventories and/or accounts receivable). In contrast, service and software businesses may have far lower working capital requirements, as they do not have inventories and may receive payments from customers upfront.

Working Capital Management

Firms estimate working capital requirements by first determining optimal working capital requirements in relation to revenue and then forecasting future working capital levels based on their revenue forecast. In doing so, firms often distinguish between, on the one hand, base levels of inventory, staffing, and receivables that are *permanent* current assets and relatively constant over time and, on the other hand, additional inventory and labor needed during a company's seasonal peak production and sales period or during a growth phase that are considered *variable* current assets. During this process, managers also weigh the cost versus benefit of different inventory and receivables management policies. For example, higher inventory levels may reduce the likelihood of a shortfall due to supplier risk or unanticipated demand but may also increase the obsolescence risk of existing inventory. Although more accommodative sales credit policies that increase receivables may help drive sales or revenue growth, they may also lead to higher billing costs and increased payment delinquencies over time.

Companies take different approaches to both the *size* of current assets and the *composition* of financing used to support those assets. Exhibit 10 outlines three different approaches to working capital management, from the highest cost (i.e., higher levels of current assets funded on a longer-term basis) to the lowest (fewer assets funded on a shorter-term basis) for a given level of sales.

Exhibit 10: Working Capital Management and Funding Approaches

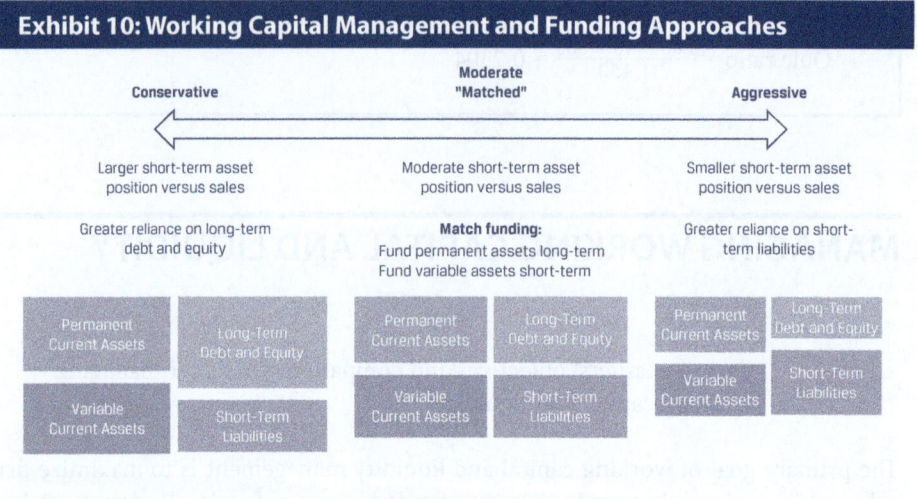

A conservative approach to working capital management involves more cash, receivables, and inventory relative to sales, with a greater reliance on long-term funding sources. While this strategy provides a firm with the most financial flexibility to meet its needs, it is also typically the costliest. The pros and cons of a conservative working capital approach are outlined in Exhibit 11.

Exhibit 11: Conservative Working Capital Approach: Pros and Cons

Pros	Cons
Stable, permanent financing avoids rollover risk associated with short-term debt	Long-term debt typically involves a higher interest rate
Financing costs are known upfront	High cost of equity
Certainty of working capital needed to purchase the necessary inventory	Permanent financing eliminates the opportunity to borrow only as needed

Pros	Cons
Extended payment term reduces short-term cash needs for debt service	A longer lead time is often required to establish the financing position
Higher flexibility during market disruptions that can be covered by larger cash or marketable securities positions	Long-term debt may involve more restrictions on business operations

Firms in an early-growth phase are more likely to consider a conservative approach due to limited access to short-term debt. More established companies with higher profit margins pursuing such a policy may also be able to pass these higher financing costs on to customers. Firms may choose to pursue a conservative working capital strategy for a number of other reasons:

- Reduced need to access capital during times of market stress
- Expectation of flat to rising interest rates
- Preference for cash flow stability over rollover risk of short-term debt
- Benefits of greater certainty and access to more permanent capital, which are perceived to offset the higher associated financing cost

An aggressive working capital approach, in contrast, seeks to minimize excess cash, receivables, and inventory relative to sales, with more reliance on short-term funding to meet variable and some permanent working capital needs. With fewer committed resources to support current assets, the firm has reduced its short-term financial flexibility in exchange for higher returns for investors.

The pros and cons of an aggressive working capital strategy are outlined in Exhibit 12.

Exhibit 12: Aggressive Working Capital Approach: Pros and Cons

Pros	Cons
Lower financing cost	Interest expense may fluctuate as rates on short-term financing change
Flexibility to borrow only as needed reduces overall interest expense	May result in higher short-term cash needs to satisfy debt maturities
Short-term debt usually involves fewer restrictions on business operations	Rollover risk of short-term debt increases bankruptcy risk, particularly during market disruptions
Flexibility to refinance if rates decline	May have to rely on more costly trade credit, tighten customer credit, or sell receivables if unable to refinance at favorable terms

Firms in industries with lower profit margins may consider pursuing a more aggressive working capital policy to gain a cost advantage over competitors. While greater reliance on short-term financing lowers debt cost versus a conservative approach, a firm also faces greater exposure to debt rollover risk in times of market stress. This exposure affected many firms during the 2008–2009 financial crisis and in early 2020 during the initial phase of the COVID-19 pandemic.

Firms choosing an aggressive working capital policy may do so for one or more of the following additional reasons:

- Ability to forecast future sales and cash needs with a high degree of precision
- Expectation of stable or falling interest rates
- Expectation that firm will shorten its cash conversion cycle (i.e., shorten its accounts receivable and inventory period and extend its accounts payable period)
- Ability to quickly liquidate inventory and minimize accounts receivable

A moderate working capital approach strikes a balance between the use of long-term financing for more permanent current asset needs and short-term debt for variable needs. Since stable, predictable needs are met with long-term financing and less predictable seasonal or growth-based needs are met with short-term resources, this method is often also referred to as a "matched" approach.

The pros and cons of a moderate working capital strategy are outlined in Exhibit 13.

Exhibit 13: Moderate Working Capital Approach: Pros and Cons

Pros	Cons
Lower financing cost versus conservative approach; lower risk than aggressive approach	Access to short-term capital may be limited for seasonal or growth needs
Flexibility to increase financing for seasonal requirements or growth as needed	Uncertain cost of short-term debt for variable needs during market disruptions
Diversified sources of funding, with a more disciplined approach to balance sheet management	May have to rely on more costly trade credit to meet seasonal or growth needs if unable to refinance at favorable terms

Under a moderate approach, firms face lower financing costs than under a more conservative policy, with lower refinancing risk relative to a more aggressive working capital strategy. While these firms may also pursue measures to reduce working capital and shorten their cash conversion cycle, the use of long-term debt and equity to support permanent needs allows for more gradual changes in doing so. Other reasons a firm might pursue a moderate approach to working capital management include the following:

- Ability to accurately forecast base current asset requirements, with less certainty surrounding variable needs
- Reduced financing costs relative to a conservative approach, with lower roll-over risk and greater financial flexibility than a more aggressive approach
- To balance the use of less costly short-term financing with the stability and certainty of permanent working capital supported by long-term financing

The interaction between a firm's sales strategy and its working capital approach is an important consideration for financial analysts. For example, extending more credit, or more generous credit terms, to customers in order to boost sales will also increase working capital. In addition to an increase in accounts receivable, a firm may well face rising customer payment delinquencies, both of which require additional financing. The added cost of monitoring, billing, and collecting receivables over a longer period, as well as higher borrowing costs, must be weighed against the additional profit generated under the new strategy.

Effective management of liquidity is a core finance function for most firms. Even profitable companies can encounter financial difficulties by failing to ensure they have sufficient liquidity to meet current liabilities.

EXAMPLE 5

Changes to Keown Corporation's Credit Policy

1. Keown Corporation is considering an increase in the line of credit it offers to new customers as its sales manager believes doing so will lead to increased sales. What would be the expected impact on Keown's short-term funding needs if this change were made?

   A. The company would reduce its inventory levels.

   B. The company would likely collect faster, reducing its receivables.

   C. The company would have an increased need for working capital.

   D. The company could pay its suppliers sooner, reducing its accounts payable.

   E. The company would not see any change in working capital needs as a result of the change.

   Solution:

   C is correct. The company would likely need more short-term funding to support the expected increase in required inventory and accounts receivable resulting from an increase in sales.

Liquidity and Short-Term Funding

As described in a prior lesson, liquidity involves a firm's relative ability to convert resources into cash to meet immediate obligations. For most firms, this ability includes using existing cash balances, cash flow from operations, or borrowings. Firms can maximize financial flexibility by developing a short-term financing strategy and regularly evaluating available alternatives to fund themselves. Companies that fail to sufficiently explore available options or to take advantage of cost savings from available forms of financing are more likely to face higher financing costs or even financial distress, in which they are unable to borrow from any source.

A prudent short-term financing strategy (when to borrow and in what form) achieves several objectives, including the following:

- Maintaining sufficient and diversified sources of credit to fund *ongoing* cash needs. While many firms have a primary source of short-term funding, such as trade credits and credit facilities, a company should ideally ensure it has additional sources of financing available to reduce reliance on one lender or type of funding.

- Securing adequate funding capacity to handle the firm's *changing* cash needs. This objective may involve accommodation of peak seasonal needs or planned growth.

- Confirming that financing rates offered, as well as associated terms and conditions, are competitive and understanding how these rates might change under different capital markets and economic conditions.

- Ensuring that both implicit (e.g., the cost of supplier financing discussed earlier) and explicit funding costs are considered in calculating the company's effective cost of borrowing.

A firm's industry, size, location, and other factors may also influence its approach to short-term funding in the following ways:

- *Size.* A company's size is an important determinant of available financing alternatives. For example, a small, privately held firm might be limited to short-term credit advances from a single bank, while very large firms are able to access short-term fixed-income markets, among other sources. Many funding alternatives involve either a minimum size or fixed costs, making them prohibitively expensive or unavailable for small and midsize companies.

- *Creditworthiness.* A firm's creditworthiness determines not only whether a loan will be approved by a lender and the rate it will pay, but also whether the loan contains terms and conditions that restrict the firm's operations. For example, a lender may impose borrowing conditions on a less credit-worthy firm that restrict its ability to sell or use its assets for different purposes. This topic will be covered in greater detail in later learning modules.

- *Legal considerations.* Some firms in emerging or frontier markets with less well-defined legal systems may have fewer funding alternatives from financial intermediaries or financial markets than firms in developed economies. As a result, they may rely more heavily on trade credits from suppliers.

- *Regulatory considerations.* Several industries in developed markets are highly regulated. Firms in these industries, such as utilities or banks, may be restricted in both how much they can borrow and the type of borrowing they can access. In other instances, they may have access to unique sources of short-term funding unavailable to other firms. For example, financial institutions can borrow and lend central bank reserves with one another and can also directly access central bank funding. The funding of financial institutions will be addressed in detail later in the curriculum.

- *Underlying assets.* Depending on their business model, companies may have assets, such as inventory, that are considered attractive as collateral for secured short-term funding.

For firms of any size, industry, or location, proper planning enables a company to manage its short-term debt needs more efficiently. For example, forecasting cash positions over a cash conversion cycle and beyond can help firms reduce the likelihood of financial distress under adverse market conditions. Matching the timing of debt maturities to expected cash receipts and spacing debt maturities out over time can also help reduce short-term funding risk.

KNOWLEDGE CHECK: EVALUATING SHORT-TERM FINANCING CHOICES

1. Which of the following factors should a company consider when evaluating short-term financing choices?

   A. The cost of the funds borrowed

   B. The flexibility offered by the source

   C. The ease with which the funds can be accessed

   D. Legal or regulatory constraints that might favor one source over another

E. All of the above

Solution:

E is correct. The cost of funds for a company is the most obvious item to consider, but it may choose to borrow at a slightly higher cost after taking all the other items into consideration.

KNOWLEDGE CHECK: MEETING KEOWN CORPORATION'S SHORT-TERM FINANCING NEEDS

1. Keown Corporation has accounts payable of CAD2 million with terms of 2/10, net 30 and accounts receivable of CAD2 million. In addition, the company holds CAD5 million in marketable securities. Keown has a short-term need of CAD200,000 to meet payroll. Which of the following choices makes the most sense for raising the CAD200,000?

   A. The company should issue long-term debt.

   B. The company should issue common stock.

   C. The company should delay paying accounts payable and forgo the 2% discount.

   D. The company should sell accounts receivable at a 10% discount.

   E. The company should sell marketable securities at a 0.5% brokerage cost (ignore capital gains tax).

   Solution:

   E is correct.
   The options for raising CAD200,000 are summarized in this table.

		Liquidation Cost	
Source of Funds	**Action**	**%**	**CAD**
C. Accounts payable (2/10, net 30)	Delay CAD200,000 in payment and forgo 2% discount	2.0	4,000
D. Accounts receivable	Sell CAD222,222 in value at 10% discount to raise CAD200,000	10.0	22,222
E. Marketable securities	Sell CAD200,000 in value	0.5	1,000

   Choosing C involves forgoing a 2% discount, which on CAD200,000 amounts to a cost of CAD4,000. To net CAD200,000 using option D, the company would have to sell CAD222,222 of accounts receivable at a cost of CAD22,222. E appears to be the best choice. Marketable securities are liquid and can be easily sold for market value, less the relatively minor brokerage cost of CAD1,000.

QUESTION SET

1. Classify each of the following in terms of approaches to working capital management:

	Conservative	Aggressive
Greater level of inventory relative to sales		
Greater reliance on long-term financing		
Greater level of cash on hand		
Greater level of marketable securities		
Greater reliance on short-term bank loans		

Solution:

	Conservative	Aggressive
Greater level of inventory relative to sales	✓	
Greater reliance on long-term financing	✓	
Greater level of cash on hand	✓	
Greater level of marketable securities	✓	
Greater reliance on short-term bank loans		✓

2. A company has USD30 million of accounts payable, for which it could delay payment to day 14, forgoing the 2% discount it would receive for paying within ten days. The liquidation cost in millions of USD is closest to:

   A. 0.6.

   B. 6.1.

   C. 8.4.

   Solution:

   A is correct. The liquidation cost is the forgone 2% discount applied to the USD30 million value of the accounts payable.

   Liquidation cost = USD 30 million × 0.02 = USD 0.6 million

   B and C are incorrect, because they represent effective annual rates of the forgone interest applied to the value of the accounts payable.

3. A company changed the credit terms it offers its customers from 1/10, net 30 to 1/15, net 30. The most likely effect of this change is:

   A. an increase in accounts receivable.

   B. no change in accounts receivable.

C. a decrease in accounts receivable.

Solution:

A is correct. The company extended the discount period by 5 days and did not change the discount amount as a percentage of the sale price (1%). More generous credit terms for its customers will likely increase accounts receivable, because customers will take longer to pay even if they take the discount. In addition, the more attractive credit terms may result in increased accounts receivable due to increased sales.

B and C are incorrect, because a more generous discount period will result in increased accounts receivable as customers will take longer to pay if they take advantage of the discount.

4. Changing its accounts receivable policy to extend credit to customers with lower creditworthiness will most likely result in:

   A. a pull on liquidity.

   B. a drag on liquidity.

   C. no effect on liquidity.

   Solution:

   B is correct. By extending credit to customers with lower creditworthiness, the company is likely to experience more delinquent or uncollectible accounts and an increase in days sales outstanding, resulting in a drag on liquidity.

   A is incorrect, because a pull on liquidity would result from an acceleration of cash outflows. In this case, the change to the company's credit policy has the effect of slowing cash inflows.

   C is incorrect, because the change in the company's accounts receivable policy would likely increase its working capital needs due to having higher accounts receivable.

5. The Lucor Corporation is seeking to raise liquidity and is evaluating two potential actions.

   Option 1   Selling accounts receivable to a financial intermediary at a 5% discount off their carrying value

   Option 2   Accelerating payments to suppliers to receive a 5% discount

   Which of the options would achieve Lucor's objective?

   A. Option 1

   B. Option 2

   C. Neither, because they both incur liquidation costs

   Solution:

   A is correct. Option 1 would increase liquidity by converting a less liquid asset (accounts receivable) into cash immediately, albeit at a cost.

   B is incorrect, because Option 2 would decrease liquidity by accelerating cash outflows.

   C is incorrect, because Option 2 would decrease liquidity by accelerating cash outflows and would not incur liquidation costs.

PRACTICE PROBLEMS

1. An issuer changing its credit terms for customers from 2/10, net 30 to 2/10, net 40 will most likely experience:

   A. a pull on its liquidity.

   B. a drag on its liquidity.

   C. no change in its liquidity.

2. Which of the following will most likely *decrease* an issuer's cash conversion cycle? An increase in its days:

   A. sales outstanding.

   B. of inventory on hand.

   C. payable outstanding.

3. An analyst gathers balance sheet information for the most recent fiscal year for three issuers.

	Issuer A	Issuer B	Issuer C
Cash	100	120	50
Marketable securities	20	10	20
Accounts receivable	300	300	200
Inventory	500	600	300
Prepaid expenses	50	0	10
Accounts payable	400	500	300
Accrued expenses	40	20	0

   Which issuer is most liquid based on the quick ratio?

   A. Issuer A

   B. Issuer B

   C. Issuer C

4. An analyst is evaluating an issuer's liquidity and calculates a negative cash conversion cycle for the issuer in the most recent fiscal year. This result is:

   A. not feasible.

   B. possible, because the issuer has sufficient cash and marketable securities on hand to support short-term needs.

   C. possible, because the investment in inventory is returned quickly and the issuer takes advantage of vendor financing.

5. An issuer eliminated the prompt-payment discount it had offered to customers. This action most likely will:

   A. increase the issuer's liquidity.

B. decrease the issuer's liquidity.

C. not affect the issuer's liquidity.

SOLUTIONS

1. B is correct. By extending the net period, the issuer will likely see its accounts receivable increase, lengthening its cash conversion cycle and producing a drag on its liquidity.

   A is incorrect, because the change will slow payments from customers (inflows) rather than pull on liquidity in terms of outflows.

   C is incorrect, because extending the net period will slow payments from customers and produce a drag on liquidity.

2. C is correct. Increasing days payable outstanding would reduce the cash conversion cycle, because payments to suppliers are delayed. Days payable outstanding is subtracted from the sum of days sales outstanding and days of inventory on hand to compute the cash conversion cycle.

   A is incorrect, because an increase in days sales outstanding will increase the issuer's cash conversion cycle.

   B is incorrect, because an increase in days of inventory on hand will increase the issuer's cash conversion cycle.

3. A is correct. The quick ratio is defined as:

   $$\text{Quick ratio} = \frac{\text{Cash} + \text{Short-term marketable instruments} + \text{Receivables}}{\text{Current liabilities}}$$

   The quick ratio for each issuer is:

   $$\text{Issuer A quick ratio} = \frac{100 + 20 + 300}{400 + 40} = \frac{420}{440} = 0.9545$$

   $$\text{Issuer B quick ratio} = \frac{120 + 10 + 300}{500 + 20} = \frac{430}{520} = 0.8269$$

   $$\text{Issuer C quick ratio} = \frac{50 + 20 + 200}{300 + 0} = \frac{270}{300} = 0.9000$$

4. C is correct. If days of inventory on hand is low, the accounts receivable collection period is short, and the issuer takes advantage of its vendors' financing, a negative cash conversion cycle is a possible result.

   A is incorrect, because issuers may have a negative cash conversion cycle if days payable outstanding is larger than the sum of days of inventory on hand and days sales outstanding.

   B is incorrect, because the amount of cash and marketable securities on hand does not affect the company's cash conversion cycle.

5. B is correct, because the elimination of the discount will likely result in customers paying later as there is no incentive to pay early without the discount. With customers paying later, this action becomes a drag on liquidity.

   A and C are incorrect, because customers likely paying later will reduce the issuer's liquidity.

Capital Investments and Capital Allocation

INTRODUCTION

The previous learning module described issuers' *short-term* investments and financing activities. In this module and the next, we turn our attention to issuers' *long-term* investment and financing activities. First, we explore the various forms of capital investment and their purposes. We then discuss the investment decision-making process and compare analytical approaches employed in that process. In the third lesson, we describe principles of capital allocation and common pitfalls. While the goals of both capital allocation and estimating expected investment returns are to select the best choice among investment alternatives, a firm's decision today may influence future investment decisions, resulting in so-called real options, which are discussed in the final lesson.

> **LEARNING MODULE OVERVIEW**
>
> - Companies make capital investments to maintain or expand operations. Capital investments can be grouped into four categories based on their risk and return characteristics: (1) going concern projects, (2) regulatory/compliance projects, (3) expansion projects, and (4) other.
>
> - Capital allocation is a process undertaken by issuers' management and board for evaluating investment opportunities based on their expected contribution to shareholder value, as well as other considerations, such as environmental, social, and governance (ESG) factors. Although

some projects might look profitable on an accounting or standalone basis, they might be uneconomical compared to alternatives or from an overall strategic perspective. Such projects should not be pursued, and capital should instead be returned to shareholders.

- Net present value (NPV) and internal rate of return (IRR) are two tools used to evaluate individual investment projects. NPV estimates the increase in firm value from a project, while IRR is an estimate of the rate of return on a project, subject to certain assumptions, which can be compared to a hurdle rate.

- Unlike NPV and IRR, return on invested capital (ROIC) is a company-wide measure and can be calculated using data available to independent analysts. ROIC is the rate of return an issuer earns over a period across all investments and can be compared to an investor's required rate of return. Like NPV and IRR, ROIC is subject to limitations and assumptions.

- Before investment projects are appraised on a quantitative basis, they should be modeled in accordance with certain principles, including measurement of cash flows on an after-tax basis, avoiding double counting, and including a project's impact on the rest of the firm. Impacts can be positive, such as cost savings, or negative, such as the loss of sales from existing products.

- Apart from deviations from these principles, capital allocation is additionally prone to behavioral biases and cognitive errors. These pitfalls can be detected by a thorough analysis of a company's financials on a historical and comparative basis, as well as an examination of corporate governance and management renumeration policies.

- Real options are like financial options in that they provide a right, not an obligation, for management to alter different aspects of capital projects in the future. Those aspects include timing and size of a project, as well as flexibility with regard to future pricing policies or operating capacity.

- The most common approach to evaluating projects with real options is to compare a project's NPV before and after inclusion of an option's value less the option's cost. More advanced methods include decision trees and option pricing models, which require assumptions about the probability of future events.

LEARNING MODULE SELF-ASSESSMENT

These initial questions are intended to help you gauge your current level of understanding of this learning module.

1. The following list contains either an example or an attribute of a capital investment project. Assign each item to either *maintenance* or *growth*.

   - Acquisition
   - Expand business scope
   - Research and development
   - Replace outdated facilities
   - High-risk investment and uncertainty

- Limited downside risk and uncertainty
- Needed to meet safety, compliance, regulatory standards

Maintenance	Growth

Solution:

Maintenance	Growth
Replace outdated facilities	Acquisition
Needed to meet safety, compliance, regulatory standards	Expand business scope
Limited downside risk and uncertainty	Research and development
	High-risk investment and uncertainty

2. When calculating IRR, the interim cash flows are assumed to be reinvested and earn a rate of return rate that is:

   A. lower than IRR.

   B. the same as IRR.

   C. higher than IRR.

   Solution:

   B is correct. An important assumption of IRR is that it represents only the (geometric) rate of return on the investment if interim cash flows are reinvested at the IRR.

   A is incorrect because if reinvestment rates are lower compared to IRR, the rate of return on the investment will be lower than the IRR.

   C is incorrect because if reinvestment rates are higher compared to IRR, the rate of return on the investment will be higher than the IRR.

3. Complete the following sentences by filling in the blanks using the terms provided.

   When calculating ROIC, an independent analyst should add _____ and _____ to calculating average invested capital. ROIC, _____ project NPV and IRR, can be calculated using data available to independent investment analysts.

   like

   unlike

   equity

   short-term assets

   long-term assets

long-term liabilities

Solution:

When calculating ROIC, an independent analyst should add _equity_ and _long-term liabilities_ to calculate average invested capital. ROIC, _unlike_ project NPV and IRR, can be calculated using data available to independent investment analysts.

4. Explain why capital allocation decisions should *not* be based on accounting measures such as earnings per share (EPS).

Solution:

Capital investments with a positive NPV can reduce rather than increase accounting measures in the near term, while cost cutting and share buybacks, in contrast, may have a positive effect on such measures. Basing investment decisions on short-term accounting numbers can lead a company to choose investments that are not in the long-run interests of its shareholders. Additionally, capital allocation should consider opportunity costs, such as by using a required rate of return for calculating NPV and an appropriate hurdle rate for an IRR. Accounting profits do not consider opportunity costs.

5. The annual report of company XYZ contains the following disclosures:

Disclosure 1: "XYZ's management compensation is based on exceeding a target EPS growth rate."

Disclosure 2: "XYZ's management does not change the required rate of return when evaluating capital projects based on whether they are financed by internal or external sources."

Disclosure 3: "When evaluating investment projects, XYZ prepares cash-flow projections based on inflation-adjusted cash flows and discounts them using real rates."

Which of the disclosed policies does *not* conform to best practices regarding capital allocation?

   A. Disclosure 1

   B. Disclosure 2

   C. Disclosure 3

Solution:

A is correct. Positive-NPV investment projects can reduce, rather than increase, EPS in the near term, even though they increase shareholder value. Management compensation should incorporate a longer-term perspective and a measure that better considers required rates of return, such as ROIC. B is incorrect because internally generated capital, such as cash flow from operations, is equity financing and it could be returned to equity investors as a dividend. Regardless of the financing source, management should use appropriate risk-adjusted required rates of return to evaluate capital investments.

C is incorrect because companies may perform analysis in either nominal or real terms, but the approach to cash flows and the discount rate should be consistent. That is, nominal cash flows should be discounted at a nominal discount rate, and real (inflation-adjusted) cash flows should be discounted at a real rate.

6. Explain what real options are and how they influence company value.

Solution:

Real options are similar to financial options, except that they deal with real, instead of financial, assets. Real options grant companies the right to make a decision (but do not impose an obligation) in the future that alters the value of capital investment decisions made today. Real options, by providing future decision-making flexibility to companies, can be an important piece of the value in many capital investments.

CAPITAL INVESTMENTS

2

☐ | describe types of capital investments

Capital investments, also referred to as *capital projects*, are investments with a life of one year or longer, which usually appear on the balance sheet as long-term assets. Like most assets, capital investments are initially recorded at cost. The expenditure is not recorded on the income statement; rather, a portion of the cost is recorded on the income statement periodically as a non-cash **depreciation** or **amortization** expense over the asset's useful life. The result is that capital spending is "smoothed" over time and aligned with the inflow of benefits from the investment. On the statement of cash flows, cash capital spending is simply reported as incurred.

In subsequent periods, capital investment assets are presented on the balance sheet on a *net* basis: cost less accumulated depreciation or amortization. As depreciation or amortization is recorded over time and accumulates, this net value declines to zero or a salvage value. The process is illustrated in Exhibit 1 and will be covered in greater detail later in the curriculum.

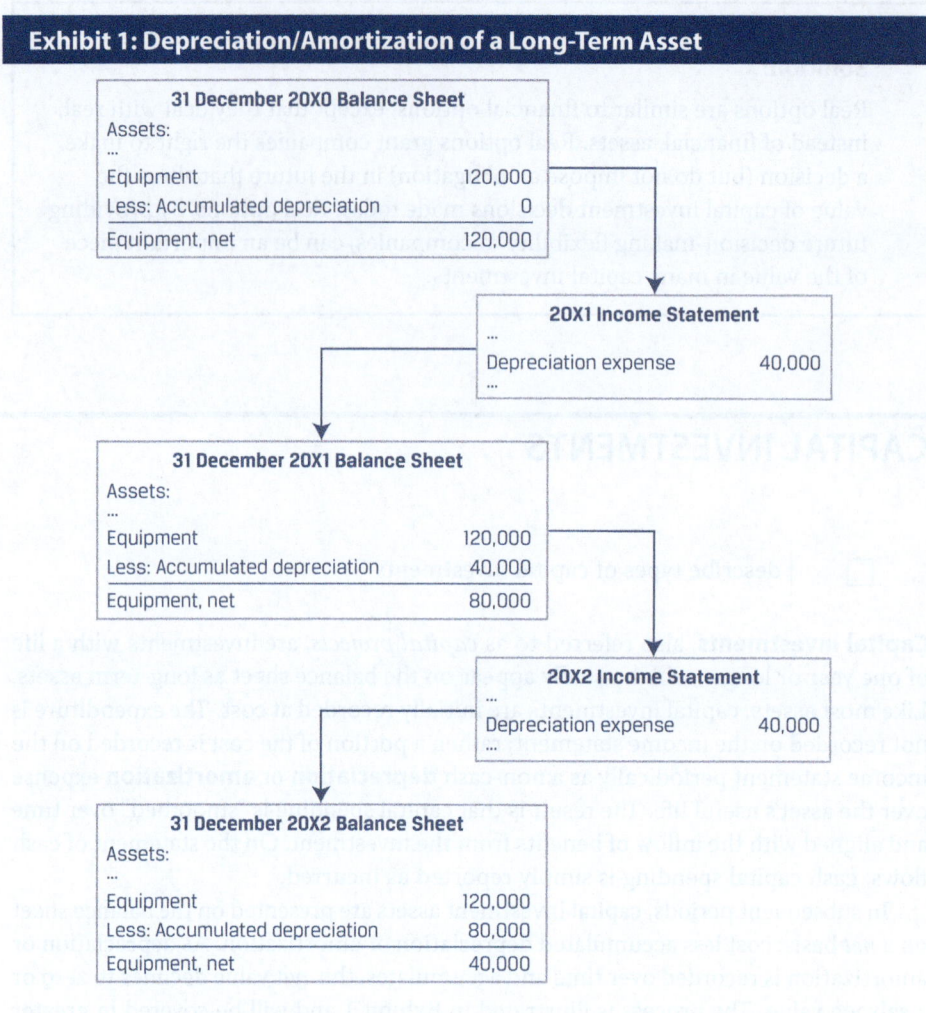

Exhibit 1: Depreciation/Amortization of a Long-Term Asset

A firm's capital investment and allocation process are central to its success and therefore important for analysts to understand. Capital investments describe a company's prospects best, providing insight into both the quality of management decisions and how the company creates value. Note that capital investments are not limited to property, equipment, and other tangible assets; increasingly, capital investments are in the form of digital capabilities and other intangible assets. Regardless of the nature of the asset, the principles in this learning module apply because we are focused on cash flows.

Four categories of capital investments and their potential uses are summarized in Exhibit 2. These investments usually link to the business model of the firm and reflect its strategic and competitive environment.

Exhibit 2: Types of Capital Projects	
Maintain Business	**Grow Business**
Going Concern (Maintenance)	**Expansion of Existing Business**
▪ Continue current operations	▪ Expand business size
▪ Improve efficiency	▪ Expand business scope
▪ Risk management	▪ Research and development and acquisitions within core business
	▪ Low to moderate risk
Regulatory/Compliance	**New Lines of Business and Other**
▪ Usually imposed by a third party, laws, etc.	▪ Research and development, investments, and acquisitions outside the firm's current business
▪ Needed to meet safety, compliance, regulatory or supervisory standards	▪ Often high risk

Going Concern Projects

Going concern projects, often known as **maintenance capital expenditures**, are investments to continue the company's current operations and maintain the existing size of the business. Common going concern projects include replacing assets nearing the end of their useful life, maintaining IT hardware and software, and continuous improvements of existing facilities. For example, a company might replace data center cooling units with newer, more efficient alternatives.

These maintenance projects are relatively easy for management to evaluate since they usually involve the replication of existing business operations. Projects aimed at improving efficiencies typically involve comparing the upfront cost to the expected periodic savings over time in the context of current operations. Typically, these projects are lower risk.

To fund these projects, managers (and debt investors who provide the financing) usually seek to match the term of incremental financing with the lifespan of new assets. For example, a utility company may issue a 30-year bond to finance replacement power generation equipment with an expected useful life of 30 years. This so-called **match funding** approach reduces financing risk, because funding long-term assets with shorter debt obligations introduces rollover risk, or uncertain financing cost or availability during the project before the capital investment reaches the end of its useful life. Similarly, a company that borrows for longer than necessary may either pay a higher long-term rate of interest or face the cost of buying back debt in the future that is no longer needed.

Issuers are not required to disclose the amount of maintenance capital expenditures or the composition of total capital expenditures generally. Analysts often estimate that annual maintenance capital expenditure is equal to the amount of depreciation and amortization expense reported on the income statement. The accuracy of this estimate depends on how closely the expected useful life of assets approximates actual useful life and whether the historical cost of an asset approximates its replacement cost; both assumptions are likely to be more accurate for shorter-lived assets.

Regulatory Compliance Projects

Unlike projects based on management discretion, regulatory compliance projects are required to meet rules and standards. For example, such projects may be driven by a new law to reduce pollution or financial regulations requiring banks to monitor and report transactions and balances to regulators.

Regulatory compliance projects often increase a firm's expenses with no added revenue but are required to avoid fines and/or to continue operations. However, industry incumbents may find that such rules and standards serve as a barrier to industry entry and therefore increase or protect their profitability. Also, when firms work directly with regulators to develop these new standards, their timing and impact may be tailored to best suit an industry's ability to adapt while continuing operations. Firms with greater financial flexibility may consider early adoption of new rules to reduce business uncertainty going forward and gain a competitive edge versus their peers. Moreover, such investments can attract new customers and are often considered to create a strategic advantage.

As standards evolve, firms must decide whether the returns on an underlying business remain attractive once additional regulatory costs are imposed. In some cases, firms may be able to pass some or all of the additional regulatory costs from these projects on to end users in the form of higher prices. In other cases, a firm may decide that a business no longer meets its minimum return requirement (once the costs of such projects are included) and it would be better off winding down or ceasing certain affected operations altogether.

EXAMPLE 1

Complying with Anti-Money-Laundering Regulations

Danske Bank A/S ("Danske"), the largest financial institution in Denmark, is subject to a large anti-money-laundering investigation after a report from a whistle blower and audit letters from Group Internal Audit. Danske acknowledged in a press release that *"major deficiencies in controls and governance made it possible to use Danske Bank's branch in Estonia for criminal activities, such as money laundering."*

The examination of Danske's anti-money-laundering policies resulted in the resignation of its CEO, the closure of the Estonian branch, and the arrests of multiple employees. Danske is also expected to pay fines of up to several billion dollars to financial regulators in the United States, Denmark, and other European countries. The scandal not only had an impact on Danske but also resulted in increasing penalties for money laundering in Denmark.

While regulatory compliance projects can be costly, they can prevent scandals and losses from fines and legal proceedings that damage firms' reputations.

Businesses seeking to grow often engage in capital projects to increase the *scale* of existing business activities, expand their *scope* to new areas of operation, or enter new areas. These expansion projects typically involve greater uncertainty, time, and amounts of capital than going concern or regulatory compliance projects.

Expansion of Existing Business

Capital projects aimed at increasing the size of a firm's existing operations may introduce execution risks, such as sourcing additional inputs, addressing unforeseen production and distribution bottlenecks, or failing to budget for the cost of acquiring new customers. These risks are highest among firms in an early phase without established operations whose expansion projects are therefore usually largely financed by equity. More established firms also spend heavily on expansion projects. For example, pharmaceutical and energy exploration companies often invest over 10% of annual revenues in pursuit of new medications and energy reserves, respectively. Similarly, technology companies typically invest heavily in expansion projects initially to accelerate product development cycles, maintain competitiveness, acquire customers and clients, and stay ahead of rivals. Established firms with an existing track record of successful expansion are more often able to use debt financing for such capital projects given investor perception of lower associated risk.

Capital investments are also usually necessary if an established firm decides to extend its existing operations to adjacent products and services or expand to new regions or markets. The expansion of business scope may take advantage of existing capabilities to meet the needs of a different customer base. Unforeseen risks related to increasing scope include the added complexity of managing multiple business lines and facing new competitors. Investors and analysts often look to a firm's competitive position and past performance by peers in executing similar strategies when gauging the likelihood of success.

EXAMPLE 2

Sony Grows Gaming Business

Sony Interactive Entertainment ("SIE") is a global, leading video game and digital entertainment company owned by Japanese multinational conglomerate Sony. SIE conducts the research and development, production, and sales of both hardware and software for the PlayStation console.

In January 2022, SIE announced it would acquire Bungie Inc. ("Bungie") for $3.6 billion. Bungie is a US-based independent videogame developer and long-time partner of SIE that has created some of the videogame industry's most highly acclaimed franchises, including Halo, Myth, and Destiny.

In the press release, SIE summarized how the acquisition would expand its business: "This acquisition will give SIE access to Bungie's world-class approach to live game services and technology expertise, furthering SIE's vision to reach billions of players."

New Lines of Business and Other Projects

A firm's management may decide to invest in an activity completely outside or only minimally related to its existing business. Usually seen as a special situation offering unusual growth, investment, or innovation opportunities for a company's business or business model, these projects are likely to be the riskiest capital investments.

Either these projects will have characteristics of a startup, such as investing capital to explore a new technology or a business idea/model for sources of new business growth, or the company will acquire a firm in a new industry or sector. Important risks include the unforeseen challenges of an unfamiliar business and the risk of overpaying.

EXAMPLE 3

Kirin Enters New Market

Kirin Holding ("Kirin") is an integrated beverage producer and the second largest brewer in Japan. Kirin's top brands include both alcoholic beverages, such as Kirin Ichiban and Honkirin, and soft drinks, such as Kirin Gogo-no-Kocha and Nama-cha.

In September 2019, Kirin invested ¥129 billion to become a top shareholder of Fancl Corp. ("Fancl"), a Japanese cosmetics and dietary supplement maker. Fancl has more than 25 years of experience as a pioneer in the supplement market and is a market leader in foods with functional claims. Both companies want to combine their research and development capabilities with their strong brands to offer a wide range of products.

Analysts should carefully examine issuers' overall level and trend of expansion capital investment, as well as the segment and market if disclosed, to analyze growth prospects, management priorities, and the rates of return on investment relative to alternatives. The level and trend of expansion capital spending may be estimated by subtracting maintenance (often estimated using depreciation and amortization expense) from total capital expenditures.

QUESTION SET

1. Match the following examples of capital projects with type of the project.

   - Project 1: An office equipment producer decides to develop a new line of computer peripherals intended for gamers.
   - Project 2: A tire producer decides to invest in solar panel production to benefit from government subsidies.
   - Project 3: A global bank migrates its on-site data storage to cloud computing data storage to improve its cost efficiency.
   - Project 4: A property management company undertakes a new capital project intended to install an advanced ventilation system in all its office buildings to meet stricter air pollution regulations.

Project Type	Capital Project
Expansion of existing business	
Going concern/maintenance	
Regulatory or compliance	
New lines of business and other	

Solution:

Project Type	Capital Project
Expansion of existing business	Project 1, because it aims to increase the size of a firm's existing operations and acquire new customers
Going concern/maintenance	Project 3, which allows the bank to continue its current operations using more efficient technology
Regulatory or compliance	Project 4, because unlike projects based on management discretion, this project is to comply with air pollution regulations.
New lines of business and other	Project 2, which is an investment into a new market not related to the company's existing business

2. It is true that the capital allocation process:

   A. involves the use of significant proprietary, non-public information about a company.

   B. aims at identifying projects with the highest absolute non-risk-adjusted rate of returns.

   C. uses less information compared to the process used to construct investment management portfolios.

   Solution:

   A is correct. The capital allocation process is the process used by a firm's management and board to make capital investment based on both internal, non-public *and* public information. The process is substantially similar to those used by investors and analysts constructing investment management portfolios but occurs at a more granular level of detail and more in "real time" because insiders do not need to wait for quarterly earnings reports.
   B is incorrect because the capital allocation process is used by a firm's management to deliver superior risk-adjusted returns, when compared to similarly risky investments.
   C is incorrect because the capital allocation process is more granular compared to the process used to construct investment management portfolios. The capital allocation process focuses on identifying profitable projects and utilizes proprietary information. The process used to construct investment portfolios involves public information and non-material, non-public information, often at the company and segment level.

3. What type of capital allocation project will *most likely* be implemented even if it has a negative estimated NPV?

   A. New lines of business and other

   B. Expansion of existing business

   C. Regulatory or compliance

   Solution:

   C is correct. Regulatory compliance projects are required by third parties, such as government regulatory bodies, to meet rules and standards and to avoid fines or other legal consequences.
   A and B are incorrect because new lines of business and other as well as expansion of existing business projects are done at management's discretion

and would generally not be pursued if they were estimated to have a negative NPV.

3 CAPITAL ALLOCATION

☐ describe the capital allocation process, calculate net present value (NPV), internal rate of return (IRR), and return on invested capital (ROIC), and contrast their use in capital allocation

Capital allocation is the process used by a firm's management and board to make capital investment and return decisions. Management seeks to deliver risk-adjusted returns greater than what investors could earn on similarly risky investments elsewhere. The process is substantially similar to those used by investors and analysts constructing investment management portfolios but occurs at a more granular level of detail. Rather than only investing in entire companies, issuers invest in projects and utilize significant proprietary, non-public information.

Investors and analysts must judge whether an issuer will manage capital wisely over the long term. To make that judgment, analysts should evaluate the issuer's capital allocation process and its adherence to first principles and, most importantly, assess the issuer's historical track record of capital allocation. The generic steps in the capital allocation process are shown in Exhibit 3.

Exhibit 3: Steps in the Capital Allocation Process

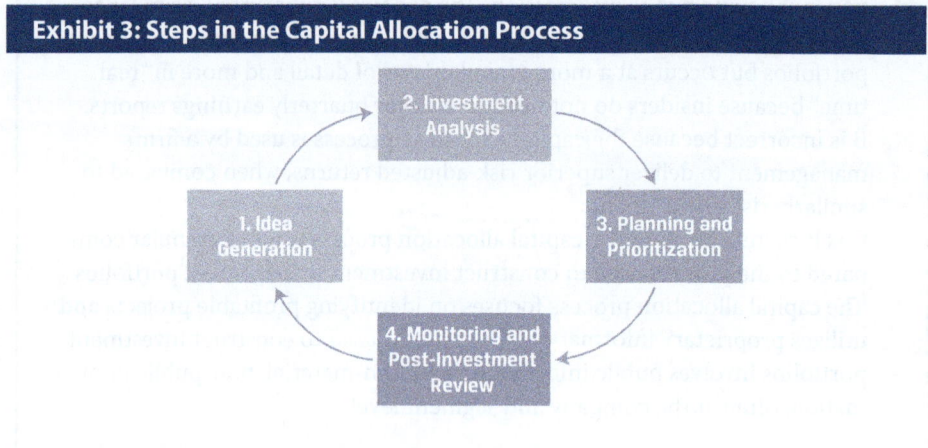

- *Idea generation:* While ideas may originate from anywhere, it is important that management has a strong understanding of the competitive environment that the prospective investment is situated in, as well as the firm's current operations, capabilities, and competitive position. Often, ideas come from managers engaged in the business and involve expanding scale and scope of existing activities or adjacent businesses. Executives may also engage external consultants for advice on idea generation. As will be discussed later, capital spending tends to be highly correlated from year to year, indicating that prior-period ideas and plans weigh heavily.

- *Investment analysis:* Following the generation of investment ideas, managers forecast the amount, timing, duration, and volatility of an investment's expected cash flows to estimate whether the investment is a wise use of capital.

- *Planning and prioritization:* Management selects and prioritizes profitable investment opportunities that, when considered together, are the most value enhancing on a risk-adjusted return basis. Only investment candidates estimated to generate returns greater than investors' opportunity cost (the returns they could earn elsewhere on similarly risky endeavors) should be pursued. Additionally, some projects that appear attractive in isolation may be less desirable when considered in the context of existing operations, other proposed projects, or constraints on financing.

When value-creative investment opportunities are exhausted, managers should return any remaining capital to shareholders. In this way, shareholders can redeploy that capital elsewhere to earn their required rate of return.

- *Monitoring and post-investment review:* This step involves monitoring the performance of the investment and related activities against projections and, often, making adjustments, such as increasing or decreasing investment levels (which will be discussed later as real options). This step is important for several reasons. First, it helps validate assumptions made in the capital allocation process, revealing systematic errors, such as overly optimistic forecasts. Second, it helps enforce discipline in business operations by focusing management attention on bringing performance into alignment with projections. Finally, it may produce ideas for future investments. Managers should seek to invest in profitable areas and scale down or dispose of assets in areas that generate suboptimal returns or may have greater value to other firms.

Two of the most widely used analytical tools in the investment analysis step are **net present value (NPV)** and **internal rate of return (IRR)**. These are applications of time-value-of-money concepts. While an independent investment analyst does not have access to the project-by-project information used by management in these calculations, an analyst should understand the rationale behind them, their strengths, and their limitations in practice (also, these tools are used elsewhere in investment management, which will be covered later in the curriculum). Analysts have access to highly aggregated consolidated financial statements, which they can use to calculate and analyze **return on invested capital (ROIC)**, a useful *aggregate*, rather than *project*, return measure.

Net Present Value (NPV)

The NPV of an investment is the present value (in currency terms) of expected future cash inflows less the investment's costs (or cash *outflows*), as shown in Exhibit 4.

Exhibit 4: Net Present Value of a Capital Investment

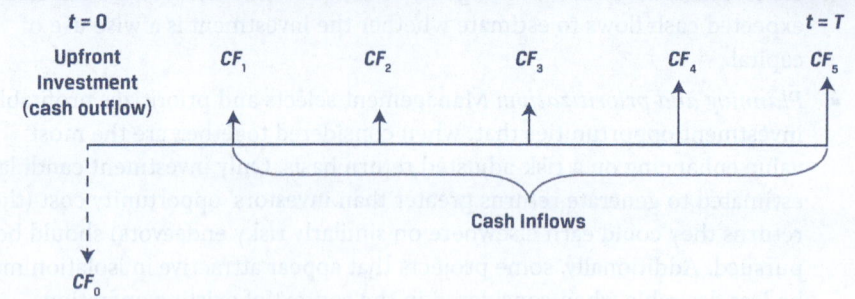

Exhibit 4 shows the simple case where a single investment ($CF_0 < 0$) occurs at inception followed by cash inflows. We may solve for the NPV using Equation 1:

$$NPV = CF_0 + \frac{CF_1}{(1+r)^1} + \frac{CF_2}{(1+r)^2} + \ldots + \frac{CF_T}{(1+r)^T}.$$

(1)

$$NPV = \sum_{t=0}^{T} \frac{CF_t}{(1+r)^t},$$

where

CF_t = After-tax cash flow at time t

   r = Required rate of return—the rate of return that a corporate issuer's investors could earn on a similarly risky investment

The calculation is illustrated in the following example.

EXAMPLE 4

Gerhardt Corporation NPV

1. Assume that Gerhardt Corporation is considering a capital investment of €50 million today that is expected to return after-tax cash flows of €16 million per year for the next four years plus another €20 million in Year 5. If the required rate of return is 10%, what is the NPV of this investment?

Solution:

Using Equation 1, we may solve for the NPV as follows:

$$NPV = CF_0 + \frac{CF_1}{(1+r)^1} + \frac{CF_2}{(1+r)^2} + \ldots + \frac{CF_T}{(1+r)^T}.$$

$$NPV = -50 + \frac{16}{(1+0.10)^1} + \frac{16}{(1+0.10)^2} + \frac{16}{(1+0.10)^3} + \frac{16}{(1+0.10)^4} + \frac{20}{(1+0.10)^5}.$$

$$NPV = -50 + 63.136 = 13.136.$$

Since this investment may be acquired today at a cost of €50 million, the company exchanges €50 million today for an investment worth €63.136 million. The investment increases the present value of the firm's wealth by a net amount of €13.136 million.

This can also be solved in Microsoft Excel or Google Sheets using the NPV function:

=NPV(rate,value1,value2,...)

where

rate = Required rate of return

value(s) = After-tax cash flows

Note that the NPV function uses $t = 1$ for the first cash flow, not $t = 0$, and assumes cash flows are evenly spaced. Therefore, cash flows at $t = 0$ (in this case, –50) need to be subtracted or added outside the function. The proper argument here is

= NPV(0.10, 16, 16, 16, 16, 20) – 50

= 13.136.

Because the NPV is the amount by which investors' wealth increases from an investment, the NPV decision rule is as follows:

Invest if	NPV ≥ 0.
Do not invest if	NPV < 0.

Positive-NPV investments increase the wealth of the shareholders, while a negative NPV reduces wealth. In the rare event that NPV is zero, a project could be accepted because it meets the required rate of return. However, because NPV analysis relies on estimated future cash flows, a zero-NPV project leaves no room for error. While the decision rule is straightforward, NPV is usually just one factor in capital allocation. There may be competing projects, intangible considerations, and so on, that factor into the decision. Therefore, NPV ≥ 0 can be viewed as a *necessary* but not *sufficient* condition for making an investment.

Many investments have unconventional cash flow patterns in which outflows may occur not only at inception but also on future dates, as in Exhibit 5. An example of this is an investment in additional capacity at a later stage.

Exhibit 5: Unconventional Cash Flow Patterns

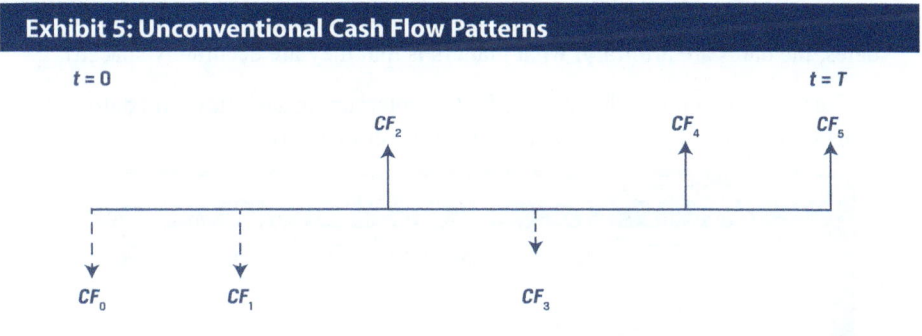

Analysis of these types of investments is best handled using spreadsheet software, such as Microsoft Excel and Google Sheets, manually, or using the XNPV function, which, unlike the NPV function, does *not* assume evenly spaced periods and allows the user to specify the timing of cash flows. This concept is illustrated in the following example.

EXAMPLE 5

Gerhardt Corporation NPV II

Assume that Gerhardt Corporation is considering a capital investment of €50 million today with the following estimated cash flow schedule over the next five years (all amounts in millions of euros).

t	0	1	1.5	2	3	4	5
Cash flow	−50	10	-5	13	16	19	23

1. If the required rate of return is 10%, what is the NPV of this investment and should Gerhardt make the investment?

Solution:

Using Equation 1, we may solve for the NPV as follows:

$$\text{NPV} = CF_0 + \frac{CF_1}{(1+r)^1} + \frac{CF_2}{(1+r)^2} + \dots + \frac{CF_T}{(1+r)^T}.$$

$$\text{NPV} = -50 + \frac{10}{(1+0.10)^1} + \frac{-5}{(1+0.10)^{1.5}} + \frac{13}{(1+0.10)^2} + \frac{16}{(1+0.10)^3} + \frac{19}{(1+0.10)^4}$$

$$+ \frac{23}{(1+0.10)^5}.$$

$$\text{NPV} = 4.78.$$

Since the NPV ≥ 0, Gerhardt should make the investment.

This problem can also be solved in Microsoft Excel or Google Sheets using the XNPV function. The XNPV function syntax is as follows:

=XNPV(rate,values,dates)

where

rate = Required rate of return

values = After-tax cash flows at each date

dates = Date of each after-tax cash flow (for a problem like this without exact dates, the dates are arbitrary; what matters is that they are accurately spaced)

The function is most clearly specified by referencing cash flow and date arrays that are aligned on a spreadsheet, as shown here:

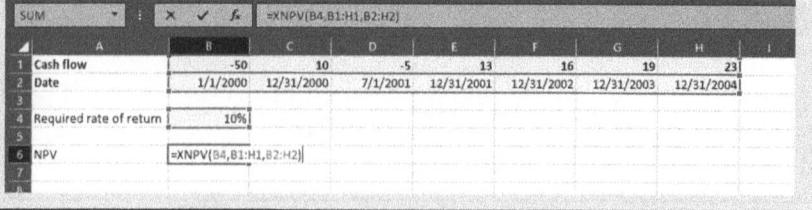

Internal Rate of Return

The **internal rate of return (IRR)** is the discount rate that makes the net present value of an investment equal to zero, as shown in Equation 2:

$$\sum_{t=0}^{T} \frac{CF_t}{(1+IRR)^t} = 0. \tag{2}$$

Note the similarity of the IRR calculation to Equation 1, which includes r (the required rate of return) in the denominator instead of IRR.

EXAMPLE 6

Gerhardt Corporation IRR

1. Assume that Gerhardt Corporation is considering a capital investment of €50 million today that is expected to return after-tax cash flows of €16 million per year for the next four years plus another €20 million in Year 5. What is the IRR of this investment?

Solution:

Recall from Equation 1 that the NPV is

$$NPV = CF_0 + \frac{CF_1}{(1+r)^1} + \frac{CF_2}{(1+r)^2} + \frac{CF_T}{(1+r)^T}$$

The IRR is the discount rate, r, that makes the NPV equal to zero. In other words,

$$NPV = CF_0 + \frac{CF_1}{(1+r)^1} + \frac{CF_2}{(1+r)^2} + \frac{CF_T}{(1+r)^T}$$

$$0 = -50 + \frac{16}{(1+IRR)^1} + \frac{16}{(1+IRR)^2} + \frac{16}{(1+IRR)^3} + \frac{16}{(1+IRR)^4} + \frac{20}{(1+IRR)^5}$$

Besides trial and error, the IRR function in Microsoft Excel and Google Sheets is a straightforward approach to solving this problem. The IRR function syntax is

=IRR(values,[guess])

where

values = After-tax cash flows

[guess] = An optional user-specified guess for the IRR (the default is 10%)

Importantly, like the NPV function, the IRR function assumes that cash flows are received or paid at the end of period and that each period is evenly spaced. Unlike the NPV function, it does not assume that the first cash flow is at $t = 1$, so the argument here is simply

= IRR (–50, 16, 16, 16, 16, 20)

= 0.1952, or 19.52%.

The IRR decision rule is to invest if the IRR *exceeds* the required rate of return (r) for a capital investment:

Invest if	$IRR \geq r$.
Do not invest if	$IRR < r$.

For this reason, the required rate of return is often referred to as the **hurdle rate**. If the IRR is equal to r, the project is *theoretically* acceptable because it meets the required return with an NPV of zero. Since the IRR of 19.52% in our example exceeds the hurdle rate of 10%, Gerhardt should invest.

An important attribute of IRR is that it will only equal an investor's (geometric) rate of return on an investment if interim cash flows are reinvested at the IRR; if reinvestment rates are in fact lower, the rate of return on the investment will be lower than the IRR and vice versa. The NPV calculation instead assumes interim cash flows are reinvested at r, the required rate of return, which is often more economically realistic. Reinvestment rates and the implications therein will be explored in depth later in the curriculum in fixed-income lessons.

For an investment for which the assumptions of end-of-period, evenly spaced cash flows are inappropriate, the XIRR function in Microsoft Excel and Google Sheets is the proper tool, as in the following example.

EXAMPLE 7

Gerhardt Corporation IRR III

1. Assume that Gerhardt Corporation is considering a capital investment of €50 million today with the following estimated cash flow schedule over the next five years (all amounts in millions of euros).

t	0	1	2	2.5	3	4	5
Cash flow	−50	0	1	3	16	20	25

What is the IRR of this investment, and should Gerhardt make the investment if its required rate of return is 10%?

Solution:

This problem can be solved in Microsoft Excel or Google Sheets using the XIRR function. The XIRR function syntax is as follows:

=XIRR(values,dates,[guess])

where

values = After-tax cash flows at each date

dates = Date of each after-tax cash flow (for a problem like this without exact dates, the dates are arbitrary; what matters is that they are accurately spaced)

[guess] = An optional user-specified guess for the IRR (the default is 10%)

The function is most clearly specified by referencing cash flow and date arrays that are aligned on a spreadsheet, as shown here:

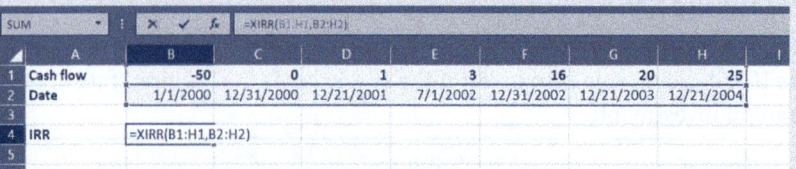

The IRR is 6.76%, which is below Gerhardt's required rate of return of 10%, so it should not invest in this project.

An important limitation with IRR is that multiple IRRs exist if cash flow signs (+/−) change more than once. We can illustrate this with the following simple example:

Time	0	1	2
Cash flow	−1,000	5,000	−6,000

The IRR for this investment satisfies this equation:

$$-1,000 + \frac{5,000}{(1 + \text{IRR})^1} + \frac{-6,000}{(1 + \text{IRR})^2} = 0.$$

Two values of IRR satisfy the equation: 100% and 200%, which are clearly quite different. In such cases, where cash flow signs change more than once, NPV should be used instead of IRR. Financial calculators and spreadsheet software will often misleadingly return a single IRR solution, defaulting to the lowest value.

WHICH TO USE: NPV OR IRR?

While NPV and IRR criteria usually indicate the same investment decision, in the case of mutually exclusive investment projects, a company could face a decision between one project with a larger NPV and another with a higher IRR. If the company can invest in only one project, which should it choose?

The correct choice is the project with the higher NPV. While NPV shows the firm's wealth increase in currency terms from a capital investment, the IRR solely indicates a project's rate of return (subject to the IRR reinvestment assumption) rather than its size or the period over which the IRR is earned.

Many practitioners find IRR easier to use than NPV. If the required return is 10%, for example, a project IRR of more than 10% is desirable, while an NPV amount in currency terms may be harder to interpret because the number needs to be in the context of firm size. As a practical matter, once a firm has the data to calculate the NPV, it is simple to also calculate the IRR. However, the most appropriate and theoretically sound criterion is the NPV.

Return on Invested Capital

Independent investment analysts do not have the necessary information to calculate or audit management's calculations of project NPVs or IRRs. Analysts of listed companies have consolidated financial statements and, sometimes, segment-level information, all of which are highly aggregated and include cash flows associated with many projects. Return on invested capital, also known as return on capital employed (ROCE), is a profitability measure for the total capital that management has invested, shown as Equation 3. Typically, an annual after-tax profit measure is used, so ROIC is measured *per year*.

$$\text{ROIC} = \frac{\text{After-tax operating profit}_t}{\text{Average invested capital}} = \frac{(1 - \text{Tax rate}) \times \text{Operating profit}_t}{\text{Average total LT liabilities and equity}_{t-1,t}}. \quad (3)$$

The denominator is a measure of total *capital* investment, so working capital is not included. From the perspective of the balance sheet, invested capital includes the amounts in the red box:

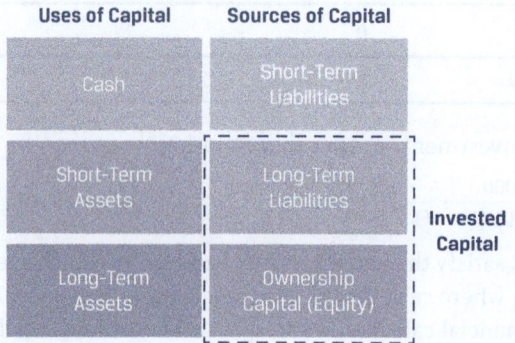

Uses of Capital	Sources of Capital
Cash	Short-Term Liabilities
Short-Term Assets	Long-Term Liabilities
Long-Term Assets	Ownership Capital (Equity)

Invested Capital

EXAMPLE 8

Return on Invested Capital

Assume that a corporate issuer reported 24,395 in Year 2 after-tax operating profits and the following balance sheet information.

Assets:	End of Year 1	End of Year 2
Cash	4,364	6,802
Short-term assets	40,529	52,352
Long-term assets	287,857	279,769
Total assets	332,750	338,923

Liabilities and Equity:	End of Year 1	End of Year 2
Accounts payable	35,221	50,766
Short-term debt	21,142	5,877
Long-term debt	112,257	106,597
Share capital	15,688	15,688
Retained earnings	148,442	159,995
Total liabilities and equity	332,750	338,923

1. Calculate ROIC for Year 2.

   Solution:

   $$ROIC = \frac{\text{After-tax operating profit}_t}{\text{Average LT liabilities and equity capital}_{t-1,t}}$$

   $$ROIC = \frac{24,395}{\frac{(112,257 + 15,688 + 148,442) + (106,597 + 15,688 + 159,995)}{2}}$$

   $ROIC = 8.73\%$.

2. If an investor has a required rate of return of 10%, is this company a promising investment candidate?

   Solution:

   No. Although the company is profitable, the company's ROIC is below the investors' required rate of return, so the investor should look to invest elsewhere. However, this is only a single historical year, and myriad other factors will have to be considered by the investor.

ROIC has several practical benefits:

- Unlike project NPV and IRR, it can be calculated using data available to independent investment analysts.

- Unlike such measures as operating profit or operating profit margin (operating profit as a percentage of sales), ROIC accounts for the capital needed to generate returns. The relationship between operating profit margin and ROIC can be illustrated by decomposing ROIC as follows:

$$\text{ROIC} = \frac{\text{After-tax operating profit}}{\text{Average invested capital}}$$

$$\text{ROIC} = \frac{\text{After-tax operating profit}}{\text{Sales}} \times \frac{\text{Sales}}{\text{Average invested capital}}$$

The term on the left is after-tax operating profit margin, and the term on the right is a measure of capital or asset turnover—how much in annual sales the company's invested capital is generating. Therefore, there are two paths to a high or increasing ROIC: profit margin and turnover. A high-margin company can earn a low ROIC if turnover is low, and a low-margin company can earn an attractive ROIC if turnover is high.

- While NPV and IRR measures allow the comparison of individual projects within a firm, ROIC is an aggregate measure to gauge a firm's ability to create value across *all* its investments. This is important because investors generally cannot invest in individual projects, only the company as a whole (some exceptions exist, such as leases and asset-backed securities, which will be discussed later in fixed-income modules).

- ROIC can be compared to investors' required rate of return. If an issuer's ROIC is greater than the investors' required rate of return over time, the issuer is creating value for investors. Conversely, if the ROIC is below the required rate of return, it is an indicator that investors would have been better off investing elsewhere; the issuer should take actions to improve turnover or profit margins, dispose of investments in underperforming areas, return capital, or seek alternative areas of investment with greater returns.

- Since ROIC measures the returns that an issuer earns on investing both debt and equity, it should be compared to a required rate of return for both its debt *and* equity investors. As discussed in prior lessons, equity is riskier than debt and therefore has a higher required return, so using solely a required return for equity investors would be an overestimate. In the next module, we will calculate a blended required rate of return as part of a broader discussion of financing.

ROIC does have limitations and shortcomings:

- ROIC, unlike NPV and IRR, is an accounting, not cash-based, measure. Operating profit and cash flows can differ materially, owing to the recognition of certain items and the difference between depreciation and capital expenditures.

- ROIC is backward looking and can be volatile from year to year based on investment activity and business conditions, so examining trends and rates of change is essential. Profitable investments can sometimes take years to earn competitive returns.

- As a highly aggregated measure, ROIC may mask profitable or unprofitable areas of the issuer.

Analysts should also be aware that there is less consensus on the measurement of ROIC than such measures as operating profit margin, particularly the denominator. Many practitioners, for example, subtract some or all intangible assets and "excess" cash from the denominator and may exclude certain long-term liabilities, such as pension and deferred tax liabilities that are not considered "invested capital." Additional calculation issues, which will be addressed later in the curriculum, include treatments of "non-recurring" expenses, leased assets, and equity from non-controlling interests.

QUESTION SET

1. True or false. During the planning and prioritization step in the capital allocation process, a firm's management should accept any investment project with an estimated positive NPV.

   Solution:

   False. Some projects that appear attractive in isolation may be less desirable when considered in the context of existing operations, other proposed projects, ESG factors, or financing constraints.

2. Which step in the capital allocation process *most likely* involves the calculation of NPV and IRR?

   A. Idea generation

   B. Investment analysis

   C. Planning and prioritization

   Solution:

   B is correct. The investment analysis step involves forecasting the amount, timing, duration, and volatility of an investment's expected cash flows and subsequently using NPV and IRR to determine whether the investment will be a wise use of capital.

   A is incorrect because during the idea generation step, management gathers ideas and chooses the most promising ones for further analysis. However, in this early phase, no forecasts or profitability analysis involving NPV or IRR is conducted.

   C is incorrect because during the planning and prioritization step, management selects and prioritizes profitable investment opportunities that, when considered together, are the most value enhancing on a risk-adjusted return basis. This step occurs after NPV and IRR analysis.

3. Which of the following relationships is true?

   A. If IRR > Required rate of return, then NPV < 0.

   B. If IRR = Required rate of return, then NPV = 0.

   C. Required rate of return = Risk-free rate.

   Solution:

   B is correct. IRR is the required rate of return that makes an investment's NPV equal to zero.

   A is incorrect because IRR is the required rate of return for which NPV = 0. If IRR is greater than the required rate of return, then NPV of cash flows discounted at the required rate of return will be greater than zero, not less than zero.

C is incorrect because when calculating NPV, expected cash flows should be discounted at the required rate of return to reflect investors' opportunity cost for similarly risky projects, not a rate that ignores risk.

4. A company is considering undertaking a new capital investment project that is expected to cost $33 million. The after-tax cash-flow projection for the next four years is shown below. Calculate NPV and IRR assuming a required rate of return of 7.5%.

Year	1	2	3	4
Cash flow	0	16	24	7

Solution:

To calculate NPV, we use the following equation:

$$NPV = CF_0 + \frac{CF_1}{(1+r)^1} + \frac{CF_2}{(1+r)^2} + \dots + \frac{CF_T}{(1+r)^T}.$$

$$NPV = -33 + \frac{0}{(1+0.075)^1} + \frac{16}{(1+0.075)^2} + \frac{24}{(1+0.075)^3} + \frac{7}{(1+0.075)^4}..$$

NPV = $5.41 million.

Using the same equation, we can also solve for IRR by assuming that NPV = 0.

$$0 = -33 + \frac{0}{(1+IRR)^1} + \frac{16}{(1+IRR)^2} + \frac{24}{(1+IRR)^3} + \frac{7}{(1+IRR)^4}.$$

IRR = 13.57%.

5. Based on the information below, calculate ROIC for year 20X2. Values in each column are as of the end of the period. Assume operating profit of 3,890 and a tax rate of 17% in Year 20X2.

Balance Sheet		
Assets:	**20X1**	**20X2**
Cash	490	700
Short-term assets	10,520	11,790
Long-term assets	22,400	23,740
Total assets	33,410	36,230
Liabilities and equity:		
Accounts payable	5,970	6,620
Short-term debt	2,470	2,840
Long-term debt	9,880	10,550
Share capital	15,090	16,220
Total liabilities and equity	33,410	36,230

Solution:

ROIC can be calculated using the following formula:

$$ROIC = \frac{(1 - \text{Tax rate}) \times \text{Operating profit}_t}{\text{Average LT liabilities and equity}_{t-1,t}}.$$

$$ROIC = \frac{(1 - 0.17) \times 3,890}{(9,880 + 15,090 + 10,550 + 16,220)/2}.$$

$$ROIC = 12.48\%.$$

6. Complete the sentences by filling in the blanks using the following terms. Note that each term can be used more than once.

   equity

   profit margin

   asset turnover

   long-term liabilities

   average invested capital

   ROIC can be increased by increasing _____ or _____. A high-_____ company can earn a low ROIC if _____ is low, and a low-_____ company can earn a high ROIC if _____ is high.

   Solution:

   ROIC can be increased by increasing *profit margin* or *asset turnover*. A high-*profit margin* company can earn a low ROIC if *asset turnover* is low, and a low-*profit margin* company can earn a high ROIC if *asset turnover* is high.

7. Explain why a government-owned company may have a low required rate of return compared to a small technology company.

   Solution:

   The required rate of return is the discount rate that investors require given the riskiness of the project or company and the rate of return available on other similarly risky investments. Considering the business risk of both companies, a government-owned company can be perceived as a lower-risk issuer compared to a small technology company. Consequently, investors would require less compensation for risk.

---

4   CAPITAL ALLOCATION PRINCIPLES AND PITFALLS

☐ | describe principles of capital allocation and common capital allocation pitfalls

Capital Allocation Principles

While the analytical tools and investment decision criteria introduced in the prior lesson are quantitative and straightforward, there is considerable latitude for errors and misjudgment. To improve the decision-making process, key principles should be followed when using these tools.

- *After-tax cash flows:* Managers should evaluate capital allocation decisions based on after-tax cash flows rather than other profit- or accounting-based measures. Managers must reflect the impact of taxation on a project's expected cash flows, specifically the tax benefits derived from non-cash deductions, such as depreciation and amortization.

- *Incremental cash flows only but examine broadly:* Capital allocation analysis should ignore **sunk costs**, or those expenses that have already been incurred (or written off), and include only incremental cash flows associated with a new investment as compared to without it. However, capital investments often have an impact on the rest of the firm, which may be positive or negative. A positive effect might include cost savings with business activities that directly result from making the investment, while a negative effect might be the loss of sales from a similar product. Both are incremental cash flows, so they should be included in the analysis.

- *Timing of cash flows:* The forecasted timing, duration, volatility, and change in the possible direction of the expected cash flows must be considered for a capital investment. Notice how the NPV and IRR can change when cash flows are moved from one period to another.

Capital Allocation Pitfalls

Despite adhering to the principles, capital allocation is challenging for most firms. We divide common capital allocation pitfalls into cognitive errors and behavioral biases. Cognitive errors include calculation and other mistakes, while behavioral biases include errors in judgment and blind spots.

Cognitive Errors in Capital Allocation

- *Internal forecasting errors:* Management may make errors in their forecasts, which may be difficult to impossible for external analysts to identify. However, if significant enough, the incorrect or flawed analysis will ultimately manifest itself in failed, or underperforming, investments. Forecasting errors include incorrect cost or required rates of return inputs. For example, overhead costs such as management time, information technology support, financial systems, can be challenging to estimate. Finally, companies often fail to incorporate competitor responses into the analysis of a planned investment.

- *Ignoring costs of internal financing:* The primary source of financing for investments by large corporate issuers is cash flows from operations (i.e., not borrowing or issuing shares). Many management teams behave as if these internally generated funds are "free" but scarce and allocate them according to a budget that is closely tied to prior-period amounts. External financing from debt or equity issuance, however, is treated differently: It is used less often, typically only for larger investments, such as acquisitions, and treated as "expensive." This is flawed logic. Internally generated capital, such as cash flow from operations, *is* equity financing because it could be returned to equity investors as a dividend. While it is not raised from equity investors by issuing shares, it is withheld from them, incurring their opportunity cost nonetheless. Regardless of financing source, management should use appropriate risk-adjusted required rates of return to evaluate capital investments; those funded by internally generated funds do not automatically get a lower *r*.

This error is hard to detect and isolate from other errors and biases, but analysts should inquire about management's capital allocation process and how the source of financing influences investment decisions. If a company has an aversion to raising external capital and to returning capital, management may potentially be affected by this.

- *Inconsistent treatment of, or ignoring, inflation:* Inflation affects capital allocation in several ways. The first is whether the investment analysis is done in nominal or in real terms. Nominal cash flows include inflation effects, whereas real cash flows are adjusted downward to remove the effect of inflation (or adjusted upward to remove the effect of deflation). Companies may perform analysis in either nominal or real terms, but the approach to cash flows and discount rate should be consistent. That is, nominal cash flows should be discounted at a nominal discount rate, and real cash flows should be discounted at a real rate.

Investment analysis embeds, explicitly or implicitly, expectations for inflation, which probably does not affect all unit prices and unit costs uniformly. For example, rising oil prices are obviously beneficial for oil producers, which sell their product at a higher price. However, rising oil prices over longer time periods can be associated with rising production and capital costs, eroding some of the benefit. Second, many oil companies also own refining and chemical businesses, for which crude oil is the main input. Profitability of those businesses tends to decline as crude prices rise. If actual inflation differs from expected inflation, after-tax cash flows will be better or worse than expected depending on how specific sales outputs or cost inputs are affected.

Behavioral Biases in Capital Allocation

- *Inertia:* In a study of more than 1,600 US listed companies, researchers from McKinsey found a 0.92 correlation between levels of capital investment in a business segment or unit from one year to the next.[1] This is the result of management anchoring capital investment budgets to prior-year amounts. Analysts identify this bias by examining the level of capital investment in total, by segment, or by business line, if disclosed, and comparing it to the prior year and the return on investment. If capital investment each year is static or rising despite falling returns on investment, analyst should question the issuer's justification for a capital investment and whether management should consider alternative uses.

- *Basing investment decisions on accounting measures, such as EPS:* Managers often have an incentive to increase accounting measures, such as earnings per share, net income, or return on equity. Many capital investments, even those with high NPVs, can reduce rather than increase these accounting results in the near term, while cost cutting and share buybacks, in contrast, may have a positive effect on such measures. Paying too much attention to short-run accounting numbers can lead a company to choose investments that are not in the long-run interests of its shareholders. Analysts may observe this behavior first by examining the direct financial incentives of management based on the structure and composition of their compensation.

---

1 Stephen Hall, Dan Lovallo, and Reiner Musters, "How to Put Your Money Where Your Strategy Is," *McKinsey Quarterly* (March 2012).

Second, analysts can compare the level of capital spending to historical and peer levels to judge whether management has prioritized shorter-term, accounting-based measures. That said, lower capital investment may be a sign of limited investment opportunities, in which case allocating capital to alternative uses is a wise decision.

- *Pet project bias:* Projects that receive preferential treatment, or so-called **pet projects**, are sometimes selected without thorough capital allocation analysis. In other cases, such analysis is conducted but overly optimistic projections are used to inflate the pet project's profitability. Identifying pet projects is difficult, because financial statements are usually aggregated and such projects may not meet the threshold of materiality. Instead, analysts should evaluate the corporate governance structure for warning signs that increase the chances of misallocation of capital: controlled companies or significant ownership concentration by a single individual or group, weak oversight by the board of directors, and executive compensation that is not aligned with stakeholders' interests.

- *Failure to consider investment alternatives or alternative scenarios:* While investment idea generation is the first step in the capital allocation process, many viable alternatives are never even considered at some companies. Firms also often fail to consider different outcomes, which can and should be incorporated through breakeven, scenario, and simulation analyses. This error may stem from limited capital investment experience, such as not making divestitures or acquisitions, or no experience with a failed investment. While failure is obviously undesirable, the lack of failure over time may reflect a management team that is not taking enough risk.

QUESTION SET

---

1. True or false: Investment projects funded using internally generated funds (e.g., cash flow from operations) should be evaluated using a lower required rate of return as compared to projects funded using debt or share issuance.

   Solution:

   False. Ignoring the cost of internal financing is a common cognitive error. Internally generated capital, such as cash flow from operations, is equity financing because it could be returned to equity investors as a dividend or share repurchase. While internally generated capital is not raised from equity investors by issuing shares, it is withheld from them, therefore incurring their opportunity cost. Regardless of financing source, management should use an appropriate risk-adjusted required rate of return to evaluate capital investments.

---

2. Alexandra Tolonen, an investment analyst, prepares forecasts for expansion of a car battery plant and wants to consider the effect of rising lithium carbonate prices. Tolonen adjusts future after-tax cashflows downward to remove the effects of an expected lithium carbonate price increase of 5%

and uses real discount rates to calculate the project's NPV. In the second year of the project, the actual lithium carbonate price increased by 10%.

True or false. Given that Tolonen has used inflation-adjusted cash flows and discount rates, the rise in lithium carbonate prices will not impact the project's profitability.

Solution:

False. Even though Tolonen was consistent in using real cash flows and real rates while preparing the forecast, this fact does not make the project immune to changes in inflation. If actual inflation differs from expected inflation, after-tax cash flows will be better or worse than expected, depending on how specific cost inputs are affected.

3. An analyst is analyzing company XYZ and has gathered annual invested capital and ROIC for each of the three XYZ business segments.

| | Capital Expenditures ($ m) | | | ROIC | | |
Segment	20X0	20X1	20X2	20X0	20X1	20X2
A	264	282	303	7.50%	7.10%	6.80%
B	297	318	340	10.00%	8.90%	7.10%
C	211	226	242	6.90%	7.80%	9.00%

Based on the information provided, XYZ's management is *most likely* prone to which of the following biases?

A. Inertia

B. Sunk cost

C. Pet project

Solution:

A is correct. Inertia can be identified by examining the level of capital investment in total, by segment, or by business line, if disclosed, and comparing it to the prior year and the return on investment. If capital investment each year is static or rising despite falling returns on investment, the analyst should question the issuer's justification for a capital investment and whether management should consider alternative uses. In the case of XYZ, we can observe that for segments A and B, ROIC is decreasing, but both segments are getting a higher capital allocation each year.

B is incorrect because sunk cost is related to the capital allocation process in determining a potential project's profitability. Sunk costs, or those expenses that have already been incurred, should be ignored when evaluating potential projects.

C is incorrect because a detailed view of individual investment projects undertaken by XYZ's management is not provided. Identifying pet projects from outside the firm is difficult, because financial statements are aggregated and such projects may not meet the threshold of materiality.

4. Bradshaw, a financial analyst, prepares a forecast of future expected gross (pre-tax) cash flows for an investment project. Bradshaw also forecasts future depreciation related to that project and assumes a required rate of return 6%. Based on the information provided and a tax rate of 18%, calculate

the NPV of the project. In this jurisdiction, depreciation is not deductible for taxes.

Cash Flow and Depreciation Forecast

Time	0	1	2	3
Gross cash flow	−7.50	4.50	4.50	6.00
Depreciation	0.00	−1.00	−1.00	−1.00

Solution:

To calculate NPV for this project, Bradshaw should first calculate after-tax cash flows and consider depreciation only to the extent that it is tax deductible and reduces taxes, because it is non-cash. After-tax cash flows can be calculated by applying the following formula to all cash flows to be received in the future.

$$\text{After-tax cash flow}_t = \text{Gross cash flow}_t \times (1 - \text{Tax rate}).$$

After-Tax Cash Flow Forecast

Time	0	1	2	3
After-tax cash flow	−7.50	3.69	3.69	4.92

The calculation of NPV is follows:

$$\text{NPV} = -7.5 + \frac{3.69}{(1+0.06)^1} + \frac{3.69}{(1+0.06)^2} + \frac{4.92}{(1+0.06)^3}.$$

$$\text{NPV} = 3.396$$

5. Explain why some managers might reject projects that significantly increase shareholder value (i.e., have a high NPV).

Solution:

Managers may have an incentive to increase accounting profitability measures, such as earnings per share, net income, or return on equity. Many capital investments, even those with high NPVs, can reduce rather than increase these measures in the near term, while cost cutting and share buybacks, in contrast, may have a positive effect on such measures. If this incentive is strong enough, management may forgo high-NPV projects in favor of actions that increase near-term earnings per share.

REAL OPTIONS

5

☐ | describe types of real options relevant to capital investments

The capital allocation process described earlier implied that firms make all capital investment decisions for a project at inception, maintaining one course of action throughout the life of a project. In practice, firms often have alternatives, known as **real options**, that can alter the value of capital investments. That is, some capital investment decisions are in fact a series of decisions; some are taken today, while others can be postponed and will be based on future economic events or information. Similar to financial options, such as derivatives, real options grant a firm the right, but not the obligation, to take an action in the future. A company should only pursue (or **exercise**) a real option if it is value enhancing.

Just as the value of a financial option depends on the future value of an underlying asset, real options are contingent on future events for a company. Real options offer flexibility to companies that can greatly enhance the NPV of companies' capital investments in one or more of the following forms:

- *Timing option:* Instead of investing now, the company can choose to delay its investing decision. In doing so, companies forgo near-term returns and hope to obtain improved information for the NPV of projects selected. Investments may be sequenced over time, so that investing in a project creates the option to make future investments.

- *Sizing option:* An **abandonment option** allows a company to abandon the investment after it is undertaken if the financial results are disappointing. At some future date, if the cash flow from abandoning an investment exceeds the present value of the cash flows from continuing the investment, the company should exercise the abandonment option. Conversely, if the company can make additional investments when future financial results are strong, the company has a **growth option**, or expansion option.

- *Flexibility option:* Companies may also benefit from operational flexibility other than abandonment or expansion once an investment is complete. For example, suppose a firm finds that demand for a product or service exceeds capacity. Management may be able to exercise a **price-setting option**. By increasing prices, the company could benefit from the excess demand, which it cannot do by increasing production. Alternatively, a firm may consider **production flexibility options** to alter production when demand differs from its forecast. For example, a firm may add overtime or extra shifts to increase production for a given capacity.

- *Fundamental option:* The entire value of an investment may depend on factors outside the firm's control, such as the price of a commodity. For example, the value of an oil well or refinery investment is contingent on the price of oil. The value of a gold mine is contingent on the price of gold. If oil prices were low, a company likely would not choose to drill a well. If oil prices were high, it would go ahead and drill. Many R&D (research and development) projects are also very similar to such options.

Firms use several approaches in evaluating capital investments with these characteristics, such as the following:

1. Investment analysis *without* considering options: If the NPV is positive without considering real options and the project involves real options that could increase its net present value, then the NPV represents a *minimum* return and the firm should make the investment.

2. Calculation of NPV with real options: Under this approach, the firm calculates a project's NPV based on expected cash flows and then subtracts the incremental cost of the real option and adds its associated value, as shown in Equation 4:

Project NPV = NPV (without options) − Option cost + Option value.   (4)

3. Decision trees and option pricing models: Either approach may be used by firms seeking to assess the value of a capital investment that involves future sequential decisions and alternative outcomes for a given investment. These models often assign a probability and expected timing to future outcomes, which are used to calculate the project's NPV.

To calculate the return on capital investments with or without real options, firms must often assume an expected probability for future events. The following example provides an illustration using a decision tree for evaluating the return on a capital investment with and without real options.

Gerhardt Corporation Capital Allocation Using a Decision Tree

Assume that Gerhardt Corporation is considering a €500 million outlay for a capital investment in a facility to produce a new product. Gerhardt assigns a 60% probability to a successful product launch, which is expected to return €750 million in one year's time. Gerhardt's finance team has also conducted an analysis of alternative facility uses, summarizing the timing and probability of cash flows associated with each real option in the following decision tree.

Gerhardt Corporation Decision Tree

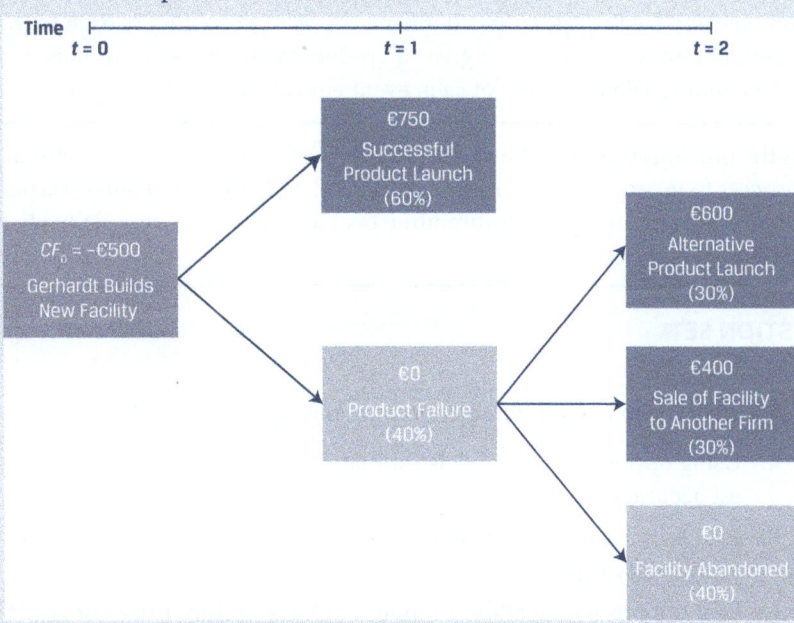

1. Calculate the NPV of Gerhardt's project *without* real options using a 10% required rate of return (r).

   Solution:

   The NPV without real options uses Equation 1 and a probability-weighted cash flow if the product is successfully launched (60%) and a 40% probability that future cash inflows are zero:

$$NPV = CF_0 + \frac{CF_1}{(1+r)^1} + \text{ , or}$$

$$NPV = -500 + \frac{(0.6 \times 750)}{(1.10)}$$

Because NPV = –€90.91, Gerhardt should not pursue the project, based on the NPV decision rule.

2. Calculate the NPV of Gerhardt's proposed project *with* real options and a 10% required rate of return.

Solution:

Calculate NPV with real options using Equation 1 and probability-weighted cash flows in future periods:

$$NPV = CF_0 + \frac{CF_1}{(1+r)^1} + \frac{CF_2}{(1+r)^2}$$

$$= -500 + \frac{(0.6 \times 750)}{(1.10)^1} + \frac{[(0.4 \times 0.3) \times 600] + [(0.4 \times 0.3) \times 400]}{(1.10)^2}$$

The NPV *with* real options equals €8.26, which implies based on the NPV decision rule that Gerhardt should invest in the new production facility if alternative uses in the future are considered. Note that the cash flow calculation for the second period is based on the conditional probabilities of specific outcomes. That is, in the case of both the possible alternative product launch and facility sale to another firm, the 30% probability of each of these mutually exclusive outcomes *given* a product failure in Period 1 (40%) makes the conditional probability of each event equal to 12% (= 0.4 × 0.3).

As the previous example shows, the inclusion of real options in the capital allocation process to incorporate different scenarios related to internal and external events and their expected impact on future after-tax cash flows can materially change the evaluation of an investment.

QUESTION SET

---

1. Which of the following statements about real options is true?

   A. Using option pricing models estimates an option's value with the highest accuracy.

   B. Real options allow companies to abandon an investment project if its profitability is poor.

   C. Real options would allow a refinery to hedge future prices of crude oil needed for production.

   Solution:

   B is correct. An abandonment option is a type of real option, which allows a company to abandon the investment after it is undertaken.

   A is incorrect because even though real options can be priced using option pricing models, the estimates require multiple unobservable inputs, such as probabilities of events and timing of their occurrence. The complexity does not necessarily improve accuracy.

   C is incorrect because real options provide companies with flexibility with regard to future decisions; however, they do not allow the hedging of commodity prices. The risk of crude oil price changes can be hedged using financial options, not real options.

2. ScolarCorp is planning a market research campaign to gauge interest in a new type of product. If interest in the new product is high, the company will need to upgrade its existing production plant to allow for product manufacturing. Alternatively, if interest is low, ScolarCorp will sell the plant for $90 million. The required rate of return for the project is 7.5%. A ScolarCorp analyst summarized the timing and probability of cash flows associated with each alternative use in the following decision tree.

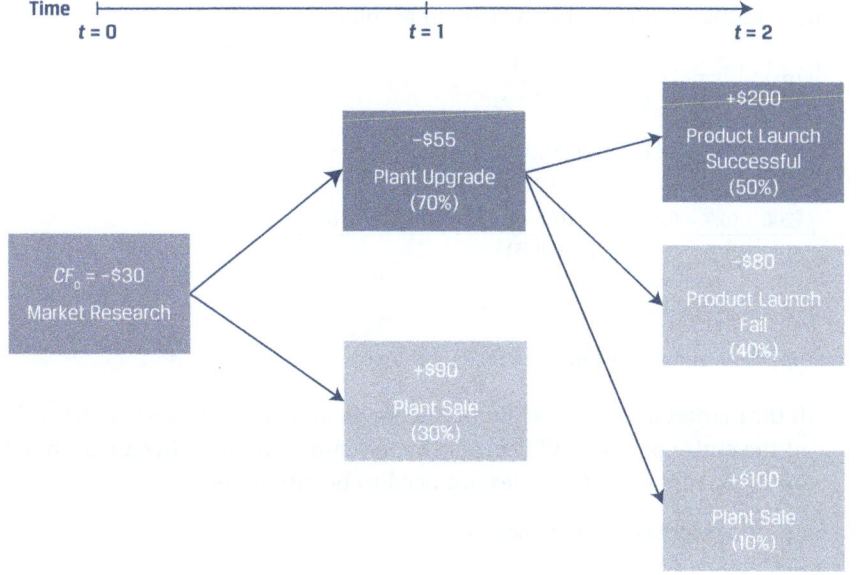

Based on the decision tree, match the following factors with the impact on the capital project's value (option value):

   Increase in market research cost

   Decrease in market research cost

   Increase in plant sale price

   Decrease in plant sale price

   Increasing required rate of return

   Decreasing required rate of return

Increases Project Value	Decreases Project Value

Solution:

Increases Project Value	Decreases Project Value
Decrease in market research cost	Increase in market research cost
Increase in plant sale price	Decrease in plant sale price
Decreasing required rate of return	Increasing required rate of return

The calculation of the NPV of the project, considering all alternatives and their probabilities, can be carried out as follows:

$$NPV = CF_0 + \frac{CF_1}{(1+r)^1} + \frac{CF_1}{(1+r)^2}.$$

$$NPV = -30 + \frac{(-55 \times 0.7 + 90 \times 0.3)}{(1+0.075)^1}$$
$$+ \frac{(200 \times (0.7 \times 0.5) - 80 \times (0.7 \times 0.4) + 100 \times (0.7 \times 0.1))}{(1+0.075)^2}.$$

$NPV = \$6.549$.

Impact of increase in market research cost

If the market research cost increases, for example, by 10 (to −40), the NPV of the entire project will decrease by the same amount. Given that initial outlay occurs at $t = 0$, it does not need to be discounted.

Impact of increase in plant sale price

If the plant sale price increases (either in Year 1 or Year 2), the NPV of the entire project will increase by a smaller amount, given that corresponding cash flow needs to be probability adjusted and discounted to T_0.

Impact of increase in required rate of return

An increase in the required rate of return will decrease the NPV of the entire project, given that it is used to discount future cash flows.

3. Company XYZ is considering expanding its distribution center in a foreign country. The local government is working on a new environmental regulation that introduces subsidies and tax breaks for investments related to renewable energy. Once the new law is approved, XYZ could upgrade the distribution center at lower cost. If the company decides to wait for the new regulation to come into effect, it will have to bear project-related costs of $1.8 million. XYZ's finance team estimates that if the company waits, the NPV of the project will be $9.7 million, compared to a current value of $8.9 million. Calculate option value.

Solution:

To determine option value, we need to compare the project value with and without the option and additionally consider option cost.

Project NPV (with option) = $9.7 million.

Project NPV (without option) = $8.9 million.

Option cost = $1.8 million.

Project NPV (with option)

= Project NPV (without option) − Option cost + Option value.

$9.7 million = $8.9 million − $1.8 million + Option value.

Option value = $2.6 million.

PRACTICE PROBLEMS

The following information relates to questions 1-5

Larissa Soroka, an analyst at ABC company, has been asked to prepare cash flow forecasts for two mutually exclusive investment projects related to new products. ABC's management asks Soroka to include the cost of market research that was recently completed as well as the potential loss of revenue from existing products that could occur if either project is undertaken. Soroka presents the forecast in Exhibit 1 and is asked to calculate IRR and NPV for both projects. Investors in ABC have a required rate of return of 8%.

Exhibit 1					
Cash Flow Forecast for Projects A and B					
Time	**0**	**1**	**2**	**3**	**4**
Project A	(18.5)	4.5	6.0	6.0	5.5
Project B	(33.5)	(2.5)	(1.0)	24.0	25.5

ABC's management asks Soroka to consider in her forecast the impact of a six-month delay in all future cash flows and estimate the impact of that event on IRR and NPV.

After reviewing the forecast, ABC's management asks Soroka to estimate ABC's ROIC for 20X2. ABC earned operating profit of $8,830, had an effective tax rate of 22%, and reported the balance sheet in Exhibit 2.

Exhibit 2		
ABC Balance Sheet **(end-of-period values)**		
Assets:	**20X1**	**20X2**
Cash	1,600	1,720
Short-term assets	30,450	29,910
Long-term assets	60,250	62,060
Total assets	92,300	93,690
Liabilities and equity:	**20X1**	**20X2**
Accounts payable	12,930	11,620
Short-term debt	8,030	8,390
Long-term debt	25,040	25,910
Share capital	39,800	40,990

Liabilities and equity:	20X1	20X2
Retained earnings	6,500	6,780
Total liabilities and equity	92,300	93,690

ABC's management has an ROIC objective of at least 9.2% and asks Soroka for her recommendation about the projects.

1. When preparing the cash-flow forecasts for both projects, Soroka should include:

   A. only the cost of the market research.

   B. only the loss of revenue from existing products.

   C. both the market research cost and the loss of revenue from existing products.

2. With regard to Project A and Project B, which of the following is true?

   A. Both projects should be invested in according to the IRR decision rule.

   B. Both projects should be invested in according to the NPV decision rule.

   C. Only Project B should be invested in according to the IRR decision rule.

3. The *most likely* impact from the cash-flow timing considered by Soroka is that:

   A. both IRR and NPV would decrease.

   B. both IRR and NPV stay unchanged.

   C. only IRR would decrease but NPV would increase.

4. Based on ABC's balance sheet presented in Exhibit 2, Soroka should calculate:

   A. average invested capital of $72,510 and ROIC of 9.50%.

   B. average invested capital of $80,720 and ROIC of 10.94%.

   C. average invested capital of $92,995 and ROIC of 9.50%.

5. Considering ABC management's ROIC-based investment criterion and the IRR and NPV of both projects, Soroka should recommend to:

   A. reject both projects A and B.

   B. invest only in Project B because it has a higher NPV.

   C. invest only in Project A because has positive cash flow during all four years.

SOLUTIONS

1. B is correct. Capital allocation analysis should include only incremental cash flows associated with a new investment. The loss of revenue from existing products is an incremental negative effect that should be included in the analysis. The market research costs in this case are a sunk cost because the research has already been completed and therefore does not affect cash-flow estimates, no matter whether ABC undertakes either of these projects or neither of them.

2. C is correct. The IRR decision rule is to invest if the IRR exceeds the required rate of return or hurdle rate. Project B's IRR is 8.97%, which exceeds the required rate of return of 8%; however, Project A's IRR is 7.04%, which is below the required rate of return of 8%.

    The NPV of both projects can be calculated as follows:

    $$NPV_A = -18.5 + \frac{4.5}{(1+0.08)^1} + \frac{6}{(1+0.08)^2} + \frac{6}{(1+0.08)^3} + \frac{5.5}{(1+0.08)^4} = -0.38.$$

    $$NPV_B = -33.5 + \frac{-2.5}{(1+0.08)^1} + \frac{-2.5}{(1+0.08)^2} + \frac{24}{(1+0.08)^3} + \frac{25.5}{(1+0.08)^4} = 1.12.$$

    Using the same equation, we can solve for the IRRs by assuming that NPV = 0.

    $$0 = -18.5 + \frac{4.5}{(1+IRR_A)^1} + \frac{6}{(1+IRR_A)^2} + \frac{6}{(1+IRR_A)^3} + \frac{5.5}{(1+IRR_A)^4}.$$

    $$IRR_A = 7.04\%.$$

    $$0 = -33.5 + \frac{-2.5}{(1+IRR_B)^1} + \frac{-2.5}{(1+IRR_B)^2} + \frac{24}{(1+IRR_B)^3} + \frac{25.5}{(1+IRR_B)^4}.$$

    $$IRR_B = 8.97\%.$$

    A is incorrect because Project B's IRR is 8.97%, which exceeds the required rate of return of 8%; however, Project A's IRR is 7.04%, which is below the required rate of return of 8%. Consequently, only Project B meets the IRR decision rule.

    B is incorrect because the NPV decision rule is to invest if the NPV is greater than 0. Project B's NPV is $1.12 million, while Project A's NPV is −$0.38. Consequently, only Project B meets the NPV decision rule.

3. A is correct. The forecasted timing of cash flow is an important factor affecting both projects' IRR and NPV. In the case of delaying all future cash flows from both projects by six months, the result would be a lower IRR and a lower NPV. Given that all future cash flows are to be received six months later, their present value decreases; hence, the NPV and IRR of an entire project also decrease.

    B is incorrect because when cash flows from the investment projects are delayed by six months, both projects' NPV and IRR would decrease, not stay unchanged.

    C is incorrect because when cash flows from the investment projects are delayed by six months, both project's NPV and IRR would decrease.

4. A is correct. To calculate ROIC, we can use the following formula:

    $$ROIC = \frac{(1 - \text{Tax rate}) \times \text{Operating profit}_t}{\text{Average invested capital}_{t-1,t}},$$

    where

$$\text{Average invested capital}_{t-1,t} = \frac{(\text{Debt} + \text{Equity})_{20X1} + (\text{Debt} + \text{Equity})_{20X2})}{2}$$

$$\text{Average invested capital}_{t-1,t} = \frac{[(25,040 + 39,800 + 6,500) + (25,910 + 40,990 + 6,780)]}{2}$$

$$\text{Average invested capital}_{t-1,t} = 72,510.$$

$$\text{ROIC} = \frac{(1 - 0.22) \times 8,830}{72,510}.$$

$$\text{ROIC} = 9.50\%.$$

5. A is correct. ABC's management aims to achieve a minimum ROIC above 9.20%, but the IRR of both projects fails to meet this investment criterion. Even though Project B has a positive NPV, if it were undertaken, it would reduce ROIC.

   B is incorrect because even though Project B's NPV is $1.12 million (which increases ABC's value to shareholders), its IRR is 8.97%, which is below the target ROIC of 9.20%. Consequently, if Project B was undertaken, it would lower ABC's ROIC.

   C is incorrect because Project A's IRR is below ABC management's target ROIC of 9.2%. Additionally, Project A's NPV is negative, so it decreases ABC's shareholder value.

6

Capital Structure

INTRODUCTION

1

Earlier lessons addressed a firm's short-term activities and longer-term capital investment decisions. We now turn to the last part of the balance sheet: long-term debt and equity financing, known as a firm's capital structure. The first lesson introduces the basic objective of most managers when choosing a capital structure: minimizing the firm's weighted-average cost of capital. The second lesson considers the internal and external factors that influence a firm's choice of—and investors' willingness to offer—debt versus equity financing. While capital structure seems like an important decision for boards and managers, it is the present value of future cash flows, rather than a firm's capital structure, that primarily drives a firm's value, a central insight in the influential work of Franco Modigliani and Merton Miller. In the third lesson, we explore the simplifying assumptions used by Modigliani and Miller to demonstrate the irrelevance of capital structure to firm value, and then we relax these assumptions to show the impact of both taxes and the cost of financial distress. In the final lesson, we discuss optimal and target capital structures for issuers.

LEARNING MODULE OVERVIEW

- An issuer's cost of capital is composed of its cost of debt and equity, which are defined as its investors' required rates of return on debt and equity financing. An issuer's cost of capital is estimated using a weighted average of the costs of debt and equity, using either current market value or management's target weights of each type of financing as the weights.

- Issuers generally aim to minimize their weighted-average cost of capital and to match the duration of their assets and financing. Managements' target capital structures are usually stated using book values or indirectly through financial leverage ratios, such as a maximum ratio of debt or net debt to EBITDA or a minimum credit rating.

- While management has some influence, the total amount and type of financing needed or the weights in the WACC calculation often depends on the issuer's business model (e.g., capital intensive or capital light) and on the company's life cycle stage.

- The component costs of debt and equity are determined by top-down factors, such as financial market and industry conditions, and by issuer-specific factors, including the stability of revenues and operating and financial leverage.

- Modigliani and Miller (MM) showed, under a restrictive set of assumptions including no taxes, that an issuer's capital structure is irrelevant to firm value. MM relaxed the assumptions by considering corporate taxes, financial distress, and bankruptcy costs and showed that capital structure does matter, although far less than an issuer's future cash flows, for firm value.

- Under MM's static trade-off theory of capital structure, the optimal capital structure occurs where the tax benefit of debt equals the financial distress costs associated with debt.

- The pecking order theory of capital structure is an alternative to the static theory and suggests that a firm will use internal financing as much as possible. If external financing is needed, the firm prefers private debt over public debt and will limit the use of equity financing if possible.

LEARNING MODULE SELF-ASSESSMENT

These initial questions are intended to help you gauge your current level of understanding of this learning module.

1. In computing WACC, the cost of equity is higher than the cost of debt because the:

   A. cost of debt is set by management.

   B. distributions to shareholders are tax deductible.

   C. debt investors take less risk than equity investors.

   Solution:

   C is correct. Debt is less risky than equity because it has a priority, contractual claim on the firm's cash flow. Additionally, some debt is secured with an underlying asset. In contrast, equity is a residual claim.

   A is incorrect because an issuer's cost of debt, like its cost of equity, is determined by financial market participants.

   B is incorrect because, generally, distributions to shareholders, such as dividends, are not tax deductible while interest expense is tax deductible in many jurisdictions.

2. Nutry, Inc., has a capital structure of 30% debt and 70% equity, and interest expense is tax deductible. Debt investors require a before-tax return of 5%,

and equity investors' required return is 10%. If the marginal corporate tax rate is 20%, the WACC is closest to:

A. 5.9%.

B. 8.2%.

C. 8.5%.

Solution:

B is correct. Nutry's WACC is calculated as follows:

WACC = (Weighting of debt × Cost of debt) + (Weighting of equity × Cost of equity)

$$= (0.3)(5\%)(1 - 0.2) + (0.70)(10\%) = 8.2\%.$$

Thus, the WACC for Nutry is 8.2%. The cost of debt is stated on an after-tax basis because interest expense is tax deductible in Nutry's jurisdiction.

3. The optimal capital structure is determined where the benefit of the debt tax shield is offset by the cost of financial distress under the:

A. pecking order theory.

B. free cash flow hypothesis.

C. static trade-off theory of capital structure.

Solution:

C is correct. The static trade-off theory of capital structure incorporates both the value-enhancing effect of the tax shield and the value-reducing impact of the costs of financial distress. At the optimal level of debt, the financial distress cost equals the tax benefit of debt.

The pecking order theory states that firms use internally generated funds first because there are no floatation costs or negative signals. If more funds are needed, firms issue debt and only as a last resort will they issue equity. There is no optimal capital structure.

The free cash flow hypothesis argues that higher debt levels discipline managers by forcing them to manage the company efficiently and use cash wisely so the company can make its interest and principal payments.

4. True or False: Managers cannot precisely estimate the optimal capital structure, but they often establish a target capital structure. An issuer's actual capital structure may differ from its target based on business and financial market conditions.

A. True

B. False

Solution:

A is correct. Since management cannot estimate the optimal capital structure in practice, it instead sets a target capital structure. The actual capital structure may deviate from the target for several reasons. First, the firm may be able to issue debt at a favorable rate, so management takes advantage of these opportunities. Second, changing market values of the firm's debt and equity may cause the firm's actual capital structure to differ from its target. Transaction costs make it costly to constantly adjust to the changing market values.

5. The amount and type of financing needed or the weights in the WACC calculation depend on the issuer's:

   A. business model.

   B. financial leverage.

   C. proportion of fixed cost to total costs.

   Solution:

   A is correct. The amount and type of financing needed or the weights in the WACC calculation depend on the business model and the stage in the company's life cycle. Some businesses require large amounts of assets and are capital intensive. Other business models require less assets and are capital light.

   B and C are incorrect because the proportion of fixed assets to total costs (operating leverage) and financial leverage are issuer-specific factors that influence the component costs of debt and equity.

6. Under Modigliani and Miller (MM), if one assumes no taxes and no financial distress cost, among other assumptions, the value of the company is:

   A. determined by its capital structure.

   B. determined solely by its expected future cash flows.

   C. set so the value of levered company is greater than that of the unlevered company.

   Solution:

   B is correct. MM showed that under a set of restrictive assumptions, including zero taxes, the firm's value is unaffected by its financing mix or capital structure. It is the firm's cash flow that is the primary determinant of value. If the market value of the company is not affected by its financing mix, then the value of the levered firm is equal to the value of the unlevered firm.

2   THE COST OF CAPITAL

☐ | calculate and interpret the weighted-average cost of capital for a company

As discussed in prior lessons, issuers make capital investments that are expected to have a return on investment greater than the required rate of return. An *issuer's* required rate of return on its capital investments is derived from its *investors'* required rates of return, adjusted for specific risks in the project. If the issuer has exhausted its positive-NPV project opportunities, it should return capital to investors so they can invest elsewhere and earn their required rate of return. Not doing so would destroy value for investors.

For an issuer, its required rate of return is also known as its **cost of capital**. Since issuers use both debt and equity, the cost of capital is composed of the **cost of debt** and the **cost of equity**. As described in prior lessons, debt is less risky than equity for investors because it is a priority, fixed claim on a firm's cash flows while equity is a residual claim of indeterminate length. Additionally, debt is sometimes secured with an underlying asset that would be transferred to the debtholder in the event of default, further reducing risk for the debt investor. Therefore, debt investors have lower required rates of return than equity investors because they take less risk; equivalently, an issuer's cost of debt is lower than its cost of equity financing.

An issuer's **weighted-average cost of capital (WACC)** blends its costs of debt and equity to obtain a single cost of capital. The WACC, after adjusting for any project-specific risks, is what issuers use as r in NPV analysis and as the hurdle rate for IRR analysis.

The calculation of WACC is shown in Equation 1:

WACC = (Cost of debt × Weighting of debt) + (Cost of equity × Weighting of equity).

$$(1)$$

The estimation of each component of Equation 1 will be covered in much greater detail in lessons on fixed income and equity later in the curriculum. For now, note the following observations.

- The cost of debt for an issuer is debt investors' required rate of return on debt financing. The interest rate on existing unsecured loans and bonds is typically a good starting point. However, if we want a forward-looking measure, meaning the interest rate on *new* debt raised to finance a new project, we might instead look to what interest rates similarly situated companies have recently borrowed at. Additionally, in jurisdictions where interest expense is tax deductible, we reduce the nominal cost of debt by multiplying by (1 − Tax rate) to obtain an after-tax amount.

- The weightings of debt and equity are either their market value proportions or target weights provided by management, which are typically on a book value basis. Market value weights are more commonly used because book values reflect historical prices of debt and equity, while investors' opportunity costs are based on current market prices of debt and equity.

- The cost of equity for an issuer is equity investors' required rate of return. Unlike the cost of debt, we do not have a historical interest rate to observe as a starting point. We do know that the cost of equity is higher than the cost of debt because of equity's riskiness and because distributions to shareholders are not tax deductible.

One simplistic approach is to simply observe the historical returns on equities in general—because perhaps equity investors are expecting a similar rate of return going forward—and adjust that rate for the company-specific considerations we will discuss in the next lesson, such as how stable a company's cash flows are.

One long-running broad market index of stocks has increased by a compound annual growth rate (CAGR) of 10% from 1928 to 2021, so 10% is a starting estimate for the cost of equity we'll use for these lessons. Expected and required rates of return for equity investors are rich topics that will be discussed in more detail later in the curriculum.

- If an issuer has additional types of financing with different risk and return characteristics from those of debt and equity—for example, preferred stock and non-controlling interests—the weighted-average after-tax cost of that financing needs to be added to Equation 1 as well.

KNOWLEDGE CHECK: COMPUTING WACC

1. Assume that ABC Corporation is financed with 40% debt and 60% equity. Also assume that interest expense is tax deductible. ABC Corporation wishes to maintain these proportions as it raises new funds.

   ABC's debt investors' required rate of return, measured before taxes, is 4%, and its equity investors' required rate of return is 10%. If the company's marginal tax rate is 23%, what is ABC's weighted-average cost of capital?

   Solution:

   ABC's weighted-average cost of capital is 7.23%:

   WACC = [(1 − Tax rate) × Pre-tax cost of debt × Weighting of debt] + (Cost of equity × Weighting of equity).

   WACC = [0.04 × (1 − 0.23) × 0.40] + (0.10 × 0.60).

   WACC = 7.23%.

DISCUSSION

If ABC's management maintains the company's current mix of financing (40% debt, 60% equity), what would happen to ABC's weighted-average cost of capital if its cost of debt decreases by 1%? If its cost of equity increases by 1%? What about if the company's tax rate changes? Write your responses on this lesson's discussion board on the LES.

As demonstrated in the prior module, capital investments increase firm value if their returns exceed required rates of return. The prior module focused on the return on investment as the main driver of value, but it is also clear that a lower required rate of return would increase NPV, too, or at least provide a lower threshold for value-creative investments. This forms the basis for one of the most common objectives for managers in **capital structure** decisions, the mix of debt and equity financing: Choose whichever one leads to the lowest WACC. However, the cost of debt and equity are not chosen by management but, rather, are determined in financial markets by investors, so it is a dynamic and non-trivial endeavor. The second objective of management in choosing a capital structure is, where possible and economical, matching the liquidity or time horizon with that of its capital investments.

QUESTION SET

1. XYZ corporation has a capital structure of 30% debt and 70% equity, and interest expense is tax deductible. Debt investors require a before-tax return of 6%, and equity investors' required return is 12%. If the marginal corporate tax rate rises from 20% to 25%, the change in the WACC is closest to:

   A. −0.09%.

   B. 0.09%.

C. 0.30%.

Solution:

A is correct. XYZ's WACC at a tax rate of 20% is calculated as follows:

WACC = (Weighting of debt × Cost of debt) + (Weighting of equity × Cost of equity)

= (0.3)(6%)(1 − 0.2) + (0.70)(12%) = 9.84%.

XYZ's WACC at a tax rate of 25% is calculated as follows:

WACC = (0.3)(6%)(1 − 0.25) +(0.70)(12%) = 9.75%.

Thus, WACC declines by 0.09% as the after after-tax cost of debt declines from 4.8% to 4.5%.

2. True or False: Since the cost of debt and equity are controlled by the firm, managers can lower the cost of capital for the firm by reduce reducing the cost of debt and equity used in their capital allocation process.

   A. True

   B. False

   Solution:

   B is correct. This statement is false because the costs of debt and equity are not selected by management but are determined in financial markets by investors, though they are influenced by management's actions.

Questions 3 and 4 relate to the following information:
   Company X has the following on the right-hand side of its balance sheet:

   Bonds $400,000

   Common stock (40,000 shares) $600,000

   Total liabilities and equity $1,000,000

   The price of Company X stock is currently $20 per share. The required return before tax on debt is 5%, and the required return on equity is 10%.

3. In calculating WACC for Company X, the weight for debt using book values for the balance sheet components is likely to be _____ than the weight for debt using market values for the balance sheet components.

   A. lower

   B. the same

   C. higher

   Solution:

   A is correct.
   The book value weights are computed as follows:

   W_d = $400,000/$1,000,000 = 0.40.

   W_e = $600,000/$1,000,000 = 0.60.

   The market value of equity is equal to $20 × 40,000 shares = $800,000.
   The market value weights are computed as follows:

   W_d = $400,000/$1,200,000 = 0.33.

W_e = $800,000/$1,200,000 = 0.67.

Thus, the book value weight for debt (0.40) is higher than the market value weight (0.33).

---

4. If the marginal corporate tax rate is 20% and the stock price increases to $25, the WACC for Company X is closest to:

   A. 7.60%.

   B. 8.26%.

   C. 8.55%.

   Solution:

   B is correct.

   The book value weights are computed as follows:

   W_d = $400,000/$1,000,000 = 0.40.

   W_e = $600,000/$1,000,000 = 0.60.

   The market value of equity is equal to $25 × 40,000 shares = $1,000,000. The market value weights are computed as follows:

   W_d = $400,000/$1,400,000 = 0.29.

   W_e = $1,000,000/$1,400,000 = 0.71.

   The appropriate weights for the WACC calculation are the market weights Company X's WACC, using the market weights, is calculated as follows:

   WACC = (weighting of debt * cost of debt) + (weighting of equity * cost of equity)

   = (0.29) (5%)(1-0.2) +(0.71)(10%) = 8.26%

---

5. Fill in the blanks using the following two terms:

   higher

   lower

   Shareholder value is increased by a _____ return on investment and a capital structure that results in a _____ WACC.

   Solution:

   Shareholder value is increased by a *higher* return on investment and a capital structure that results in a *lower* WACC.

---

3   FACTORS AFFECTING CAPITAL STRUCTURE

☐ | explain factors affecting capital structure and the weighted-average cost of capital

Issuers desire a capital structure that minimizes its weighted-average cost of capital and generally matches the duration of its assets. The total amount and type of financing needed are generally determined by the issuer's business model and its position in the corporate life cycle. The costs of debt and equity are determined in financial markets by top-down factors that affect debt and equity markets generally, as well as investors' assessments of issuer-specific risk factors, as summarized in Exhibit 1.

Exhibit 1: Factors Affecting Capital Structure

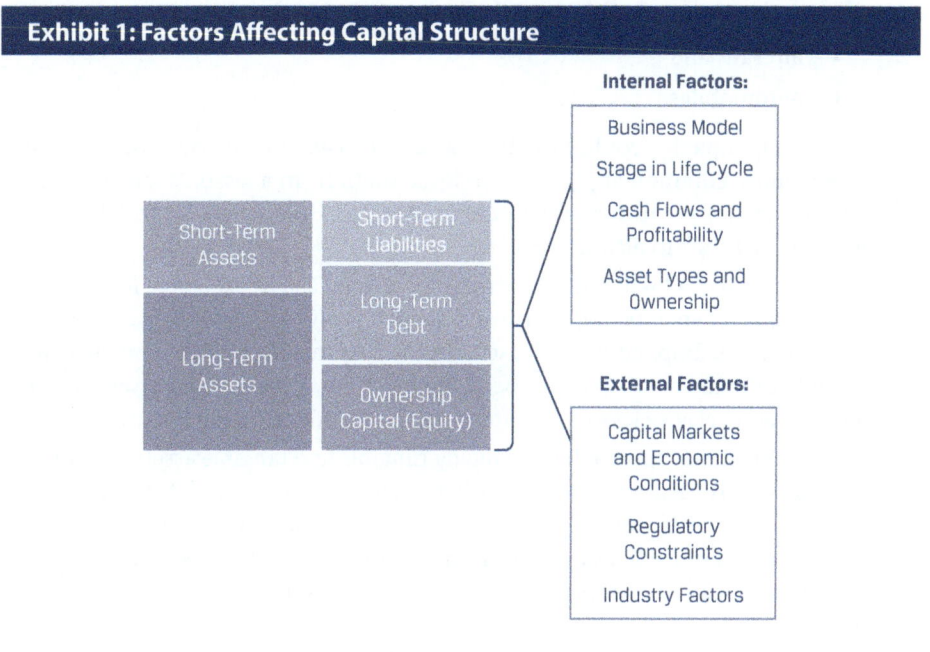

Determinants of the Amount and Type of Financing Needed

The total amount and type of financing needed (thus, the weightings in the WACC calculation) generally depend on the issuer's business model and its position in the corporate life cycle.

Capital-Intensive Businesses

Some businesses require a lot of assets—for example, those in utilities; transportation; real estate; some types of manufacturing, such as semiconductors; and natural resource production. These are known as **capital-intensive businesses**. This need for lots of assets is evident from low asset turnover (low sales-to-total-assets ratio), high capital expenditures to sales, and high net-working-capital-to-sales ratios.

While many businesses were once vertically integrated and more capital intensive, many have separated into multiple, focused companies where the capital-intensive business is separate from the customer-facing brand or service businesses. The businesses then have contractual rather than ownership relations. For example, Hilton Worldwide, one of the world's largest hotel companies, operates almost all its hotel rooms through long-term franchise or management agreements, with the hotels themselves owned by others. Similarly, NVIDIA designs and tests its products but does not manufacture semiconductor wafers; that capital-intensive activity is instead done by Taiwan Semiconductor Manufacturing Company Limited and Samsung Electronics Co. Ltd.

EXAMPLE 1

Leases as Debt Financing

Many business models require fungible and tangible assets, such as

- office space,
- data centers,
- IT devices, such as PCs, phones, and tablets,
- aircraft, and
- automobiles.

While companies could buy these assets for cash or borrow cash and buy them, a more common approach is to lease them from a lessor, such as a bank or specialized asset lessor—for example, AerCap Holdings N.V., which leases over 1,000 aircraft to airlines.

A lease is like a loan, but rather than receiving cash in exchange for interest and principal payments, the borrower (lessee) receives an asset in exchange for lease payments. Implicit in the lease is an interest rate that is often much lower than what the lessee would have been lent cash for, because the leased asset is collateral and because lessors are often large companies that can borrow cheaply.

Another similar approach to financing fungible and tangible assets is through secured debt. By using the asset as collateral for a loan or bond, the issuer may be able to obtain a far lower cost of debt than on an unsecured basis. This is true of a downtown office building but probably not for a highly specialized factory in a remote location or a consumable asset that has little value to investors as collateral.

The capital structures of some firms can be regulated by governments. For example, banks must adhere to regulatory capital standards by maintaining a certain percentage of equity as a proportion of assets. Similarly, regulatory oversight of public utility companies by local governments can influence their capital structures through rules and regulations relating to setting pricing/rates. This generally increases WACC because it results in higher equity financing.

"Capital-Light" Businesses

Some business models—notably in the technology sector, as well as service businesses that have shed their capital-intensive businesses—have low capital needs (i.e., high fixed asset turnover and/or low capital-expenditures-to-sales-ratios), known as **capital-light businesses**, or asset-light businesses. Their assets might be primarily composed of excess cash and some intangibles. This reflects several factors:

- They simply operate a network for others that own assets and thus do not need to seek financing for them from financial markets. For example, Uber and Airbnb operate global ridesharing and hospitality networks, respectively, that connect drivers and hosts who own the automobile and real estate assets with riders and guests. The companies earn commissions and fees from network users.

- The company may charge its customers upfront for services or have a very short or negative cash conversion cycle, thus obviating the need for external financing for working capital.

- The company may compensate employees and management primarily with stock, which the employees and management are happy to accept based on a rising stock price, again obviating the need for cash. This is technically a form of equity financing, but from employees rather than formal financial markets.

- If the company is profitable from an early stage and is capital light, it may not need to raise significant external financing unless management intends to expand quickly.

Corporate Life Cycle

Besides the business model determining the amount of financing needed, a large determinant of the type of financing (debt versus equity) used is based on the company's life cycle stage. Rather than a static capital structure, most firms have a capital structure that changes over time. The framework in Exhibit 2 describes the relationship between a company's life cycle stage, its cash flow characteristics, and its ability to support debt.

Exhibit 2: Capital Structure and Company Life Cycle

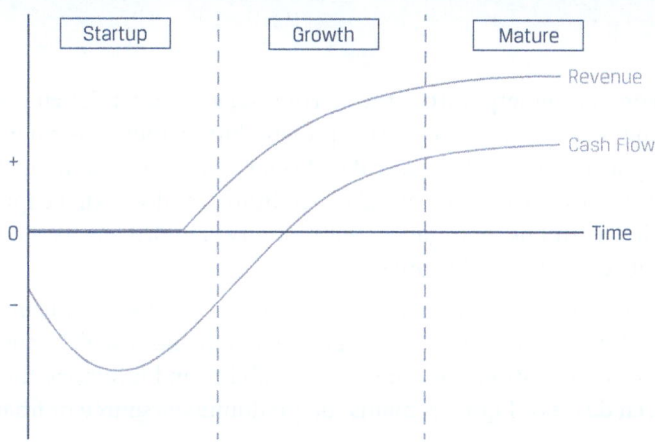

Feature / Phase	Startup	Growth	Mature
Revenue Growth	Initial	Rising	Slowing
Free Cash Flow	Negative	Rising	Stable
Business Risk	High	Medium	Low
Debt Availability	Little or None	Rising	High
Debt Type	Convertible	Secured	Unsecured

As companies mature, business risk typically declines and a firm's cash flows turn positive and stabilize, allowing for greater use of debt financing on better terms and at lower cost. Note that the framework considers free cash flow, which is net of capital investment. Profitable, high-growth businesses may have negative free cash flow once greater investments are considered. While the life cycle stages of a company often mirror those of an industry, both startup and growth companies can often be found in mature industries. Examples include restaurants and apparel, with new concepts, formats, and fashions appearing regularly, as well as technology-driven disruption of established industries, such as advertising (TikTok and Douyin), retail (Shopify), and automobiles (Tesla and BYD).

Early Stage/Startup

- Early in its life, a company requires funding to develop and launch its first product or service. Revenues are zero or minimal, and the risk of business failure is high. The uncertain prospects and negative free cash flow lead most startups to seek equity rather than debt financing. Many stock exchanges have minimum size and profitability requirements and costly regulatory requirements, so equity financing for startups is usually sourced from founders, employees, and venture capital investors rather than through an IPO.

- At this early stage, the only types of debt financing that might be available are leases and convertible debt. Leased assets commonly include office or retail real estate that can be leased at a low cost. Second, in some cases, startups may be able to raise **convertible debt**, or debt that offers investors the right to convert the debt to equity in the future at a predetermined price, while usually deferring interest payments until maturity. Convertible debt and other instruments combining debt and equity features are covered later in the curriculum.

Growth

- As a company emerges from the startup stage, product demand may result in rising revenue and accelerating growth, but further investment is needed to support growth and build scale. This includes sales and marketing expenses, growth-related capital expenditures, and working capital. Free cash flow is still likely negative, but visibility is improving as the firm establishes its customer and supplier base.

- As business risk declines and free cash flow improves, the business becomes more attractive to lenders. Many growth companies use debt conservatively to preserve operational and financial flexibility and minimize the risk of financial distress. Equity remains the predominant source of financing.

Mature Phase

- As a firm reaches maturity, revenue growth slows but also becomes more predictable. A mature firm usually generates reliable and positive free cash flow and likely has an established customer and supplier base. There is typically a decline or a deceleration in growth-related investment spending. Consistent free cash flow allows the company to borrow more cheaply, which is usually more attractive than higher-cost equity.

- In practice, large, mature public companies commonly use significant debt in their capital structures, although many seek to maintain an investment-grade credit rating to preserve maximum financial flexibility and minimize the cost of debt. Mature companies may elect to distribute capital to shareholders by increasing dividends or repurchasing shares.

Determinants of the Costs of Debt and Equity

The costs of debt and equity are determined in financial markets by top-down factors that affect debt and equity markets generally, as well as investors' assessments of issuer-specific factors. While the cost of debt is lower than the cost of equity, these costs are influenced by the same risk factors and thus tend to move together because they are claims on the same cash flows.

Top-Down Factors

Top-down factors affecting the cost of capital include financial market conditions and industry conditions.

Economic conditions can significantly influence debt and equity investors' expected returns, whether in private or public markets. Debt investors can invest on a nearly risk-free basis in sovereign government debt and will demand a spread over that as compensation for assuming the issuer-specific risks. Macroeconomic and country-specific factors (real growth, inflation, monetary policy, and exchange rate changes) can increase both interest rates on sovereign governments debt and credit spreads across issuers. As recession risk increases, debt investors may charge borrowers much higher spreads, owing to the increasing possibility of default. This effect is often more pronounced among firms in cyclical sectors, such as mining, materials, or industrials, in which revenues and cash flows vary widely through the economic cycle. The same is true for equity investors; companies ideally want to borrow when interest rates are low, and they want to issue equity when stock prices are high. This tends to follow the same conditions as when credit spreads are low.

The industry in which a firm operates is likely to have a significant effect as well. Exposure to economic factors is generally based on the products or services the issuer sells. For example, higher oil prices might lead to lower credit spreads and greater investor willingness to increase financial leverage for oil producers, while the opposite may happen for airlines, for which fuel is a significant expense.

Issuer-Specific Factors

Debt and equity investors consider the risk and return profile of an issuer and adjust their required rates of return relative to base rates or broad averages by evaluating risk factors, including the following:

1. Sales risks
2. Profitability risks (operating leverage)
3. Financial leverage and interest coverage
4. Collateral/type of assets owned by the firm.

Investors are more confident, all else equal, in firms with stable, predictable, and growing revenues and so will extend financing at lower costs to these types of firms. This is generally the result of size and the characteristics of the firm's products and services. For example, established firms in the telecommunications or software industries have stable cash flow streams from recurring subscription-based revenues from many customers, so no single customer represents more than a small fraction of total revenues. In contrast, such industries as automobile and construction equipment manufacturing have more volatile cash flows that are highly sensitive to economic conditions, increasing the risk of default should business conditions worsen.

Besides stability of revenues, stability of profit margins is also an important factor, which is determined by a company's proportion of fixed versus variable costs. This is often measured using a firm's **operating leverage**, or its proportion of fixed costs to total costs:

$$\text{Operating leverage} = \text{Fixed costs/Total costs.} \tag{2}$$

Companies with higher operating leverage experience a greater change in cash flow and profitability for a given change in revenue than firms with low operating leverage, as shown in the following example.

KNOWLEDGE CHECK: FIXED VS. VARIABLE COST AND FIRM PROFITABILITY

Consider two companies fully financed by equity. Each firm has revenue of 100 over a particular period and expenses of 70.

- The first company ($Firm_{FC+}$) has fixed costs (FC) of 50 and variable costs (VC) equal to 20% of sales, or 20.
- The second company ($Firm_{FC-}$) has fixed costs of 20 and variable costs equal to 50% of sales.

1. Calculate profit (revenue – total costs) for each firm, and compare their returns on equity (profit/total equity).

   Solution:

   Solve for profit by subtracting fixed costs (FC) and variable costs from revenue and dividing the profit by total equity to calculate the one-period return on equity:

$Firm_{FC+}$ (Primarily Fixed Cost)		$Firm_{FC-}$ (Primarily Variable Cost)	
Revenue	100	Revenue	100
Less: Fixed Costs	−50	Less: Fixed Costs	−20
Variable Cost (20%)	−20	Variable Cost (50%)	−50
Profit	30	Profit	30
Total Equity	100	Total Equity	100
Return on Equity	**30%**	**Return on Equity**	**30%**

2. Calculate the return on equity (ROE) for each firm if both firms experience a 25% increase in sales.

   Solution:

$Firm_{FC+}$ (Primarily Fixed Cost)	25% Sales Decline	Base Case	25% Sales Rise
Revenue	75	100	125
Less: Fixed Costs	50	50	50
Variable Cost (20%)	15	20	25
Profit	10	30	50
Total Equity	100	100	100
Return on Equity	**10%**	**30%**	**50%**

$Firm_{FC-}$ (Primarily Variable Cost)	25% Sales Decline	Base Case	25% Sales Rise
Revenue	75	100	125
Less: Fixed Costs	20	20	20
Variable Cost (50%)	37.5	50	62.5
Profit	17.5	30	42.5

Firm$_{FC-}$ (Primarily Variable Cost)	25% Sales Decline	Base Case	25% Sales Rise
Total Equity	100	100	100
Return on Equity	**18%**	**30%**	**43%**

3. Calculate the ROE for each firm if both firms experience a 25% decrease in sales.

   Solution:

Firm$_{FC+}$ (Primarily Fixed Cost)	25% Sales Decline	Base Case	25% Sales Rise
Revenue	75	100	125
Less: Fixed Costs	50	50	50
Variable Cost (20%)	15	20	25
Profit	10	30	50
Total Equity	100	100	100
Return on Equity	**10%**	**30%**	**50%**

Firm$_{FC-}$ (Primarily Variable Cost)	25% Sales Decline	Base Case	25% Sales Rise
Revenue	75	100	125
Less: Fixed Costs	20	20	20
Variable Cost (50%)	37.5	50	62.5
Profit	17.5	30	42.5
Total Equity	100	100	100
Return on Equity	**18%**	**30%**	**43%**

4. Which firm might debt investors be willing to extend credit to at a lower cost of debt? Explain your answer.

   Solution:

   Based on the information provided, debt investors might be willing to extend credit at a lower cost of debt to Firm$_{FC-}$ because its profits and profitability are more stable, especially in the downside case of a 25% decline in sales. The firm's stability of profits makes it more likely than Firm$_{FC+}$ to be able to make promised interest and principal payments even if sales decline. The stability of profits results from a higher percentage of costs that are variable; in other words, it has lower operating leverage.

   In practice, debt investors would, among other things, evaluate the stability of sales and develop an outlook for sales growth for both firms. While Firm$_{FC-}$ has lower operating leverage, it could have greater sales risk than Firm$_{FC+}$.

Financial leverage and interest coverage are important considerations because a company with significant indebtedness already is less able to support *incremental* debt because it has already committed to interest and principal payments. Additionally, for equity investors, high levels of indebtedness mean that there are significant priority claims ahead of them. Financial leverage, covered in a prior lesson, is often measured using a ratio of either total debt or debt net of cash and marketable securities to a profit measure, such as operating income, or to total equity. Interest coverage measures an issuer's ability to make interest payments from its core business profits:

Interest coverage = Profit before interest and taxes/Interest expense.   (3)

KNOWLEDGE CHECK: FINANCIAL LEVERAGE AND FIRM PROFITABILITY

Consider two companies both with assets of 100.

- Firm A is financed with 80 in equity and 20 in debt, while Firm B is financed with 40 equity and 60 debt.
- Each firm has revenue of 100 over a particular period and non-interest expenses of 70. Firm A has interest expense of 2, while Firm B has interest expense of 9. Ignore income taxes.

1. Calculate profit, interest coverage, and ROE for each firm.

   Solution:

Firm A (Majority Equity)		Firm B (Majority Debt)	
Revenue	100	Revenue	100
Less: Operating expenses	−70	Less: Operating expenses	−70
Operating income	30	E	30
Less: Interest expense	−2	Less: Interest expense	−9
Interest coverage	**15**	**Interest coverage**	**3.3**
Profit	**28**	**Profit**	**21**
Total Equity	80	Total Equity	40
Return on Equity	**35%**	**Return on Equity**	**53%**

2. Calculate ROE and interest coverage for each firm if both experience a 25% increase in operating income.

   Solution:

Firm A (Majority Equity)	25% OI Decline	Base Case	25% OI Rise
Operating income	22.5	30	37.5
Less: Interest expense	−2	−2	−2
Interest coverage	**11**	**15**	**19**
Profit	20.5	28	35.5
Total Equity	80	80	80
Return on Equity	**26%**	**35%**	**44%**

Firm B (Majority Debt)	25% OI Decline	Base Case	25% OI Rise
Operating income	22.5	30	37.5
Less: Interest expense	−9	−9	−9

Firm B (Majority Debt)	25% OI Decline	Base Case	25% OI Rise
Interest coverage	2.5	3.3	4.2
Profit	13.5	21	28.5
Total Equity	40	40	40
Return on Equity	34%	53%	71%

3. Calculate ROE and interest coverage for each firm if both experience a 25% decrease in operating income.

Solution:

Firm A (Majority Equity)	25% OI Decline	Base Case	25% OI Rise
Operating income	22.5	30	37.5
Less: Interest expense	−2	−2	−2
Interest coverage	11	15	19
Profit	20.5	28	35.5
Total Equity	80	80	80
Return on Equity	26%	35%	44%

Firm B (Majority Debt)	25% OI Decline	Base Case	25% OI Rise
Operating income	22.5	30	37.5
Less: Interest expense	−9	−9	−9
Interest coverage	2.5	3.3	4.2
Profit	13.5	21	28.5
Total Equity	40	40	40
Return on Equity	34%	53%	71%

4. Which firm might investors require lower rates of return for on debt and equity? Explain your answer.

Solution:

Firm A, which is primarily financed with equity. While Firm B has greater profitability (ROE) in the base case and higher upside for equity investors if operating income increases, it has a much wider range of outcomes owing to its substantially higher leverage. Even in the downside case, Firm A's interest coverage ratio is over 10; therefore, it can withstand a >90% decline in operating income before its ability to make interest payments is seriously imperiled.

In practice, investors would, among other things, evaluate the stability of sales and operating leverage in developing an outlook for both firms. So while Firm A has lower financial leverage and higher interest coverage, it could have greater operating leverage and higher sales risk than Firm B.

Finally, the underlying assets associated with a firm's business model are also an important consideration. In general, assets that support the greater use of debt include those that are considered strong collateral, generate cash, or are fungible or liquid, such as real estate, automobiles, aircraft, and receivables from creditworthy customers. Secured debt and leases are covered in detail later in the curriculum.

QUESTION SET

1. Match each of the following phases of the company life cycle with the debt type:

Phase of company life cycle	Likely debt type
A. Startup	i. Unsecured
B. Growth	ii. Convertible
C. Mature	iii. Secured

Solution:

A. ii. Convertible: In the early stages of the corporate life cycle, the only types of debt available are leases and convertible debt.

B. iii. Secured: Business risk declines and free cash flow improves in the growth phase but is still likely negative, so secured debt financing is most likely.

C. i. Unsecured: Free cash is now positive and predictable. The firm is able to use a significant amount of debt, including unsecured debt.

---

2. The cost of debt and equity is likely to be higher for a firm with

    A. stable revenue growth.

    B. high operating leverage.

    C. high interest coverage.

Solution:

B is correct. Operating leverage is the firm's proportion of fixed costs to total costs and measures the stability of profits. Firms with high operating leverage experience a greater change in operating profits for a given change in revenues. Thus, firms with high operating margins are riskier and likely to have higher debt and equity costs.

A and C are incorrect. Stable revenue growth and high interest coverage suggest a lower risk profile for the firm and a lower cost of debt and equity. A high interest coverage ratio indicates the firm has lower financial leverage and less risk.

Jason Jayman, a financial analyst, is preparing a report on two companies. Newtech is an early-stage company with a primarily variable operating cost structure, and its assets are largely cash and intangibles. Oldtech is a mature company with high fixed costs, low capital turnover, and a high capital expenditure to sales ratio. Jayman expects GDP growth to slow over the next year, which will lower the growth rate of revenues for both companies.

---

3. Newtech will likely finance activity by issuing:

    A. unsecured debt.

    B. equity through an IPO.

> **C.** equity sourced from founders and employees.
>
> **Solution:**
>
> C is correct. Newtech is in the early stages of its corporate life cycle. Equity financing for early-stage firms is sourced from founders, employees through share-based compensation, and venture capital. Generally, the only sources of debt financing available for these firms are leases and convertible debt. Equity financing through an IPO is unlikely given that most stock exchanges have minimum size and profitability requirements.
>
> 4. Given the forecast of deteriorating business conditions, which company will experience a greater change in cash flow and profitability?
>
> **A.** Newtech
>
> **B.** No difference
>
> **C.** Oldtech
>
> **Solution:**
>
> C. is correct. With revenue growth slowing, Oldtech is likely to experience a greater change in cash flow and profitability. Despite being in the mature phase of the corporate life cycle, during which one would expect stable profits, Oldtech has high operating leverage given its high degree of fixed cost. This will result in a greater change in profits for a given change in revenues. In contrast, Newtech's costs are variable, with low operating leverage.
>
> 5. The business model used by Oldtech can best be described as:
>
> **A.** capital light.
>
> **B.** capital intensive.
>
> **C.** contractual rather than ownership relationships.
>
> **Solution:**
>
> B is correct. Oldtech's business model can best be described as capital intensive given its high fixed costs, low capital turnover, and high capital-expenditure-to-sales ratio. The firm requires a lot of assets and has significant financing requirements. Newtech is capital light since most of its costs are variable and its assets are largely cash and intangibles.

MODIGLIANI–MILLER CAPITAL STRUCTURE PROPOSITIONS

4

☐ explain the Modigliani–Miller propositions regarding capital structure

In a classic 1958 paper, Nobel Prize–winning economists Franco Modigliani and Merton Miller argued that under certain assumptions, a company's choice of capital structure does not affect (or is "irrelevant" in determining) its value, where firm value is equal to the present value of the firm's expected future cash flows, discounted by its weighted-average cost of capital. In short, managers *cannot* change a company's value by simply changing its capital structure. The assumptions used by Modigliani and Miller (MM) are shown in Exhibit 3.

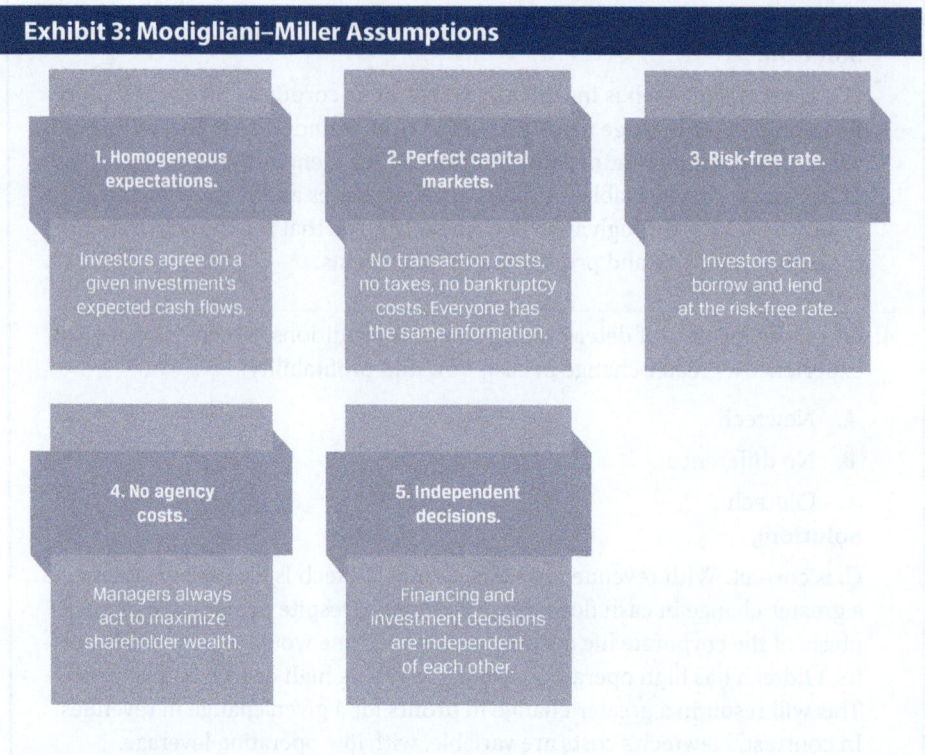

Exhibit 3: Modigliani–Miller Assumptions

1. Homogeneous expectations.

Investors agree on a given investment's expected cash flows.

2. Perfect capital markets.

No transaction costs, no taxes, no bankruptcy costs. Everyone has the same information.

3. Risk-free rate.

Investors can borrow and lend at the risk-free rate.

4. No agency costs.

Managers always act to maximize shareholder wealth.

5. Independent decisions.

Financing and investment decisions are independent of each other.

Modigliani and Miller then relaxed their assumptions to show how taxes and financial distress costs *do* result in capital structure having an impact on firm value, though relatively modest in practice. While their assumptions do not hold in practice—which ultimately does alter MM's original conclusion of capital structure irrelevance—their theoretical framework remains a popular starting point for considering the use of debt in a company's capital structure. What is clear is that it's a firm's future cash flows that are the primary driver of value, not capital structure.

Capital Structure Irrelevance (MM Proposition I without Taxes)

Modigliani and Miller demonstrated that changing the capital structure does not affect firm value based on investors being able to create any capital structure they wish for a company by simply borrowing and lending themselves in addition to owning a firm's shares. This "homemade" leverage argument relies on the assumption that investors can lend and borrow at the risk-free rate.

Say, for example that a company has a capital structure consisting of 50% debt and 50% equity and that an individual investor would prefer that the company's capital structure be 70% debt and 30% equity. The investor could borrow money to finance her share purchases so that her ownership of company assets would reflect her preferred 70% debt financing. This action would be equivalent to buying stock on margin and would have no effect on either the company's expected operating cash flows or company value.

Modigliani and Miller used the concept of arbitrage to demonstrate their point: If the value of an unlevered company (i.e., a company without any debt) is not equal to that of a levered company, investors could make a riskless arbitrage profit at no cost by selling shares of the overvalued company and using the proceeds to buy shares of the undervalued company, forcing their values to become equal. The value of a firm is thus determined not by how it finances itself but, rather, by its expected future cash flows. Their conclusion is summarized next.

MM PROPOSITION I WITHOUT TAXES

If the market value of a company is not affected by the company's capital structure, then the following is true:

1. The value of the levered company (V_L) is equal to the value of the unlevered company (V_U), or $V_L = V_U$.

2. The value of a company is determined solely by its expected future cash flows (not its relative use of debt versus equity capital).

3. In the absence of taxes, the weighted-average cost of capital is unaffected by capital structure.

Higher Financial Leverage Raises the Cost of Equity (MM Proposition II without Taxes)

Debt is less costly than equity because debtholders have a priority claim. Therefore, one might expect a company's WACC to *decline* by increasing the proportion of debt in its capital structure. However, adding financial leverage increases risk, because more debt increases the probability of bankruptcy. As a result, equity investors will demand a higher return on equity to offset the increase in risk.

MM Proposition II without taxes tells us that adding any amount of lower-cost debt capital to the capital structure is always perfectly offset by an increase in the cost of equity, resulting in *no* change in the company's WACC. MM Proposition II explains why investors require higher returns on levered equity; their required returns should match the increased risk from leverage. Specifically, MM Proposition II without taxes implies that a firm's equity cost is a linear function of its debt-to-equity ratio (D/E):

$$r_e = r_0 + (r_0 - r_d)\frac{D}{E},\qquad(4)$$

where r_e is the cost of equity, r_0 is the cost of capital for a company financed *only* with equity, r_d is the cost of debt, D is the market value of debt, and E is the market value of equity. Exhibit 4 shows this relationship.

Exhibit 4: Equity Cost as a Function of the Debt-to-Equity Ratio

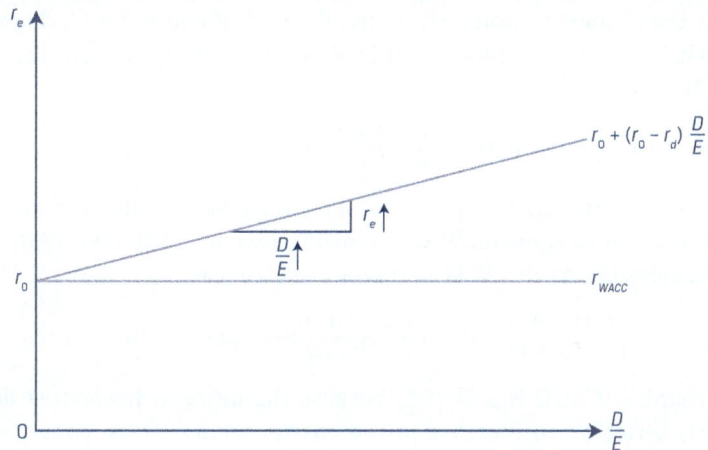

Note that r_e increases with the debt-to-equity ratio with an intercept equal to r_0 and slope equal to the quantity $(r_0 - r_d)$, while the WACC (r_{WACC}) does not change as debt levels change.

Given that capital structure changes do not affect the company's future cash flow stream and the company's weighted-average cost of capital remains unchanged for any chosen capital structure, there is no change in the value of the company. Note that Modigliani and Miller did not assume away the possibility of bankruptcy but simply assumed it occurs at zero cost.

MM PROPOSITION II WITHOUT TAXES

If the cost of equity is assumed to be a linear function of the company's debt-to-equity ratio, then the following is true:

1. Higher leverage raises the cost of equity but does not change firm value or WACC.

2. The increase in the cost of equity must exactly offset the greater use of lower-cost debt.

EXAMPLE 2

Gerhardt Corporation Cost of Equity

Assume that Gerhardt Corporation has an all-equity capital structure. Gerhardt has expected annual cash flows (or CF_e) of EUR5,000 and a cost of equity of 10%, which is also its WACC since equity is the firm's only source of capital. For simplicity, we assume that all cash flows are perpetual. Therefore, Gerhardt's value is equal to

$$V = \frac{CF_e}{r_{wacc}} = \frac{EUR5,000}{0.10} = EUR50,000.$$

Now suppose that Gerhardt plans to issue EUR15,000 in debt at a cost of 5% and use the proceeds to buy back and reduce its outstanding equity by EUR15,000. This action leaves total invested capital unchanged at EUR50,000.

Under MM Proposition I, $V_L = V_U$, the value of Gerhardt must remain the same at EUR50,000 after the change in capital structure. Under MM Proposition II, after the change in capital structure, the cost of equity for Gerhardt—now with EUR15,000 in debt capital and EUR35,000 in equity capital—increases to 12.143%:

$$r_e = 0.10 + (0.10 - 0.05)\frac{EUR15,000}{EUR35,000} \approx 0.12143 = 12.143\%.$$

To prove that Gerhardt's firm value is unchanged under the new capital structure, we must show its WACC remains unchanged at 10%. With the new cost of equity, Gerhardt's WACC is now calculated as

$$r_{wacc} = \left(\frac{EUR15,000}{EUR50,000}\right)0.05 + \left(\frac{EUR35,000}{EUR50,000}\right)0.12143 = 0.10 = 10\%.$$

Gerhardt's WACC is still 10%, because the move to lower-cost debt was perfectly offset by an increase in the cost of equity. Thus, consistent with MM Proposition I, the value of the firm remains unchanged, at EUR50,000. Furthermore, the value of Gerhardt must equal the sum of the present values of cash flows to debtholders (CF_d) and shareholders (CF_e). With EUR15,000 debt at a cost of 5% (r_d), Gerhardt makes the following debtholder and shareholder payments:

$$CF_d = D \times r_d.$$

$$EUR750 = EUR15,000 \times 5\%.$$

This leaves EUR5,000 – EUR750 = EUR4,250 remaining for shareholders (CF_e). Therefore, the total value of the company can also be expressed as

$$V = D + E$$

$$V = \frac{CF_d}{r_d} + \frac{CF_e}{r_e}$$

$$V = \frac{EUR750}{0.05} + \frac{EUR4,250}{0.12143} = EUR50,000.$$

Firm Value with Taxes (MM Proposition II with Taxes)

In most jurisdictions, interest expense is deductible from a company's income for tax purposes. In other words, debt provides a tax shield for companies that are earning profits, and the money saved in taxes enhances the value of the company. Ignoring other factors, such as the costs of financial distress and bankruptcy, for now, let us explore the two MM propositions when we relax the assumption of no corporate taxes.

The value of the company increases with increasing levels of debt, and the actual cost of debt is reduced by the amount of the tax benefit:

After-tax cost of debt = Before-tax cost of debt × (1 − Marginal tax rate).

Modigliani and Miller's Proposition I with corporate taxes states that in the presence of corporate taxes (but not personal taxes), the value of the levered company is greater than that of the all-equity company by an amount equal to the tax rate multiplied by the value of the debt (tD), defined as the present value of the **debt tax shield**:

$$V_L = V_U + tD, \tag{5}$$

where t is the marginal tax rate and tD is the present value of the debt tax shield. When there are corporate taxes, a profitable company can increase its value by using debt financing, as shown in Exhibit 5.

Exhibit 5: Firm Value with Corporate Taxes and Debt

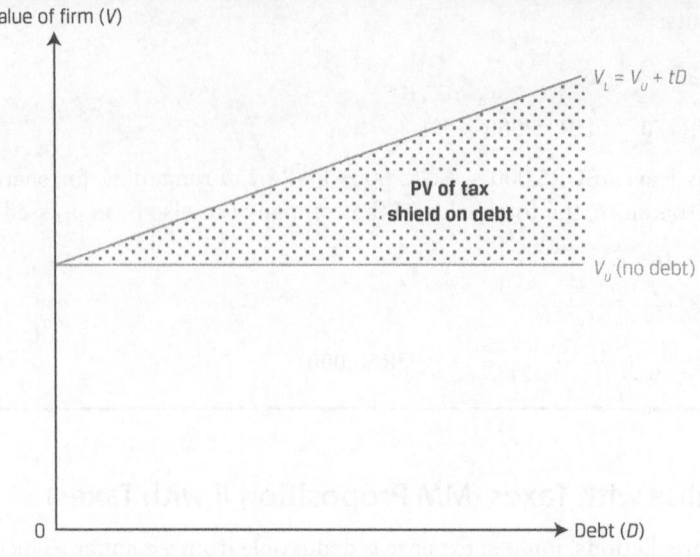

As noted in Proposition I with corporate taxes, the increase in firm value, V, is solely attributable to the tax shield. Taken to its (unrealistic) extreme, Equation 5 predicts a value-maximizing capital structure of 100% debt.

MM PROPOSITION I WITH CORPORATE TAXES

If the market value of a levered company is equal to the value of an unlevered company plus the value of the debt tax shield, then the following is true:

1. In the presence of taxes, a profitable company can increase its value (V) by using debt.

2. The higher the tax rate, the greater the benefit of using debt in the capital structure.

Cost of Capital (MM Proposition II with Taxes)

If the value of the company increases as it uses more debt, the company's WACC must decrease as it uses more debt. That is, in the earlier propositions without corporate taxes, the lower cost of debt was fully offset by an increase in the cost of equity. Now, in the presence of corporate taxes, the cost of debt is further lowered by the tax benefit such that the lower debt cost outweighs the increase in the cost of equity and results in a lower WACC.

To demonstrate this idea, let's begin with the revised cost of equity under MM Proposition II with corporate taxes:

$$r_e = r_0 + (r_0 - r_d)(1 - t)\frac{D}{E}. \tag{6}$$

Notice that the only difference between Equation 6 and Equation 4 (MM Proposition II with no taxes) is the presence of the term $(1 - t)$. When t is zero, the two equations are identical. When t is not zero, the term $(1 - t)$ is less than 1 and serves to reduce the cost of levered equity. The cost of equity still rises as the company increases the amount of debt in its capital structure, but it rises at a slower rate than in the no-tax case. as shown in Exhibit 6.

Exhibit 6: Equity Cost, Debt-to-Equity Ratio, and WACC with Taxes

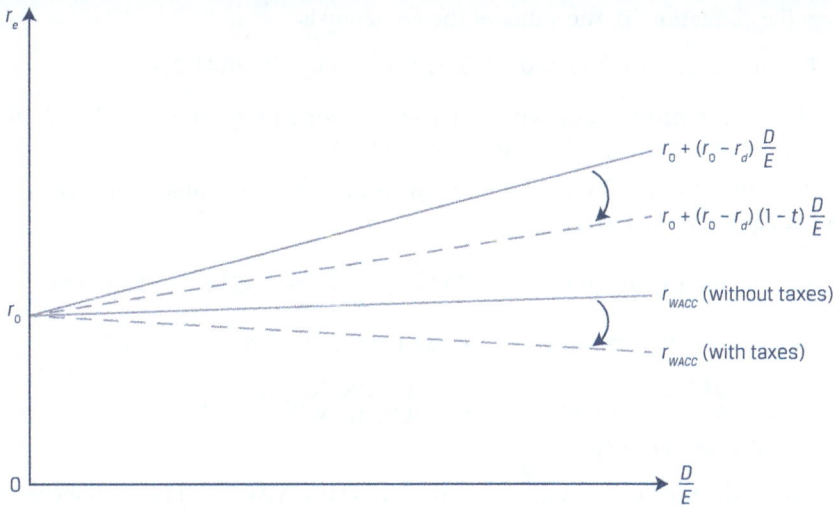

Consequently, as debt increases, the company's r_{WACC} decreases and the company's value increases. This result implies that when there are taxes (and no financial distress or bankruptcy costs), debt financing is highly advantageous. Taken to an extreme, this result also suggests that a company's optimal capital structure is 100% debt—a conclusion that is at odds with reality and a direct result of Modigliani and Miller's restrictive assumptions.

MM PROPOSITION II WITH CORPORATE TAXES

If the cost of equity is a linear function of the company's debt-to-equity ratio with an adjustment for the tax rate, then the following is true:

1. In the presence of taxes, the cost of equity rises as the company uses more debt but at a slower rate than in the no-tax case.

2. As the company's use of debt increases, its WACC decreases and its value increases.

3. In the presence of taxes (but no financial distress or bankruptcy costs), the use of debt is value enhancing and, at the extreme, 100% debt is optimal.

EXAMPLE 3

Gerhardt Corporation under Corporate Taxes

Recall from the previous example that annual cash flows to Gerhardt shareholders were EUR5,000 and the cost of equity (and WACC) was 10%. As before, Gerhardt is planning to issue EUR15,000 of 5% debt to buy back an equivalent amount of equity. Now, however, assume that Gerhardt pays corporate taxes at a rate of 25%.

Since the company does not currently have debt, the after-tax cash flows are now EUR5,000(1 − 0.25), or EUR3,750. Because the cash flows are assumed to be perpetual, the value of the company is EUR37,500 (= EUR3,750/0.10), considerably less than the amount when there were no corporate taxes, EUR50,000.

Now, suppose Gerhardt proceeds to issue EUR15,000 of debt and uses the proceeds to repurchase equity. According to MM Proposition II with corporate taxes (i.e., Equation 5), the value of the company is

$$V_L = V_U + tD = \text{EUR37,500} + 0.25(\text{EUR15,000}) = \text{EUR41,250}.$$

The total company value is now EUR41,250, consisting of debt of EUR15,000 and equity of EUR26,250 (= EUR41,250 – EUR15,000).

According to MM Proposition II with corporate taxes (Equation 6), the new cost of equity for Gerhardt is

$$r_e = 0.10 + (0.10 - 0.05)(1 - 0.25)\frac{\text{EUR15,000}}{\text{EUR26,250}} = 0.12143 = 12.143\%.$$

Using this new cost of equity, we can compute the new WACC:

$$r_{wacc} = \frac{\text{EUR15,000}}{\text{EUR41,250}}(0.05)(1 - 0.25) + \frac{\text{EUR26,250}}{\text{EUR41,250}}(0.12143)$$
$$= 0.09091 = 9.091\%.$$

Unlike the previous example, where Gerhardt's WACC did not change with the change in capital structure, Gerhardt's WACC decreased in this example from 10% to 9.091%. This reduction in WACC resulted in an increase in company value to EUR41,250:

$$V_L = \frac{CF_e(1 - t)}{\text{WACC}} = \frac{\text{EUR5,000}(1 - 0.25)}{0.09091} \approx \text{EUR41,250}.$$

As shown in the previous example, the value of the company must also equal the present value of cash flows to debtholders and shareholders:

$$V_L = D + E = \frac{r_d D}{r_d} + \frac{(CF_e - r_d D)(1 - t)}{r_e}$$
$$V = \frac{\text{EUR750}}{0.05} + \frac{(\text{EUR5,000} - \text{EUR750})(1 - 0.25)}{0.12143} \approx \text{EUR41,250}.$$

Of course, in the real world, taxes are not the only factor affecting the value of a levered company. The analysis becomes more complex when we consider the costs of financial distress, among other real-world considerations.

Cost of Financial Distress

Financial distress refers to the heightened uncertainty regarding a company's ability to meet its obligations because of diminished earnings power or actual current losses. Operating and financial leverage can magnify profits but also increase losses and the likelihood of financial distress. Even before filing for bankruptcy, companies under financial distress may lose customers, creditors, suppliers, and employees.

Direct costs of financial distress are cash expenses associated with bankruptcy, such as legal and administrative fees, while indirect costs include forgone business and investment opportunities, reputational risk, and costs arising from conflicts of interest between managers and debtholders, or agency costs of debt, when a firm is near or in bankruptcy.

Costs of financial distress are lower for firms whose assets have a ready secondary market. Airlines, shipping companies, and some manufacturers have tangible assets that can be easily sold. Technology, pharmaceutical, and information technology firms, as well as those in the service sector, usually lack such assets and have higher costs associated with financial distress. The probability of financial distress and bankruptcy rises with more debt in the capital structure, higher sales risk and operating leverage, and lower liquidity. The task of optimizing a firm's capital structure by taking these and other factors into consideration is the subject of the next lesson.

EXAMPLE 4

The Costs of Financial Distress

Rite Aid Corporation, listed on the NYSE, operates over 2,000 retail pharmacies in the United States. The company has a highly leveraged balance sheet, with a ratio of net debt to annual earnings before interest, taxes, depreciation, and amortization over 5.0 for many years. During the COVID-19 pandemic, the company performed well, exceeding profit expectations largely due to brisk COVID-19 testing and vaccine revenues. However, as the pandemic entered its third year, vaccine and testing revenue began to fall, and other issues, such as pricing declines from insurance companies and wage pressures, accelerated. Owing to its high financial leverage, the ensuing reduction in analysts' profit estimates resulted in large declines in the prices of Rite Aid debt and equity: Over the first five months of 2022, the price of its 02/15/2027 unsecured notes fell from 94 to 60 and its stock price fell from $15 to $6 per share. By May 2022, Rite Aid's cost of debt exceeded 20%.

In April 2022, one equity analyst lowered the estimated fair value of Rite Aid stock from $16 to $1 and warned that the stock may in fact be worthless. According to the analyst, the company faced $200 million per year in interest expenses and another $225 million per year in maintenance capital expenditures. The analyst estimated that next fiscal year, the company would achieve only $370 million in earnings before interest, taxes, depreciation, and amortization, and the analyst warned that it faces considerable challenges in growing beyond that. Continued net losses would render the stock worthless and likely require the company to restructure its obligations with its bondholders.

During its quarterly earnings call, management was upbeat, but it intends to close 145 underperforming stores to lower its expenses and further cut corporate costs to improve profitability.

QUESTION SET

---

1. The view that debt financing is highly advantageous and the optimal capital structure is 100% debt is consistent with:

    A. MM without taxes.

    B. MM with taxes and financial distress costs.

    C. MM with taxes and no financial distress cost.

    Solution:

    C is correct. MM with taxes and no distress cost leads to the conclusion that the optimal capital structure is 100% debt. This is because tax law favors debt financing over equity financing since the interest expense on debt financing is tax deductible. Ignoring financial distress costs, the value of the company increases with increasing levels of debt. The value of the levered firm (V_L) is greater than that of the unlevered one (V_U) by the amount equal to the tax rate multiplied by the level of debt (tD).

---

2. True or False: What is clear from MM is that the primary driver of firm value is capital structure.

    A. True

B. False

Solution:

B is correct. This statement is false since it is future cash flows that are the primary driver of value. Under a set of restrictive assumptions, MM's conclusion of capital structure irrelevance is obtained. Relaxing these assumptions, MM showed that capital structure does impact value, but it has only a modest impact compared to future cash flows.

3. MM Proposition II without taxes differs from MM Proposition I without taxes since it concludes that:

   A. WACC is unaffected by capital structure.

   B. the value of the levered firm is equal to that of the unlevered firm.

   C. higher leverage raises the cost of equity, which exactly offsets the lower cost of debt.

   Solution:

   C is correct. MM Proposition II without taxes differs from MM Proposition I without taxes in that the cost of equity will rise with leverage and completely offset the lower cost of debt. Debt has a lower cost relative to equity because debtholders have a priority claim on the cash flow of the firm. So, one would expect WACC to decline with more debt. MM Proposition II without taxes argues that the cost of equity is a linear function of the debt-to-equity ratio. The addition of more low-cost debt to the capital structure will increase the debt-to-equity ratio and raise the cost of equity, offsetting the lower debt cost. As a result, the firm's WACC is unchanged.

Company Y has an unlevered WACC of 10%. It has a cost of debt equal to 5.5% and a debt-to-equity ratio of 0.75. The corporate tax rate is 25%.

4. Fill in the blanks: The cost of equity for Company Y will be _____ if it pays no corporate taxes and _____ if it pays corporate taxes.

   Solution:

   The cost of equity for Company Y will be <u>13.37%</u> if it pays no corporate taxes and <u>12.53%</u> if it pays corporate taxes.
   The cost of equity is a linear function of its debt-to-equity ratio and without taxes is calculated as follows:

   $$r_e = r_0 + (r_0 - r_d)\frac{D}{E}$$

   $$= 10\% + (10\% - 5.5\%)(0.75) = 13.37\%.$$

   The cost of equity with taxes is calculated as

   $$r_e = r_0 + (r_0 - r_d)(1 - t)\frac{D}{E}$$

   $$= 10\% + (10\% - 5.5\%)(1 - 0.25)(0.75) = 12.53\%.$$

5. If Company Y is an all-equity-financed firm, its cost of equity will be _____ its WACC.

   A. greater than

   B. equal to

C. lower than

Solution:

B is correct. Since Company Y is an unlevered firm and has no debt in its capital structure, the cost of equity will be the same as WACC. Since the weighting of debt is zero, the WACC formula is simply WACC = Weighting of equity × Cost of equity.

OPTIMAL CAPITAL STRUCTURE

5

☐ | describe optimal and target capital structures

While the Modigliani–Miller propositions offer an initial framework for capital structure decisions, a company's managers facing capital structure choices must address trade-offs simultaneously while incorporating those factors outlined in prior lessons. For example, consider a more real-world-appropriate scenario with *both* corporate taxes and bankruptcy/financial distress costs. The value-enhancing effect of the tax shield from leverage is offset by the value-reducing impact of the present value of expected (or probability-weighted) costs of financial distress or bankruptcy. We can show this trade-off by incorporating the potential cost of financial distress or bankruptcy into the value of a levered firm:

$$V_L = V_U + tD - PV(\text{Costs of financial distress}). \tag{7}$$

Equation 7 represents what is sometimes referred to as the **static trade-off theory of capital structure**, which is illustrated in Exhibit 7.

Exhibit 7: Static Trade-Off Theory of Capital Structure

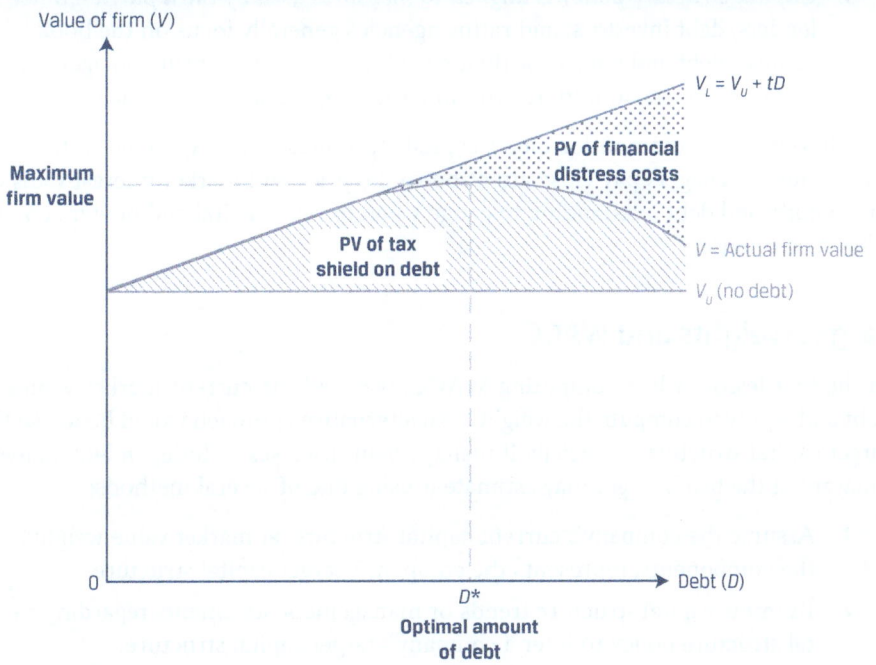

V_U represents the value of an unlevered or all-equity firm. As debt is added to the capital structure, the new levered firm value is derived from Equation 7. At low debt levels, the tax benefit of debt usually outweighs potential financial distress costs, resulting in a higher firm value. However, as debt increases, the possible financial distress costs rise substantially and equal the tax benefit of debt at D^*. Beyond this point, greater leverage reduces firm value, and the present value of financial distress costs outweighs the tax benefit. The debt level corresponding to D^*, which maximizes firm value, and the associated level of equity are referred to as the **optimal capital structure**.

Managers cannot precisely estimate D^* in practice but, rather, establish a **target capital structure** based on these two considerations, as well as the internal and external factors outlined in earlier lessons. There are several reasons why a firm's actual capital structure may differ from its target. For example, management may exploit short-term opportunities in a particular financing source. A company able to issue debt at attractive rates, for instance, may borrow more than planned in response to strong investor demand. Also, changing market values of the company's debt and equity securities can cause the firm's actual capital structure to deviate from a target. Transaction costs and minimum deal sizes make it impractical for firms to constantly align capital structure to a specific number. As a result, firm managers usually set an optimal capital range: for example, 30%–50% debt rather than 40%.

While prior WACC calculations and debt and equity weights were made with the *market* value of equity and debt, target capital structure is often expressed using the *book* value of equity and debt for the following reasons:

1. *Market values can fluctuate substantially and seldom impact the appropriate level of borrowing.* On the contrary, a company whose share price has risen rapidly may take advantage of this by raising equity capital rather than debt to maintain a certain debt-to-equity ratio.

2. *For management, the primary concern is the amount and types of capital invested* by *the company, not* in *the company.* This perspective includes how working capital and capital projects will be funded. It differs from that of a shareholder who has purchased shares at the prevailing market price seeking a return on that investment.

3. *Capital structure policy is aligned to measures used by third parties.* Since lenders, debt investors, and rating agencies generally focus on the book value of debt and equity for their calculation measures, firm managers take this fact into account in determining their capital structure policies.

Although it is common for target capital structures to be expressed in terms of book values, managers pay close attention to the price and market interest rates on their equity and debt outstanding to gauge when to raise capital and how much and what type to raise.

Target Weights and WACC

In the first lesson, when computing WACC, we used the current market values of debt and equity to compute the weights. An alternative approach would be to use the target capital structure, especially if management discloses it. Independent analysts unaware of the firm's target may estimate it using one of several methods:

1. Assume the company's current capital structure, at market value weights for the components, represents the company's target capital structure.

2. Examine capital structure trends or management statements regarding capital structure policy to infer a company's target capital structure.

3. Use averages of comparable companies' capital structures as the target.

Note that a simple way of transforming a debt-to-equity ratio (D/E) into a weight—that is, $D/(D + E)$—is to divide D/E by $1 + D/E$.

KNOWLEDGE CHECK ESTIMATING PROPORTIONS OF CAPITAL FOR GERHARDT CORPORATION

A financial analyst seeks to estimate Gerhardt Corporation's weighted-average cost of capital using the following information:

- Market value of debt: EUR50 million
- Market value of equity: EUR60 million

Primary competitors and their capital structures (in millions):

Competitor	Market Value of Debt	Market Value of Equity
A	EUR25	EUR50
B	EUR101	EUR190
C	GBP40	GBP60

---

1. Calculate the proportions of debt and equity for the WACC analysis using Gerhardt's current capital structure.

    Solution:

    Current capital structure:

    $$w_d = \frac{€50 \text{ million}}{€50 \text{ million} + €60 \text{ million}} = 0.4545.$$
    $$w_e = \frac{€60 \text{ million}}{€50 \text{ million} + €60 \text{ million}} = 0.5454.$$

---

2. Calculate the proportions of debt and equity for the WACC analysis using the capital structure of Gerhardt's competitors.

    Solution:

    Competitors' capital structure:

    $$w_d = \frac{\left(\frac{€25}{€25 + €50}\right) + \left(\frac{€101}{€101 + €190}\right) + \left(\frac{£40}{£40 + £60}\right)}{3} = 0.3601.$$
    $$w_e = \frac{\left(\frac{€50}{€25 + €50}\right) + \left(\frac{€190}{€101 + €190}\right) + \left(\frac{£60}{£40 + £60}\right)}{3} = 0.6399.$$

---

3. Calculate the proportions of debt and equity for the WACC analysis if Gerhardt announces that a debt-to-equity ratio of 0.7 reflects its target capital structure.

    Solution:

    A debt-to-equity ratio of 0.7 represents a weight on debt of 0.7/1.7 = 0.4118, so $w_d = 0.4118$ and $w_e = 1 - 0.4118 = 0.5882$. These would be the preferred weights to use in a cost-of-capital calculation.

Pecking Order Theory and Agency Costs

Investors and issuers have **asymmetric information**. Issuer management has access to more information about its business and its prospects than is publicly available, and managers are likely to use this information to their advantage when seeking financing.

Debt and equity investors demand higher returns from companies with higher information asymmetry because they may be concerned that new securities are overpriced; that is, a company will either issue equity when its shares are expensive or issue new debt when the firm's creditworthiness is about to deteriorate.

Since investors often closely watch manager behavior for insight into a company's prospects, managers consider what their actions might signal to outsiders. The signaling model of capital structure suggests a hierarchy (or pecking order) of methods for financing new investments.

The **pecking order theory**, developed by Stewart C. Myers and Nicholas S. Majluf in 1984, suggests that managers give first preference to financing methods with the least potential information content (internally generated funds) and last preference to methods with the most potential information content (public equity offerings). Public equity offerings often raise skepticism among investors because existing owners would seem less likely to want to share ownership of a company with strong future prospects. As a result, managers prefer internal financing, and if external financing is needed, they prefer private debt to public debt and prefer equity issuance least of all.

Another implication of the work of Myers and Majluf is that issuers tend to issue equity when management believes the stock is overvalued and are reluctant to issue equity if they believe the stock is undervalued, potentially choosing instead to repurchase shares. Thus, additional issuance of equity, usually to finance an acquisition, is often interpreted by investors as a negative signal. The issuance of debt commits the company to future interest and principal payments, which (along with recurring dividends) may be interpreted as a sign of management confidence in the company's future ability to make such payments. These signals are considered too costly for poorly performing companies to afford.

Alternatively, the signal of issuing equity at the bottom of the pecking order holds other clues. If, for instance, the company's cost of capital increases after an equity issuance, we can interpret this effect as an indication that management needs capital beyond what comes cheaply; in other words, this is a negative signal regarding the company's prospects. Managers may hesitate to issue new equity when they believe the company's shares are underpriced, because they wish to avoid signaling that they believe the shares are overpriced and also to avoid the cost and effort involved with new equity issuance.

Agency costs were introduced in an earlier lesson as the incremental costs arising from conflicts of interest between managers, shareholders, and bondholders. In the case of capital structure decisions, savings in the agency costs of equity may arise with the increased use of debt. Similarly, the more financially leveraged a company, the less freedom for managers to either take on more debt or spend cash unwisely. This is the foundation of Michael Jensen's (1986) **free cash flow hypothesis**: Higher debt levels discipline managers by forcing them to manage the company efficiently and use cash wisely so the company can make its interest and principal payments.

EXAMPLE 5

Agency Costs, Asymmetric Information, and Signaling

CLP AG, a small, listed biopharmaceutical company, is conducting a clinical trial of its drug, which is already approved for treatment of an autoimmune disorder, to be used in a new application for which it was not originally intended: treatment of a type of viral infection. Management hopes this new application for the drug will result in a big increase in sales and the value of the company. The company has been consistently profitable and debt free. The following events occur:

- In July, management receives notice from the clinical trial investigators that results look promising. Anticipating that it might have to scale up production quickly, the company negotiates and announces a large increase in its credit line.

- In August, CLP announces successful test results by public press release. CLP shares increase by 35%.

Explain how asymmetric information and signaling are represented here.

1. Asymmetric information

Solution

Asymmetric information is represented by management's knowledge of the positive trial results in July, before they were publicly announced in August. Signaling is represented by the company's announcement in July that it was increasing its credit line. The announcement could reasonably be taken as a signal of management's confidence that the trial results will be positive and that the company will need to expand production capacity. This is true whether or not the signaling is intentional.

QUESTION SET

---

1. True or False: Under the pecking order theory, the firm has no optimal capital structure and a firm's capital structure reflects its historic need for external financing.

   A. True

   B. False

   Solution:

   A is correct. The pecking order theory is based on asymmetric information held by investors and issuers and the idea that managers consider what their actions may signal to investors. The signaling model suggests a hierarchy in methods in financing the firm. Internal funds are used first, then debt is used, and finally, reluctantly, firms use equity. There is no optimal capital structure, and a firm's capital structure reflects its historic need for external financing.

---

2. Company Z announces that a debt-to-equity ratio of 1.2 is consistent with its target capital structure. Given this value, the weight for equity in the WACC calculation is:

   A. 45%.

   B. 55%.

   C. 83%.

   Solution:

   A is correct. A simple way of transforming a debt-to-equity ratio (D/E) into a weight—that is, $D/(D + E)$—is to divide D/E by $1 + D/E$. Therefore, a debt-to-equity ratio of 1.2 represents a weight on debt of $1.2/2.2 = 0.5455$, so $w_d = 0.5455$ and $w_e = 1 - 0.5455 = 0.4545$. Thus, the weight for equity in the WACC calculation is 45%.

3. Match each of the following concepts on the left with a capital structure theory/hypothesis on the right:

Concepts	Capital Structure Theory/Hypothesis
1. Optimal capital structure	A. Free cash flow hypothesis
2. Agency costs	B. Pecking order theory
3. Asymmetric information	C. Static trade-off theory of capital structure

Solution:

1. C. The static trade-off theory of capital structure determines the optimal capital structure.

2. A. The free cash flow hypothesis is based on agency costs and the idea that higher debt levels impose discipline on managers to avoid perks and non-value-adding acquisitions.

3. B. The pecking order theory is based on asymmetric information held by investors and issuers and the important role of signaling.

4. The value-reducing impact of financial distress or bankruptcy increases if the firm has:

   A. higher business risk.

   B. lower operating and financial leverage.

   C. assets with a ready secondary market.

Solution:

A is correct. The probability and cost of financial distress rise for firms with higher business risk and more debt in the capital structure. In contrast, the cost of financial distress is lower for firms with lower operating and financial leverage and for firms with assets that have a secondary market and can be easily sold.

5. True or False: The target capital structure should be estimated using the market value of equity and debt in calculating WACC.

   A. True

   B. False

Solution:

B is correct. Target capital structure is often estimated using book values because market values can fluctuate significantly and are unlikely to impact borrowing capacity. Issuers will often aim for a certain credit rating, such as investment grade, which is strongly influenced by the issuer's (book value) level of indebtedness relative to cash flows.

PRACTICE PROBLEMS

The following information relates to questions 1-4

A financial analyst is evaluating the capital structure for Boulder, Inc. Boulder, Inc., is a US-based unleveraged firm with a constant (perpetual) cash flow of $6 million per year before taxes. The firm has a market value of $45 million and a corporate tax rate of 30%. Boulder plans to issue $15 million in debt to retire an equivalent amount of equity. The debt will have a cost of 5.5%.

The financial analyst notes that the tax shield advantage of debt is offset due to the risk of financial distress. He estimates the present value of the cost of financial distress at various debt levels as follows:

Value of Debt	Present Value of Cost of Distress
$5 million	$0.1 million
$10 million	$0.2 million
$15 million	$0.5 million
$20 million	$1.5 million
$25 million	$6.0 million
$30 million	$12.0 million

1. The WACC of the unleveraged firm, prior to the debt issue, is closest to:

   A. 4.00%.

   B. 9.33%.

   C. 13.33%.

2. The use of the $15 million of debt financing increases the value of Boulder by _____ over its unlevered value. Ignore the costs of financial distress.

   A. $4.5 million

   B. $10.5 million

   C. $15 million

3. Including the present value of the cost of distress, the value of Boulder is closest to:

   A. $49 million.

   B. $55 million.

   C. $59.5 million.

4. The level of debt that will maximize the value of Boulder Inc. is closest to:

   A. $15 million.

B. $20 million.

C. $30 million.

---

5. A financial analyst is evaluating the capital structure for Plover, Inc., a European-based unleveraged firm with a constant (perpetual) cash flow of EUR10.0 million per year before taxes. The firm has a market value of EUR100.0 million and a corporate tax rate of 20%. Plover plans to issue EUR35.0 million in debt to retire an equivalent amount of equity, so the size of the firm will remain unchanged. The debt will have a cost of 4.5%. Assume the cost of financial distress is close to zero.

   After the debt issuance and change in the capital structure, Plover's WACC is closest to:

   A. 5.47%.

   B. 7.48%.

   C. 8.82%.

SOLUTIONS

1. B is correct. The after-tax cash flows for the company are $6 million $\times$ (1 – 0.30) = $4.2 million. Since the cash flows are assumed to be perpetual, WACC is calculated as follows:

   $r_{WACC} = CF(1 - t)/V = \$4.2/\$45 = 9.33\%$.

   Since this is an all-equity firm, the cost of equity is equal to WACC.

2. A is correct. According to MM Proposition I with corporate taxes, the value of the levered company is greater than that of the unlevered company by an amount equal to the tax rate multiplied by the value of the debt (tD), defined as the present value of the debt tax shield.

   $V_L = V_U + tD = \$45$ million $+ 0.30(\$15$million$) = \$49.5$ million.

   Thus, the use of debt financing will increase the value of Boulder by $4.5 million over the unlevered firm. Note that the firm's value increases continuously as additional debt is added to the capital structure, and the optimal capital structure is 100% debt.

3. A is correct. With financial distress included, as debt is added to the capital structure, the levered value of the firm is given by:

   $V_L = V_U + tD - PV$(Costs of financial distress).

   The levered value of Boulder financed with $15 million in debt is

   $V_L = \$45$ million $+ 0.30(\$15$ million$) - \$0.5$ million $= \$49$ million.

4. B is correct. With financial distress included, as debt is added to the capital structure, the levered value of the firm is given by:

   $V_L = V_U + tD - PV$(Costs of financial distress).

   The following shows calculations of the levered value of Boulder at various debt levels, in $millions.

D	PV(Costs of financial distress)	$V_L = V_U + tD - PV$(Costs of financial distress).
5	0.1	$V_L = 45 + 0.3(5) - 0.1$ $V_L = 46.4$
10	0.2	$V_L = 45 + 0.3(10) - 0.2$ $V_L = 47.8$
15	0.5	$V_L = 45 + 0.3(15) - 0.5$ $V_L = 49$
20	1.5	$V_L = 45 + 0.3(20) - 1.5$ $V_L = 49.5$
25	6.0	$V_L = 45 + 0.3(25) - 6.0$ $V_L = 46.5$
30	12.0	$V_L = 45 + 0.3(30) - 12.0$ $V_L = 42$

Thus, the optimal amount of debt is $20 million, which maximizes the value of Boulder at a level of $49.5 million. Beyond $20 million in debt, greater leverage reduces the firm value because the present value of financial distress costs more than the offsetting tax benefit.

5. B is correct. The calculations to determine the WACC are as follows:

The after-tax cash flows for the company are EUR10.0 million (1 − 0.20) = EUR8.0 million. Since the cash flows are assumed to be perpetual, WACC for the unlevered firm is calculated as

$$r_{WACC} = CF(1 − t)/V = \text{EUR8.0 million}/\text{EUR100.0 million} = 8.0\%.$$

The market value of Plover with the debt financing is EUR107 million:

$$V_L = V_U + tD = \text{EUR100.0 million} + 0.20(\text{EUR35.0 million}) = \text{EUR107.0 million}.$$

To find the cost of equity, we first need to find the market value of equity:

$V_L = D + E$, where D and E are market values of debt and equity, respectively.

$$E = \text{EUR107.0 million} − \text{EUR35.0 million} = \text{EUR72.0 million}.$$

The cost of equity is given by

$$r_e = r_0 + (r_0 − r_d)(1 − t)\frac{D}{E}$$

$$= 8.0\% + (8.0\% − 4.5\%)(0.80)(\text{EUR35.0 million}/\text{EUR72.0 million}) = 9.36\%.$$

Plover's WACC is calculated as follows:

WACC = (Weighting of debt × Cost of debt) + (Weighting of equity × Cost of equity)

$$= (\text{EUR35 million}/\text{EUR107.0 million})(4.5\%)(1 − 0.2) + (\text{EUR72.0 million}/\text{EUR107.0 million})(9.36\%)$$

= 7.48%, which is lower than the 8.0% for the unlevered firm.

Business Models

INTRODUCTION

1

A clearly described business model helps the analyst understand a business: its strategy, operations, target markets, key customers, suppliers, and ultimately prospects, risks, and financial profile. Many firms have conventional business models that are easily understood and have long existed, such as manufacturers and retailers. However, many business models are complex, novel, or a combination of models. Technological innovation, particularly digitalization, has enabled significant business model innovation over the past decades. Analysts need to develop their own understanding of an issuer's business model to inform their outlook and risk assessment; analysts should not rely solely on management's description of its business model.

LEARNING MODULE OVERVIEW

- A business model addresses four key parts of a business: the customers (the."who"), the firm's product and service offerings (the "what" and often the "why"), channels for reaching customers (the "where"), and pricing (the "how much").

- A pricing model describes the amount customers are billed for units of products or services. A firm's value proposition refers to the product attributes that lead customers to purchase the product rather than those of competitors. A firm's value chain refers to how a firm structures its systems and processes to create value for its customers.

- Conventional business models are common and long established, while unconventional business models are based on innovations or industry-specific combinations and variations of conventional models.

- Digital technology has been particularly influential for business model innovation by generating new products, new channels, new ways to communicate and exchange information, and new methods for handling financial transactions.

LEARNING MODULE SELF-ASSESSMENT

These initial questions are intended to help you gauge your current level of understanding of this learning module.

1. _____ refers to characterizing types of customers a firm may serve according to attributes such as geography, demographics, behavior, preferences, income, affinity for technology, and self-image.

   A. Channeling

   B. Segmenting

   C. Direct selling

   Solution:

   B is correct. Companies often identify and group prospective or current customers into segments based on attributes useful for sales, marketing, and product design.

2. The objective of _____ is to maximize profit in situations where different customers have different willingness or ability to pay.

   A. unit economics

   B. price discrimination

   C. functional separation

   Solution:

   B is correct. Firms can price the same or similar products and services differently by customer segment, volume purchased, season, time of day, channel, and so on, based on perceived customer preferences to expand their addressable market.

3. Companies selling in markets with many competitors and little or no product differentiation are often _____; in contrast, companies selling differentiated products with few competitors tend to have _____.

   A. crowdsourcing; bundling

   B. price takers; pricing power

   C. omnichannel; direct sales

   Solution:

   B is correct. Markets with many competitors and homogeneous products are characterized by having perfect or near-perfect competition market structures, with prices determined by market supply and demand.

4. Two examples of pricing models for complex products are _____, which refers to incentivizing or requiring the purchase of multiple products or services, and _____, which combines a low price on an initial purchase of a durable good with high-margin prices on associated consumables.

   A. bundling; razor, razorblade

B. fractional ownership; subscriptions

C. horizontal integration; network effects

Solution:

A is correct. Companies often bundle complementary products and services by offering a discount for their combined purchase versus the sum of the individual prices, such as a product and a repair/maintenance package. A razor, razorblade model, named for Gillette's business model of selling a razor with disposable razorblades, combines a durable good sold at near cost with high-margin, possibly proprietary consumables needed to use the durable good. Other examples include Nespresso and Keurig coffee machines, printers and toner/ink, and diagnostic instruments and reagents.

---

5. _____ refers to the increase in the value of a network to its users as more users join.

A. "Value chain"

B. "Network effects"

C. "Value proposition"

Solution:

B is correct. A network in which participants interact or transact with one another increases in value as more participants join. Examples of companies or services with network effects include financial instrument exchanges, payment networks, social media, and phone and other communication networks. Network effects can be a strong barrier to new industry entrants.

---

6. _____ involves user communities that enable voluntary collaboration between users of a product with generally a small amount of moderation and oversight by the community host or operator.

A. Franchising

B. Crowdsourcing

C. A loyalty program

Solution:

B is correct. Generically, crowdsourcing means obtaining contributions from multiple parties. Many digital business models incorporate or utilize crowdsourcing as their defining feature, whereby the company creates a service that users build, while the company simply creates rules and moderates user contributions. Common examples include social media, product reviews, open source software, and Wikis.

DEFINING THE BUSINESS MODEL

2

☐ | describe key features of business models

Successful new businesses may be based on a new product or technology, but there are many success stories based on familiar products or services and a new **business model**. For example, IKEA successfully combines existing business concepts—low-cost self-assembly furniture, modernist Scandinavian design, and big box retailing—in a unique and successful way. Similarly, Google did not invent online search but found a way to improve the accuracy of search results and to generate revenues through advertising based on user search data.

Often, successful business models are neither new nor unique but proven. Many businesses, such as wholesalers, retailers, law firms, building contractors, banks, and insurers, have conventional business models. Success for these firms hinges not on business model innovation but on superior execution, skill, proprietary technology, a strong brand, scale, scope economies, or other factors.

While there is no precise generally accepted definition of a business model, it is a description of how a business works and includes the following:

- The customer base for the business ("who?")
- The product or service the business offers to customers ("what?" and often "why?")
- Where is the firm selling and how do its products and services reach customers ("where?")
- The pricing strategy ("how much?")
- The key assets, partners, and suppliers the business requires ("how?")

A business model should provide enough detail so that the basic elements and relationships are clear, without providing so much detail as to become a business plan. A clear business model should have the elements included in Exhibit 1.

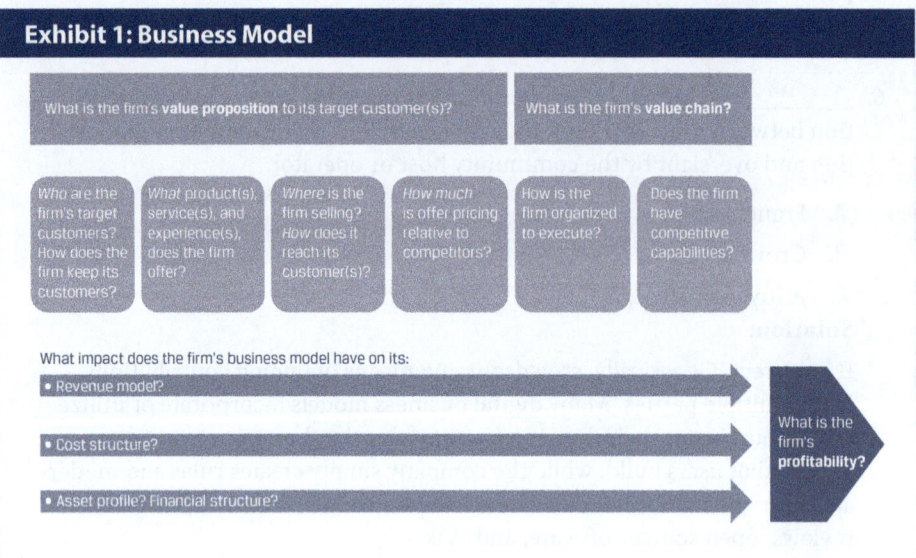

Exhibit 1: Business Model

Business Model Features

Information needed to determine the business model of public corporate issuers is often provided in annual reports and presentations; management may even provide its own description of the issuer's business model. The beginning of Tesla's annual report provides a good example.

EXAMPLE 1

Tesla Management's Description of its Business

"We design, develop, manufacture, sell and lease high-performance fully electric vehicles and energy generation and storage systems, and offer services related to our products. We generally sell our products directly to customers, including through our website and retail locations. We also continue to grow our customer-facing infrastructure through a global network of vehicle service centers, Mobile Service technicians, body shops, Supercharger stations and Destination Chargers to accelerate the widespread adoption of our products. We emphasize performance, attractive styling and the safety of our users and workforce in the design and manufacture of our products and are continuing to develop full self-driving technology for improved safety. We also strive to lower the cost of ownership for our customers through continuous efforts to reduce manufacturing costs and by offering financial and other services tailored to our products. Our mission to accelerate the world's transition to sustainable energy, engineering expertise, vertically integrated business model and focus on user experience differentiate us from other companies."

We can identify two business model elements from this paragraph.

What: "high-performance fully electric vehicles and energy generation and storage systems, and offer services related to our products" and "emphasize performance, attractive styling and . . . safety . . . and are continuing to develop full self-driving technology."

Where: "sell our products directly to customers, including through our website and retail locations. We also continue to grow our customer-facing infrastructure through a global network of vehicle service centers, Mobile Service technicians, body shops, Supercharger stations and Destination Chargers."

In the quote from Tesla, it describes its products and their attributes; venues in which it sells its products, known as sales channels or simply **channels**; and its emphasis on innovation. Analysts use a business model to begin their evaluation of how effectively it has been implemented, the company's prospects for future success, and understanding its implications for exposures to risks and opportunities. Management can change an issuer's business model or launch new businesses with distinct models within the same company, so this must be an ongoing analysis.

Let's explore the features of a business model further.

The Customers and the Market ("Who")

A business model should identify target customers:

- Are there specific types, or segments, of customers served?
- Are customers other businesses (business-to-business or B2B model) or consumers (business-to-consumer or B2C model)?
- What geographies will be served?

Tesla management's description is silent on which customer segments it is targeting, most likely because its target is shifting gradually toward the mass market with lower-cost and lower-price models. For an analyst, this type of inference can guide inputs for financial models, such as unit and price forecasts.

It is common in consumer markets to think of demographic segments, such as high-income suburban families. In many cases, segmentation is even narrower and is unique to the product or service category—for instance, "affluent early adopters of technology with homes that support plug-in charging in countries with EV subsidies."

Business opportunities often arise because established firms may not effectively serve—or even recognize—certain prospective customer segments. At the same time, choices made concerning a firm's target customers may introduce other related considerations or risks to the firm, such as high barriers to entry, changes in customer segment(s), or greater competition.

EXAMPLE 2

Segmenting Customers

Customers can be classified or segmented in numerous ways, including by their geography, demographics, seasonal or life-cycle timing, and behavior. Sophisticated market analytics can be used in **segmenting** to further break out smaller, homogeneous markets. Such analyses help such companies as Tesla to develop products and market them effectively.

Tesla positioned its products as the "new technology for clean energy" and moved away from being a company that solely produced expensive, premium electric sports cars to a company that defined what a practical, attractive, electric vehicle could look like. By targeting aspirational middle- and upper-class consumers who not only thrive on status-seeking behavior but also seek to be perceived to be environmentally friendly, socially and environmentally progressive, and cost conscious, Tesla expanded its customer markets.

Tesla and other companies can drill down to the postal code level for their customers and segment customers based on their social group, life-cycle stage, and wealth. This allows companies to identify customer cohorts across geographies and combine them into larger homogeneous markets that are easier to access and penetrate using targeted digital advertising.

Product or Service Offering ("What" and Often "Why")

The business model should define what product or service the firm offers and how, if at all, it is different from competitor offerings by referencing the needs of its target customers. This helps the analyst identify the addressable market for the business and to understand key opportunities and risks. For example, there may be a high risk of imitation or substitution. Understanding why customers buy the product or service, or the "job" that customers are "hiring" the product or service to fulfill, can help analysts identify current and potential competitors. While trucks and railroads do not seem like competitors, they both fulfill the same customer need: the transportation of goods. A more thoughtful analysis would identify which types of customers and in which scenarios customers would choose truck versus rail transportation (as well as air and marine transportation).

Generally, business customers have straightforward needs (e.g., ship goods), are sophisticated buyers, and are motivated to earn a profit. Consumer customers have diverse needs that can be impossible to quantify. Some consumers purchase whichever car is the most economical on a cost per mile basis, while others look to purchase aesthetically pleasing, high-performance, or low-emission vehicles. Certain products can satisfy these needs, and companies can use advertising, promotions, and product placement in media to create these needs in the first place.

For Tesla, management describes its products quite precisely: "high-performance fully electric vehicles and energy generation and storage systems." Some companies, however, will use overly broad terms in describing their offerings and addressable markets, overstate differentiation, or reference platforms and networks that may be very weakly developed—all in an attempt to convince investors that everyone could be a customer and inflate the value of the business. It is important for analysts to scrutinize management's assertions and supplement them with independent research.

EXAMPLE 3

Business Model Evolution: Netflix

Netflix's evolution since its start in 1997 is a prime example of how the "what" evolves over time. It started as a DVD rental by mail business in 1998, when the home movie rental business was dominated by brick-and-mortar rental stores and only 2% of the US households owned a DVD player. Netflix created and operated a website for customers to select DVDs to rent and delivered them through the mail. Subsequently, the company introduced a subscription model, where customers could rent several DVDs at one time for a fixed monthly fee. This new service disrupted the entire video rental industry.

Netflix's direct rival at the time was Blockbuster, but it took Blockbuster years to offer the same service as Netflix. By that time, Netflix had launched a new business model: a subscription-based, online-streaming video platform, and began to de-emphasize its DVD rental business. Through substantial investment in video content and improving streaming technology, Netflix grew to millions of monthly subscribers. The monthly subscription fee is substantially lower than monthly cable service fees, though Netflix has increased prices significantly over time. Netflix has differentiated its platform by producing exclusive content.

Blockbuster filed for bankruptcy in 2010 and ceased operations in 2014.

Channels ("Where")

A firm's channel strategy refers to "where" the firm is selling its offering; that is, how does it reach its customers? Channel strategy usually includes two main functions: selling the firm's products and services ("sales and marketing") and delivering them to customers ("distribution" or "logistics").

In assessing a firm's channel strategy, it is important to distinguish between what functions the firm can perform internally and what functions are better done by strategic partners and suppliers. For example, many business software companies do not install their software on customers' systems. Instead, customers hire a third-party consulting firm, which often provides additional ongoing services. Exhibit 2 provides examples of the functions, assets, and firms that may be part of the channel strategy for a firm.

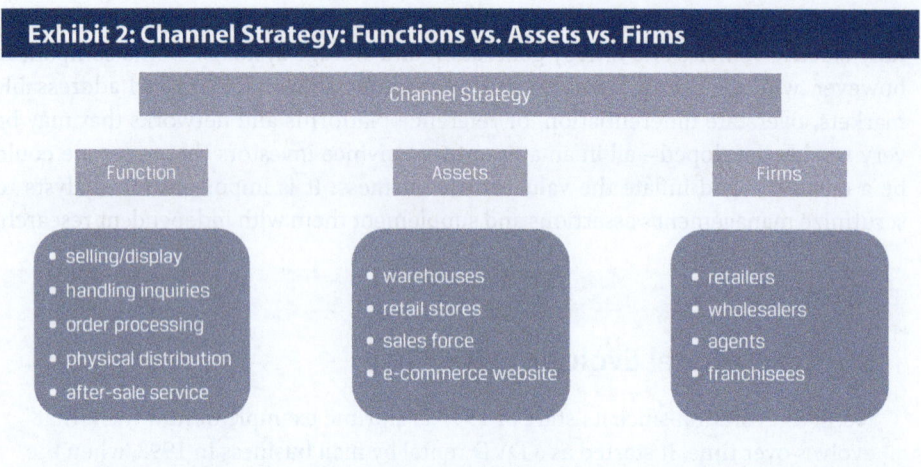

Exhibit 2: Channel Strategy: Functions vs. Assets vs. Firms

For companies that sell physical products, the traditional channel strategy is typically reflected in the flow of inventory through a series of intermediaries before reaching the final customer. Firms at each stage have their own physical facilities, and the product is purchased and then re-sold by the intermediaries at each stage until it is sold to the final customer.

Some companies, however, employ a **direct sales** strategy, selling directly to the end customer. Direct sales is a common and longstanding channel strategy for complex or high-margin products or services, such as medical devices, industrial equipment, and luxury goods. It is common in B2B models where the universe of potential customers is relatively small and easily reached. Historically, direct sales involved a significant investment in salespeople, but this is increasingly either substituted or supplemented with digital sales capabilities. Exhibit 3 contrasts the interactions of a traditional channel strategy with a direct sales strategy.

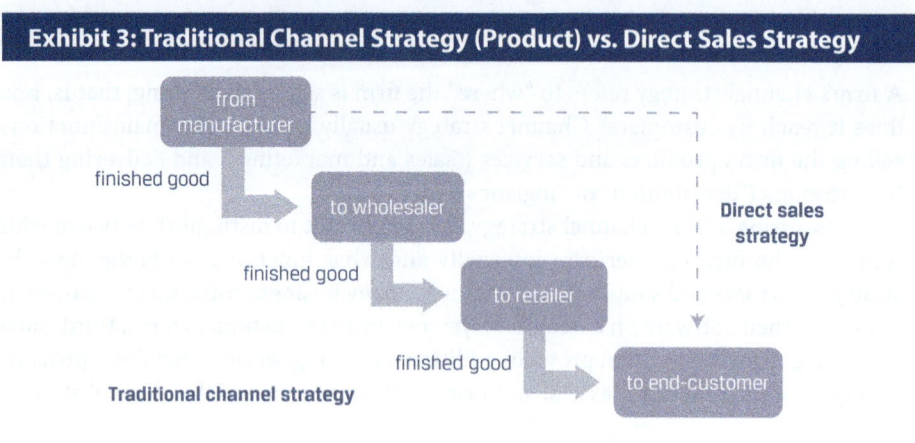

Exhibit 3: Traditional Channel Strategy (Product) vs. Direct Sales Strategy

Often, channels are used in combination. A so-called **omnichannel** strategy, common for apparel and consumer packaged goods, relies on both digital and physical channels to complete a sale. For example, a customer might order an item online and pick it up in a store or select an item in a store and have it delivered.

EXAMPLE 4

Adidas

Adidas is the world's second largest sportswear brand and combines four channels to distribute its products: retail shops, franchise outlets, wholesale business, and its own e-commerce. The following excerpt from its annual report summarizes its channel strategy:

> "With more than 2,500 own-retail stores, more than 15,000 mono-branded franchise stores and more than 150,000 wholesale doors, we have an unrivaled network of consumer touchpoints within our industry. In addition, through our own e-commerce channel, our single biggest store available to consumers in over 40 countries, we are leveraging a consistent global framework."

Source: Adidas AG Annual Report 2019 https://report.adidas-group.com/2019/en/group-management-report-our-company/corporate-strategy/sales-and-distribution-strategy.html

---

The channels used by a business are material drivers of revenues and cost behavior, profitability, and sensitivity to internal and external risk factors. Companies that employ a direct sales strategy have the advantage of a close relationship to customers and do not risk their products being shown alongside competitors on a shelf. However, direct sales impose significant cost, an important portion of which is fixed salaries and benefits.

How a firm's channel strategy differs from those of its competitors is an important factor to consider. For example, Tesla references its direct sales strategy, which is different from its US competitors, which sell to franchised dealers. This difference will affect comparability of financial results between Tesla and US automakers.

Pricing ("How Much")

A business model needs to provide sufficient detail about pricing so that the logic of the business is clear.

- Does the firm price at a premium, at parity, or at a discount relative to competitors?
- How do prices and costs compare?
- How is the firm's pricing justified in its business model?

Companies selling in markets with many competitors and little or no product differentiation are price takers that simply receive the market price determined by supply and demand; they are known as **commodity producers**. Examples of **commodities** include oil and gas, pharmaceuticals that are no longer patented, and many types of loans. Companies selling in markets with few competitors or with highly **differentiated products** enjoy more **pricing power**, or the ability to maintain prices above costs or increase prices without negatively impacting customer demand. A business that does not have pricing power is likely to pursue a cost leadership strategy, seeking to be the lowest-cost producer, such as discount retailers Costco and Lidl and the low-cost airline Ryanair.

Companies charging premium prices may justify doing so by emphasizing cost savings for customers elsewhere or by adding services for a reduced price (or free). For example, while Tesla's vehicles are priced at a premium, the annual report references a lower total cost of ownership, which refers to the aggregate direct and indirect costs associated with owning an asset over its life span. After considering government subsidies and the lower costs of electric charging compared with petroleum, the price is more competitive (though there is a risk of subsidies decreasing or ceasing in the future). This value proposition— the reduced total cost of ownership through some combination of product capabilities, reliability, ease of maintenance and operation, training, and so on—is common to business models in many sectors.

In some cases, however, companies do not "justify" premium pricing but, rather, establish strong brands and distinctiveness that customers value. While some of Tesla's prices can be justified based on lower total costs of ownership, much of it is owed to the aesthetic, performance, and intangible characteristics valued by customers and created by the company and its advertising. The same is true for most premium and luxury goods and services.

Pricing and Revenue Models

A pricing model describes how much money customers are billed for units of products or services. There are many models because there are many ways to specify a unit of product or service, and varying prices can be established, known as **price discrimination**, based on such factors as quality or grade, units sold, channel, customer size and type, and unit cost. The objective of price discrimination is to maximize profit in a situation where different customers have different willingness to pay. It may also be less costly to serve certain customer segments, such as large-volume buyers.

Rather than changing list or published prices, companies often implement pricing strategies using variable discounting, promotions, and bundles. For example, a customer may be offered a discount that other customers are not offered, and companies may adjust prices by changing the generosity of promotions rather than changing list prices. Prices adjusted for these are typically referred to as net prices.

Common pricing models include the following:

- **Tiered pricing**: Charging different prices to different buyers, often based on volume purchased but also based on product features (e.g., base versus premium trims of vehicles)

- **Dynamic pricing**: Charging different prices at different times and for different types of customers depending on such variables as available supply levels and demand. Specific examples include seasonal pricing for hotels, where prices may be high in the summer for beachfront properties and low in the winter, and surge pricing by ride-sharing companies Uber and Lyft, in which prices are raised in periods of exceptionally high demand.

- **Value-based pricing**: Setting prices based on the value received by the customer, which often involves estimating opportunity cost. This approach is commonly attempted in pharmaceuticals, where, for example, the price of a new drug that reduces the risk of stroke by 33% would reflect the savings from avoided hospitalization and death. Such an approach leads to different prices for different drugs since drugs vary in effectiveness and the type of disease they treat, and the prices of hospitalizations, physician services, and so on, that may be avoided from their use also vary by country.

- **Auction/reverse auction models**: These models establish prices through a bidding process. Digital technology enables this process to be automated, making these models feasible in new categories (e.g., Google and Baidu for digital advertising and eBay for consumer merchandise).

Some pricing models are used by firms selling multiple or complex products:

- **Bundling** refers to combining multiple products or services so that customers are incentivized or required to buy them together. Bundling can be effective, particularly for products that are complementary and that have high incremental profit margins and high marketing costs relative to the cost of the product itself. Examples include phone, cable TV, and internet services or application software with cloud-based storage.

- **Razor, razorblade pricing**combines a low price on an initial purchase of equipment (e.g., razor, printer, gaming console, diagnostic equipment) with high-margin prices on repeat-purchase consumables associated with the equipment (razorblades, printer ink, games, reagents). Often, companies design the equipment to work only with their proprietary consumables. Other companies selling generic consumables can render this pricing model unprofitable.

- **Add-on pricing** applies when a customer buys additional but optional services or product features, either at the time of purchase or during product use. A common strategy is to seek profitable pricing on the add-on when the customer is "captive" after the initial purchase decision has been made, such as in-game or in-app purchases of content and features. Firms that take this strategy too far, however, can damage customer goodwill and their reputation.

Businesses that seek to expand their footprint quickly may select an approach in which they use **penetration pricing**, or discounting willingly to build scale and market share, albeit at the cost of margins. It can be thought of as effectively a marketing expense to acquire customers. Examples include mobile phone providers discounting smartphones and Amazon discounting its Alexa-enabled tablets, e-readers, and speakers. However, penetration pricing can be controversial if implemented for a long period, because regulators may see the practice as unfair or anti-competitive and investors may question when or if the company will achieve profitability.

For digital businesses, growing a user base is often a critical objective, since the incremental costs associated with one more customer subscription are often minimal and the benefits can be enormous, including promotion through word of mouth and, potentially, network effects. Trial and adoption can be encouraged through pricing strategies that include the following:

- The pricing in a **freemium business model** allows customers a certain level of usage or functionality at no charge or with ads, for example with news content, a software application, or a game. This model is widely used in digital services with network effects when the company is seeking to scale up.

- A **hidden revenue business model** provides services to users at no charge and generates revenues elsewhere. This is a common feature of both legacy and digital business models in the media sector, with "free" content and paid advertising. Examples can also be found in online marketplaces, where sellers pay and buyers do not, and financial services with debit cards, checking accounts, and security trading that appear free.

Some business models create value by providing an alternative to ownership and provide use of the product without purchasing an asset or product. The simplicity of electronic invoicing and payments and the value that businesses and investors place on predictable, recurring revenue streams have driven the introduction of subscription pricing models in new areas.

- Subscriptions deliver products or services—or access to them—in exchange for recurring fees. Traditionally, the subscription model is associated with media and utilities. However, subscription models have been extended broadly to many sectors, notably application software and cloud computing infrastructure. Subscription fees can be fixed, discounted for promotional offers, tiered according to features, or based on customer usage, such as in utilities, payment processing, and cloud computing.

- Leasing, licensing, and franchising, while all different, are also all like subscriptions but involve the transfer of property or access to it rather than a product. Leasing is typically used when the property is real estate or another physical asset, licensing is for intellectual property, and **franchising** is a more comprehensive form of licensing, in which the franchisor typically gives the franchisee the right to sell or distribute its product or service in a specified territory and to receive marketing and other support. Specifics on these important but complicated forms of recurring-revenue models will be covered in greater detail in later lessons.

The Value Proposition (Who + What + Where + How Much)

A **value proposition** refers to the product or service attributes valued by customers that lead them to purchase the product and prefer one firm's offering over those of its competitors, given relative pricing. These vary greatly and relate to factors such as the following:

- Product and service itself—its capability, performance, features, and style
- Service and support behind the product and service—whether it is "high-touch" or "low-touch" customer service, depending on the requirements of the customer and the type of product or service, access to repairs, spare parts, and so on
- Sale process (e.g., purchasing convenience, no-hassle returns)
- The pricing relative to competitors

Crafting a compelling value proposition requires management to carefully consider these factors. For instance, Tesla's value proposition goes beyond transportation: It emphasizes the benefits of its electric propulsion system, zero emissions, and high performance with strong and silent acceleration, as well as technological sophistication, including self-driving capabilities and other enhancements via ongoing software upgrades. Additionally, an important part of Tesla's value proposition is its proprietary network of high-speed charging stations. It is a major undertaking for Tesla to build this network in multiple countries, but doing so can provide a competitive advantage against market entrants. Finally, Tesla has engendered significant customer loyalty from the aesthetics of its vehicles, the personality of its founder, and word-of-mouth marketing from customers and online influencers.

EXAMPLE 5

HD Tools Business Model

The fictional firm HD Tools sells tools. It is considering two business models, A and B. Elements of each are presented in the following table.

	Business Model A	Business Model B
Customer segment	- Apartment dwellers and new homeowners	- Do-it-yourself/professional trades
Products	- Simple, low-priced kit of tools	- A full assortment of high-quality tools for individual purchase

	Business Model A	**Business Model B**
Channel	■ They do not shop at home improvement stores and are likely to buy a kit online or from a mass retailer.	■ They frequent large home improvement stores and specialty trade distributers.
Customer profile, need	■ They may not know what tools they need and may have none to start with. ■ Occasional use to do everyday repairs	■ Their time is valuable. ■ They know and can differentiate between tools and brands. ■ Heavy-use, high-quality requirement
Relative pricing	■ Low and affordable price point	■ Premium priced tools
Customer value	■ A single kit contains several tools they are likely to need. ■ A simple and compact toolbox given limited storage space	■ Will pay a premium for a tool that they are confident will be durable and will perform
Service expectations	■ After-sales support is not critical, provided there is an acceptable return policy	■ After-sales support not critical, but prefers interacting with knowledgeable staff ■ Product availability important

Each of these business models is valid for its respective customer segment. Both require distribution to disparate customer bases. However, Model A (low-priced kits) could potentially be established at a smaller scale online or by gaining shelf space at a handful of large retailers.

With Model A, the challenge will be to have a low-enough product cost to generate an acceptable margin for the business. Differentiation against other kit providers might be also achievable through better online customer reviews, product aesthetics, a better selection of tools, or perhaps an extra feature not offered by competitors—for example, by bundling with a selection of common fasteners, aimed at maximizing customer convenience at a low price point.

With Model B, the more critical factor is likely to be product quality, price, and distribution. The professional market requires tools that are of demonstrably high quality so that their customers, who are knowledgeable, will choose them over established rival brands. This might be difficult for a new brand, such as HD. However, HD might be able to overcome this, with objective statements about the quality of materials used in making the tools, their strength and durability, a lifetime warranty and generous return policy, marketing aimed at professionals, and working with specialist retailers to promote the product.

Businesses can be constrained in their value proposition by regulations, customers that prioritize price above all other factors, or the firm selling a commodity product with thin margins.

Business Organization and Capabilities

Evaluating a firm's business model requires consideration not only of the value proposition but also "how" the firm is structured to deliver. Specifically, what labor and capital resources, relationships, intellectual property, and other capabilities and assets does the firm require to execute on its business model, and will the firm need to own them or can they be contracted for. If a firm is dependent on other firms for critical inputs, those supplier relationships can become key elements of its strategy and a potential risk.

EXAMPLE 6

Both a Key Supplier and Competitor

Netflix, the digital entertainment company, sells a streaming video service through its website and mobile applications. While it produces and licenses content, it relies on the services provided by internet service providers, such as broadband and wireless telecom companies, to reach its customers. Additionally, Netflix relies on digital infrastructure companies to enable the delivery of content to its more than 200 million subscribers globally whenever and wherever they want. One digital infrastructure company is Amazon, which, through its Prime Video streaming service, is also a significant competitor for Netflix.

In its annual report, Netflix noted the following under its risk factors:

"Amazon Web Services ("AWS") provides a distributed computing infrastructure platform for business operations, or what is commonly referred to as a "cloud" computing service. We have architected our software and computer systems to utilize data processing, storage capabilities and other services provided by AWS. Currently, we run the vast majority of our computing on AWS. Given this, along with the fact that we cannot easily switch our AWS operations to another cloud provider, any disruption of or interference with our use of AWS would impact our operations and our business would be adversely impacted. While the retail side of Amazon competes with us, we do not believe that Amazon will use the AWS operation in such a manner as to gain competitive advantage against our service, although if it were to do so, it could harm our business."

The auto business has traditionally been organized with automakers supplied by networks of parts manufacturers. Parts manufacturers might supply very specific components, such as tires, or complete assemblies, such engines. There is generally a very close relationship between automakers and their suppliers because parts or assemblies are often custom designed for a particular vehicle. When the supplier becomes involved at the design stage and throughout the production stage, it improves quality and interoperability, though specificity of parts increases reliance on single manufacturers and the risk of supply interruptions. For instance, in the wake of the COVID-19 pandemic, undersupply of some semiconductor inputs resulted in significant supply disruptions and lost sales for automakers. In some cases, automakers outsource vehicle production entirely, as in the case of Porsche outsourcing to Valmet and Magna Steyr.

Tesla's business model is different because it emphasizes vertical integration, with in-house development and production of key components, such as batteries and software/electronics. This requires substantial capital and effort and is therefore an unusual choice for a new company but is consistent with Tesla's strategy of proprietary technology.

The "how" aspect of a business model is also referred to as a firm's **value chain**—that is, the systems and processes in a firm that create value for its customers. The value chain includes only those functions performed by a single firm, including functions that are valued by customers but may not involve physical transformation or handling the product. Note that a firm's value chain is different from its **supply chain**, which refers to the sequence of processes involved in the creation of a product, both within and external to a firm. A supply chain includes all the steps involved in producing and delivering a physical product to the end customer, regardless of whether those steps are performed by a single firm. For businesses, where marketing and sales are strategically critical functions, the "value proposition" includes the channels used to reach customers, the value the firm might deliver through the sales and service functions.

Value chain analysis provides a link between the firm's value proposition for customers and its profitability, as Exhibit 4 shows, and was originally conceptualized by Porter in 1985.

Exhibit 4: Business Value Chain Components: Support and Primary Activities

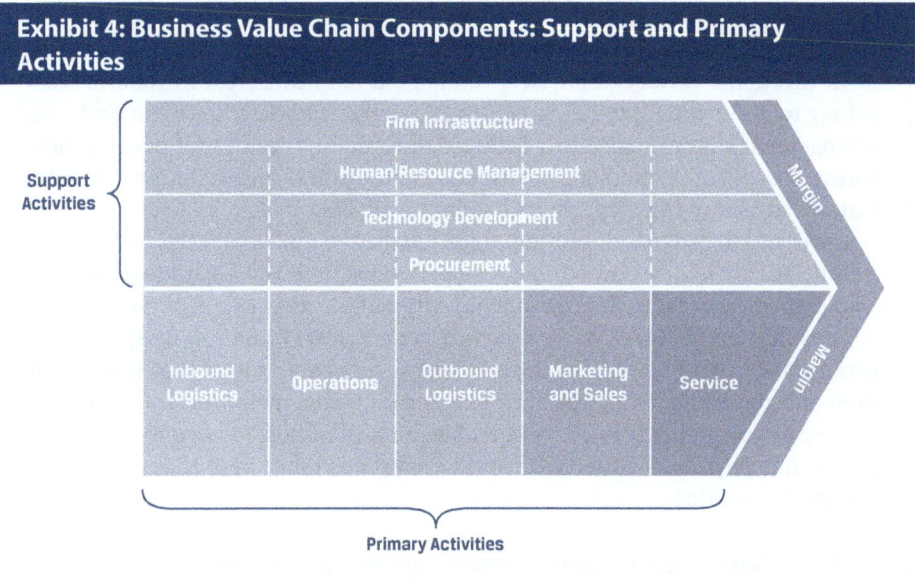

These activities are core to each firm, and the extent and significance each of these roles play in the day-to-day activities of firms depend on the scale of the business and its operations. Additionally, the firm's four primary "support" activities include procurement, human resource management, technology development, and firm infrastructure. This provides a useful starting point for evaluating the value chain of a company, although dramatic advances in digital technology have radically changed the way that some of these functions are carried out in many businesses. When analyzing the value chain, each component should be evaluated by first identifying the specific activities carried out by the firm, then estimating the value added and costs associated with each activity, and finally identifying opportunities for competitive advantage.

Finally, a business model should reveal how the firm expects to generate a profit. That is, how and why prices and volumes not only cover but exceed variable and fixed costs today or in the future at a greater scale. An analyst will want to examine margins, break-even points, and **unit economics**, which expresses revenues and costs on a per-unit basis. For example, Amazon Web Services and the cloud infrastructure business model is based on a *decline over time* in both unit costs and unit prices as volumes increase and technology improves. This would be expected to create a virtuous cycle: Lower prices enable cloud computing providers to expand customers and usage, which in turn lowers costs because most costs are fixed; in fact, unit costs fall faster than prices, so profits increase. Overall, this is a considerable barrier to competition, because a new entrant that matched the prevailing price would suffer losses because they did not have the economies of scale to have low costs.

In summary, a business model answers several key questions:

- What is the firm selling?
- To whom?
- For how much?

- How is the company going to execute?
- How much does it cost, and how will costs behave as size and conditions change?

QUESTION SET

An analyst is evaluating two bicycle manufacturing companies: Winston Bikes and Carbondash.

Winston Bikes manufactures inexpensive, mass-market bicycles and sells them through a variety of physical retailers. It uses the latest in robotic technology to do its manufacturing, and it leases the robotic equipment under an arrangement where it can easily increase or decrease the amount of equipment it uses. It uses conventional, established, common, and simple designs and uses materials that are inexpensive and widely available.

Carbondash produces premium, high-quality, complex bicycles by hand. Its technicians are highly trained over long periods of time and are under long-term employment contracts. It uses unconventional, sophisticated, highly precise designs. It manufactures its frames with a proprietary and highly specialized variant of carbon fiber that is infused with a rare earth metal that is available from only one mine in the world. Everything is custom measured and custom fit to the rider by highly trained salespeople in retail outlets located in expensive, prestigious physical locations. It serves a loyal customer base that is relatively insensitive to price.

---

1. If a sudden change in market demand happens, which company will be better able to handle it?

   Guideline solution:

   If there is a sudden change in market demand, whether an increase or a decrease in demand, Winston Bikes will most likely be able to handle it better than Carbondash. Because of Winston Bikes' flexible lease arrangements with its manufacturing robots, it can easily scale its manufacturing up or down in response to changes in market demand. Carbondash, however, has a heavy dependence on skilled human labor. It can't scale up quickly because its technicians require long periods of training, and it can't scale down easily because of its long-term labor contracts.

---

2. Why might the risks of supplier disruption be lower for Winston Bikes than for Carbondash?

   Guideline solution:

   Carbondash faces higher risk of supplier disruption because it single-sources its materials from one company, uses a proprietary design that requires specialized manufacturing techniques, and uses a special ingredient that is available from only one source in the world. Winston Bikes, in contrast, uses many suppliers and has simple designs and widely available materials that can be used by many suppliers.

---

3. Why might the risks of increases in material costs be lower for Carbondash than for Winston Bikes?

   Guideline solution:

   Winston Bikes is a low-cost business that competes on price and has thin margins. It is a price taker and so is unable to raise its prices without suffering a decrease in sales. Its thin margins mean that it can't absorb cost increases and remain profitable. Carbondash, in contrast, relies on differentiation of its products and has a loyal customer base that is less sensitive to price. Because its margins are higher, it is better able to absorb an increase in the cost of its materials, and because its customer base is loyal and less sensitive to price, it is able to raise its prices without a significant adverse impact on its sales.

4. Which company will most likely:

   a. be larger?

   b. have higher prices?

   c. have higher costs?

   Guideline solution to a:

   Winston Bikes will most likely be larger than Carbondash, at least in terms of units sold. Winston Bikes operates on thin margins and so must have a high volume in order to generate sufficient profitability to survive. Carbondash, in contrast, is likely a high-price, low-volume manufacturer. Winston Bikes has omnichannel distribution, which puts its products in front of more customers. Carbondash uses direct sales in physical stores using salespeople to create relationships.

   Guideline solution to b:

   Carbondash will most likely have higher prices. It pursues a product differentiation strategy, and it targets a customer base that is relatively price insensitive. Winston Bikes competes on price and so must have low prices.

   Guideline solution to c:

   Carbondash most likely has higher costs per unit because of all the human labor involved throughout the manufacturing and sales process. The bikes are assembled by hand and are sold using direct sales in its own stores with its own sales staff. Winston Bikes uses the latest in software and robot manufacturing technology in order to keep costs as low as possible, and it uses distribution channels whereby it doesn't need to pay for stores or sales staff.

5. An analyst sits down for a meeting with the management team of Luggo Corporation, who is describing their business. The CEO makes the following statement:

   Luggo makes premium parts to secure wheels onto cars and trucks. We differentiate ourselves from our competitors by using premium designs and building our products from the finest titanium to ensure strength and light weight. We distribute our products through wholesalers that supply physical retail stores, and we price at parity with the market.

   What parts of the business model did the CEO not describe?

   Guideline solution:

   The CEO did not describe the firm's customers. This is one of the key attributes of a business model and describes how the firm segments its customer base and which segments it is targeting with its products. Customers can be segmented in numerous ways, including by their geography, demographics, seasonal or life-cycle timing, behavior, social group, and wealth. Segmenting allows companies to identify customer cohorts across geographies and combine them into larger homogeneous markets that are easier to access and penetrate using targeted marketing. Business opportunities often arise

> because established firms may not effectively serve—or even recognize—
> customer segments.

3

BUSINESS MODEL TYPES

☐ | describe various types of business models

Conventional Business Models

Some business models are common and have existed for a long time. Alone or in combination with one another, these conventional models make up most business models in practice and are thus essential for analysts to understand. We briefly describe eight conventional models in Exhibit 5 using the framework in the prior lesson. In practice, each industry sector tends to have its own version of these conventional models, with specific features, such as "athletic apparel manufacturer."

Business Model Variations

While the conventional business models are enough to describe many companies, there are many others in practice. Most of them are simply combinations of the conventional models or industry-specific variations.

- Private label or **contract manufacturers** that produce goods to be marketed by others. This is a common arrangement, particularly for offshore production. Apple and NVIDIA, for example, do not manufacture their own branded products but instead contract with many specialized contract manufacturers in Asia. Apple and NIVIDIA manage a web of complex relationships, while specializing in R&D, product design, and sales and marketing.

- **Value added resellers** not only distribute a product but also handle more complex aspects of product installation, customization, service, or support. This is common with complex, service-intensive products, such as construction machinery, IT hardware, and enterprise software.

- **Licensing arrangements** in which a company will produce a product using someone else's brand name in return for a royalty: This is common in toys and apparel, for example, when manufacturers might pay for the right to use the name of a famous film character, a sports team, or a brand that has become popular in a related category, such as sporting goods.

- Franchise models in which franchisees have a tightly defined and exclusive relationship with a franchisor to operate under a specific brand with proprietary products and processes. Restaurants, retailers, and auto dealerships are common types of franchises. The franchisor earns a royalty on the franchisee's sales. The franchisor is responsible for product development and advertising, for which it often collects an additional fee from franchisees.

Exhibit 5: Conventional Business Models

Conventional Model	Customers	Products	Channel	Pricing	Key Inputs Required	Example
Natural Resource Producer	▪ Refiners ▪ Distributors	▪ Usable natural resources and raw material	▪ Contracts with refiner or distributor, based on spot or forward prices	▪ Spot or forward market prices in contracts	▪ Rights to natural resources with profitable economics ▪ Technical expertise	▪ Total Energies, a French oil and gas producer
Manufacturer	▪ Distributors ▪ End-users (direct)	▪ Finished goods	▪ Distributors ▪ Direct salespeople or digital	▪ Price per product sold ▪ Subscription	▪ Raw materials ▪ Brands ▪ Creative and technical expertise	▪ L'Oréal SA, a French cosmetics and beauty company
Distributor	▪ Retailers	▪ Transportation and storage	▪ Retailers	▪ Spread on purchase price vs. sales price ▪ Delivery or service fee	▪ Transportation assets ▪ Selection of products	▪ McKesson, a US distributor of pharmaceuticals and medical supplies
Retailer	▪ End-users	▪ Finished goods • Customer experience	▪ Stores ▪ Direct salespeople or digital	▪ Mark-up on products sold ▪ Member service fees	▪ Selection of product ▪ Physical or digital storefront	▪ JD.com, a Chinese first-party e-commerce company
Broker	▪ Buyers and sellers	▪ Connecting buyers and sellers	▪ Salespeople ▪ Digital	▪ Commissions ▪ Listing fees	▪ Large numbers of both buyers and sellers ▪ Digital platform	▪ Pinduoduo, a Chinese e-commerce platform for third-party merchants
Bank	▪ Borrowers	▪ Loans ▪ Leases	▪ Digital ▪ Branches, Loan officers	▪ Loan and lease interest rate spread over interest rate paid for funding	▪ Deposits and other sources of funding ▪ Borrower relationships	▪ HSBC, a UK-based global financial services company

Conventional Model	Customers	Products	Channel	Pricing	Key Inputs Required	Example
Service Producer	▪ Services ▪ Businesses	▪ Services	▪ Direct salespeople or digital	▪ Service fees ▪ Mark-ups on product used or sold	▪ Customer relationships ▪ Technical expertise	▪ Infosys Ltd., an Indian technology consulting and outsourcing company
Software	▪ Services ▪ Businesses	▪ Software	▪ Direct salespeople or digital	▪ Subscription fee ▪ License costs▪ ◆ Maintenance fee	▪ Technical expertise ▪ Channel partner ▪ Digital support infrastructure	▪ Shopify Inc., a Canadian software and services company for e-commerce merchants

Business Model Innovation

Most discussion of business models focuses on innovation: how new business models can be introduced or adapted to existing markets. While not requiring it, business model innovation is often combined with technological innovation and pioneered by new market entrants rather than industry incumbents.

Exhibit 6 identifies several historical cases of business model innovations in various industries. Notice how innovation becomes convention over time.

Exhibit 6: Business Model Innovation Historical Examples		
Industry	**Business Model Innovation**	**Innovative Features**
Airlines	▪ Low-cost and ultra-low-cost airlines	▪ Customer: leisure, mass market ▪ Product: Point-to-point flights ▪ Low prices ▪ No frills, low costs ▪ Channel: direct, digital sales
Software	▪ Software as a service (SaaS)	▪ Price: monthly fees rather than upfront license ▪ Customer: broader, owing to pricing
Retailing	▪ Discount retailing ▪ E-commerce ▪ Digital marketplaces	▪ Prices ▪ Product selection ▪ Channel
Securities brokerage	▪ Discount brokers	▪ Customer: individuals ▪ Low or free commissions ▪ No extra services or research, low costs ▪ Channel: direct, digital sales

Digital technology has generated many new products, such as streaming video, digital advertising, social media, and dating apps and has enabled many business model innovations, such as digital marketplaces. While large-scale business model innovation did not start with digital technology, the rapid and open-ended advance of digital technology has dramatically changed how businesses operate by radically reducing the cost of communicating, exchanging information, and financially transacting. This had several direct implications for many businesses:

- Location matters less. Digital communications and e-commerce enable customers to shop and purchase more easily from firms having no local physical presence.
- Outsourcing is easier, for similar reasons.
- Digital marketing makes it easy and cost effective to reach very specific groups of customers, regardless of location, and to engage more deeply with them than was possible with traditional advertising.
- Network effects, discussed next, have become more powerful and accessible to more firms.

Network Effects and Platform Business Models

Network effects refer to the increase in value of a network to its users as more users join. Many internet-based businesses are built on network effects; for example, China's WeChat messaging and payment platform is valuable to its users in large part because it is used by so many people. Once it achieved a high enough number of users, it also became available to marginal users, further increasing user growth. Online classifieds, social media, and ride-sharing services are other examples. Network effects capitalize on both economics of scale and scope. Network effects are also at work in many older, pre-internet businesses, such as telephone service, payment systems including credit cards, and financial infrastructure, such as stock exchanges. In all these businesses, the key metric is the number of users and the growth rate of users.

"One-sided" network effects apply in networks where it is only one *type* of user that is valuable to other users: for example, telephone services and peer-to-peer payment systems, such as Venmo, a mobile app owned by PayPal that enables users to easily transfer, deposit, and withdraw money. Connections between users are crucial, but there is one type of user. Depending on the size and the connections of the network, the marginal cost of acquiring each additional user is lower than the revenue generated by adding the user to the network.

In some cases, networks are composed of two or more *types* of users, which can be described as "two-sided" or "multi-sided" networks, such as buyers and sellers in an online marketplace. The typical example for these multi-sided platforms includes credit and debit card networks, such as Visa and China Union Pay, composed of both merchant and cardholder users. Other examples include digital marketplaces, such as Airbnb, composed of both hosts and guests. As these multi-sided networks grow—more users join the service, which attracts more merchants, which in turn attracts more users—these businesses can grow exponentially. The growth of food delivery services connects restaurants, independent drivers, and customers and has evolved through multiple interdependent network effects. As each of the three groups has grown, they in turn increase the aggregate size of their networks, as Exhibit 7 shows. Network effects create strong barriers to entry and are a form of competitive advantage.

Exhibit 7: Multiple Network Effects for Multi-Sided Platforms

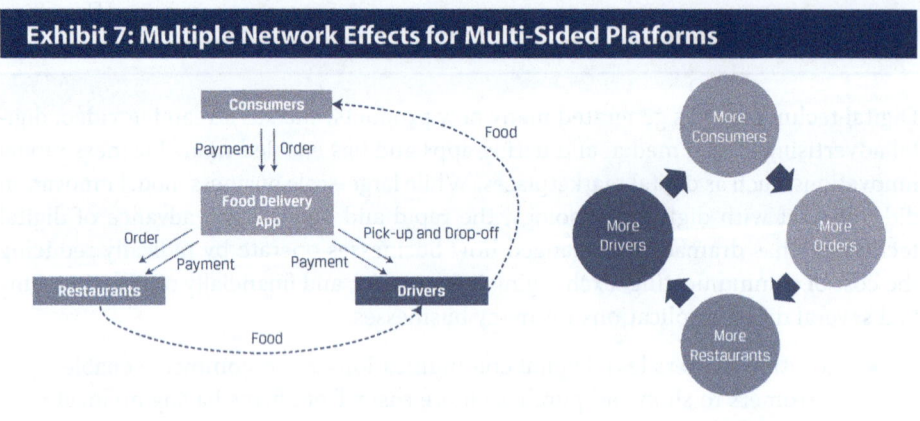

Network business models often include **crowdsourcing**, where users contribute directly to a product or service. Examples include social media, such as TikTok/Douyin and Reddit; open-source software; knowledge aggregators, such as Wikipedia; and customer reviews and feedback on, for example, Yelp, Amazon, and TripAdvisor. These businesses facilitate "user communities" that enable voluntary collaboration between users of a product with a small amount of moderation and oversight by the company.

EXAMPLE 7

Business Model Evolution in the Hotel and Travel Industry

The hotel industry provides a good illustration of business model evolution over time and the emergence of different business models, with varying financial characteristics. Until the 20th century, business model evolution was slow. In response to increasing scale and specialization demanded by a growing market, hotels became larger and more numerous but with little change in the basic business model. The 20th century brought major changes to business models in the industry. The single-property hotel business remained a relevant business model, due to the inherent uniqueness of certain hotel properties.

However, with a much larger and highly mobile customer base, hotel operators saw an opportunity, with the need to serve a growing corporate travel market, increase the scale and footprint of their businesses, and provide convenience and consistency to customers, thereby increasing operating efficiency. Some specific examples are outlined below.

Impact		Example
Scale	Large, global hotel chains and brands with multiple locations that serve highly mobile customers in numerous market segments.	Intercontinental Hotels & Resorts has more than 15 brands in approximately 6,000 locations. Brands range from basic to luxury and extended stay.
Specialization	Specialized lodging businesses to serve specific market segments	Resort hotels, vacation packages (bundled flights + lodging + meals), casinos, weekly/monthly accommodation (for out-of-town executives)
Franchising	Applying the franchise approach to the hotel business	Most Hilton Hotels properties are not owned or leased by Hilton but are operated by franchisees who pay fees.
Functional separation	Specialized businesses handling such functions as branding and marketing, property ownership, management, and development	REITs and property ownership: The largest hotel companies seldom own all their hotels; some own none. Host Hotels & Resorts, the world's largest hotel REIT, owns close to 100 hotel properties and is the largest third-party owner of Marriott and Hyatt hotels.
Fractionalized ownership	Fractionalized ownership in the form of time-sharing, creating a new lodging category between the hotel and the vacation home	Wyndham Destinations is the largest vacation ownership company. The company develops, sells, and manages time-share properties under various vacation ownership clubs.
Loyalty programs	The introduction of programs to increase brand loyalty among high-value, frequent travelers	Hotel loyalty programs first introduced by Holiday Inn and Marriott in 1983

The digital transformation of business models has also impacted the hotel business. To increase the efficiency in marketing and distribution of hotel and travel-related services, Online Travel Agency (OTA) reducedthe complexities of travel planning and bookings. In both its traditional and online forms, the travel agency business is a two-sided network.

Like a traditional travel agent, OTA assists travelers with research and planning, price comparisons, bookings, and logistics. For hotels, it provides exposure, leads, bookings, customer information, feedback, and competitive intelligence. Automating these functions and delivering them as a web-based service so greatly improved their convenience, speed, and efficiency that the business model was transformed, shifting the relationship and the balance of power between agencies and their hotel customers. Effectively, through network effects, OTA disintermediated the traditional travel agency model and forced the remaining agencies to specialize. Examples of differing OTA business models are shown below.

OTA Business Model	Description	Examples
Price-comparison "aggregators"	These network-based businesses offer buyers and sellers in the hotel and travel community travel-related price comparison services and bookings.	Booking.com, Expedia, Ctrip, eDreams
Crowdsourcing	These platform businesses provide crowd-sourced reviews and information on hotels and other travel services.	TripAdvisor.com
Home sharing/short-term rental service	These platform businesses have challenged and disrupted the traditional hotel model by supplying a variety of temporary, often unique, accommodations.	Airbnb; Vrbo (acquired in 2006 by HomeAway, which in turn was acquired by Expedia in 2015)

Hotel operators have responded to these challenges by investing in their own websites, customer data, and direct booking capabilities or selling directly to various sites. Some traditional hotel chains, which have historically emphasized consistency and uniformity, have launched so-called soft brands, which are hotels that operate under their own name but with a greater degree of local operator autonomy. Moreover, they have created hybrid hotel solutions, such as condo-hotels (condos in a hotel that are at the disposal of the owner but are rented out otherwise by the hotel).

QUESTION SET

Bynta is a new entrant in the retail clothing industry. It is competing against Ocean Hill Inc., an established industry incumbent that uses a conventional business model.

---

1. What attributes of a conventional retail business model will Bynta and Ocean Hill Inc. likely share?

Solution:

The four major components of a business model framework are customers, products, channels, and pricing. Bynta and Ocean Hill Inc. will likely be similar in that their customers will be end users of the products, their products will be finished goods, and their pricing will be based on markup on products sold.

---

2. What most likely would distinguish Bynta from Ocean Hill Inc.?

Solution:

Bynta can distinguish itself from Ocean Hill Inc. by using digital technology to reduce the cost of communicating, exchanging information, and financially transacting. With digital technology, location matters less because e-commerce allows for shopping and purchasing without the need for a physical storefront.

Outsourcing to private label or contract manufacturers is also made easier with digital technology and will allow Bynta to focus more on product design, sales, and marketing.

Improved customer segmentation is also enabled by digital technology, allowing for segments that are narrower and unique to Bynta's product categories. Digital technology in marketing will make it easier and more cost effective for Bynta to reach very specific customer segments, regardless of location, and to engage more deeply with them than is possible with traditional advertising. Sophisticated market analytics can be used to break out smaller, homogeneous markets. This will allow Bynta to identify customer cohorts across geographies and combine them into larger homogeneous markets that are easier to access and penetrate using targeted digital advertising.

Bynta can also benefit from network effects and crowdsourcing by facilitating user communities that enable voluntary collaboration between its customers.

3. Given an increase in the price of raw materials/commodities, what is the difference in revenue/profit impact for producers versus manufacturers versus distributors and retailers?

Solution:

A supply chain includes all the steps involved in producing and delivering a physical product to the end customer, regardless of whether those steps are performed by a single firm. Different firms at different points in the supply chain may attempt to mitigate the impact of raw materials/commodity price increases in different ways. Some firms may try to stabilize revenues by entering long-term customer or hedging contracts.

While these are often available for firms at the beginning of the supply chain, where there are established markets for contracts on raw materials, it is less possible further down the chain. For example, producers that sell natural resources or commodities and manufacturers that buy them can enter derivative contracts in the forward markets to secure more stable pricing for the products they sell or the key inputs that they need.

Further down the supply chain, distributors and retailers may secure long-term contracts to ensure stabilized prices, though they are unlikely to have access to structured and highly liquid derivative contracts. The manufacturing stage of the supply chain creates products that are too differentiated to support broad derivative markets as there are with commodities.

One risk is that if a firm locks in a sale price for its products while not locking in a purchase price for its raw material key inputs, it faces the risk of substantial loss if the cost of raw materials increases in the spot market. Some firms may attempt to minimize fixed operating costs—for example, through outsourcing or flexible contracts with workers and suppliers.

Firms whose revenue/profit may be impacted by fluctuations in materials prices may also use more conservative capital structure policies, with relatively little debt and therefore smaller fixed financing obligations compared with firms that are less sensitive to such fluctuations.

Questions 4 and 5 expand on the earlier example of business model evolution in the hotel and travel industry.

4. Describe the differences in features between the hotel business model and the home-sharing business model.

Solution:

Many hotels use a franchise model in which franchisees have a tightly defined and exclusive relationship with a franchisor to operate under a specific brand with proprietary products and processes. The franchisor earns a royalty on the franchisee's sales.

Homesharing follows an Online Travel Agency (OTA) business model and has challenged and disrupted the traditional hotel model by enabling homeowners and hosts to supply a variety of temporary, often unique, accommodations.

5. Explain why there might be so many fewer OTA companies than hotel companies.

Solution:

One reason why there might be so many fewer OTA companies than hotel companies is that OTA companies are aggregators that benefit much more from network effects than hotel companies. "Network effects" refers to the exponential increase in value to a network's users as the number of its users grows. A large network is valuable to its users in large part because it is used by so many people. As more users join the network, more merchants are attracted to the network, which in turn attracts more users. Hence, there are fewer OTA companies and each one attracts many users.

Network business models also often include crowdsourcing, where users contribute directly to a product or service. These businesses facilitate "user communities" that enable voluntary collaboration between users of a product via customer reviews and feedback and require only a small amount of moderation and oversight by the company.

PRACTICE PROBLEMS

1. The sequence of processes involved in the creation of a product, both within and external to a firm, including all the steps involved in producing a physical product and delivering it to the end customer, regardless of whether those steps are performed by a single firm, is referred to as the:

   A. value chain.

   B. supply chain.

   C. business model.

The following information relates to questions 2-5

An analyst is reviewing investor presentations from the management teams of two companies with unconventional business models: HealthyPet and DiaSera.

HealthyPet is a pet medical insurer that has a differentiated approach in a business dominated by incumbent property & casualty insurers, for which pet insurance is a niche business relative to business, home, and auto insurance lines. HealthyPet targets the high-income, young, urban, busy professional pet owner segment. It bundles coverage for owners of multiple pets, including exotic pets that incumbents are typically reluctant to insure. The industry incumbents sell insurance policies that reimburse pet owners for a percentage of veterinarian and other medical costs incurred, subject to restrictions and limits. HealthyPet, however, pays veterinarians directly for pet medical costs. It has a preferred network of veterinarians it recommends and for which it negotiates lower prices, but policyholders face relatively few restrictions. It sells through veterinarian referrals and boutique pet stores to maintain an image of exclusivity and prestige and maintains an online storefront for customer convenience. It avoids mass market retail to protect its image. It charges more than its competitors for monthly insurance premiums because it is a better product. The pricing has worked so far because HealthyPet has a strong brand and a distinctiveness that its customers value.

DiaSera designs, makes, and sells a medical device that delivers insulin to people with insulin-dependent diabetes known as an insulin pump. DiaSera's pump is differentiated from those of its competitors in its design and operation; it is far smaller and more aesthetically pleasing than competitors' pumps. It is a single, small device adhered to a user's skin, while competitors' pumps consist of separate handheld controllers attached to a delivery device on a user's skin with tubing.

Insulin pumps are used primarily by people with Type 1 diabetes, which is a smaller market that has complex medical needs, including close management of insulin. The insulin pump market is complex, with several competitors; complement products, such as insulin monitoring devices; and an inexpensive substitute: using multiple daily injections of insulin.

DiaSera is looking to expand its customer reach to include Type 2 diabetics who are on multiple daily insulin injections, which is a market several times the size of the Type 1 diabetics market. DiaSera's pump product is priced at a small premium to competitors. Management says that given significant economies of scale in manufacturing, unit costs will fall substantially as the customer base grows and, even with unchanged pricing, margins will rise significantly. Besides the differentiated product design, the company also offers substantial customer service from highly trained nurses both before and after the sale. Access to customer service is available 24/7 and does not have any additional cost to the customer.

DiaSera makes direct sales to customers and markets to both customers and physicians, because customers must receive a prescription for the pump from a physician before purchase. Products are shipped directly to customers' homes.

2. Complete the grid of business model features for HealthyPet.

Customers

Products

Channels

Pricing strategy

3. Complete the table of business model features for DiaSera.

Customers

Products

Channels

Pricing strategy

4. Discuss key risks, opportunities, and questions regarding the HealthyPet business model.

5. Discuss key risks, opportunities, and questions regarding DiaSera's business model.

SOLUTIONS

1. B is correct. A company's supply chain is the network or system inside and outside the company involved in producing a product or service and delivering it to an end user.

    A is incorrect because *value chain* refers to the systems and processes within a firm that create value for its customers. It is the "how" aspect of a business model.

    C is incorrect because the business model is a description of how a business works. It includes descriptions of the core customer base, the product or service that the business offers, the key resources and assets the business uses, and the main partners and suppliers of the business.

2.

Customers	• High-income, young, urban, busy professional pet owners • Own multiple pets and exotic pets
Products	• Insurance policy for pets that are sick or injured • Provides peace of mind to customers • Handles billing directly with veterinarians
Channels	• Veterinarian referrals • Boutique pet stores, online storefront
Pricing strategy	• Premium pricing because it is a premium product • Monthly premiums, similar to subscription

3.

Customers	• Diabetics who need insulin • Expanding customer base to include Type 2 diabetics who are on multiple daily insulin injections
Products	• Differentiated insulin pump for diabetics • Substantial customer service over the phone from highly trained experts both before and after sales • Complex market with complements and substitutes
Channels	• Direct sales to customers • Maintain close relationship with customers • Product shipped directly to customers
Pricing strategy	• Bundling • Premium pricing because it is a premium product and with service

4. There are several apparent risks to HealthyPet's business model. It is not clear that their offering is sufficiently differentiated to build a large-enough customer base to provide the diversification that an insurance company depends on (insurance requires a large pool of policyholders such that there is enough premiums to cover losses). It may incur an adverse selection problem in covering exotic pets because they may be uneconomical to insure as evidenced by the reluctance of established companies to insure them. Finally, if its model is successful, it will likely face competition in the form of imitators, possibly from the incumbent insurers because it is probably possible for them to copy the model of pay veterinarians directly.

    HealthyPet could see opportunity in building a loyal base of customers and a loyal base of veterinarians. Its image of prestige, premium service, and not needing to worry when a pet gets sick could appeal to many pet owners.

Questions include how difficult it would be for other insurers to copy the business model, how HealthyPet plans to establish relationships with veterinarians and how many it has and needs, and whether relationships with veterinarians can be exclusive. It is also questionable whether referrals and boutique pet stores will deliver a sufficient flow of new customers to support the business or whether HealthyPet will instead need to invest in large advertising campaigns directly to consumers.

5. A major risk is the possible incompatibility between DiaSera's pricing strategy and its emphasis on customer service. It is priced only slightly higher than parity with competitors but aims to provide substantially better customer service by using highly trained experts. If customer growth and sales disappoint or take longer than expected, the economies of scale in manufacturing will as well, potentially imperiling profitability or forcing management to raise prices. A second major risk is targeting Type 2 diabetics who have historically not used insulin pumps. While DiaSera's insulin pump seems more convenient than multiple daily injections of insulin, it is more expensive and requires customers to navigate a potentially complicated prescription, purchasing, and service scenario. DiaSera management should discuss key factors that give it confidence in the strategy—such as a segment of customers in the Type 2 market who have tried a pump before, patients who are younger and more likely to try a new product—and establish relationships with key physicians who can recommend the product to patients.

The clear major opportunities are market share gains in Type 1 diabetes from inferior competitor products and the new market opportunity of Type 2 diabetics who require multiple daily injections. If competitors have not segmented the market to explicitly target this cohort, DiaSera could realize a competitive advantage.

Key questions include details on its manufacturing strategy, such as estimating unit costs or gross margins at different levels of volume, how experienced the manufacturing management and staff are in this setting, to what extent the company owns the manufacturing resources, and whether there are key suppliers it relies on. Additionally, an analyst will have to develop an outlook for market penetration and sales based on customer segmenting, historical data, precedent product launches, and realistic expectations for customer demand at the current price point. Finally, additional details on how many service professionals are needed per number of customers and at what cost will be essential to modeling operating costs.

Glossary

Abandonment option   The option to terminate an investment at some future time if the financial results are disappointing.

Abnormal return   The return on an asset in excess of the asset's required rate of return; the risk-adjusted return.

Absolute dispersion   The amount of variability present without comparison to any reference point or benchmark.

Accelerated book build   An offering of securities by an investment bank acting as principal that is accomplished in only one or two days.

Accounting profit   Income as reported on the income statement, in accordance with prevailing accounting standards, before the provisions for income tax expense. Also called *income before taxes* or *pretax income*.

Accredited investors   Investors that meet certain minimum regulatory net worth or other requirements in order to invest in certain types of alternative assets.

Accrued interest   The amount of interest in currency or par value terms of a fixed-income instrument that accumulates from the last coupon payment until the trade settlement date. The amount is paid by the buyer to the seller.

Action lag   Delay from policy decisions to implementation.

Active investment   An approach to investing in which the investor seeks to outperform a given benchmark.

Active return   The return on a portfolio minus the return on the portfolio's benchmark.

Activist   Short for "activist shareholder." Managers secure sufficient equity holdings to allow them to seek a position in a company's board and influence corporate policies or direction.

Activity ratios   Ratios that measure how well a company is managing key current assets and working capital over time.

Ad hoc committee   A small group of lenders or bondholders who negotiate with an issuer on debt restructuring and refinancing before the issuer submits a final proposal to the wider group of all lenders and bondholders.

Add-on pricing   A pricing approach based on high-margin optional features, customizations, and additional content.

Add-on rate   A yield or pricing convention for money market instrument quotations. It is the interest earned on an instrument, derived from the difference between the price and face value, expressed as a percentage of the price and multiplied by the periodicity of the annual rate.

Agency costs   Direct and indirect costs borne by the principal in a principal-agent relationship owing primarily to information asymmetries. Agency costs include the costs of monitoring and assessing the agent as well as missed opportunities.

Agency RMBS   Securities created by the pooling of residential mortgage-backed securities in the United States by either the Federal National Mortgage Association (Fannie Mae) or the Federal Home Loan Mortgage Corporation (Freddie Mac). These RMBS carry the full faith and credit of the government, essentially a guarantee with respect to timely payment of interest and repayment of principal.

All-or-nothing (AON) orders   An order that includes the instruction to trade only if the trade fills the entire quantity (size) specified.

Allocationally efficient   A characteristic of a market, a financial system, or an economy that promotes the allocation of resources to their highest value uses.

Altcoin   A cryptocurrency other than Bitcoin.

Alternative data   Data that are generated from non-traditional sources, such as social media and sensor networks.

Alternative hypothesis   The hypothesis that is accepted if the null hypothesis is rejected.

Alternative investment markets   Market for investments other than traditional securities investments (i.e., traditional common and preferred shares and traditional fixed income instruments). The term usually encompasses direct and indirect investment in real estate (including timberland and farmland) and commodities (including precious metals); hedge funds, private equity, and other investments requiring specialized due diligence.

Alternative trading systems   Trading venues that function like exchanges but that do not exercise regulatory authority over their subscribers except with respect to the conduct of the subscribers' trading in their trading systems. Also called *electronic communications networks* or *multilateral trading facilities*.

American depository receipt   A US dollar-denominated security that trades like a common share on US exchanges.

American depository share   The underlying shares on which American depository receipts are based. They trade in the issuing company's domestic market.

American options   Options that may be exercised at any time from contract inception until maturity.

American-style   Type of option contract that can be exercised at any time up to the option's expiration date.

Amortization   The process of allocating the cost of intangible long-term assets having a finite useful life to accounting periods; the allocation of the amount of a bond premium or discount to the periods remaining until bond maturity.

Amortizing debt   A loan or bond with a payment schedule that calls for periodic payments of interest and repayments of principal.

Analysis of variance (ANOVA)   A table that presents the sums of squares, degrees of freedom, mean squares, and F-statistic for a regression model.

Analytical duration   Estimates of duration using mathematical formulas. Estimates of the impact of yield changes on bond prices using analytical duration implicitly assume that benchmark yields and spreads are independent variables and are uncorrelated.

Anchoring and adjustment bias   An information-processing bias in which the use of a psychological heuristic influences the way people estimate probabilities.

Annual general meeting (AGM)   A yearly meeting of the corporate board of directors and shareholders, typically held in person and digitally, during which votes on directors, compensation plans, shareholder resolutions, and any other matters properly brought forward at the meeting are held. Issuer management may also make presentations and hold events.

Anomalies   Apparent deviations from market efficiency.

Antidilutive   With reference to a transaction or a security, one that would increase earnings per share (EPS) or result in EPS higher than the company's basic EPS—antidilutive securities are not included in the calculation of diluted EPS.

Arbitrage   1) The simultaneous purchase of an undervalued asset or portfolio and sale of an overvalued but equivalent asset or portfolio, in order to obtain a riskless profit on the price differential. Taking advantage of a market inefficiency in a risk-free manner. 2) The condition in a financial market in which equivalent assets or combinations of assets sell for two different prices, creating an opportunity to profit at no risk with no commitment of money. In a well-functioning financial market, few arbitrage opportunities are possible. 3) A risk-free operation that earns an expected positive net profit but requires no net investment of money.

Arbitrageurs   Traders who engage in arbitrage. See *arbitrage*.

Arithmetic mean   The sum of the observations divided by the number of observations.

Artificial intelligence (AI)   Computer systems that are capable of performing tasks that previously required human intelligence. AI methods are sometimes better suited to identify complex, non-linear relationships than are traditional quantitative and statistical methods.

Ask   The price at which a dealer or trader is willing to sell an asset, typically qualified by a maximum quantity (ask size). See *offer*.

Ask size   The maximum quantity of an asset that pertains to a specific ask price from a trader. For example, if the ask for a share issue is $30 for a size of 1,000 shares, the trader is offering to sell at $30 up to 1,000 shares.

Asset allocation   The process of determining how investment funds should be distributed among asset classes.

Asset class   A group of assets that have similar characteristics, attributes, and risk–return relationships.

Asset utilization ratios   Ratios that measure how efficiently a company performs day-to-day tasks, such as the collection of receivables and management of inventory.

Asset-backed commercial paper   Secured form of commercial paper issuance. Loans or receivables are sold to a special purpose entity that issues the ABCP and makes interest and principal payments to investors from asset cash flows.

Asset-backed securities (ABS)   A type of bond issued by a legal entity called a special purpose entity created solely to own assets such as loans, receivables, and mortgages and to distribute cash flows to ABS investors. Generally, ABS backed by mortgages are known as mortgage-backed securities (MBS) while ABS refer to non-mortgage ABS.

Asset-backed token   A token that represents the ownership of a physical asset that does not exist on the blockchain and whose value is based on the underlying asset.

Asset-based valuation models   Valuation based on estimates of the market value of a company's assets.

Asymmetric information   Also known as *information asymmetry*; the differential of information between corporate insiders and outsiders regarding the company's performance and prospects. Managers typically have more information about the company's performance and prospects than owners and creditors.

At-the-money   Describes a unique situation in which the price of the underlying is equal to an option's exercise price. Like an out-of-the-money option, the intrinsic value is zero.

Auction/reverse auction models   Pricing models that establish prices through bidding (by sellers in the case of reverse auctions).

Autarky   Countries seeking political self-sufficiency with little or no external trade or finance. State-owned enterprises control strategic domestic industries.

Automatic stabilizer   A countercyclical factor that automatically comes into play as an economy slows and unemployment rises.

Availability bias   An information-processing bias in which people take a heuristic approach to estimating the probability of an outcome based on how easily the outcome comes to mind.

Available-for-sale   Under US GAAP, debt securities not classified as either held-to-maturity or held-for-trading securities. The investor is willing to sell but not actively planning to sell. In general, available-for-sale debt securities are reported at fair value on the balance sheet, with unrealized gains included as a component of other comprehensive income.

Average revenue (AR)   Total revenue divided by quantity sold.

Backfill Bias   A problem whereby certain surviving hedge funds may be added to databases and various hedge fund indexes only after they are initially successful and start to report their returns. Also see *survivorship bias*.

Backup line of credit   A type of credit enhancement provided by a bank to an issuer of commercial paper to ensure that the issuer will have access to sufficient liquidity to repay maturing commercial paper if issuing new paper is not a viable option.

Backwardation   A downward-sloping, or inverted, forward curve in a futures market.

Balance sheet ratios   Financial ratios involving balance sheet items only.

Balanced   With respect to a government budget, one in which spending and revenues (taxes) are equal.

Balloon payment   A large payment required at maturity to retire a bond's outstanding principal amount.

Base rates   The reference rate on which a bank bases lending rates to all other customers.

Base-rate neglect   A type of representativeness bias in which the base rate or probability of the categorization is not adequately considered.

Basic EPS   Net earnings available to common shareholders (i.e., net income minus preferred dividends) divided by the weighted average number of common shares outstanding.

Basis risk   The possibility that the expected value of a derivative differs unexpectedly from that of the underlying.

Basket of listed depository receipts (BLDR)   An exchange-traded fund (ETF) that represents a portfolio of depository receipts.

Bayes' formula   The rule for updating the probability of an event of interest—given a set of prior probabilities for the event, information, and information given the event—if you receive new information.

Bearer bonds   Bonds for which ownership is not recorded; only the clearing system knows who the bond owner is.

Behavioral finance   A field of finance that examines the psychological variables that affect and often distort the investment decision making of investors, analysts, and portfolio managers.

Behind the market Said of prices specified in orders that are worse than the best current price; e.g., for a limit buy order, a limit price below the best bid.

Benchmark A bond used to compare against another bond to discern attributes, often a government bond with the same or similar time-to-maturity as the bond under analysis.

Benchmark spread The difference in yield-to-maturity between a bond and that of a benchmark bond.

Best bid The highest bid in the market.

Best effort offering An offering of a security using an investment bank in which the investment bank, as agent for the issuer, promises to use its best efforts to sell the offering but does not guarantee that a specific amount will be sold.

Best offer The lowest offer (ask price) in the market.

Best-in-class An ESG implementation approach that seeks to identify the most favorable companies in an industry based on ESG considerations.

Beta A measure of systematic risk that is based on the covariance of an asset's or portfolio's return with the return of the overall market; a measure of the sensitivity of a given investment or portfolio to movements in the overall market.

Bid The price at which a dealer or trader is willing to buy an asset, typically qualified by a maximum quantity.

Bid size The maximum quantity of an asset that pertains to a specific bid price from a trader.

Big data The vast amount of information being generated by both traditional sources—for example, stock exchanges, companies, governments—and non-traditional sources—for example, electronic devices, social media, sensor networks, and company exhaust.

Bilateralism The conduct of political, economic, financial, or cultural cooperation between two countries. Countries engaging in bilateralism may have relations with many different countries but in one-at-a-time agreements without multiple partners. Typically, countries exist on a spectrum between bilateralism and multilateralism.

Bimodal A distribution that has two most frequently occurring values.

Bitcoin A cryptocurrency using blockchain technology that was created in 2009.

Bivariate correlation Also known as Pearson correlation. A parametric measure of the relationship between two variables.

Black swan risk An event that is rare and difficult to predict but has an important impact.

Block brokers A broker (agent) that provides brokerage services for large-size trades.

Blockchain A type of digital ledger in which information is recorded sequentially and then linked together and secured using cryptographic methods.

Blue chip Widely held large market capitalization companies that are considered financially sound and are leaders in their respective industry or local stock market.

Board of directors A body or individual selected by a limited company's member(s) or shareholder(s), in a manner determined by the company's charter, that manages the company. Typically, for larger companies, boards of directors appoint and oversee executive management.

Bond equivalent yield A money market interest rate quoted on a 365-day add-on rate basis.

Bond indenture A legal document between a bond issuer and investors that governs each party's rights and responsibilities.

Bond market vigilantes Bond market participants who might reduce their demand for long-term bonds, thus pushing up their yields.

Bondholders Investors in an entity's securitized debt claims, such as commercial paper, notes, and bonds. Common types of bondholders include investment funds and institutional investors.

Bonds Contractual agreements between an issuer and bondholders.

Bonus issue of shares A type of dividend in which a company distributes additional shares of its common stock to shareholders instead of cash.

Book building Investment bankers' process of compiling a "book" or list of indications of interest to buy part of an offering.

Book value The net amount shown for an asset or liability on the balance sheet; book value may also refer to the company's excess of total assets over total liabilities. Also called *carrying value.*

Boom An expansionary phase characterized by economic growth "testing the limits" of the economy.

Bootstrap A resampling method that repeatedly draws samples with replacement of the selected elements from the original observed sample. Bootstrap is usually conducted by using computer simulation and is often used to find standard error or construct confidence intervals of population parameters.

Bottom-up analysis An investment selection approach that focuses on company-specific circumstances rather than emphasizing economic cycles or industry analysis.

Box and whisker plot A graphic for visualizing the dispersion of data across quartiles. It consists of a box with "whiskers" connected to the box.

Breakeven point Represents the price of the underlying in a derivative contract in which the profit to both counterparties would be zero.

Bridge financing Interim financing that provides funds until permanent financing can be arranged.

Broker An agent who executes orders to buy or sell securities on behalf of a client in exchange for a commission.

Brokered market A market in which brokers arrange trades among their clients.

Broker–dealer A financial intermediary (often a company) that may function as a principal (dealer) or as an agent (broker) depending on the type of trade.

Brownfield investments The third stage of development of an infrastructure asset. Brownfield investments involve expanding existing facilities and may involve privatization of public assets or a sale leaseback of completed greenfield projects. They are characterized by a shorter investment period with immediate cash flows and an operating history.

Budget surplus/deficit The difference between government revenue and expenditure for a stated fixed period of time.

Bullet bond A bond whose principal repayment is made entirely at maturity.

Bundling A pricing approach that refers to combining multiple products or services so that customers are incentivized or required to buy them together.

Business cycles Are recurrent expansions and contractions in economic activity affecting broad segments of the economy.

Business model A concise description of how a business works and makes revenues and profits, including its customers, products or services, channels for reaching customers, and pricing.

Businesses Organization entities formed and managed for the purpose of providing a return or economic benefits to its investors and owners.

Buy-side firm An investment management company or other investor that uses the services of brokers or dealers (i.e., the client of the sell side firms).

Buyback A transaction in which a company buys back its own shares. Unlike stock dividends and stock splits, share repurchases use corporate cash.

Cabotage The right to transport passengers or goods within a country by a foreign firm. Many countries—including those with multilateral trade agreements—impose restrictions on cabotage across transportation subsectors, meaning that shippers, airlines, and truck drivers are not allowed to transport goods and services within another country's borders.

Call market A market in which trades occur only at a particular time and place (i.e., when the market is called).

Call money rate The interest rate that buyers pay for their margin loan.

Call option The right to buy an underlying.

Call period The time during which the issuer of a callable bond can exercise the call option.

Call price The price at which the issuer of a callable bond has the right to purchase the bond from investors.

Call protection period The time during which the issuer of a callable bond is not allowed to exercise the call option.

Call risk The uncertain maturity and limited price appreciation associated with callable bonds.

Callable bond A bond containing an embedded call option that gives the issuer the right to buy the bond back from the investor at specified prices on predetermined dates.

Cannibalization A transfer of sales or market share from one product to another product owned by the same company. It tends to occur when the two products are actual or perceived substitutes.

Capacity The ability of the borrower to make its debt payments on time.

Capital Other company resources available that reduce reliance on debt.

Capital allocation The process that companies use for decision making on capital investments—those projects with a life of one year or longer.

Capital allocation line (CAL) A graph line that describes the combinations of expected return and standard deviation of return available to an investor from combining the optimal portfolio of risky assets with the risk-free asset.

Capital asset pricing model (CAPM) An equation describing the expected return on any asset (or portfolio) as a linear function of its beta relative to the market portfolio.

Capital expenditure Expenditure on physical capital (fixed assets).

Capital investments An expenditure for an asset or resource with a useful life of more than one year.

Capital market expectations (CME) Expectations concerning the risk and return prospects of asset classes.

Capital market line (CML) The line with an intercept point equal to the risk-free rate that is tangent to the efficient frontier of risky assets; represents the efficient frontier when a risk-free asset is available for investment.

Capital market securities Fixed-income securities with original maturities greater than one year.

Capital markets Financial markets that trade securities of longer duration, such as bonds and equities.

Capital restrictions Controls placed on foreigners' ability to own domestic assets and/or domestic residents' ability to own foreign assets.

Capital structure The mix of debt and equity that a company uses to finance its business; a company's specific mix of long-term financing.

Capital-indexed bond A type of index-linked bond for which changes in the index are captured with adjustments to the principal. A common example is Treasury Inflation Protected Securities (TIPS) issued by the United States government.

Capital-intensive businesses Companies or business activities that are characterized by a relatively low fixed asset turnover, a high percentage of capital expenditures to sales, or a high net-working-capital-to-sales ratio.

Capital-light businesses Also known as *asset light businesses*, companies or business activities characterized by relatively high fixed asset turnover, a low percentage of capital expenditures to sales, or a low net-working-capital-to-sales ratio.

Carried interest A performance fee (also referred to as an incentive fee, or carry) that is applied based on excess returns above a hurdle rate.

Carrying Investing and holding an asset for a period of time.

Carrying amount The amount at which an asset or liability is valued according to accounting principles.

Carrying value Of a fixed-income instrument is the purchase price plus (minus) the amortized amount of the discount (premium) if the bond is purchased at a price below (above) par value.

Cartel Participants in collusive agreements that are made openly and formally.

Cash conversion cycle The amount of time between an issuer paying its suppliers in cash and receiving cash from its customers.

Cash flow additivity principle The principle that dollar amounts indexed at the same point in time are additive.

Cash flow from operations A cash profit measure over a period for an issuer's primary business activities. It includes cash from customers as well as interest and dividends received from financial investments, less cash paid to employees and suppliers as well as taxes paid to governments and interest paid to lenders.

Cash flow hedge Refers to a specific **hedge accounting** classification in which a derivative is designated as absorbing the variable cash flow of a floating-rate asset or liability, such as foreign exchange, interest rates, or commodities.

Cash markets Markets in which specific assets are exchanged at current prices. Cash markets are often referred to as **spot markets**.

Cash prices The current prices prevailing in **cash markets**.

Cash ratio A measure of liquidity that is the ratio of cash and marketable securities to current liabilities.

Catch-up clause A clause in an agreement that favors the GP. For a GP who earns a 20% performance fee, a catch-up clause allows the GP to receive 100% of the distributions above the hurdle rate *until* she receives 20% of the profits generated, and then every excess dollar is split 80/20 between the LPs and GP.

CDS credit spread Reflects the credit spread of a credit default swap (CDS) derivative contract. As with cash bonds, CDS credit spreads depend on the probability of default (POD) and the loss given default (LGD).

Central bank digital currencies (CBDCs)   A tokenized version of the currency issued by the central bank, such as a digital bank note or coin, and a digital liability of the central bank.

Central bank funds market   The market in which deposit-taking banks that have an excess reserve with their national central bank can lend money to banks that need funds for maturities ranging from overnight to one year. Called the federal or fed funds market in the United States.

Central bank funds rate   The interest rate at which central bank funds are bought (borrowed) and sold (lent) for maturities ranging from overnight to one year. Called federal or fed funds rate in the United States.

Central clearing mandate   A requirement instituted by global regulatory authorities following the 2008 global financial crisis that most **over-the-counter (OTC)** derivatives be **cleared** by a **central counterparty (CCP)**.

Central counterparty (CCP)   An economic entity that assumes the **counterparty credit risk** between derivative **counterparties**, one of which is typically a financial intermediary. CCPs provide **clearing** and **settlement** for most **derivative contracts**.

Central limit theorem   The theorem that states the sum (and the mean) of a set of independent, identically distributed random variables with finite variances is normally distributed, whatever distribution the random variables follow.

Certificate of deposit (CD)   An instrument that represents a specified amount of funds on deposit with a bank for a specified maturity and interest rate. CDs are issued in various denominations and can be negotiable or non-negotiable.

Channels   Venues where a company markets and/or delivers its products and services.

Character   The quality of a debt issuer's management.

Checking accounts   Bank deposits with no stated maturity available for transactional purposes that pay little or no interest. Also known as a *demand deposit*.

Circuit breaker   A pause in intraday trading for a brief period if a price limit is reached.

Classical cycle   Refers to fluctuations in the level of economic activity when measured by GDP in volume terms.

Clawback   A requirement that the general partner return any funds distributed as incentive fees until the limited partners have received their initial investment and a percentage of the total profit.

Clearing   An exchange's process of verifying the execution of a transaction, exchange of payments, and recording of participants.

Clearing instructions   Instructions that indicate how to arrange the final settlement ("clearing") of a trade.

Clearinghouse   An entity associated with a futures market that acts as middleman between the contracting parties and guarantees to each party the performance of the other.

Closed-end fund   A mutual fund in which no new investment money is accepted. New investors invest by buying existing shares, and investors in the fund liquidate by selling their shares to other investors.

Cluster sampling   A procedure that divides a population into subpopulation groups (clusters) representative of the population and then randomly draws certain clusters to form a sample.

Co-investing   In co-investing, the investor invests in assets *indirectly* through the fund but also possesses rights (known as co-investment rights) to invest *directly* in the same assets. Through co-investing, an investor is able to make an investment *alongside* a fund when the fund identifies deals.

Code of ethics   An established guide that communicates an organization's values and overall expectations regarding member behavior. A code of ethics serves as a general guide for how community members should act.

Coefficient of determination (R^2)   The percentage of the variation of the dependent variable that is explained by the independent variable. It is a measure of goodness of fit of a regression model.

Coefficient of variation   The ratio of a set of observations' standard deviation to the observations' mean value.

Cognitive cost   The effort involved in processing new information and updating beliefs.

Cognitive dissonance   The mental discomfort that occurs when new information conflicts with previously held beliefs or cognitions.

Cognitive errors   Behavioral biases resulting from faulty reasoning; cognitive errors stem from basic statistical, information-processing, or memory errors.

Coincident economic indicators   Turning points that are usually close to those of the overall economy; they are believed to have value for identifying the economy's present state.

Collateral   Assets or financial guarantees underlying a debt obligation that are above and beyond the issuer's promise to pay.

Collateral manager   Buys and sells debt obligations for and from the CDO's collateral pool to generate sufficient cash flows to meet the obligations to the CDO bondholders.

Collateralized bond obligations (CBOs)   CDOs backed by high-yield corporate and emerging market bonds.

Collateralized debt obligations (CDOs)   Securities backed by a diversified pool of one or more debt obligations. CDOs can be backed by a broad range of debt.

Collateralized loan obligations (CLOs)   CDOs backed by leveraged bank loans.

Collateralized mortgage obligations   Securitize mortgage pass-through securities or multiple pools of loans. CMOs are structured to redistribute the cash flows to different bond classes or tranches and create securities that have different exposures to prepayment risk.

Commercial paper (CP)   Short-term, negotiable, unsecured promissory note that represents a debt obligation of the issuer.

Committed (regular) lines of credit   Bank commitments to extend credit; the commitment is considered a short-term liability and is usually in effect for 364 days (one day short of a full year).

Committed capital   The amount that the limited partners have agreed to provide to the private equity fund.

Commodities   A product or service from a firm that is indistinguishable from products or services of competing firms, usually conforming to a common standard or grade imposed by convention or regulation.

Commoditization   A process by which competing products become less differentiated over time and become interchangeable "commodities" in the eyes of customers. This process is typically associated with declining profitability for the selling firms.

Commodity producers   A firm that makes and/or sells commodities.

Commodity swap   A type of swap involving the exchange of payments over multiple dates as determined by specified reference prices or indexes relating to commodities.

Common market Level of economic integration that incorporates all aspects of the customs union and extends it by allowing free movement of factors of production among members.

Common shares A type of security that represents an ownership interest in a company. Also called *common stock*.

Common stock A type of security that represents an ownership interest in a company. Also called *common shares*.

Common-size analysis The restatement of financial statement items using a common denominator or reference item that allows one to identify trends and major differences; an example is an income statement in which all items are expressed as a percent of revenue.

Companies Organization entities formed and managed for the purpose of providing a return or economic benefits to its investors and owners.

Company research report A document that presents an analyst's investment recommendation on an issuer and its securities, supported by financial modeling, industry overviews and competitive analyses, valuation scenarios, ESG considerations, and investment risks.

Complete markets Informally, markets in which the variety of distinct securities traded is so broad that any desired payoff in a future state-of-the-world is achievable.

Concession agreement A contractual arrangement under which an entity (also known as a grantor) establishes terms and conditions with a developer or operator (referred to as a concessionaire) to plan, build, operate, finance, and maintain an infrastructure asset for a specific period.

Conditional expected value The expected value of a stated event given that another event has occurred.

Conditional pass-through covered bonds Convert to pass-through securities after the original maturity date if all bond payments have not yet been made.

Conditional variances The variance of one variable, given the outcome of another.

Conditions The general economic, competitive, and business environment faced by all borrowers that may affect their ability to service or refinance debt.

Confidence level The complement of the level of significance.

Confirmation bias A belief perseverance bias in which people tend to look for and notice what confirms their beliefs, to ignore or undervalue what contradicts their beliefs, and to misinterpret information as support for their beliefs.

Consensus protocol A set of rules governing how blocks can join the blockchain that is designed to resist attempts at malicious manipulation up to a certain level of security; it can be either a proof of work or a proof of stake.

Conservatism bias A belief perseverance bias in which people maintain their prior views or forecasts by inadequately incorporating new information.

Constant yield-price trajectory A graphical depiction of the relationship between time to maturity and a bond price, assuming no default, that shows that a bond price approaches par as time passes.

Constituent securities With respect to an index, the individual securities within an index.

Contango Refers to spot price below forward price in a futures market.

Contingency provision Clause in a legal document that allows for some action if a specific event or circumstance occurs.

Contingency table A table of the frequency distribution of observations classified on the basis of two discrete variables.

Contingent claim A type of derivative in which one of the *counterparties* determines whether and when the trade will settle. An *option* is a common type of contingent claim.

Contingent convertible bonds Bonds that automatically convert to equity if a specific event or circumstance occurs, such as the issuer's equity capital falling below the minimum requirement set by regulators.

Continuous trading market A market in which trades can be arranged and executed any time the market is open.

Continuously compounded return The natural logarithm of 1 plus the holding period return, or equivalently, the natural logarithm of the ending price over the beginning price.

Contract manufacturers Companies that make products for other companies that meet specific terms and specifications.

Contract size Amount(s) used for calculation to price and value the derivative. The contract size is often referred to as "notional amount or notional principal."

Contraction The period of a business cycle after the peak and before the trough; often called a *recession* or, if exceptionally severe, called a *depression*.

Contraction risk The risk of earlier repayment of a mortgage-backed security than expected.

Contractionary Tending to cause the real economy to contract.

Contractionary fiscal policy A fiscal policy that has the objective to make the real economy contract.

Contribution margin A profitability measure using variable costs: unit price less unit variable cost. It can also be expressed as a percentage of price or sales.

Controlling shareholder An individual or entity that owns a majority of the voting rights in a corporation.

Convenience sampling A procedure of selecting an element from a population on the basis of whether or not it is accessible to a researcher or how easy it is for a researcher to access the element.

Convenience yield A non-cash benefit of holding a physical commodity versus a derivative.

Conversion price For a convertible bond, the price per share at which the bond can be converted into shares.

Conversion ratio Number of common shares received in exchange for each preferred share after a predetermined period.

Conversion value For a convertible bond, the value of the bond if it is converted at the market price of the shares. Also called *parity value*.

Convertible bond A bond that gives the bondholder the right to exchange the bond for a specified number of common shares in the issuing company.

Convertible debt A debt instrument that gives the holder the right to exchange the instrument for a specified number of common shares in the issuing company.

Convertible preference shares A type of equity security that entitles shareholders to convert their shares into a specified number of common shares.

Convexity An interest rate risk measure used in conjunction with duration; captures the degree of nonlinearity (curvature) in the relation between price change and yield change.

Convexity adjustment A measure that is used to complement modified duration to capture the second-order effect of yield changes on a bond's price. It is equal to the annual convexity statistic times one-half times the given change in the yield-to-maturity squared.

Convexity bias Refers to the difference in price changes for a given change in yield between interest rate futures and interest rate forward contracts. That is, interest rate forwards exhibit a non-linear or convex relationship between price and yield, while the price–yield relationship is linear for interest rate futures.

Cooperation   The process by which countries work together toward some shared goal or purpose. These goals may, and often do, vary widely—from strategic or military concerns, to economic influence, to cultural preferences.

Cooperative country   A country that engages and reciprocates in rules standardization; harmonization of tariffs; international agreements on trade, immigration, or regulation; and allowing the free flow of information, including technology transfer.

Core real estate strategies   Strategies with exposure to well-leased, high-quality commercial and residential real estate in the best markets, generally offered by open-end funds. Investors expect core real estate to deliver stable returns, primarily from income from the property.

Core-plus real estate strategies   Value-add investments that require modest redevelopment or upgrades to lease any vacant space together with possible alternative use of the underlying properties. Compared to core real estate strategies, these may be appealing for investors seeking higher returns and willing to accept additional risks from development, redevelopment, repositioning, and leasing.

Corporate issuers   Limited companies or corporations that seek financing in financial markets by, for example, issuing debt or equity securities.

Corporations   Another term for limited companies, though often used to refer to public limited companies. See *limited company*, *private limited company*, and *public limited company*.

Correlation   A measure of the linear relationship between two random variables.

Correlation coefficient   A number between −1 and +1 that measures the consistency or tendency for two investments to act in a similar way. It is used to determine the effect on portfolio risk when two assets are combined.

Cost averaging   The periodic investment of a fixed amount of money.

Cost of capital   The cost of financing for a company; the rate of return that suppliers of capital require as compensation for their contribution of capital (also called *opportunity cost of funds*).

Cost of carry   The net of the costs and benefits related to owning an underlying asset for a specific period.

Cost of debt   The required return on debt financing for a company, such as when it issues a bond, takes out a bank loan, or leases an asset through a finance lease.

Cost of equity   The return required by equity investors to compensate for both the time value of money and the risk. Also referred to as the required rate of return on common stock or the required return on equity.

Counterparty   Legal entities entering a **derivative contract**.

Counterparty credit risk   The likelihood that a **counterparty** is unable to meet its financial obligations under the contract.

Counterparty risk   The risk that the other party to a contract will fail to honor the terms of the contract.

Country   The geopolitical environment as well as the legal and political system faced by all issuers in a jurisdiction that may affect debt payment.

Coupon   Periodic interest payments paid by a bond issuer to investors, typically expressed as a percentage of par on an annual basis.

Cournot assumption   Assumption in which each firm determines its profit-maximizing production level assuming that the other firms' output will not change.

Covariance   A measure of the co-movement (linear association) between two random variables.

Covenants   The terms and conditions of lending agreements that the issuer must comply with; they specify the actions that an issuer is obligated to perform (affirmative covenant) or prohibited from performing (negative covenant).

Credit default swap (CDS)   A type of credit derivative in which one party, the credit protection buyer who is seeking credit protection against a third party, makes a series of regularly scheduled payments to the other party, the credit protection seller. The seller makes no payments until a credit event occurs.

Credit enhancements   Provisions or methods that allow a borrower improve their creditworthiness in a structured transaction.

Credit event   An event that defines a payout in a credit derivative. Events are usually defined as bankruptcy, failure to pay an obligation, or an involuntary debt restructuring.

Credit facilities   Loan agreements with pre-specified terms and limits but with fluctuating balances based on borrower-specific needs at different points in time, analogous to a credit card.

Credit migration risk   The risk that a bond issuer's creditworthiness deteriorates, or migrates lower, leading investors to believe the risk of default is higher. Also called **downgrade risk**.

Credit rating   Letter-grade, qualitative measures of an issuer's ability to meet its debt obligations based on both the probability of default and the expected loss under a default scenario.

Credit rating agencies   Institutions that issue and maintain credit ratings. The three largest are Standard & Poor's, Moody's, and Fitch Ratings.

Credit risk   The expected economic loss under a potential borrower default over the life of the contract

Credit spread   A premium over and above the current government bond yield.

Credit spread risk   The risk of greater expected loss due to changes in credit conditions as a result of macroeconomic, market, and/or issuer-related factors.

Credit tranching   Internal credit enhancement where cash flows into a senior/subordinate structure.

Credit-linked notes   Bonds whose coupon changes when the bonds' credit rating changes.

Critical values   Values of the test statistic at which the decision changes from fail to reject the null hypothesis to reject the null hypothesis.

Cross-default clause   Covenant or contract clause that specifies borrowers are considered in default if they default on another debt obligation.

Cross-sectional analysis   Also called relative analysis. Analysis that involves comparisons across individuals in a group over a given time period or at a given point in time.

Crossing networks   Trading systems that match buyers and sellers who are willing to trade at prices obtained from other markets.

Crowdsourcing   A business model that enables users to contribute directly to a product, service, or online content.

Cryptocurrency   An electronic medium of exchange that lacks physical form.

Cryptocurrency wallet A storage unit for public and/or private keys for cryptocurrency transactions. These wallets may be a physical device, program, or service.

Cryptography An algorithmic process to encrypt data, making the data unusable if received by unauthorized parties.

Cumulative preference shares Preference shares for which any dividends that are not paid accrue and must be paid in full before dividends on common shares can be paid.

Cumulative voting A voting process whereby shareholders can accumulate and vote all their shares for a single candidate in an election, as opposed to having to allocate their voting rights evenly among all candidates.

Currencies Monies issued by national monetary authorities.

Currency Money issued by national monetary authorities.

Currency swap A swap in which each party makes interest payments to the other in different currencies.

Current government spending With respect to government expenditures, spending on goods and services that are provided on a regular, recurring basis including health, education, and defense.

Current ratio A measure of liquidity that is the ratio of current assets to current liabilities.

Current yield The sum of the coupon payments received over the year divided by the flat price. Also called the income, interest yield, or running yield.

Customs union Extends the free trade area (FTA) by not only allowing free movement of goods and services among members, but also creating a common trade policy against nonmembers.

CVaR Conditional VaR, a tail loss measure. The weighted average of all loss outcomes in the statistical distribution that exceed the VaR loss.

Daily settlement A specific process of *mark-to-market* by a central clearing party in which the profits and losses of all counterparties to derivatives contracts are determined using settlement prices for each contract.

Dark pools Alternative trading systems that do not display the orders that their clients send to them.

Data mining The practice of determining a model by extensive searching through a dataset for statistically significant patterns.

Data science An interdisciplinary field that harnesses advances in computer science, statistics, and other disciplines for the purpose of extracting information from big data (or data in general).

Data snooping The practice of determining a model by extensive searching through a dataset for statistically significant patterns.

Day order An order that is good for the day on which it is submitted. If it has not been filled by the close of business, the order expires unfilled.

Days of inventory on hand (DOH) The average number of days it would take to sell the amount of inventory on hand. It is calculated as either the ending or average balance of inventories divided by (cost of goods sold/days in the period).

Days payable outstanding (DPO) The average number of days it takes a company to pay its suppliers. It is calculated as either the ending or average balance of accounts payable divided by (cost of goods sold/days in the period).

Days sales outstanding (DSO) The average number of days it takes for a company to receive payment from customers who purchase goods or services on credit. It is calculated as either the ending or average balance of accounts receivable divided by (revenues/days in the period).

Dealers Financial intermediaries, such as commercial banks or investment banks, who transact as **counterparties** with derivative end users.

Debt A claim against an entity to receive cash, stock, or other assets at a future date. From the perspective of the debtor or borrower, an obligation to pay cash, stock, or other assets at a future date. Generally, debt claims are unconditional and are senior to equity claims.

Debt service coverage ratio A ratio in which the net operating income of a real estate investment for a specific period is divided by the amount of debt service to be paid during the same time period.

Debt tax shield The tax benefit from interest paid on debt being tax deductible from income, equal to the marginal tax rate multiplied by the value of the debt.

Debt-to-assets ratio A solvency ratio calculated as total debt divided by total assets.

Debt-to-capital ratio A solvency ratio calculated as total debt divided by total debt plus total shareholders' equity.

Debt-to-equity ratio A solvency ratio calculated as total debt divided by total shareholders' equity.

Debt-to-income ratio (DTI) Residential lending metric that compares an individual's monthly debt payments to their monthly pre-tax, gross income.

Debut issuer An issuer approaching the bond market for the first time.

Deciles Quantiles that divide a distribution into 10 equal parts.

Declaration date The day that the corporation issues a statement declaring a specific dividend.

Decreasing returns to scale When a production process leads to increases in output that are proportionately smaller than the increase in inputs.

Deductible temporary differences Temporary differences that result in a reduction of or deduction from taxable income in a future period when the balance sheet item is recovered or settled.

Deep learning An area of artificial intelligence in which a system uses neural networks to perform multistage, non-linear data processing to identify patterns. Also called *deep learning nets*.

Deep learning nets See *Deep learning*.

Deep-in-the-money option An option that is highly likely to be exercised.

Deep-out-of-the-money option An option that is highly unlikely to be exercised.

Default When a borrower on a mortgage loan fails to meet the obligations of the loan.

Default risk premium An extra return that compensates investors for the possibility that the borrower will fail to make a promised payment at the contracted time and in the contracted amount.

Defeasance Mechanism that allows prepayment on mortgage, but the borrower must purchase a portfolio of government securities that fully replicates the cash flows of the remaining scheduled principal and interest payments, including the balloon loan balance, on the loan.

Defensive interval ratio A liquidity ratio that estimates the number of days that an entity could meet cash needs from liquid assets; calculated as (cash + short-term marketable investments + receivables) divided by daily cash expenditures.

Deferred coupon bonds   Bonds that pay no coupons for their first few years but then pay a higher coupon than they otherwise normally would for the remainder of their life. Also called *split coupon bonds*.

Deferred tax assets   A balance sheet asset that arises when an excess amount is paid for income taxes relative to accounting profit. The taxable income is higher than accounting profit and income tax payable exceeds tax expense. The company expects to recover the difference during the course of future operations when tax expense exceeds income tax payable.

Deferred tax liabilities   A balance sheet liability that arises when a deficit amount is paid for income taxes relative to accounting profit. The taxable income is less than the accounting profit and income tax payable is less than tax expense. The company expects to eliminate the liability over the course of future operations when income tax payable exceeds tax expense.

Defined benefit pension plans (DB plans)   Plans in which the company promises to pay a certain annual amount (defined benefit) to the employee after retirement. The company bears the investment risk of the plan assets.

Defined contribution pension plans   Individual accounts to which an employee and typically the employer makes contributions during their working years and expect to draw on the accumulated funds at retirement. The employee bears the investment and inflation risk of the plan assets.

Deflation   Negative inflation.

Degree of financial leverage   The ratio of percentage change in net income to percentage change in operating income over a period. It is a measure of how sensitive net income is to changes in operating income, driven by the firm's use of debt in its capital structure.

Degree of operating leverage (DOL)   The ratio of percentage change in operating income to percentage change in sales over a period. It is a measure of how sensitive operating income is to changes in sales, driven by the fixed and variable cost composition of operating expenses.

Delta   The relationship between the option price and the underlying price, which reflects the sensitivity of the price of the option to changes in the price of the underlying. Delta is a good approximation of how an option price will change for a small change in the stock.

Demand shock   A typically unexpected disturbance to demand, such as an unexpected interruption in trade or transportation.

Dependent variable   The variable that is explained by a regression model.

Depository bank   A bank that raises funds from depositors and other investors and lends it to borrowers.

Depository institutions   Commercial banks, savings and loan banks, credit unions, and similar institutions that raise funds from depositors and other investors and lend it to borrowers.

Depository receipt   A security that trades like an ordinary share on a local exchange and represents an economic interest in a foreign company.

Depreciation   The process of systematically allocating the cost of long-lived (tangible) assets to the periods during which the assets are expected to provide economic benefits.

Derivative   A financial instrument that derives its value from the performance of an underlying asset.

Derivative contract   A legal agreement between counterparties with a specific **maturity**, or length of time, until the closing of the transaction, or **settlement**.

Derivative pricing rule   A pricing rule used by crossing networks in which a price is taken (derived) from the price that is current in the asset's primary market.

Derivatives   A financial instrument whose value depends on the value of some underlying asset or factor (e.g., a stock price, an interest rate, or exchange rate).

Differentiated products   A product or service from a firm that is distinguishable or distinct from those of competing firms. It is customers who determine and value whether a product is differentiated.

Diffuse prior   The assumption of equal prior probabilities.

Diffusion index   Reflects the proportion of the index's components that are moving in a pattern consistent with the overall index.

Digital assets   The umbrella term covering assets that can be created, stored, and transmitted electronically and have associated ownership or use rights. Digital assets include a variety of assets, such as cryptocurrencies, tokens (security and utility), and digital collectables.

Diluted EPS   The EPS that would result if all dilutive securities were converted into common shares.

Dilution   An increase in the number of shares outstanding from share issuance that decreases the percentage of shares owned by existing shareholders.

Direct investing   Occurs when an investor makes a direct investment in an asset without the use of an intermediary.

Direct lending   Providing capital directly from private debt investors.

Direct listing   Where the equity of a security is floated on the public markets directly, without underwriters, reducing the complexity and cost of the transaction.

Direct sales   Marketing and/or delivering products and services to customers without an intermediary or third party between the customer and seller.

Direct taxes   Taxes levied directly on income, wealth, and corporate profits.

Discount factor   The price equivalent of a zero rate. Also may be stated as the present value of a currency unit on a future date.

Discount rate   A yield or pricing convention for money market instrument quotations. It is the interest earned on an instrument, derived from the difference between the price and face value, expressed as a percentage of the face value and multiplied by the periodicity of the annual rate.

Discounted cash flow models   Valuation models that estimate the intrinsic value of a security as the present value of the future benefits expected to be received from the security.

Discriminatory pricing rule   A pricing rule used in continuous markets in which the limit price of the order or quote that first arrived determines the trade price.

Diseconomies of scale   Increase in cost per unit resulting from increased production.

Dispersion   The variability of a population or sample of observations around the central tendency.

Display size   The size of an order displayed to public view.

Disposition effect   As a result of loss aversion, an emotional bias whereby investors are reluctant to dispose of losers. This results in an inefficient and gradual adjustment to deterioration in fundamental value.

Distressed debt   Debt of mature companies in financial difficulty, in bankruptcy, or likely to default on debt.

Distressed/restructuring These strategies focus on securities of companies either in or perceived to be near bankruptcy. In one approach, hedge funds simply purchase fixed-income securities trading at a significant discount to par but that are still senior enough to be backed by sufficient corporate assets.

Distributed ledger A type of database that can be shared among entities in a network.

Distributed ledger technology (DLT) Technology based on a distributed ledger.

Diversification ratio The ratio of the standard deviation of an equally weighted portfolio to the standard deviation of a randomly selected security.

Dividend A distribution paid to shareholders based on the number of shares owned.

Dividend discount model (DDM) A present value model of stock value that views the intrinsic value of a stock as present value of the stock's expected future dividends.

Dividend payout ratio The ratio of cash dividends paid to earnings for a period.

Dividends Distributions of profits and/or net assets from a corporation to its shareholders. While often in cash, dividends can be also be paid in stock or assets, such as property.

Divisor A number (denominator) used to determine the value of a price return index. It is initially chosen at the inception of an index and subsequently adjusted by the index provider, as necessary, to avoid changes in the index value that are unrelated to changes in the prices of its constituent securities.

Domestic bonds A type of bond for which the issuer's domicile and jurisdiction of issuance are the same.

Domestic content provisions Stipulate that some percentage of the value added or components used in production should be of domestic origin.

Double taxation The taxation of business income at both the entity and personal or owner levels. In most jurisdictions, this taxation scheme applies to public limited companies.

Downside risk The potential for loss.

Drag on liquidity An action or event that reduces available funds or delays cash inflows.

Drivers Causative factors that explain the level of and changes in an output variable.

DSC ratio A property's annual net operating income (NOI) divided by the debt service.

Dual-class structure A capital structure that includes at least two classes of equity shares with unequal voting rights.

Dupont analysis An approach to decomposing return on investment, e.g., return on equity, as the product of other financial ratios.

Duration The percentage change in bond price given an unanticipated small change in interest rates.

Duration gap The difference between a bond's Macaulay duration and its investor's investment horizon.

Dynamic pricing A pricing approach that charges different prices at different times. Specific examples include off-peak pricing, "surge" pricing, and "congestion" pricing.

Early repayment option May entitle the borrower to prepay all or part of the outstanding mortgage principal prior to maturity. This creates a risk from the lender's or investor's viewpoint because the cash flow amounts and timing cannot be known with certainty.

Earnings surprise The portion of a company's earnings that is unanticipated by investors and, according to the efficient market hypothesis, merits a price adjustment.

Economic indicators Economic statistics provided by government and established private organizations that contain information on an economy's recent past activity or its current or future position in the business cycle.

Economic infrastructure investments A category of infrastructure investments that support economic activity through transportation assets, information and communication technology assets, and utility and energy assets.

Economic stabilization Reduction of the magnitude of economic fluctuations.

Economic union Incorporates all aspects of a common market and in addition requires common economic institutions and coordination of economic policies among members.

Economies of scale A decline in costs per unit as output grows, generally resulting from having fixed costs in the cost structure that are spread over more units of output.

Economies of scope A decline in costs per unit as the number of product or business lines increases, generally resulting from having shared costs between the product lines.

Effective annual rate An interest rate with a periodicity of one.

Effective convexity An interest rate risk statistic that measures the non-linear/second-order effect of changes in the benchmark yield curve on a bond's price.

Effective duration The sensitivity of the bond's price to an instantaneous parallel shift in a benchmark yield curve—for example, the government par curve.

Efficient market A market in which asset prices reflect new information quickly and rationally. See also, *informationally efficient market*.

Either/or fee A custom fee arrangement whereby major investors are offered a structure where managers agree to charge *either* a lower management fee *or* a higher incentive fee, whichever is greater.

Electronic communications networks (ECNs) See *alternative trading systems* and *multilateral trading facilities*.

Embedded derivative A derivative within an underlying, such as a callable, putable, or convertible bond.

Embedded options Contingency provisions found in a bond's indenture representing rights that enable their holders to take advantage of interest rate movements. They can be exercised by the issuer, by the bondholder, or automatically depending on the course of interest rates.

Emotional biases Behavioral biases resulting from reasoning influenced by feelings; emotional biases stem from impulse or intuition.

Empirical duration Estimates of duration calculated over time and in different interest rate environments. Unlike analytical duration, empirical duration estimates do not assume that benchmark yields and spreads are independent variables and are uncorrelated.

Employee stock ownership plan (ESOP) A type of employee benefit plan in which a company sets up a trust fund to receive contributions of newly issued shares or cash to buy existing shares. Contributions are tax deductible up to certain limits. Shares in the trust fund are allocated to individual employees based on relative pay or a formula.

Endowment bias An emotional bias in which people value an asset more when they hold rights to it than when they do not.

Enterprise risk management An overall assessment of a company's risk position. A centralized approach to risk management sometimes called firmwide risk management.

Enterprise value (EV)   Total company value (the market value of debt, common equity, and preferred equity) minus the value of cash and investments.

Equal weighting   An index weighting method in which an equal weight is assigned to each constituent security at inception.

Equity   Ownership interest in an entity. A residual claim on the assets of an entity after more senior claims, such as debt, have been satisfied. Also known as *net assets*.

Equity swap   A swap transaction in which at least one cash flow is tied to the return on an equity portfolio position, often an equity index.

Error term   Represents the difference between the observed value of the independent variable and that expected from the true underlying population relation between the dependent and independent variable.

Estimated parameters   In a simple linear regression, the estimated parameters are the intercept and slope of the fitted line.

Ether   A programmable cryptocurrency created on the Ethereum blockchain in 2015 that allows for the execution of smart contracts.

Ethical principles   Beliefs regarding what is good, acceptable, or obligatory behavior and what is bad, unacceptable, or forbidden behavior.

Ethics   The study of moral principles or of making good choices. Ethics encompasses a set of moral principles and rules of conduct that provide guidance for our behavior.

Eurobonds   A type of bond issued internationally, outside the jurisdiction of the country in whose currency the bond is denominated.

European options   Options that may be exercised only at contract maturity.

European-style   Said of an option contract that can only be exercised on the option's expiration date.

Event risk   Risk that evolves around set dates, such as elections, new legislation, or other date-driven milestones, such as holidays or political anniversaries, known in advance. Example: Brexit referendum.

Ex-dividend date   The first date that a share trades without (i.e., "ex") the right to receive the declared dividend for the period.

Excess kurtosis   Degree of kurtosis (fatness of tails) relative to the kurtosis of the normal distribution.

Excess spread   Surplus difference of yield remaining after payments to bondholders are made after expenses are made and losses are covered.

Exchange   A rules-based, open access market venue where financial instruments are traded, with price and volume transparency accessible by issuers, investors, and their intermediaries.

Exchange-traded derivative (ETD)   Futures, options, and other financial contracts available on exchanges.

Exchanges   Places where traders can meet to arrange their trades.

Execution instructions   Instructions that indicate how to fill an order.

Exercise   The decision to transact the underlying by an option holder.

Exercise date   The day that an option is exercised by its holder. For a call option, the day the strike price is paid and underlying is purchased. For a put option, when the strike price is received and the underlying is sold.

Exercise price   The pre-agreed execution price specified in an option contract. Sometimes, this price is referred to as the strike price.

Exogenous risk   A sudden or unanticipated risk that impacts either a country's cooperative stance, the ability of non-state actors to globalize, or both. Examples include sudden uprisings, invasions, or the aftermath of natural disasters.

Expansion   The period of a business cycle after its lowest point and before its highest point.

Expansionary   Tending to cause the real economy to grow.

Expansionary fiscal policy   Fiscal policy aimed at achieving real economic growth.

Expected exposure (EE)   The size of the investor's claim at the time of default.

Expected loss (EL)   Default probability times loss severity given default.

Expected return on the portfolio   Denoted as $(E(R_p))$. The weighted average of the expected returns $(R_1$ to $R_n)$ on the component securities using their respective weights $(w_1$ to $w_n)$.

Expected value of a random variable   The probability-weighted average of the possible outcomes of a random variable.

Expert system   A type of computer programming, often based on "if–then" rules, that attempts to simulate the knowledge base and analytical abilities of human experts in specific problem-solving contexts.

Export subsidy   Paid by the government to the firm when it exports a unit of a good that is being subsidized.

Exposure at default (EAD)   The size of the investor's claim at the time of default.

Extension risk   The risk of later repayment of a mortgage-backed security than expected.

External credit enhancements   Provisions or methods from a third party that allow a borrower improve their creditworthiness in a structured transaction.

External debt   Sovereign debt owed to foreign creditors.

Extra dividend   A dividend paid by a company that does not pay dividends on a regular schedule, or a dividend that supplements regular cash dividends with an extra payment.

Extraordinary general meetings (EGMs)   Meetings besides an AGM of the corporate board and shareholders, typically held to deliberate and vote on urgent matters. Corporate charters and bylaws specify who can call an EGM and under what conditions.

Extreme value theory   A branch of statistics that focuses primarily on extreme outcomes.

Face value   The amount of principal on a bond, also known as par value.

Factoring arrangement   When a company sells its accounts receivable to a lender (known as a factor) that assumes responsibility for the credit-granting and collection process.

Fair value   A market-based measure of an investment based on observable or derived assumptions to determine a price that market participants would use to exchange an asset or liability in an orderly transaction at a specific time.

Fair value hedge   Refers to a specific **hedge accounting** designation that applies when a derivative is deemed to offset the fluctuation in fair value of an asset or liability.

Fallen angels   Formerly investment-grade issuers whose credit quality has deteriorated since the time of issuance.

Fat-Tailed   Describes a distribution that has fatter tails than a normal distribution (also called leptokurtic).

Fed funds rate   The US interbank lending rate on overnight borrowings of reserves.

Federal funds rate   The US interbank lending rate on overnight borrowings of reserves. Also known as *Fed Funds rate.*

Fiat money   Money that is not convertible into any other commodity.

Fiduciary call   A combination of a purchased call option and investment in a risk-free bond with face value of the option's exercise price.

Fill or kill   See *immediate or cancel order.*

Finance lease   A type of lease which is more akin to the purchase or sale of the underlying asset.

Financial leverage   The use of debt in the capital structure. Measured using ratios such as operating income to operating income less interest expense, total assets to total equity, or debt to equity.

Financial leverage ratio   A measure of financial leverage calculated as average total assets divided by average total equity.

Financial risk   The risk arising from a company's capital structure and, specifically, from the level of debt and debt-like obligations.

Fintech   Technological innovation in the financial services industry, specifically with the design and delivery of financial services and products. It may also refer more broadly to companies involved in developing the new technologies and their applications, as well as the business sector that includes such companies.

Firm commitment   A pre-determined amount (price and quantity) is agreed to be exchanged at settlement. Examples of firm commitments include forward contracts, futures contracts, and swaps.

First lien   Security interest in a property that gives the lender the right to seize the collateral if the borrower does not pay as agreed.

First lien debt   Debt secured by a pledge of certain assets that could include buildings, but it may also include property and equipment, licenses, patents, brands, etc.

First mortgage debt   Debt secured by a pledge of a specific property.

Fiscal multiplier   The ratio of a change in national income to a change in government spending.

Fiscal policy   The use of taxes and government spending to affect the level of aggregate expenditures.

Fixed charge coverage   A solvency ratio measuring the number of times interest and lease payments are covered by operating income, calculated as (EBIT + lease payments) divided by (interest payments + lease payments).

Fixed charge coverage ratio   A measure of how well a company's earnings covers its fixed expenses, which may include debt payments, interest expense, and lease costs.

Fixed-income instruments   Debt instruments such as loans or bonds.

Fixed-income securities   Fixed-income instruments designed to be more easily tradeable than a loan, such as a bond.

Fixed-price call   A contingency provision that grants an issuer the right to buy back a bond at a predetermined price in the future.

Fixed-rate payer   The counterparty paying fixed cash flows in a swap contract. May also be referred to as the floating-rate receiver.

Flat price   The full price of a bond minus accrued interest. Flat prices are usually quoted by bond dealers.

Float-adjusted market-capitalization weighting   An index weighting method in which the weight assigned to each constituent security is determined by adjusting its market capitalization for its market float.

Floating-rate notes   Notes on which interest payments are not fixed but instead vary from period to period depending on the current level of a reference interest rate. Also known as *floaters.*

Floating-rate payer   The counterparty paying the variable cash flows in a swap contract. May also be referred to as the fixed-rate receiver.

Forecast object   A variable on or related to an issuer's financial statements that an analyst makes a projection for. Examples include drivers of financial statements, financial statement lines, and summary measures like EBITDA.

Foreclosure   Allows a lender to take possession of the property and ultimately sell the property to recover funds toward satisfying the outstanding debt obligation.

Foreign bonds   A type of bond for which the issuer's domicile and jurisdiction of issuance are different.

Foreign currency reserves   Holding by the central bank of non-domestic currency deposits and non-domestic bonds.

Foreign direct investments (FDI)   Long-term investments in the productive capacity of a foreign country.

Foreign exchange gains (or losses)   Gains (or losses) that occur when the exchange rate changes between the investor's currency and the currency that foreign securities are denominated in.

Forward contract   A **derivative contract** for the future exchange of an **underlying** at a fixed price set at contract signing.

Forward price   Represents the price agreed upon in a forward contract to be exchanged at the contract's maturity date, T. This price is shown in equations as $F_0(T)$.

Forward price-to-earnings ratio   A P/E calculated on the basis of a forecast of EPS; a stock's current price divided by next year's expected earnings.

Forward rate agreement (FRA)   An OTC derivatives contract in which counterparties agree to apply a specific interest rate to a future time period.

Founders class shares   A way to entice early participation in startup funds whereby managers offer incentives that entitle investors to a lower fee structure and/or other favorable terms.

Framing bias   An information-processing bias in which a person answers a question differently based on the way in which it is asked (framed).

Franchising   A situation where an owner of an asset and associated intellectual property divests the asset and licenses intellectual property to a third-party operator (franchisee) in exchange for royalties. Franchisees operate under the constraints of a franchise agreement.

Free cash flow   The actual cash that would be available to the company's investors after making all investments necessary to maintain the company as an ongoing enterprise (also referred to as free cash flow to the firm); the internally generated funds that can be distributed to the company's investors (e.g., shareholders and bondholders) without impairing the value of the company.

Free cash flow hypothesis   The hypothesis that higher debt levels discipline managers by forcing them to make fixed debt service payments and by reducing the company's free cash flow.

Free float   The portion of a listed company's equity securities that are not held by insiders, strategic investors, sponsors, founders, and so on, that are more freely available for trading.

Free trade areas One of the most prevalent forms of regional integration, in which all barriers to the flow of goods and services among members have been eliminated.

Free-cash-flow-to-equity models Valuation models based on discounting expected future free cash flow to equity.

Freemium business model A pricing approach that allows customers a certain level of usage or functionality at no charge. Those who wish to use more must pay.

Frequency table A representation of the frequency of occurrence of two discrete variables.

Full price The price of a bond including any accrued interest owed to the seller. It is the flat price plus accrued interest.

Fully amortizing loan A loan or bond with a payment schedule that calls for the complete repayment of principal over the instrument's time to maturity.

Fund investing In fund investing, the investor invests in assets indirectly by contributing capital to a fund as part of a group of investors. Fund investing is available for all major alternative investment types.

Fund of funds Funds that hold a portfolio of hedge funds; also called *funds of hedge funds*.

Fundamental analysis The examination of publicly available information and the formulation of forecasts to estimate the intrinsic value of assets.

Fundamental growth These strategies use fundamental analysis to identify companies expected to exhibit high growth and capital appreciation.

Fundamental long/short In this strategy, the hedge fund takes a long position in companies that are trading at inexpensive levels compared to their potential intrinsic value and shorts those that trade in the other direction, with the intention of reversing this trade to obtain alpha.

Fundamental value These strategies use fundamental analysis to identify undervalued and unloved companies for which there is a possibility that a corporate turnaround, with future revenue and cash flow growth, will result in higher valuations.

Fundamental weighting An index weighting method in which the weight assigned to each constituent security is based on its underlying company's size. It attempts to address the disadvantages of market-capitalization weighting by using measures that are independent of the constituent security's price.

Fungible Freely exchangeable, interchangeable, or substitutable with other things of the same type. Money and commodities are the most common examples.

Futures contract A variation of a forward contract that has essentially the same basic definition but with some additional features, such as a clearinghouse guarantee against credit losses, a daily settlement of gains and losses, and an organized electronic or floor trading facility.

Futures contract basis point value (BPV) The change in price of a futures contract given a 1 basis point (0.01%) change in yield.

Futures contracts Forward contracts with standardized sizes, dates, and underlyings that trade on futures exchanges.

Futures margin account An account held by an exchange clearinghouse for each derivatives counterparty. The funds in such an account are used to ensure that counterparties do not default on their contract obligation.

Futures price The pre-agreed price at which a futures contract buyer (seller) agrees to pay (receive) for the underlying at the maturity date of the futures contract.

FX swap The combination of a spot and a forward FX transaction.

G-spread Yield spread in basis points between a bond's yield-to-maturity and that of an actual or interpolated government bond. It represents the return for bearing risks relative to the government bond.

Game theory The set of tools decision makers use to incorporate responses by rival decision makers into their strategies.

Gamma A numerical measure of how sensitive an option's delta (the sensitivity of the derivative's price) is to a change in the value of the underlying.

Gate A provision that when implemented limits or restricts redemptions for a period of time.

General collateral repo Rather than involving a specific security, a repo that instead references a specific group of securities as eligible collateral (such as government bonds of a specific maturity).

General collateral repo rate The interest rate on a general collateral repo.

General obligation (GO) bonds Unsecured bonds issued by a non-sovereign government which are backed by the taxing authority of the issuer.

General obligation bonds Also known as GO bonds. Bonds issued by non-sovereign governments for general purposes and repaid from tax cash flows.

General partners (GPs) Owners of a general partnership or limited partnership with unlimited liability and other attributes as specified in the partnership agreement.

General partnership A business organizational form owned entirely by general partners.

Geophysical resource endowment Includes such factors as livable geography and climate as well as access to food and water, which are necessary for sustainable growth. Geophysical resource endowment is highly unequal among countries.

Geopolitics The study of how geography affects politics and international relations. These relations matter for investments because they contribute to important drivers of investment performance, including economic growth, business performance, market volatility, and transaction costs.

Gilts Bonds issued by the UK government.

Global depository receipt (GDR) A depository receipt that is issued outside of the company's home country and outside of the United States.

Global minimum-variance portfolio The portfolio on the minimum-variance frontier with the smallest variance of return.

Global registered share (GRS) A common share that is traded on different stock exchanges around the world in different currencies.

Globalization The process of interaction and integration among people, companies, and governments worldwide. It is marked by the spread of products, information, jobs, and culture across borders.

Gold standard With respect to a currency, if a currency is on the gold standard a given amount can be converted into a prespecified amount of gold.

Good-on-close An execution instruction specifying that an order can only be filled at the close of trading. Also called *market-on-close*.

Good-on-open An execution instruction specifying that an order can only be filled at the opening of trading.

Good-till-cancelled order An order specifying that it is valid until the entity placing the order has cancelled it (or, commonly, until some specified amount of time such as 60 days has elapsed, whichever comes sooner).

Goodwill An intangible asset that represents the excess of the purchase price of an acquired company over the value of the net identifiable assets acquired.

Governance tokens In permissionless networks, governance tokens serve as votes to determine how the particular network is run.

Government debt management Government policies that relate to the issuance of debt securities, typically handled by a treasurer or finance ministry.

Government equivalent yield Measures quoted using actual/actual day counts.

Grant date The day that terms of compensation are communicated by an issuer and accepted by an employee recipient.

Green bonds Bonds used in green finance whereby the proceeds are earmarked toward environmental-related products.

Greenfield investments The first stage of development of an infrastructure asset. Greenfield investments involve developing new assets and new infrastructure with the intention either to lease or sell the assets to the government after construction or to hold and operate the assets. Greenfield investors typically invest alongside strategic investors or developers that specialize in developing the underlying assets.

Gross profit margin The ratio of gross profit to revenues.

Groupthink The practice of thinking or making decisions as a group in a way that discourages creativity or individual responsibility. For scenario analysis to be useful in portfolio management, teams must work hard to build creative processes, identify scenarios, track these scenarios, and assess the need for action on a regular cadence.

Growth cycle Refers to fluctuations in economic activity around the long-term potential trend growth level, focusing on how much actual economic activity is below or above trend growth in economic activity.

Growth option The option to make additional investments in a project at some future time if the financial results are strong. Also called an *expansion option*.

Growth rate cycle Refers to fluctuations in the growth rate of economic activity.

Haircut The difference between the market value of the security used as collateral and the value of the loan. Also called *repo margin*.

Halo effect An emotional bias that extends a favorable evaluation of some characteristics to other characteristics.

Hard commodities Traded natural resources, such as crude oil and metals, with markets often involving the physical delivery of the underlying upon settlement.

Hard hurdle rate Hurdle rate where the manager earns fees on annual returns in excess of the hurdle rate.

Hard-bullet covered bonds Type of security where if payments do not occur according to the original schedule of a covered bond, a bond default is triggered and bond payments are accelerated.

Harmonic mean A type of weighted mean computed as the reciprocal of the arithmetic average of the reciprocals.

Hedge The **derivative contract** used in **hedging** an exposure.

Hedge accounting Accounting standard(s) that allow an issuer to offset a hedging instrument (usually a derivative) against a hedged transaction or balance sheet item to reduce financial statement volatility.

Hedge funds Private investment vehicles that may invest in public equities or publicly traded fixed-income assets, private capital, and/or real assets, but they are distinguished by their investment *approach* rather than by the investments themselves.

Hedge ratio The proportion of an underlying that will offset the risk associated with a derivative position.

Hedging The use of a derivative contract to offset or neutralize existing or anticipated exposure to an **underlying**.

Hegemony Countries that are regional or even global leaders and use their political or economic influence of others to control resources.

Held-to-maturity Debt (fixed-income) securities that a company intends to hold to maturity; these are presented at their original cost, updated for any amortisation of discounts or premiums.

Herding Clustered trading that may or may not be based on information.

Herfindahl-Hirschman Index (HHI) A measure of market concentration, calculated as the sum of the squares of competitor market shares. Antitrust regulators in some countries consider markets with an HHI between 1,500 and 2,500 moderately concentrated and consider markets with an HHI over 2,500 highly concentrated.

Heteroskedasticity Non-constant variance across all observations.

Hidden order An order that is exposed not to the public but only to the brokers or exchanges that receive it.

Hidden revenue business model Business models that provide services to users at no charge and generate revenues elsewhere.

High yield Bond issuers and issues rated BB+ (Ba1 on Moody's scale) or lower. Also known as speculative grade and junk.

High-water mark The highest value, net of fees, that a fund has reached in history. It reflects the highest cumulative return used to calculate an incentive fee.

Hindsight bias A bias with selective perception and retention aspects in which people may see past events as having been predictable and reasonable to expect.

Holder-of-record date The date that a shareholder listed on the corporation's books will be deemed to have ownership of the shares for purposes of receiving an upcoming dividend.

Holding period return The single-period internal rate of return for a real estate property that includes property income and the change in property value over the period.

Home bias A preference for securities listed on the exchanges of one's home country.

Homogeneity of expectations The assumption that all investors have the same economic expectations and thus have the same expectations of prices, cash flows, and other investment characteristics.

Homoskedasticity Constant variance across all observations.

Horizon yield An investor's total rate of return on a fixed income instrument over their holding period, including reinvested coupon payments. It is an internal rate of return expressed as an annualized rate.

Hostile takeover   When a potential acquirer seeks to acquire a company (the target) against the wishes of the target's board of directors. Typically, a tender offer is used to carry out the hostile takeover, against which a board might use a poison pill in its defense.

Household   A person or a group of people living in the same residence, taken as a basic unit in economic analysis.

Human capital   The present value of an individual's future expected labor income.

Hurdle rate   The rate of return that a project's IRR must exceed for the project to be accepted by the company.

Hypothesis   A proposed explanation or theory that can be tested.

Hypothesis testing   The process of testing of hypotheses about one or more populations using statistical inference.

I-spread   Also known as interpolated spread, it is the yield spread for a bond over the standard swap rate in that currency of the same tenor.

Iceberg order   An order in which the display size is less than the order's full size.

If-converted method   A method for accounting for the effect of convertible securities on earnings per share (EPS) that specifies what EPS would have been if the convertible securities had been converted at the beginning of the period, taking account of the effects of conversion on net income and the weighted average number of shares outstanding.

Illusion of control bias   A bias in which people tend to believe that they can control or influence outcomes when, in fact, they cannot.

Immediate or cancel order   An order that is valid only upon receipt by the broker or exchange. If such an order cannot be filled in part or in whole upon receipt, it cancels immediately. Also called *fill or kill*.

Impact lag   The lag associated with the result of actions affecting the economy with delay.

Implied forward rate   An interest rate or yield over a future period implied by the current term structure of interest rates.

Import license   Specifies the quantity of a good that can be imported into a country.

In-the-money   Describes an option with a positive intrinsic value.

Income tax paid   The actual amount paid for income taxes in the period; not a provision, but the actual cash outflow.

Income tax payable   The income tax owed by the company on the basis of taxable income.

Increasing returns to scale   When a production process leads to increases in output that are proportionally larger than the increase in inputs.

Incurrence test   A financial ratio or other measurement taken prior to an action such as debt issuance, usually on a pro forma basis taking the action into account. Satisfaction of the test (e.g., leverage ratio below a certain value) is linked to covenants between the issuer and investors.

Indenture   A written contract between a lender and borrower that specifies the terms of the loan, such as interest rate, interest payment schedule, or maturity.

Independent   With reference to events, the property that the occurrence of one event does not affect the probability of another event occurring. With reference to two random variables X and Y, they are independent if and only if $P(X,Y) = P(X)P(Y)$.

Independent directors   Members of a corporation's board of directors who do not have an employment or familial relationship with the company, nor do they have a relationship that would impair their independence such as an economic interest in a vendor or competitor of the company.

Independent variable   An explanatory variable in a regression model.

Independently and identically distributed   With respect to random variables, the property of random variables that are independent of each other but follow the identical probability distribution.

Index-linked bonds   A bond whose coupon payments or principal repayment is linked to a specified index.

Indexing   An investment strategy in which an investor constructs a portfolio to mirror the performance of a specified index.

Indicator variable   A variable that takes on only one of two values, 0 or 1, based on a condition. In simple linear regression, the slope is the difference in the dependent variable for the two conditions. Also referred to as a *dummy variable*.

Indifference curve   A curve representing all the combinations of two goods or attributes such that the consumer is entirely indifferent among them.

Indirect taxes   Taxes such as taxes on spending, as opposed to direct taxes.

Inflation premium   An extra return that compensates investors for expected inflation.

Inflation reports   A type of economic publication put out by many central banks.

Inflation-linked bonds   Debt instruments that link the principal and interest to inflation.

Information cascade   The transmission of information from those participants who act first and whose decisions influence the decisions of others.

Information-motivated traders   Traders that trade to profit from information that they believe allows them to predict future prices.

Informationally efficient market   A market in which asset prices reflect new information quickly and rationally.

Infrastructure   A type of real asset that is intended for public use and provides essential services. These assets are typically long-lived fixed assets, such as bridges and toll roads.

Initial coin offering (ICO)   An unregulated process whereby companies raise capital by selling crypto-tokens to investors in exchange for fiat money or another agreed-upon cryptocurrency.

Initial margin   The ratio of the price of collateral to the value of cash exchanged in a repo; a value over 1.0 or 100% indicates overcollateralization.

Initial margin requirement   The margin requirement on the first day of a transaction as well as on any day in which additional margin funds must be deposited.

Initial public offering (IPO)   The first issuance of common shares to the public by a formerly private corporation.

Inside directors   Members of a corporation's board of directors who are not independent. Typically, inside directors are employees or founders (and their family) of the company.

Insolvency   Refers to the condition in which firm value is below the face value of debt used to finance the firm's assets.

Institution   An established organization or practice in a society or culture. An institution can be a formal structure, such as a university, organization, or process backed by law; or it can be informal, such as a custom or behavioral pattern important to society. Institutions can, but need not be, formed by national governments. Examples of institutions include non-governmental organizations, charities, religious customs, family units, the media, political parties, and educational practice.

Intangible assets   Assets without a physical form, such as patents and trademarks.

Interbank market   The market of loans and deposits between banks for maturities ranging from overnight to one year.

Intercept   The estimated value of the dependent variable when the independent variable is zero.

Interest coverage   A solvency ratio calculated as EBIT divided by interest payments.

Interest coverage ratio   A measure of an issuer's ability to service its debt, typically the ratio of operating income or EBIT to interest expense.

Interest rate   A rate of return that reflects the relationship between differently dated cash flows; a discount rate.

Interest rate swap   A swap in which the underlying is an interest rate. Can be viewed as a currency swap in which both currencies are the same and can be created as a combination of currency swaps.

Interest-indexed bond   A type of index-linked bond for which changes in the index are captured with adjustments to interest payments.

Internal credit enhancements   Provisions or methods a borrower initiates to improve their creditworthiness in a structured transaction, such as overcollateralization or excess spread.

Internal rate of return   The discount rate that makes net present value equal 0; the discount rate that makes the present value of an investment's costs (outflows) equal to the present value of the investment's benefits (inflows).

Internal rate of return (IRR)   The discount rate that makes net present value equal 0; the discount rate that makes the present value of an investment's costs (outflows) equal to the present value of the investment's benefits (inflows).

Internet of things   The vast array of physical devices, home appliances, smart buildings, vehicles, and other items that are embedded with electronics, sensors, software, and network connections that enable the objects in the system to interact and share information.

Interquartile range   The difference between the third and first quartiles of a dataset.

Intrinsic value   The amount gained (per unit) by an option buyer if an option is exercised at any given point in time. May be referred to as the exercise value of the option.

Investment banks   Financial intermediaries that provide advice to their mostly corporate clients and help them arrange transactions such as initial and seasoned securities offerings.

Investment grade   Bond issuers and issues rated BBB- (Baa3 on Moody's scale).

Investment policy statement   A written planning document that describes a client's investment objectives and risk tolerance over a relevant time horizon, along with the constraints that apply to the client's portfolio.

Issue rating   A rating which seeks to capture the probability of default or expected loss of the issuer's senior unsecured bonds.

Issuer rating   A rating which seeks to capture the credit risk of a specific financial obligation of an issuer which takes such factors as seniority into account.

J-curve effect   Represents the initial negative return in the capital commitment phase followed by an acceleration of returns through the capital deployment phase.

Jackknife   A resampling method that repeatedly draws samples by taking the original observed data sample and leaving out one observation at a time (without replacement) from the set.

January effect   Calendar anomaly that stock market returns in January are significantly higher compared to the rest of the months of the year, with most of the abnormal returns reported during the first five trading days in January. Also called *turn-of-the-year effect*.

Joint probability function   A function giving the probability of joint occurrences of values of stated random variables.

Judgmental sampling   A procedure of selectively handpicking elements from the population based on a researcher's knowledge and professional judgment.

Junior debt   Debt obligation with lower priority of payment than senior debt obligations.

Key rate duration   Also known as partial duration, is a measure of a bond's sensitivity to a change in the benchmark yield at a specific maturity.

Keynesians   Economists who believe that fiscal policy can have powerful effects on aggregate demand, output, and employment when there is substantial spare capacity in an economy.

Kurtosis   The statistical measure that indicates the combined weight of the tails of a distribution relative to the rest of the distribution.

Lagging economic indicators   Turning points that take place later than those of the overall economy; they are believed to have value in identifying the economy's past condition.

Law of one price   A principle that states that if two investments have the same or equivalent future cash flows regardless of what will happen in the future, then these two investments should have the same current price.

Lead underwriter   The lead investment bank in a syndicate of investment banks and broker–dealers involved in a securities underwriting.

Leading economic indicators   Turning points that usually precede those of the overall economy; they are believed to have value for predicting the economy's future state, usually near-term.

Legal tender   Something that must be accepted when offered in exchange for goods and services.

Lender of last resort   An entity willing to lend money when no other entity is ready to do so.

Leptokurtic   Describes a distribution that has fatter tails than a normal distribution (also called fat-tailed).

Lessee   Tenant or property user that enters a lease with a property owner or lessor.

Lessor   Property owner or manager that leases a property to a tenant or property user.

Level of significance   The probability of a Type I error in testing a hypothesis.

Leverage   A measure for identifying a potentially influential high-leverage point.

Leveraged buyout   A transaction whereby the target company management team converts the target to a privately held company by using heavy borrowing to finance the purchase of the target company's outstanding shares.

Leveraged buyout (LBO) An acquirer (typically an investment fund specializing in LBOs) uses a significant amount of debt to finance the acquisition of a target and then pursues restructuring actions, with the goal of exiting the target with a sale or public listing.

Leveraged buyouts Buyout equity transactions that utilize a high proportion of debt financing to make a company acquisition.

Leveraged loan Where private debt investor firms borrow money to make a direct loan to a borrower.

Leveraged loans Loans made to a borrower or issuer with relatively lower credit quality and/or higher leverage.

Liability-driven investing An investment industry term that generally encompasses asset allocation that is focused on funding an investor's liabilities in institutional contexts.

Licensing arrangements Rights to produce a product or have access to intangible assets using someone else's brand name in return for a royalty (often a percentage of revenues).

Lien A legal right or claim to property by a creditor.

Likelihood The probability of an observation, given a particular set of conditions.

Limit order Instructions to a broker or exchange to obtain the best price immediately available when filling an order, but in no event accept a price higher than a specified (limit) price when buying or accept a price lower than a specified (limit) price when selling.

Limit order book The book or list of limit orders to buy and sell that pertains to a security.

Limited company A business organizational form owned by shareholders or members with limited liability who elect a board of directors to appoint management. Generally, limited companies have indefinite life and easier transfer of ownership interests than limited partnerships.

Limited liability partnership (LLP) A business organizational form available in some jurisdictions owned entirely by limited partners with limited liability.

Limited partners (LPs) Owners of a limited partnership with limited liability and other attributes as specified in the partnership agreement.

Limited partnership A business organizational form owned by a general partner and limited partners.

Limited partnership agreement (LPA) A legal document that outlines the rules of the partnership and establishes the framework that ultimately guides the fund's operations throughout its life.

Lin-log model A functional form for transforming regression model data in which the dependent variable is linear but the independent variable is logarithmic.

Linear derivatives Firm commitment derivative contracts in which the contract's payoff/profit function is linear with respect to the price of the underlying.

Liquid market Said of a market in which traders can buy or sell with low total transaction costs when they want to trade.

Liquidity The extent to which a company is able to meet its short-term obligations using cash flows and those assets that can be readily transformed into cash.

Liquidity premium An extra return that compensates investors for the risk of loss relative to an investment's fair value if the investment needs to be converted to cash quickly.

Liquidity ratios Financial ratios measuring the company's ability to meet its short-term obligations to creditors as they come due.

Liquidity risk A divergence in the cash flow timing of a derivative versus that of an underlying transaction.

Liquidity trap A condition in which the demand for money becomes infinitely elastic (horizontal demand curve) so that injections of money into the economy will not lower interest rates or affect real activity.

Load fund A mutual fund in which, in addition to the annual fee, a percentage fee is charged to invest in the fund and/ or for redemptions from the fund.

Loan-to-value ratio (LTV) Ratio of the amount of the mortgage to the property's value. The lower the LTV, the higher the borrower's equity. From the lender's perspective, the higher the borrower's equity, the less likely the borrower is to default.

Loans Debt instruments agreed to between a borrower and lender, typically a bank.

Lockout or revolving period For an ABS with a non-amortizing collateral pool, such as credit card debt, is the period in which the cash proceeds from principal repayments are reinvested in additional loans with a principal equal to the principal repaid. During this period, there is no prepayment risk and potential default risk is generally limited. When the lockout period is over, principal repayments are used to pay off the outstanding principal on the ABS. Lockout period and revolving period are interchangeable.

Lockup period The minimum holding period before investors are allowed to make withdrawals or redeem shares from a fund. Its purpose is to allow the hedge fund manager the required time to implement and potentially realize a strategy's expected results.

Log-lin model A functional form for transforming regression model data in which the dependent variable is logarithmic but the independent variable is linear.

Log-log model A functional form for transforming regression model data in which both the dependent and independent variables are in logarithmic form.

Long A trading position in a **derivative contract** that gains value as the price of the **underlying** moves higher.

Long position A position in an asset or contract in which one owns the asset or has an exercisable right under the contract.

Long-run average total cost The curve describing average total cost when no costs are considered fixed.

Loss aversion The tendency of people to dislike losses more than they like comparable gains.

Loss given default (LGD) The investor's loss conditional on an issuer event of default.

Loss severity Portion of a bond's value (including unpaid interest) an investor loses in the event of default.

Loss-aversion bias A bias in which people tend to strongly prefer avoiding losses as opposed to achieving gains.

Low-cost producer A firm with lower production costs than its industry competitors.

M^2 An appraisal measure that indicates what a portfolio would have returned, assuming the same total risk as the market index.

M^2 alpha Difference between the risk-adjusted performance of the portfolio and the performance of the benchmark.

Macaulay duration The present-value weighted average time to receipt of cash flows for fixed-income instrument, also the holding period needed to balance coupon reinvestment risk and price risk for a one-time instantaneous "parallel" shift in the yield curve once the bond purchase is settled. It is named after Frederick Macaulay, the Canadian economist who introduced the concept in 1938.

Machine learning (ML)   Involves computer-based techniques that seek to extract knowledge from large amounts of data without making any assumptions about the data's underlying probability distribution. The goal of ML algorithms is to automate decision-making processes by generalizing, or "learning," from known examples to determine an underlying structure in the data.

Maintenance capital expenditures   Investments in assets to keep them in operation or increase their efficiency without extending their useful lives.

Maintenance margin   Minimum balance set below the initial margin that each contract buyer and seller must hold in the futures margin account from trade initiation until final settlement at maturity.

Maintenance margin requirement   The margin requirement on any day other than the first day of a transaction.

Management buy-in   A type of leveraged buyout where the current management team is replaced with the acquiring team involved in managing the company.

Management buyout   A type of leveraged buyout where the current management team participates in the acquisition.

Management guidance   Management of public companies may publicly provide targets for earnings, revenues, and other measures (e.g., capital expenditures) for the next quarter, year, or longer term. Guidance can be detailed or rather directional and is often updated throughout the year. Initial guidance for next fiscal year might be provided during the fourth-quarter earnings call and updated for completed quarters, and new information provided at the first-, second-, and third-quarter earnings calls. Also known simply as *guidance*.

Margin call   Request to a derivatives contract counterparty to immediately deposit funds to return the futures margin account balance to the initial margin.

Margin financing   A financing arrangement whereby the prime broker lends shares, bonds, or derivatives and the hedge fund (or investment manager) deposits cash or other collateral into a margin account at the prime broker based on certain fractions of the investment positions.

Margin loan   Money borrowed from a broker to purchase securities.

Marginal propensity to consume   The proportion of an additional unit of disposable income that is consumed or spent; the change in consumption for a small change in income.

Marginal propensity to save   The proportion of an additional unit of disposable income that is saved (not spent).

Mark to market (MTM)   The practice in which a central clearing party assigns profits and losses to counterparties to derivative contracts. In exchange-traded markets, this practice takes place daily and is often referred to as daily settlement.

Market anomaly   Change in the price or return of a security that cannot directly be linked to current relevant information known in the market or to the release of new information into the market.

Market bid–ask spread   The difference between the best bid and the best offer.

Market discount rate   The rate of return required by investors given the risk of the bond investment, also known as the required yield or required rate of return.

Market float   The number of shares that are available to the investing public.

Market makers   **Over-the-counter (OTC) dealers** who typically enter into offsetting bilateral transactions with one another to transfer risk to other parties.

Market model   A regression equation that specifies a linear relationship between the return on a security (or portfolio) and the return on a broad market index.

Market multiple models   Valuation models based on share price multiples or enterprise value multiples.

Market neutral   These strategies use quantitative, fundamental, and technical analysis to identify under- and overvalued equity securities. The hedge fund takes long positions in undervalued securities and short positions in overvalued securities, while seeking to maintain a market-neutral net position.

Market order   Instructions to a broker or exchange to obtain the best price immediately available when filling an order.

Market reference rate   A market-determined interest rate used as the underlying in financial instruments and contracts such as variable-rate debt and interest rate swaps. An example is the Secured Overnight Financing Rate (SOFR), which is an overnight cash borrowing rate collateralized by US Treasuries. Other MRRs include the euro short-term rate (€STR) and the Sterling Overnight Index Average (SONIA).

Market reference rate (MRR)   The interest rate underlying used in interest rate swaps. These rates typically match those of loans or other short-term obligations. Survey-based Libor rates used as reference rates in the past have been replaced by rates based on a daily average of observed market transaction rates. For example, the Secured Overnight Financing Rate (SOFR) is an overnight cash borrowing rate collateralized by US Treasuries. Other MRRs include the euro short-term rate (€STR) and the Sterling Overnight Index Average (SONIA).

Market risk   Risk related to market movements, e.g., unexpected changes in share prices, interest rates, currency exchange rates, and commodity prices.

Market share   A company's or product's revenue expressed as a percentage of its market size.

Market size   Total sales for a good or service, which can be calculated on a global or more regional basis.

Market value   The price at which an asset or security can currently be bought or sold in an open market.

Market-capitalization weighting   An index weighting method in which the weight assigned to each constituent security is determined by dividing its market capitalization by the total market capitalization (sum of the market capitalization) of all securities in the index. Also called *value weighting*.

Market-on-close   An execution instruction specifying that an order can only be filled at the close of trading.

Marketable limit order   A buy limit order in which the limit price is placed above the best offer, or a sell limit order in which the limit price is placed below the best bid. Such orders generally will partially or completely fill right away.

Markowitz efficient frontier   The graph of the set of portfolios offering the maximum expected return for their level of risk (standard deviation of return).

Master limited partnership (MLP)   Has similar features to limited partnerships but is usually a more liquid investment that is often publicly traded.

Master repurchase agreement   A legal document governing all repo trades between two parties.

Match funding   Financing an asset with a source, such as a loan or bond, that is aligned with certain attributes of the asset, such as duration and the respective streams of income and financing costs.

Material   (materiality) Refers to information that is decision-useful for a reasonable investor.

Matrix pricing An estimation process for financial instruments based on the prices of comparable instruments.

Maturity The date of a fixed-income instrument's final payment to investors.

Maturity premium An extra return that compensates investors for the increased sensitivity of the market value of debt to a change in market interest rates as maturity is extended.

Maturity structure of interest rates Also known as the term structure of interest rates, refers to the difference in interest rates or benchmark yields by time-to-maturity.

Mean absolute deviation With reference to a sample, the mean of the absolute values of deviations from the sample mean.

Mean square error (MSE) Calculated as the sum of squares error (SSE) divided by the degrees of freedom, which are the number of observations minus the number of independent variables minus one. Since simple linear regression has just one independent variable, the degrees of freedom calculation is the number of observations minus 2.

Mean square regression (MSR) Calculated as the sum of squares regression (SSR) divided by the number of independent variables in the regression model. In simple linear regression, there is only one independent variable, so MSR equals SSR.

Mean–variance analysis An approach to portfolio analysis using expected means, variances, and covariances of asset returns.

Measure of central tendency A quantitative measure that specifies where data are centered.

Measures of location Quantitative measures that describe the location or distribution of data. They include not only measures of central tendency but also other measures, such as percentiles.

Median The value of the middle item of a set of items that has been sorted into ascending or descending order (i.e., the 50th percentile).

Meme coin A type of altcoin that is often inspired by a joke.

Mental accounting bias An information-processing bias in which people treat one sum of money differently from another equal-sized sum based on which mental account the money is assigned to.

Merger arbitrage Generally, these strategies involve going long (buying) the stock of the company being acquired at a discount to its announced takeover price and going short (selling) the stock of the acquiring company when the merger or acquisition is announced.

Mesokurtic Describes a distribution with kurtosis equal to that of the normal distribution, namely, kurtosis equal to three.

Mezzanine debt Refers to private credit subordinated to senior secured debt but senior to equity in the borrower's capital structure.

Mezzanine-stage financing Mezzanine venture capital that prepares a company to go public as it continues to expand capacity and enhance its growth trajectory. It represents the bridge financing needed to fund a private firm until it can execute an IPO or be sold.

Miner A validator of transactions on the blockchain that locks blocks of transactions into the blockchain and receives compensation for this process in the form of a digital asset.

Minimum efficient scale The smallest output that a firm can produce such that its long-run average total cost is minimized.

Minimum-variance portfolio The portfolio with the minimum variance for each given level of expected return.

Minority shareholder An individual or entity that owns less than a majority of the voting rights in a corporation.

Mode The most frequently occurring value in a distribution.

Modern portfolio theory (MPT) The analysis of rational portfolio choices based on the efficient use of risk.

Modified duration The first derivative of a bond's price with respect to its yield, this statistic is a measure of interest rate risk used to estimate the percentage price change for a given change in yield-to-maturity.

Monetarists Economists who believe that the rate of growth of the money supply is the primary determinant of the rate of inflation.

Monetary policy Actions taken by a nation's central bank to affect aggregate output and prices through changes in bank reserves, reserve requirements, or its target interest rate.

Monetary transmission mechanism The process whereby a central bank's interest rate gets transmitted through the economy and ultimately affects the rate of increase of prices.

Monetary union An economic union in which the members adopt a common currency.

Money convexity A measure that is used to complement modified duration to capture the second-order effect of yield changes on a bond's price, expressed in currency terms.

Money duration A measure of the price change of a fixed-income instrument in currency units from a change in yield-to-maturity. The money duration can be stated per 100 of par value or in terms of the actual position size. In the United States, money duration is commonly called "dollar duration."

Money market The market for short-term debt instruments (one-year maturity or less).

Money market securities Fixed-income securities with original maturities of one year or less.

Money-weighted return The internal rate of return on a portfolio, taking account of all cash flows.

Moneyness Expresses the relationship between an option's value and its exercise price across the full range of possible underlying prices.

Monopolistic competition Highly competitive form of imperfect competition; the competitive characteristic is a notably large number of firms, while the monopoly aspect is the result of product differentiation.

Monopoly In pure monopoly markets, there are no substitutes for the given product or service. There is a single seller, which exercises considerable power over pricing and output decisions.

Monte Carlo simulation A technique that uses the inverse transformation method for converting a randomly generated uniformly distributed number into a simulated value of a random variable of a desired distribution. Each key decision variable in a Monte Carlo simulation requires an assumed statistical distribution; this assumption facilitates incorporating non-normality, fat tails, and tail dependence as well as solving high-dimensionality problems.

Moral principles Beliefs regarding what is good, acceptable, or obligatory behavior and what is bad, unacceptable, or forbidden behavior.

Mortgage loan Agreement to finance real estate by the collateral of a specified property that obliges the borrower to make a predetermined series of payments to the lender.

Mortgage pass-through security   Security created when mortgage lenders pool mortgages together and sell securities to investors. The cash flow from the mortgage pool—monthly payments of principal, interest, and prepayments—are "passed through" to the security holders.

Mortgage-backed securities   Debt obligations that represent claims to the cash flows from pools of mortgage loans, most commonly on residential property.

Mortgage-backed securities (MBS)   Bonds created from the securitization of mortgages.

Multi-factor model   A model that explains a variable in terms of the values of a set of factors.

Multi-market indexes   Comprised of indexes from different countries, designed to represent multiple security markets.

Multilateral trading facilities   See *alternative trading systems*.

Multilateralism   The conduct of countries who participate in mutually beneficial trade relationships and extensive rules harmonization. Private firms are fully integrated into global supply chains with multiple trade partners. Examples of multilateral countries include Germany and Singapore.

Multiple of invested capital (MOIC)   A simplified calculation that measures the total value of all distributions and residual asset values relative to an initial total investment; also known as a *money multiple*.

Multiple-price auction   A debt securities auction in which bidders receive distinct prices based on their bids.

Multiplier models   Valuation models based on share price multiples or enterprise value multiples.

Mutual fund   A comingled investment pool in which investors in the fund each have a pro-rata claim on the income and value of the fund.

Nash equilibrium   When two or more participants in a non-coop-erative game have no incentive to deviate from their respective equilibrium strategies given their opponent's strategies.

Nationalism   The promotion of a country's own economic interests to the exclusion or detriment of the interests of other nations. Nationalism is marked by limited economic and financial cooperation. These actors may focus on national production and sales, limited cross-border investment and capital flows, and restricted currency exchange.

Natural language processing (NLP)   A field of research within the field of text analytics and at the intersection of computer science, AI, and linguistics that focuses on developing computer programs to analyze and interpret human language.

Natural resources   These include commodities (hard and soft), agricultural land (farmland), and timberland.

Negative externalities   A cost to a third party because of the production or consumption of a good or service.

Negative pledge clause   Limitations on investments, the disposal of assets, or issuance of debt senior to existing obligations. Negative covenants seek to ensure that an issuer maintains the ability to make interest and principal payments.

Net cash   An issuer's total debt less cash and marketable securities. When the balance is negative it is referred to as net cash.

Net debt   An issuer's total debt less cash and marketable securities. When the balance is positive it is referred to as net debt.

Net investment hedge   Refers to a specific **hedge accounting** designation that applies when either a foreign currency bond or a derivative, such as an FX swap or forward, is used to offset the exchange rate risk of the equity of a foreign operation.

Net present value (NPV)   The present value of an investment's cash inflows (benefits) minus the present value of its cash outflows (costs).

Net profit margin   An indicator of profitability, calculated as net income divided by revenue; indicates how much of each dollar of revenues is left after all costs and expenses. Also called *profit margin* or *return on sales*.

Net tax rate   The tax rate net of transfer payments.

Net working capital   Working capital excluding short-term items unrelated to business operations, such as cash, marketable securities, and short-term debt.

Network effects   A business model that enables users to contribute directly to a product, service, or online content.

Neural networks   A type of computer program design based on how the human brain learns and processes information.

Neutral rate of interest   The rate of interest that neither spurs on nor slows down the underlying economy.

No-load fund   A mutual fund in which there is no fee for investing in the fund or for redeeming fund shares, although there is an annual fee based on a percentage of the fund's net asset value.

Node   Each value on a binomial tree from which successive moves or outcomes branch.

Non-agency RMBS   MBS backed by residential mortgages that are issued by private entities and not guaranteed by a federal agency or a GSE.

Non-amortizing loans   Type of debt where there are no scheduled principal repayments.

Non-cooperative country   A country with inconsistent and even arbitrary rules; restricted movement of goods, services, people, and capital across borders; retaliation; and limited technology exchange.

Non-cumulative preference shares   Preference shares for which dividends that are not paid in the current or subsequent periods are forfeited permanently (instead of being accrued and paid at a later date).

Non-financial risks   Risks that arise from sources other than changes in the external financial markets, such as changes in accounting rules, legal environment, or tax rates.

Non-fungible token (NFT)   A unique cryptographic token on the blockchain that cannot be replicated and is used to represent ownership of physical assets, such as artwork, real estate, or other assets.

Non-linear derivatives   Derivatives, such as options or other contingent claims, with payoff/profit profiles that are non-linear (asymmetric) with respect to the price of the underlying.

Non-participating preference shares   Preference shares that do not entitle shareholders to share in the profits of the company. Instead, shareholders are only entitled to receive a fixed dividend payment and the par value of the shares in the event of liquidation.

Non-probability sampling   A sampling plan dependent on factors other than probability considerations, such as a sampler's judgment or the convenience to access data.

Non-recourse loan   Loan in which the lender does not have a claim against the borrower and thus can look only to the property to recover the outstanding mortgage balance.

Non-state actors Those that participate in global political, economic, or financial affairs but do not directly control national security or country resources. Examples of non-state actors are non-governmental organizations (NGOs), multinational companies, charities, and even influential individuals, such as business leaders or cultural icons.

Nonparametric test A test that is not concerned with a parameter or that makes minimal assumptions about the population from which a sample comes.

Nonsystematic risk Unique risk that is local or limited to a particular asset or industry that need not affect assets outside of that asset class.

Normal distribution A continuous, symmetric probability distribution that is completely described by its mean and its variance.

Normalized earnings The expected level of mid-cycle earnings for a company in the absence of any unusual or temporary factors that affect profitability (either positively or negatively).

Notching Ratings adjustment methodology where specific issues from the same borrower may be assigned different credit ratings.

Notice period The length of time (typically 30–90 days) in advance that investors may be required to notify a fund of their intent to redeem some or all of their investment. This allows a fund manager to liquidate a position in an orderly fashion without magnifying losses.

Novation process A process thatsubstitutes the initial **swap execution facility(SEF)** contract with identical trades facing the **central counterparty (CCP)**. The CCP serves as **counterparty** for both financial intermediaries, eliminating bilateral **counterparty credit risk** and providing **clearing** and **settlement** services.

Null hypothesis The hypothesis that is tested.

Off-the-run Seasoned government bonds that are often less liquid.

Off-the-run securities Sovereign debt securities outstanding other than on-the-sun securities. Off-the-run securities are less liquid than on-the-run securities.

Offer The price at which a dealer or trader is willing to sell an asset, typically qualified by a maximum quantity (ask size).

Official interest rate An interest rate that a central bank sets and announces publicly; normally the rate at which it is willing to lend money to the commercial banks. Also called *official policy rate* or *policy rate*.

Official policy rate An interest rate that a central bank sets and announces publicly; normally the rate at which it is willing to lend money to the commercial banks.

Oligopoly Market structure with a relatively small number of firms supplying the market.

Omnichannel Refers to a company selling its products or services in multiple channels, such as in store and online.

On-the-run Most recently issued, and liquid, government bonds.

On-the-run securities The most recently issued and liquid sovereign debt securities.

Open interest The number of outstanding contracts.

Open market operations The purchase or sale of bonds by the national central bank to implement monetary policy. The bonds traded are usually sovereign bonds issued by the national government.

Open-end fund A mutual fund that accepts new investment money and issues additional shares at a value equal to the net asset value of the fund at the time of investment.

Operating cycle The length of time between a company's acquisition of goods or raw materials and the collection of cash from sales to customers.

Operating efficiency ratios Ratios that measure how efficiently a company performs day-to-day tasks, such as the collection of receivables and management of inventory.

Operating leases A type of lease which is more akin to the rental of the underlying asset.

Operating leverage The sensitivity of a firm's operating profit to a change in revenues, determined by the composition of fixed and variable operating costs.

Operating profit margin A profitability ratio calculated as operating income (i.e., income before interest and taxes) divided by revenue. Also called *operating margin*.

Operational deposits Bank deposits generated by clearing, custody, and cash management activities.

Operational independence A bank's ability to execute monetary policy and set interest rates in the way it thought would best meet the inflation target.

Operational risk The risk that arises from inadequate or failed people, systems, and internal policies, procedures, and processes, as well as from external events that are beyond the control of the organization but that affect its operations.

Operationally efficient Said of a market, a financial system, or an economy that has relatively low transaction costs.

Opportunistic real estate strategies Include major redevelopment, repurposing of assets, taking on large vacancies, or speculating on significant improvement in market conditions. These may be appealing for investors seeking higher returns and willing to accept additional risks from development, redevelopment, repositioning, and leasing.

Opportunity cost The value that investors forgo by choosing a particular course of action; the value of something in its best alternative use.

Optimal capital structure The capital structure at which the value of the company is maximized.

Option A primary example of a **contingent claim**. A **derivative contract** that provides the buyer the right, but not the obligation, to buy or sell an **underlying**.

Option contract See *option*.

Option premium An amount that is paid upfront from the option buyer to the option seller. Reflects the value of the option buyer's right to exercise in the future.

Option-adjusted price The sum of a bond's flat price and value of an embedded option.

Option-adjusted spread Or OAS for a bond is its Z-spread adjusted for the value of an embedded option.

Option-adjusted yield A yield measure for a bond adjusted for embedded options.

Order A specification of what instrument to trade, how much to trade, and whether to buy or sell.

Order precedence hierarchy With respect to the execution of orders to trade, a set of rules that determines which orders execute before other orders.

Order-driven markets A market (generally an auction market) that uses rules to arrange trades based on the orders that traders submit; in their pure form, such markets do not make use of dealers.

Ordinary shares Equity shares that are subordinate to all other types of equity (e.g., preferred equity). Also called *common stock* or *common shares*.

Organizational form A legal and tax classification of a business, specific to a jurisdiction, that determines the organization's legal identity, owner–manager relationship, owner liability, taxation, and access to financing.

Out-of-the-money Describes an option with zero intrinsic value because the option buyer would not rationally exercise the option. An example of such would be the case in which the price of the underlying is less than the option's exercise price for a call option.

Over-the-counter (OTC) Refers to derivative markets in which **derivative contracts** are created and traded between derivatives end users and **dealers**, or financial intermediaries, such as commercial banks or investment banks.

Overcollateralization Credit enhancement technique where collateral underlying the transaction exceeds the face value of the issued bonds.

Overconfidence bias A bias in which people demonstrate unwarranted faith in their own intuitive reasoning, judgments, and/or cognitive abilities.

Overfitting When a machine learning model learns the input and target dataset too precisely, making the system more likely to discover false relationships or unsubstantiated patterns that will lead to prediction errors.

P-value The smallest level of significance at which the null hypothesis can be rejected.

Par rate A yield-to-maturity that makes the present value of a bond's cash flows equal to par.

Par swap rate The fixed swap rate that equates the present value of all future expected floating cash flows to the present value of fixed cash flows.

Par value The amount of principal on a bond, also known as face value.

Parallel shift When all maturities along a yield curve increase or decrease in yield in the same direction by the same magnitude. A parallel shift in the yield curve is implicitly assumed in analytical duration and convexity.

Parameter A descriptive measure computed from or used to describe a population of data, conventionally represented by Greek letters.

Parametric test Any test (or procedure) concerned with parameters or whose validity depends on assumptions concerning the population generating the sample.

Pari passu clause A covenant or contract clause that ensures a debt obligation is treated the same as the borrower's other senior debt instruments and is not subordinated to similar obligations.

Partially amortizing bond A loan or bond with a payment schedule that calls for the complete repayment of principal over the instrument's time to maturity.

Participating preference shares Preference shares that entitle shareholders to receive the standard preferred dividend plus the opportunity to receive an additional dividend if the company's profits exceed a pre-specified level.

Pass-through businesses Businesses that, by virtue of their organizational form and/or other legal and regulatory attributes, do not pay entity-level taxes on income or loss; income or loss is passed through to owners, who pay personal taxes.

Pass-through rate The coupon rate of a mortgage pass-through security that is received by the investor after administrative charges. It is lower than the weighted average mortgage rate earned on the underlying pool of mortgages because of administrative charges. The pass-through rate that the investor receives is said to be "net interest" or "net coupon."

Passive investment In the fixed-income context, it is investment that seeks to mimic the prevailing characteristics of the overall investments available in terms of credit quality, type of borrower, maturity, and duration rather than express a specific market view.

Payable date The day that the company actually mails out (or electronically transfers) a dividend payment.

Payment date The day that the company actually mails out (or electronically transfers) a dividend payment.

Payment-in-kind A bond feature whereby coupon payments can be fully or partially paid in the form of additional issuance or added to the principal amount.

Payments system The system for the transfer of money.

Pearson correlation A parametric measure of the relationship between two variables.

Pecking order theory The theory that managers consider how their actions might be interpreted by outsiders and thereby order their preferences for various forms of corporate financing. Forms of financing that are least visible to outsiders (e.g., internally generated funds) are most preferable to managers, and those that are most visible (e.g., equity issuance) are least preferable.

Penetration pricing A discount pricing approach used when a firm willingly sacrifices margins in order to build scale and market share.

Percentiles Quantiles that divide a distribution into 100 equal parts that sum to 100.

Perfect competition A market structure in which the individual firm has virtually no impact on market price, because it is assumed to be a very small seller among a very large number of firms selling essentially identical products.

Performance evaluation The measurement and assessment of the outcomes of investment management decisions.

Performance fee Fee paid to the general partner from the limited partner(s) based on realized net profits.

Period costs Costs (e.g., executives' salaries) that cannot be directly matched with the timing of revenues and which are thus expensed immediately.

Periodicity Number of periods in a year, used for compound interest. The periodicity of a fixed-income instrument usually matches the frequency of its coupon payments.

Permanent differences Differences between tax and financial reporting of revenue (expenses) that will not be reversed at some future date. These result in a difference between the company's effective tax rate and statutory tax rate and do not result in a deferred tax item.

Permissioned networks Networks that are fully open only to select participants on a DLT network.

Permissionless networks Networks that are fully open to any user on a DLT network.

Perpetual bonds Bonds with no stated maturity date.

Perpetuity A perpetual annuity, or a set of never-ending level sequential cash flows, with the first cash flow occurring one period from now.

PESTLE analysis A framework for analyzing factors that influence an industry's economic outcomes.

Pet projects A capital investment that is pursued by management but is not economically justifiable by a disinterested party. Motivations for pet projects include self-dealing and vanity.

Physical risks Economic and financial losses from the increase in the severity and frequency of extreme weather due to climate change—for example, the loss of coastal real estate from a storm.

PIPE (private investment in public equity) A private offering to select investors with fewer disclosures and lower transaction costs that allows the issuer to raise capital more quickly and cost effectively.

Platykurtic Describes a distribution that has relatively less weight in the tails than the normal distribution (also called thin-tailed).

Pledge A legal right or claim to property by a creditor. Also called a lien.

Poison pill Officially known as a shareholder rights plan, a poison pill is a hostile-takeover defense adopted by boards of directors according to rules specified in the corporate charter. There are several types of poison pills. Generally, they allow shareholders, *excluding* the shareholder making the hostile bid and their affiliates, to buy newly issued shares at a discounted price. The share issuance would dilute the bidder's ownership percentage, rendering it impossible for the bidder to attain control.

Policy rate An interest rate that a central bank sets and announces publicly; normally the rate at which it is willing to lend money to the commercial banks.

Portfolio companies The individual companies owned by a private equity firm.

Portfolio investment flows Short-term investments in foreign assets, such as stocks or bonds.

Portfolio planning The process of creating a plan for building a portfolio that is expected to satisfy a client's investment objectives.

Position The quantity of an asset that an entity owns or owes.

Posterior probability An updated probability that reflects or comes after new information.

Power of a test The probability of correctly rejecting the null—that is, rejecting the null hypothesis when it is false.

Pre-funding period Allows the trust to acquire during a certain period of time after the close of the transaction.

Preference shares A type of equity interest which ranks above common shares with respect to the payment of dividends and the distribution of the company's net assets upon liquidation. They have characteristics of both debt and equity securities. Also called *preferred stock*.

Preferred stock See *preference shares*.

Premium In the case of bonds, premium refers to the amount by which a bond is priced above its face (par) value. In the case of an option, the amount paid for the option contract.

Prepayment option May entitle the borrower to prepay all or part of the outstanding mortgage principal prior to maturity. This creates a risk from the lender's or investor's viewpoint because the cash flow amounts and timing cannot be known with certainty.

Prepayment risk The risk that the some or all of a mortgage-backed security's principal is repaid at a different speed than expected, either in the form of contraction risk (or earlier repayment than expected) or extension risk (later repayment).

Present value models Valuation models that estimate the intrinsic value of a security as the present value of the future benefits expected to be received from the security. Also called *discounted cash flow models*.

Pretax margin A profitability ratio calculated as earnings before taxes divided by revenue.

Price discrimination A pricing approach that charges different prices to different customers based on their willingness to pay.

Price index Represents the average prices of a basket of goods and services.

Price limits Establish a band relative to the previous day's settlement price within which all trades must occur.

Price multiple A ratio that compares the share price with some sort of monetary flow or value to allow evaluation of the relative worth of a company's stock.

Price priority The principle that the highest priced buy orders and the lowest priced sell orders execute first.

Price return Measures *only* the price appreciation or percentage change in price of the securities in an index or portfolio.

Price return index An index that reflects *only* the price appreciation or percentage change in price of the constituent securities. Also called *price index*.

Price stability In economics, refers to an inflation rate that is low on average and not subject to wide fluctuation.

Price takers Producers that must accept whatever price the market dictates.

Price value of a basis point (PVBP) An estimate of the change in the full price of a bond given a 1 bp change in its yield-to-maturity. The PVBP is also called the "PV01," standing for the "price value of an 01" or "present value of an 01," where "01" means 1 bp. In the United States, it is commonly called the "DV01" for the "dollar value" of 1 bp.

Price weighting An index weighting method in which the weight assigned to each constituent security is determined by dividing its price by the sum of all the prices of the constituent securities.

Price-setting option The option to adjust prices when demand or supply varies from what is forecast.

Price-to-earnings ratio (P/E) The ratio of share price to earnings per share.

Pricing power A company's ability to set prices and other economic terms with customers without affecting its sales volumes.

Primary bond markets Fixed-income markets comprised of issuers issuing bonds to investors to raise capital, often intermediated by a third-party such as an investment bank.

Primary capital markets (primary markets) The market where securities are first sold and the issuers receive the proceeds.

Primary dealer Financial institution that is authorized to deal in new issues of sovereign bonds and that serves primarily as a trading counterparty of the office responsible for issuing sovereign bonds.

Primary market The market where securities are first sold and the issuers receive the proceeds.

Prime broker A broker that provides services that commonly include custody, administration, lending, short borrowing, and trading.

Prime loans Lending made to borrowers of high credit quality with strong employment and credit histories, a low DTI, substantial equity in the underlying property, and a first lien on the mortgaged property serving as the collateral for the loan.

Principal The amount that an issuer agrees to repay the debtholders on the maturity date.

Principal-agent relationship An arrangement in which one party (the agent) has authority to act for or on behalf of another party (the principal). Such an arrangement imposes a duty on the agent to act in the principal's best interest.

Prior probabilities Probabilities reflecting beliefs prior to the arrival of new information.

Priority of claims   Priority of payment, with the most senior or highest ranking debt having the first claim on the cash flows and assets of the issuer.

Private capital   Funding provided to companies that is not sourced from the public markets.

Private company   A company, typically a limited company, that does not list its equity securities on an exchange.

Private debt   Capital extended to companies through a loan or other form of debt.

Private debtholders   Investors in an entity's non-securitized debt claims, such as a loan or lease. The most common type of private debtholder is a bank.

Private equity   Equity investment capital raised from sources other than public markets and traditional institutions.

Private equity fund   A hedge fund that seeks to buy, optimize, and ultimately sell portfolio companies to generate profits. See *venture capital fund*.

Private equity securities   Securities that are not listed on public exchanges and have no active secondary market. They are issued primarily to institutional investors via non-public offerings, such as private placements.

Private investment in public equity (PIPE)   An investment in the equity of a publicly traded firm that is made at a discount to the market value of the firm's shares.

Private limited company   A type of limited company in many jurisdictions with pass-through taxation but restrictions on the number of shareholders or members and on the transfer of ownership interest.

Private placement   A sale of debt or equity securities to a small group of investors on an unregulated basis. The terms of the offering are negotiated by the issuer and investors.

Probability of default (POD)   The likelihood that an issuer fails to make full and timely payments of principal and interest; typically an annualized measure.

Probability sampling   A sampling plan that allows every member of the population to have an equal chance of being selected.

Probability tree diagram   A diagram with branches emanating from nodes representing either mutually exclusive chance events or mutually exclusive decisions.

Production flexibility option   The option to alter production when demand varies from what is forecast.

Profession   An occupational group that has specific education, expert knowledge, and a framework of practice and behavior that underpins community trust, respect, and recognition.

Profit margin   An indicator of profitability, calculated as net income divided by revenue; indicates how much of each dollar of revenues is left after all costs and expenses.

Profitability ratios   Ratios that measure a company's ability to generate profitable sales from its resources (assets).

Prospectus   Legal document in securitization that describes the structure of the transaction, including the priority and amount of payments to be made to the servicer, administrators, and the ABS holders, as well as the credit enhancements used in the securitization.

Protective put   A strategy of purchasing an underlying asset and purchasing a put on the same asset.

Proxy contest   When a shareholder or group of shareholders campaigns for certain matters they have submitted to a shareholder vote, often a slate of directors who oppose the incumbent board and management. The incumbent board and management simultaneously campaign for their side.

Proxy voting   A form of casting a ballot in an election in which a voter authorizes a representative to vote on their behalf according to instructions. In corporate elections, proxy ballots are cast by shareholders that direct a representative, typically the corporate secretary, to enter their votes as instructed.

Public (listed) company   A company with its equity securities traded on an exchange.

Public limited companies   A type of limited company in many jurisdictions with entity-level taxation but no restrictions on the number of shareholders or transferability of ownership interest; the most suitable organizational form for a company that seeks to go public.

Public–private partnership   A long-term contractual relationship between the public and private sectors for the purpose of having the private sector deliver a project or service traditionally provided by the public sector. Infrastructure is increasingly being financed privately through public–private partnerships by local, regional, and national governments.

Public–private partnership (PPP)   An agreement between the public sector and the private sector to finance, build, and operate public infrastructure, such as hospitals and toll roads.

Pull on liquidity   An action or event that accelerates cash outflows.

Purchase agreement   Legal document in a securitization transaction that outlines the representations and warranties that the seller makes about the assets sold.

Pure discount bonds   Bonds that do not pay interest during their life. They are issued at a discount to par value and redeemed at par. Also called zero-coupon bonds.

Put   An option that gives the holder the right to sell an underlying asset to another party at a fixed price over a specific period of time.

Put option   The right to sell an underlying.

Putable bonds   Bonds that give the bondholder the right to sell the bond back to the issuer at a predetermined price on specified dates.

Put–call forward parity   Describes the no-arbitrage condition in which at $t = 0$ the present value of the price of a long forward commitment plus the price of the long put must equal the price of the long call plus the price of the risk-free asset (with face value of the exercise price of both the call and the put).

Put–call parity   Describes the no-arbitrage condition in which at $t = 0$ the price of the long underlying asset plus the price of the long put must equal the price of the long call plus the price of the risk-free asset (with face value of the exercise price of both the call and the put).

Quantile   A value at or below which a stated fraction of the data lies. Also referred to as a fractile.

Quantitative easing   An expansionary monetary policy based on aggressive open market purchase operations.

Quartiles   Quantiles that divide a distribution into four equal parts.

Quick ratio   A measure of liquidity that is the ratio of cash, marketable securities, and receivables to current liabilities.

Quintiles   Quantiles that divide a distribution into five equal parts.

Quota rents   Profits that foreign producers can earn by raising the price of their goods higher than they would without a quota.

Quotas Government policies that restrict the quantity of a good that can be imported into a country, generally for a specified period of time.

Quote-driven market A market in which dealers acting as principals facilitate trading.

Quoted margin Specified spread of a floating rate instrument over a market reference rate or benchmark.

Range The difference between the maximum and minimum values in a dataset.

Rapid amortization provisions Provisions in receivable ABS that may require early principal amortization if specific events occur. Such provisions are referred to as early amortization and are included to safeguard the credit quality of the issue, particularly during the revolving period.

Razor, razorblade pricing A pricing approach that combines a low price on a piece of equipment and high-margin pricing on repeat-purchase consumables.

Real assets Generally, these are tangible physical assets, such as real estate, infrastructure, and natural resources, but they also include such intangibles as patents, intellectual property, and goodwill. Real assets generate current or expected future cash flows and/or are considered a store of value.

Real estate Includes borrowed or ownership capital in buildings or land. Developed land includes commercial and industrial real estate, residential real estate, and infrastructure.

Real option A right, but not an obligation, for management to make a decision with respect to a capital investment that alters future cash flows from the original forecasted scenario.

Real risk-free interest rate The single-period interest rate for a completely risk-free security if no inflation were expected.

Rebalancing In the context of asset allocation, a discipline for adjusting the portfolio to align with the strategic asset allocation.

Rebalancing policy The set of rules that guide the process of restoring a portfolio's asset class weights to those specified in the strategic asset allocation.

Recapitalization Recapitalization via private equity describes the steps a firm takes to increase or introduce leverage to its portfolio company and pay itself a dividend out of the new capital structure.

Recognition lag The lag in government response to an economic problem resulting from the delay in confirming a change in the state of the economy.

Recourse loan Loan in which the lender has a claim against the borrower for the shortfall (deficiency) between the amount of the outstanding mortgage balance and the proceeds received from the sale of the property.

Recovery rate (RR) The percentage of an outstanding debt claim recovered when an issuer defaults

Redemption fee A fee charged to discourage redemptions and to offset the transaction costs for remaining investors in the fund.

Refinancing rate A type of central bank policy rate.

Regionalism In between the two extremes of bilateralism and multilateralism. In regionalism, a group of countries cooperate with one another. Both bilateralism and regionalism can be conducted at the exclusion of other groups. For example, regional blocs may agree to provide trade benefits to one another and increase barriers for those outside of that group.

Registered bonds Bonds for which ownership is recorded by either name or serial number.

Regression analysis Allows us to test hypotheses about the relationship between two variables, by quantifying the strength of the relationship between the two variables, and to use one variable to make predictions about the other variable.

Regression coefficients The collective term for the intercept and slope coefficients in the regression model.

Regret The feeling that an opportunity has been missed; typically, an expression of *hindsight bias*.

Regret-aversion bias An emotional bias in which people tend to avoid making decisions that will result in action out of fear that the decision will turn out poorly.

Relative dispersion The amount of dispersion relative to a reference value or benchmark.

Reopening Issuing bonds by increasing the size of an existing bond issue with a price significantly different from par.

Replication A strategy in which a derivative's cash flow stream may be recreated using a combination of long or short positions in an underlying asset and borrowing or lending cash.

Repo rate The interest rate on a repurchase agreement.

Representativeness bias A belief perseverance bias in which people tend to classify new information based on past experiences and classifications.

Repurchase agreement (Repo) A form of collateralized loan involving the sale of a security with a simultaneous agreement by the seller to buy back the same security from the purchaser at an agreed-on price and future date. The party who sells the security at the inception of the repurchase agreement and buys it back at maturity is borrowing money from the other party, and the security sold and subsequently repurchased represents the collateral.

Repurchase date The date when the party who sold the security at the inception of a repurchase agreement buys back the security from the cash lending counterparty.

Repurchase price The price at which the party who sold the security at the inception of the repurchase agreement buys back the security from the cash lending counterparty.

Required margin Yield spread of a floating rate instrument such that the instrument is priced at par value on a rate reset date.

Required rate of return The rate of return required by investors given the risk of the bond investment, also known as the market discount rate or required yield.

Required yield The rate of return required by investors given the risk of the bond investment, also known as the market discount rate of required rate of return.

Required yield spread The difference in yield-to-maturity between a bond and that of a government benchmark bond with the same or similar time-to-maturity.

Resampling A statistical method that repeatedly draws samples from the original observed data sample for the statistical inference of population parameters.

Reserve currency A currency held by global central banks in significant quantities and widely used to conduct international trade and financial transactions.

Reserve requirement The requirement for banks to hold reserves in proportion to the size of deposits.

Residual The amount of deviation of an observed value of the dependent variable from its estimated value based on the fitted regression line.

Restricted domestic currency A currency with limited convertibility into other currencies due to illiquidity.

Return on assets (ROA)   A profitability ratio calculated as net income divided by average total assets; indicates a company's net profit generated per dollar invested in total assets.

Return on equity (ROE)   A profitability ratio calculated as net income divided by average shareholders' equity.

Return on invested capital (ROIC)   A measure of the profitability of a company relative to the amount of capital invested by the equityholders and debtholders.

Return on sales   An indicator of profitability, calculated as net income divided by revenue; indicates how much of each dollar of revenues is left after all costs and expenses. Also referred to as *net profit margin*.

Return-generating model   A model that can provide an estimate of the expected return of a security given certain parameters and estimates of the values of the independent variables in the model.

Revenue bonds   Bonds issued by non-sovereign governments related to a government sponsored project expected to generate future cash flow as a primary source of repayment.

Reverse repurchase agreement   A repurchase agreement viewed from the perspective of the cash lending counterparty.

Reverse stock split   A reduction in the number of shares outstanding with a corresponding increase in share price, but no change to the company's underlying fundamentals.

Revolving credit agreements   The most reliable form of short-term bank borrowing facilities; they are in effect for multiple years (e.g., three to five years) and can have optional medium-term loan features. Also known as *revolvers*.

Rho   The change in a given derivative instrument for a given small change in the risk-free interest rate, holding everything else constant. Rho measures the sensitivity of the option to the risk-free interest rate.

Ricardian equivalence   An economic theory that implies that it makes no difference whether a government finances a deficit by increasing taxes or issuing debt.

Risk   Exposure to uncertainty. The chance of a loss or adverse outcome as a result of an action, inaction, or external event.

Risk averse   The assumption that an investor will choose the least risky alternative.

Risk aversion   The degree of an investor's inability and unwillingness to take risk.

Risk budgeting   The establishment of objectives for individuals, groups, or divisions of an organization that takes into account the allocation of an acceptable level of risk.

Risk exposure   The state of being exposed or vulnerable to a risk. The extent to which an organization is sensitive to underlying risks.

Risk governance   The top-down process and guidance that directs risk management activities to align with and support the overall enterprise.

Risk management   The process of identifying the level of risk an organization wants, measuring the level of risk the organization currently has, taking actions that bring the actual level of risk to the desired level of risk, and monitoring the new actual level of risk so that it continues to be aligned with the desired level of risk.

Risk management framework   The infrastructure, process, and analytics needed to support effective risk management in an organization.

Risk premium   An extra return expected by investors for bearing some specified risk.

Risk shifting   Actions to change the distribution of risk outcomes.

Risk tolerance   the level of risk an investor is willing and able to bear.

Risk transfer   Actions to pass on a risk to another party, often, but not always, in the form of an insurance policy.

Risk-neutral pricing   A no-arbitrage derivative value established separately from investor views on risk that uses underlying asset volatility and the risk-free rate to calculate the present value of future cash flows.

Risk-neutral probability   The computed probability used in binomial option pricing by which the discounted weighted sum of expected values of the underlying equal the current option price. Specifically, this probability is computed using the risk-free rate and assumed up gross return and down gross return of the underlying.

Rollover risk   The likelihood that a property owner will lose an existing tenant and forgo income until a new one is found.

Safety-first rules   Rules for portfolio selection that focus on the risk that portfolio value or portfolio return will fall below some minimum acceptable level over some time horizon.

Sample correlation coefficient   A standardized measure of how two variables in a sample move together. It is the ratio of the sample covariance to the product of the two variables' standard deviations.

Sample covariance   A measure of how two variables in a sample move together.

Sample excess kurtosis   A sample measure of the degree of a distribution's kurtosis in excess of the normal distribution's kurtosis.

Sample mean   The sum of the sample observations divided by the sample size.

Sample skewness   A sample measure of the degree of asymmetry of a distribution.

Sample standard deviation   The positive square root of the sample variance.

Sample variance   The sum of squared deviations around the mean divided by the degrees of freedom.

Sample-size neglect   A type of representativeness bias in which financial market participants incorrectly assume that small sample sizes are representative of populations (or "real" data).

Sampling distribution   The distribution of all distinct possible values that a statistic can assume when computed from samples of the same size randomly drawn from the same population.

Sampling error   The difference between the observed value of a statistic and the estimate resulting from using subsets of the population.

Sampling plan   The set of rules used to select a sample.

Saving deposits   Bank deposits typically held for non-transactional purposes that often have a stated term.

Scatter plot   A two-dimensional graphical plot of paired observations of values for the independent and dependent variables in a simple linear regression.

Scenario analysis   A variation of the valuation process combining a base case with alternative outcomes, allowing the incorporation of more favorable or adverse scenarios in the valuation process.

Scraping   An automated, large-scale, algorithm-driven approach that retrieves otherwise unstructured data available on websites and creates data in a more structured format.

Seasoned offering   An offering in which an issuer sells additional units of a previously issued security.

Secondary bond markets Fixed-income markets comprised of investors trading existing bonds amongst themselves.

Secondary market The market where securities are traded among investors.

Secondary precedence rules Rules that determine how to rank orders placed at the same time.

Secondary sale Sale of a private company stake to another private equity firm or group of financial buyers.

Secondary-stage investments The second stage of development of an infrastructure asset. Secondary-stage investments involve existing infrastructure facilities or fully operational assets that do not require further investment or development over the investment horizon. These assets generate immediate cash flow and returns expected over the investment period.

Sector indexes Indexes that represent and track different economic sectors—such as consumer goods, energy, finance, health care, and technology—on either a national, regional, or global basis.

Secured With collateral; secured debt is backed by the cash flows of the issuer and the collateral as a secondary source of repayment.

Secured loans Loans collateralized by an asset of the borrower.

Security Evidence of equity or debt interest or in an entity or a related right, such as a derivative. Often standardized to conform to security exchange requirements.

Security characteristic line A plot of the excess return of a security on the excess return of the market.

Security market index A portfolio of securities representing a given security market, market segment, or asset class.

Security market line The graphical representation of the CAPM formula, showing the relationship between expected return and beta.

Security selection The process of selecting individual securities; typically, security selection has the objective of generating superior risk-adjusted returns relative to a portfolio's benchmark.

Security tokens Digitizes the ownership rights associated with publicly traded securities.

Segmenting A process of identifying and grouping customers by decision-useful attributes.

Self-attribution bias A bias in which people take too much credit for successes (*self-enhancing*) and assign responsibility to others for failures (*self-protecting*).

Self-control bias A bias in which people fail to act in pursuit of their long-term, overarching goals because of a lack of self-discipline.

Self-investment limits With respect to investment limitations applying to pension plans, restrictions on the percentage of assets that can be invested in securities issued by the pension plan sponsor.

Sell-side firm A broker/dealer that sells securities and provides independent investment research and recommendations to their clients (i.e., buy-side firms).

Semi-strong-form efficient market A market in which security prices reflect all publicly known and available information.

Semiannual bond basis yield Also known as a semiannual bond equivalent yield, it is an annualized interest rate with a periodicity of two.

Semiannual bond equivalent yield Also known as a semiannual bond basis yield, it is an annualized interest rate with a periodicity of two.

Senior debt A debt obligation with higher priority of payment than junior debt obligations.

Senior unsecured debt The highest-ranked debt in an issuer's capital structure which is a general obligation of the borrower.

Seniority Priority of payment of various debt obligations.

Sensitivity analysis A form of analysis used to determine the impact of a change in one or more key variables affecting investment returns or valuation.

Separately managed account (SMA) An investment portfolio managed exclusively for the benefit of an individual or institution.

Separately managed accounts Accounts that are managed in accordance with an investor's specific investment preferences and risk tolerance.

Service period The time between the grant and vesting dates for an employee share-based award, usually measured in years.

Settlement The closing date at which the counterparties of a derivative contract exchange payment for the underlying as required by the contract.

Settlement price The price determined by an exchange's clearinghouse in the daily settlement of the mark-to-market process. The price reflects an average of the final futures trades of the day.

Share class Types of equity securities that have different voting rights—for example, an issuer may issue Class A shares that carry one vote per share and Class B shares that carry ten votes per share.

Share repurchase A transaction in which a company buys back its own shares. Unlike stock dividends and stock splits, share repurchases use corporate cash.

Shareholder activism A range of actions by a corporation's shareholders that are intended to result in some change in the corporation, typically a change in the board of directors, management, or business strategy.

Shareholder derivative lawsuit A legal action by a shareholder on behalf of a company, not the shareholder personally, against a third party. Often, the third party is a director or manager who the shareholder believes has harmed the company.

Shareholder engagement Shareholder engagement reflects active ownership by investors in which the investor seeks to influence a corporation's decisions on ESG matters, either through dialogue with corporate officers or votes at a shareholder assembly (in the case of equity).

Shareholder theory of corporate governance Espoused by Milton Friedman in his famous 1970 essay, the shareholder theory holds that the objective of a business is to increase profits and shareholder value.

Shareholders Hold a direct equity position in a firm, and both individual persons and financial institutions can be shareholders. The term comes from the individual or investment firm literally having a share of the company. It is most commonly used when talking about the rights and responsibilities that come with being an "owner" of a company, such as stewardship, voting, and engagement. This differentiates it from a situation where an individual or an investment firm lends money or invests in a bond (in other words, they are not an equityholder of a company). Because bond investors do not have a share and are not owners of a company, they cannot vote. Nonetheless, expectations around engagement are increasing for those who invest in loans and bonds as well, making the difference between the two terms more subtle.

Shares Units of ownership interest in a limited company.

Sharpe ratio The average return in excess of the risk-free rate divided by the standard deviation of return; a measure of the average excess return earned per unit of standard deviation of return. Also known as the *reward-to-variability ratio*.

Shelf registration A type of public offering that allows the issuer to file a single, all-encompassing offering circular that covers a series of bond issues.

Short A trading position in a **derivative contract** that gains value as the price of the **underlying** moves lower.

Short biased These strategies use quantitative, technical, and fundamental analysis to short overvalued equity securities with limited or no long-side exposures.

Short position A position in an asset or contract in which one has sold an asset one does not own, or in which a right under a contract can be exercised against oneself.

Short selling A transaction in which borrowed securities are sold with the intention to repurchase them at a lower price at a later date and return them to the lender.

Short-run average total cost The curve describing average total cost when some costs are considered fixed.

Shortfall risk The risk that portfolio value or portfolio return will fall below some minimum acceptable level over some time horizon.

Shutdown point The point at which average revenue is equal to the firm's average variable cost.

Side letter A side agreement created between the GP and specific LPs. These agreements exist *outside* the LPA. These agreements provide additional terms and conditions related to the investment agreement.

Signpost An indicator, market level, data piece, or event that signals a risk is becoming more or less likely. An analyst can think of signposts like a traffic light.

Simple linear regression (SLR) An approach for estimating the linear relationship between a dependent variable and a single independent variable by minimizing the sum of the squared deviations between the fitted line and the observed values.

Simple random sample A subset of a larger population created in such a way that each element of the population has an equal probability of being selected to the subset.

Simple random sampling The procedure of drawing a sample to satisfy the definition of a simple random sample.

Simple yield The sum of the coupon payments plus the straight-line amortized share of the gain or loss divided by the bond's flat price. Simple yields are used mostly to quote JGBs.

Simulation A technique for exploring how a target variable (e.g. portfolio returns) would perform in a hypothetical environment specified by the user, rather than a historical setting.

Simulation trial A complete pass through the steps of a simulation.

Single-price auction A debt securities auction in which all bidders pay the same price.

Sinking fund Provisions that reduce the credit risk of a bond issue by requiring the issuer to retire a portion of the bond's principal outstanding each year.

Situational influences External factors, such as environmental or cultural elements, that shape our behavior.

Skewed Not symmetrical.

Skewness A quantitative measure of skew (lack of symmetry); a synonym of skew. It is computed as the average cubed deviation from the mean standardized by dividing by the standard deviation cubed.

Slope coefficient The change in the estimated value of the dependent variable for a one-unit change in the value of the independent variable.

Small country A country that is a price taker in the world market for a product and cannot influence the world market price.

Smart beta Involves the use of transparent, rules-based strategies as a basis for investment decisions.

Smart contracts Computer programs that are designed to self-execute on the basis of pre-specified terms and conditions agreed to by parties to a contract.

Social infrastructure investments A category of infrastructure investments that are directed toward human activities and include such assets as educational, health care, social housing, and correctional facilities, with the focus on providing, operating, and maintaining the asset infrastructure.

Soft commodities Standardized agricultural products, such as cattle and corn, with markets often involving the physical delivery of the underlying upon settlement.

Soft hurdle rate Hurdle rate where the fee is calculated on the entire return when the hurdle is exceeded. With a soft hurdle, GPs are able to catch up performance fees once the hurdle threshold is exceeded.

Soft power A means of influencing another country's decisions without force or coercion. Soft power can be built over time through actions, such as cultural programs, advertisement, travel grants, and university exchange.

Soft-bullet covered bonds Delay the bond default and payment acceleration of bond cash flows until a new final maturity date, which is usually up to a year after the original maturity date.

Solvency Refers to the condition in which firm value exceeds the face value of debt used to finance the firm's assets.

Solvency ratios Ratios that measure a company's ability to meet its long-term obligations.

Solvency risk The risk that an organization does not survive or succeed because it runs out of cash, even though it might otherwise be solvent.

Sophisticated investors Individuals or entities that are permitted in a jurisdiction to trade unregistered or, generally, less regulated securities, including shares of privately held companies; also called *accredited investors*.

Sovereign immunity A principle limiting the legal recourse of bondholders holding national government debt from forcing the issuer to declare bankruptcy or liquidate assets to settle debt claims.

Spearman rank correlation coefficient A measure of correlation applied to ranked data.

Special dividend A dividend paid by a company that does not pay dividends on a regular schedule, or a dividend that supplements regular cash dividends with an extra payment.

Special purpose acquisition company A "blank check" company that exists solely for the purpose of acquiring an unspecified private company within a predetermined period or return capital to investors.

Special purpose entity (SPE) Also referred to as a special purpose vehicle or SPV, this legal entity is created for a specific economic purpose. In the case of a project SPV, the entity's sole purpose is to facilitate the construction, operation, and financing of an infrastructure asset over its contractual life.

Special purpose vehicle   See *special purpose entity*.

Special situations   An area of private capital investment which targets return by investing in stressed, distressed, or event-driven opportunities.

Split ratings   Complex risks viewed very differently by rating agencies

Sponsored   A type of depository receipt in which the foreign company whose shares are held by the depository has a direct involvement in the issuance of the receipts.

Spot curve   Yields-to-maturity on a series of default-risk-free zero-coupon bonds.

Spot markets   Markets in which specific assets are exchanged at current prices. Spot markets are often referred to as **cash markets.**

Spot prices   The current prices prevailing in **spot markets.**

Spot rates   Yields-to-maturity on default-risk-free zero-coupon bonds.

Spread   The difference in yield-to-maturity between a bond and that of a another bond.

Spread risk   Bond price risk arising from changes in the yield spread on credit-risky bonds; reflects changes in the market's assessment and/or pricing of credit migration (or downgrade) risk and market liquidity risk.

Spurious correlation   Refers to: 1) correlation between two variables that reflects chance relationships in a particular dataset; 2) correlation induced by a calculation that mixes each of two variables with a third variable; and 3) correlation between two variables arising not from a direct relation between them but from their relation to a third variable.

Stablecoin   A cryptocurrency that aims to maintain a stable value relative to a specified asset or to a pool or basket of assets.

Stackelberg model   A prominent model of strategic decision making in which firms are assumed to make their decisions sequentially.

Staggered board   A structure of board elections in which only part of the board is elected simultaneously—for example, only one-third of the board may be up for election each year, so the board can be replaced over three years, not in one year if all seats were elected annually. This structure fosters greater continuity of board members but is an obstacle for shareholders seeking to effect change.

Stakeholder theory of corporate governance   An expansion of the shareholder theory of corporate governance under which the objective of a business is to maximize value for, and balance the interests of, a broad group of stakeholders, including shareholders, employees, society, and the non-human environment.

Stakeholders   Any party with an interest, financial or non-financial, in an entity or its actions.

Standard deviation   The positive square root of the variance; a measure of dispersion in the same units as the original data.

Standard error of the estimate   A measure of the distance between the observed values of the dependent variable and those predicted from the estimated regression. The smaller this value, the better the fit of the model. Also known as the standard error of the regression and the root mean square error.

Standard error of the forecast   Used to provide an interval estimate around the estimated regression line. It is necessary because the regression line does not describe the relationship between the dependent and independent variables perfectly.

Standard error of the slope coefficient   Calculated for simple linear regression by dividing the standard error of the estimate by the square root of the variation of the independent variable.

Standardization   The process of creating protocols for the production, sale, transport, or use of a product or service. Standardization occurs when relevant parties agree to follow these protocols together. It helps support expanded economic and financial activities, such as trade and capital flows that support higher economic growth and standards of living, across borders.

Standards of conduct   Behaviors required by a group; established benchmarks that clarify or enhance a group's code of ethics.

Standing limit orders   A limit order at a price below market and which therefore is waiting to trade.

State actors   Typically national governments, political organizations, or country leaders that exert authority over a country's national security and resources. The South African President, Sultan of Brunei, Malaysia's Parliament, and the British Prime Minister are all examples of state actors.

Statement of cash flows   A financial statement that details the movement of cash over a period. The statement is classified into operating, investing, and financing activities.

Static trade-off theory of capital structure   A theory pertaining to a company's optimal capital structure; the optimal level of debt is found at the point where additional debt would cause the costs of financial distress to increase by a greater amount than the benefit of the additional tax shield.

Statistically significant   A result indicating that the null hypothesis can be rejected; with reference to an estimated regression coefficient, frequently understood to mean a result indicating that the corresponding population regression coefficient is different from zero.

Status quo bias   An emotional bias in which people do nothing (i.e., maintain the status quo) instead of making a change.

Statutory voting   A common method of voting where each share represents one vote.

Step-up bonds   Bonds for which the coupon, be it fixed or floating, increases by specified margins at specified dates.

Stock dividend   A type of dividend in which a company distributes additional shares of its common stock to shareholders instead of cash.

Stock exchange   An exchange in which equity securities are traded. See *exchanges*.

Stock split   An increase in the number of shares outstanding with a consequent decrease in share price, but no change to the company's underlying fundamentals.

Stockholder overhang   The downward pressure on the share price of stock as large blocks of shares are being sold on the open market.

Stop order   An order in which a trader has specified a stop price condition. Also called *stop-loss order*.

Stop-loss order   See *stop order*.

Stranded assets   A resource that is no longer economically valuable owing to changes in demand, regulations, or availability of substitutes—for example, a newly discovered oil well that will not be brought into production.

Strategic asset allocation A long-term strategy that establishes target allocations for various asset classes and aims to optimize the balance between risk and reward by diversifying investments.

Stratified random sampling A procedure that first divides a population into subpopulations (strata) based on classification criteria and then randomly draws samples from each stratum in sizes proportional to that of each stratum in the population.

Street convention For yield measures on fixed-income instruments that assume payments are made on scheduled dates and ignore weekends and holidays.

Stress testing A specific type of scenario analysis that estimates losses in rare and extremely unfavorable combinations of events or scenarios.

Strong-form efficient market A market in which security prices reflect all public and private information.

Structural budget deficit Also known as the cyclically adjusted budget deficit. The deficit that would exist if the economy was at full employment (or full potential output).

Structural subordination Arises in a holding company structure when the debt of operating subsidiaries is serviced by the cash flow and assets of the subsidiaries before funds can be passed to the holding company to service debt at the parent level.

Structured notes A broad category of securities that incorporate the features of debt instruments and one or more embedded derivatives designed to achieve a particular issuer or investor objective.

Subordinated debt A class of unsecured debt that ranks below a firm's senior unsecured obligations.

Subordination A form of internal credit enhancement that relies on creating more than one bond tranche and ordering the claim priorities for ownership or interest in an asset between the tranches. The ordering of the claim priorities is called a senior/subordinated structure, where the tranches of highest seniority are called senior, followed by subordinated or junior tranches. Also called **credit tranching**.

Subprime loans Lending to borrowers with lower credit quality, high DTI, and/or are loans with higher LTV, and include loans that are secured by second liens otherwise subordinated to other loans.

Sum of squares error (SSE) A measure of the total deviation between observed and estimated values of the dependent variable. It is calculated by subtracting each estimated value $\hat{Y}_i$ from its corresponding observed value Y_i, squaring each of these differences, and then summing all of these squared differences.

Sum of squares regression (SSR) A measure of the explained variation in the dependent variable, calculated as the sum of the squared differences between the predicted value of the dependent variable, $\hat{Y}_i$, based on the estimated regression line, and the mean of the dependent variable, $\bar{Y}$.

Sum of squares total (SST) A measure of the total variation in the dependent variable in a simple linear regression. It is calculated by subtracting the mean of the observed values $\bar{Y}$ from each of the observed values Y_i, squaring each of these differences, and then summing all of these squared differences.

Sunk costs A cost that has already been incurred.

Supervised learning A type of machine learning in which the system attempts to learn to model relationships based on labeled training data.

Supervisory board In some jurisdictions, a corporation's board of directors is formally composed of a supervisory board and a management board. The supervisory board appoints and oversees the management board and often includes representatives of employees and other non-shareholder stakeholders.

Supply chain The sequence of processes involved in the creation and delivery of a physical product to the end customer, both within and external to a firm, regardless of whether those steps are performed by a single firm.

Supply shock A typically unexpected disturbance to supply.

Survivorship bias Relates to the inclusion of only current investment funds in a database. As such, the returns of funds that are no longer available in the marketplace (have been liquidated) are excluded from the database. Also see *backfill bias*.

Swap A firm commitment involving a periodic exchange of cash flows.

Swap contract An agreement between two parties to exchange a series of future cash flows.

Swap execution facility (SEF) A swap trading platform accessed by multiple **dealers**.

Swap rate The fixed rate to be paid by the fixed-rate payer specified in a swap contract.

Syndicate A group of lenders, typically made up of banks.

Synthetic protective put The combination of a synthetic long underlying position (i.e., a long forward and risk-free borrowing) and a purchased put on the underlying.

Systematic risk The risk of severe damage to the real economy caused by the impairment of (parts of) the financial system.

Systematic sampling A procedure of selecting every kth member until reaching a sample of the desired size. The sample that results from this procedure should be approximately random.

Systemic risk Refers to risks supervisory authorities believe are likely to have broad impact across the financial market infrastructure and affect a wide swath of market participants.

Tactical asset allocation A proactive strategy that adjusts asset class allocations within a portfolio based on short-term market trends, economic conditions, or valuation changes to capitalize on temporary market inefficiencies or opportunities to improve returns or manage risk more effectively.

Target capital structure Management's desired proportions of debt and equity financing, usually stated on a book value basis or indirectly using a financial leverage metric, such as net or gross debt to EBITDA or credit rating.

Target independent A bank's ability to determine the definition of inflation that they target, the rate of inflation that they target, and the horizon over which the target is to be achieved.

Target semideviation A measure of downside risk, calculated as the square root of the average of the squared deviations of observations below the target (also called target downside deviation).

Tariffs Taxes that a government levies on imported goods.

Tax base The amount at which an asset or liability is valued for tax purposes.

Tax expense An aggregate of an entity's income tax payable (or recoverable in the case of a tax benefit) and any changes in deferred tax assets and liabilities. It is essentially the income tax payable or recoverable if these had been determined based on accounting profit rather than taxable income.

Taxable income The portion of an entity's income that is subject to income taxes under the tax laws of its jurisdiction.

Taxable temporary differences Temporary differences that result in a taxable amount in a future period when determining the taxable profit as the balance sheet item is recovered or settled.

Technical analysis A form of security analysis that uses price and volume data, often displayed graphically, in decision making.

Tender offer A solicitation by a current or prospective shareholder to other shareholders to acquire a substantial percentage, including 100%, of shares at a specified price. This action is usually undertaken by a potential acquirer whose bid was rejected by the issuer's board of directors, prompting the potential acquirer to appeal directly to shareholders.

Tenor The remaining time to maturity for a bond or derivative contract. Also called term to maturity.

Term repos Repos with a maturity longer than one day.

Term structure of interest rates Also known as the maturity structure of interest rates, refers to the difference in interest rates or benchmark yields by time-to-maturity.

Terminal stock value The expected value of a share at the end of the investment horizon—in effect, the expected selling price. Also called *terminal value.*

Terminal value The expected value of a share at the end of the investment horizon—in effect, the expected selling price.

Test of the mean of the differences A statistical test for differences based on paired observations drawn from samples that are dependent on each other.

Text analytics Involves the use of computer programs to analyze and derive meaning typically from large, unstructured text- or voice-based datasets, such as company filings, written reports, quarterly earnings calls, social media, email, internet postings, and surveys.

Thematic risks Known risks that evolve and expand over a period of time. Climate change, pattern migration, the rise of populist forces, and the ongoing threat of terrorism fall into this category.

Thin-tailed Describes a distribution that has relatively less weight in the tails than the normal distribution (also called platykurtic).

Tiered pricing A pricing approach that charges different prices to different buyers, commonly based on volume purchased.

Timberland investment management organizations Entities that support institutional investors by managing their investments in timberland by analyzing and acquiring suitable timberland holdings.

Time tranching Structure of a securitization that allows for the redistribution of "prepayment risk" among bond classes by creating bond classes of different expected maturities.

Time value The difference between an option's premium and its intrinsic value.

Time value decay The process by which the time value of an option declines toward zero as the option's expiration date is approached.

Time-weighted rate of return The compound rate of growth of one unit of currency invested in a portfolio during a stated measurement period; a measure of investment performance that is not sensitive to the timing and amount of withdrawals or additions to the portfolio.

Tokenization The process of representing ownership rights to physical assets on a blockchain or distributed ledger.

Top-down analysis An investment selection approach that begins with consideration of macroeconomic conditions and then evaluates markets and industries based upon such conditions.

Total probability rule for expected value A rule explaining the expected value of a random variable in terms of expected values of the random variable conditional on mutually exclusive and exhaustive scenarios.

Total return Measures the price appreciation, or percentage change in price of the securities in an index or portfolio, plus any income received over the period.

Total return index An index that reflects the price appreciation or percentage change in price of the constituent securities plus any income received since inception.

Total working capital The difference between current assets and current liabilities.

Tracking error The standard deviation of the differences between a portfolio's returns and its benchmark's returns; a synonym of active risk. Also called *tracking risk.*

Tracking risk The standard deviation of the differences between a portfolio's returns and its benchmark's returns. Also called *tracking error* and *active risk.*

Trade creation When regional integration results in the replacement of higher cost domestic production by lower cost imports from other members.

Trade diversion When regional integration results in lower-cost imports from non-member countries being replaced with higher-cost imports from members.

Trade sale A portion or division of a private company sold via either direct sale or auction to a strategic buyer interested in increasing the scale and scope of an existing business.

Trade settlement date The date when the buyer and seller transfer consideration and securities.

Traditional investment markets Markets for traditional investments, which include all publicly traded debts and equities and shares in pooled investment vehicles that hold publicly traded debts and/or equities.

Tranches A grouping of securities within an issue with characteristics that vary from other tranches, such as different credit quality and seniority.

Transfer payments Welfare payments made through the social security system that exist to provide a basic minimum level of income for low-income households.

Transition risks Economic and financial losses from the transition to a lower-carbon economy in response to climate change—for example, the abandonment of an oil well that is no longer economical.

Treasury Inflation-Protected Securities (TIPS) US Treasury bonds with a principal that is adjusted for changes in the Consumer Price Index. TIPS are issued in 5-, 10-, and 30-year maturities.

Treynor ratio A measure of risk-adjusted performance that relates a portfolio's returns in excess of the risk-free rate to a portfolio's beta.

Trimmed mean A mean computed after excluding a stated small percentage of the lowest and highest observations.

Triparty repo A repurchase agreement in which the transacting parties agree to use a third-party agent that provides access to a larger collateral pool and multiple counterparties, as well as valuation and safekeeping of assets.

True yield Measures on fixed-income instruments use actual payment dates, accounting for weekends and holidays. The true yield on an instrument is always lower than the street convention yield.

Turn-of-the-year effect Calendar anomaly that stock market returns in January are significantly higher compared to the rest of the months of the year, with most of the abnormal returns reported during the first five trading days in January.

Two-fund separation theorem The theory that all investors regardless of taste, risk preferences, and initial wealth will hold a combination of two portfolios or funds: a risk-free asset and an optimal portfolio of risky assets.

Two-way table A table of the frequency distribution of observations classified on the basis of two discrete variables. Also known as *Contingency table*.

Two-week repo rate The interest rate on a two-week repurchase agreement; may be used as a policy rate by a central bank.

Type I error The error of rejecting a true null hypothesis; a false positive.

Type II error The error of not rejecting a false null hypothesis; false negative.

Uncommitted lines of credit Sources of bank credit that a bank can refuse to honor. Uncommitted credit lines are made up to a certain principal amount for a pre-determined maximum maturity, charging a market reference rate plus an issuer-specific spread on only the principal outstanding for the period of use.

Underfitted When a machine learning model treats true parameters as if they are noise and is unable to recognize relationships in the training data, making the model more likely to fail to fully discover patterns that underlie the data.

Underlying The asset referred to in a **derivative contract**.

Underwritten offering A type of securities issue mechanism in which the investment bank guarantees the sale of the securities at an offering price that is negotiated with the issuer. Also known as *firm commitment offering*.

Unearned revenue A liability account for money that has been collected for goods or services that have not yet been delivered; payment received in advance of providing a good or service. Also called *deferred revenue* or *deferred income*.

Unimodal A distribution with a single value that is most frequently occurring.

Unit economics The expression of revenues and costs on a per-unit basis.

Unitranche debt A hybrid or blended loan structure combining different tranches of secured and unsecured debt into a single loan with a single, blended interest rate.

Unsecured Without collateral; unsecured debt is backed only by cash flows of the issuer.

Unsponsored A type of depository receipt in which the foreign company whose shares are held by the depository has no involvement in the issuance of the receipts.

Unsupervised learning A type of machine learning in which the system tries to learn the structure of unlabeled data.

Utility tokens Tokens that provide services within a network, such as paying for services and network fees.

Validity instructions Instructions which indicate when the order may be filled.

Value added resellers Businesses that distribute a product and also handle more complex aspects of product installation, customization, service, or support.

Value at risk A money measure of the minimum value of losses expected during a specified time period at a given level of probability.

Value chain The systems and processes in a firm that create value for its customers.

Value proposition The product or service attributes valued by a firm's target customer that lead those customers to prefer that firm's offering.

Value-add real estate strategies Strategies that involve larger-scale redevelopment and repositioning of existing assets and that may allow the investor to earn a higher return compared with core-plus real estate strategies.

Value-based pricing Pricing set primarily by reference to the value of the product or service to customers.

VaR See *value at risk*.

Variance The expected value (the probability-weighted average) of squared deviations from a random variable's expected value.

Variance of a random variable The expected value (the probability-weighted average) of squared deviations from a random variable's expected value.

Variation margin The difference between current margin required and the current collateral price in a repurchase agreement.

Vega The change in a given derivative instrument for a given small change in volatility, holding everything else constant. A sensitivity measure for options that reflects the effect of volatility.

Velocity The pace at which geopolitical risk impacts an investor portfolio.

Venture capital Private equity investment in a startup or early-stage company involving high risk and a high rate of failure.

Venture capital fund A hedge fund that seeks to buy, optimize, and ultimately sell portfolio companies to generate profits. See *private equity fund*.

Venture debt Private debt funding that provides venture capital backing to start-up or early-stage companies that may be generating little or negative cash flow.

Vest To become unconditionally entitled to.

Vesting date The day that an employee becomes unconditionally entitled to compensation.

Vintage year The year in which a private capital fund makes its first investment.

Volatility The standard deviation of the continuously compounded returns on the underlying asset.

Vote by proxy A mechanism that allows a designated party—such as another shareholder, a shareholder representative, or management—to vote on the shareholder's behalf.

Voting rights The power of shareholders to cast votes in corporate elections for directors and other matters submitted to a shareholder vote.

Warrant An attached option that gives its holder the right to buy the underlying stock of the issuing company at a fixed exercise price until the expiration date.

Waterfall structures These represent the distribution order for cash flows and risk to different tranches in a financing structure.

Weak-form efficient market hypothesis The belief that security prices fully reflect all past market data, which refers to all historical price and volume trading information.

Weighted average cost of capital (WACC) The expected cost of debt and equity weighted by the proportion of each used in a company's capital structure.

Weighted average coupon rate (WAC) Rate calculated for a mortgage pass-through security by weighting the mortgage rate of each mortgage in the pool by the percentage of the outstanding mortgage balance relative to the outstanding amount of all the mortgages in the pool.

Weighted average maturity (WAM)   Calculated for a mortgage pass-through security by weighting the remaining number of months to maturity of each mortgage in the pool by the outstanding mortgage balance relative to the outstanding amount of all the mortgages in the pool.

Winsorized mean   A mean computed after assigning a stated percentage of the lowest values equal to one specified low value and a stated percentage of the highest values equal to one specified high value.

Write-off/liquidation   Refers to a transaction that has not gone well, and the investment is likely to lose value. The private equity firm revises the value of its investment downward or liquidates the portfolio company.

Yield curve   A graphical depiction of yields-to-maturity of bonds from the same issuer across maturities.

Yield spread   The difference in yield-to-maturity between a bond and that of a another bond.

Yield-to-call   An internal rate of return on a fixed-income instrument's cash flows assuming cash flows are received on scheduled dates and the bond is called at a certain call price and date.

Yield-to-maturity   The internal rate of return that an investor earns on a bond assuming no default, the bond is held to maturity, and periodic cash flows are reinvested at the yield-to-maturity. Also called yield-to-redemption or redemption yield.

Yield-to-worst   The lowest among a fixed-income instrument's yields-to-call and yield-to-maturity. A commonly cited yield measure for fixed-rate callable bonds.

Z-spread   or zero-volatility spread is a constant yield spread for a bond over a government or swap curve.

Zero-coupon bond   A bond that does not pay a coupon but is priced at a discount and pays its full face value at maturity.

Zero-coupon bonds   Bonds that do not pay interest during their life. They are issued at a discount to par value and redeemed at par. Also called pure discount bond.